# Dimensions of Human Behavior

## *The Changing Life Course*

**TITLES OF RELATED INTEREST FROM PINE FORGE PRESS**

*The Social Worlds of Higher Education: Handbook for Teaching in a New Century*
edited by Bernice Pescosolido and Ronald Aminzade

*Adventures in Social Research: Data Analysis Using SPSS® for Windows 95/98™
Versions 7.5, 8.0, or Higher* by Earl Babbie and Fred Halley

*Exploring Social Issues Using SPSS® for Windows 95/98™ Versions 7.5, 8.0, or Higher*
by Joseph Healey, John Boli, Earl Babbie, and Fred Halley

*Social Work in the 21st Century* by Eileen Gambrill and Michael Reisch

*Critical Thinking for Social Workers: Exercises for the Helping Professions,* Revised Edition,
by Leonard Gibbs and Eileen Gambrill

*Social Work Practice: Cases, Activities, and Exercises* by Kim Strom-Gottfried

*The Social WorkOut Book: Strength-Building Exercises for the Pre-Professional*
by Alice Lieberman

*Community Resources for Older Adults: Programs and Services in an Era of Change*
by Robbyn Wacker, Karen Roberto, and Linda Piper

*Investigating the Social World: The Process and Practice of Research,* Second Edition,
by Russell K. Schutt

*Aging, Social Inequality, and Public Policy* by Fred C. Pampel

# Dimensions of Human Behavior

## The Changing Life Course

### Elizabeth D. Hutchison

*Virginia Commonwealth University*

Visual Essays edited by Shelley Kowalski

*University of Oregon*

Pine Forge Press

*Thousand Oaks, California • London • New Delhi*

*For information, address:*

**Pine Forge Press**
A Sage Publications Company
2455 Teller Road
Thousand Oaks, California 91320
(805) 499-4224
E-mail: sales@pfp.sagepub.com

Sage Publications Ltd.
6 Bonhill Street
London EC2A 4PU
United Kingdom

Sage Publications India Pvt. Ltd.
M-32 Market
Greater Kailash I
New Delhi 110 048 India

*Production Management:* Scratchgravel Publishing Services
*Copy Editor:* Margaret C. Tropp
*Typesetter:* Scratchgravel Publishing Services
*Visual Essays Design:* Lisa Mirski Devenish
*Cover Designer:* Deborah Davis and Greg Draus
*Production Coordinator:* Windy Just

*Printed in the United States of America*
    00  01  02  03  10  9  8  7  6  5  4  3

**Library of Congress Cataloging-in-Publication Data**

Dimensions of human behavior. The changing life course / [edited] by
  Elizabeth Hutchison.
        p.   cm.
    Includes bibliographical references and index.
    ISBN 0-7619-8614-6
    1. Social psychology.   2. Human behavior.   3. Life cycle, Human.
  4. Social service.   I. Hutchison, Elizabeth.   II. Title: Changing
  life course.
  HM251.D55   1999
  302—dc21                                         98-31534
                                                      CIP

This book is printed on acid-free paper that meets Environmental Protection Agency standards for recycled paper.

## ABOUT THE AUTHOR

Elizabeth D. Hutchison, M.S.W., Ph.D., is an Associate Professor in the School of Social Work at Virginia Commonwealth University. She has practiced in health, mental health, and child welfare. Her major areas of interest are child welfare, social work practice with nonvoluntary clients, and the human behavior curriculum. She teaches human behavior courses at the B.S.W., M.S.W., and doctoral levels.

## ABOUT THE PUBLISHER

Pine Forge Press is a new educational publisher, dedicated to publishing innovative books and software throughout the social sciences. On this and any other of our publications, we welcome your comments. Please call or write us at:

**Pine Forge Press**
A Sage Publications Company
2455 Teller Road
Thousand Oaks, CA 91320
(805) 499-4224
E-mail: sales@pfp.sagepub.com

Visit our new World Wide Web site, your direct link to a multitude of online resources:
**http://www.pineforge.com**

*To Brad and Abby, who are the spice of my life's journey.*

# BRIEF CONTENTS

# CONTENTS

**PART II**  The Changing Life Course

**VISUAL ESSAY**  *Tracking Time / 72*

**CHAPTER 3**  Conception, Pregnancy, and Birth / 79

*by Marcia Harrigan and Suzanne Baldwin*

**CHAPTER 4**  ## Infancy and Early Childhood / 117

*by Debra J. Woody*

**CHAPTER 5**  ## Middle Childhood / 151

*by Leanne Wood Charlesworth and Pamela Viggiani*

CHAPTER 6    **Adolescence / 183**

*by Susan A. McCarter*

CHAPTER 7

# Adulthood / 221

CHAPTER 8

# Late Adulthood / 257

*by Matthias J. Naleppa*

# BRIEF CONTENTS: PERSON AND ENVIRONMENT

# PREFACE

I started work on this book and its companion volume before my daughter graduated from high school; before my son graduated from college; before my father-in-law died; before my mother's fight with cancer; before a merger/acquisition propelled my husband to return to school; about the time Bill Clinton started his first term as U.S. President; before the U.S. Supreme Court ruled that mental health professionals, including clinical social workers, may not be compelled to reveal details of counseling sessions with clients; before Aid to Families with Dependent Children was eliminated as a federal entitlement program; and in the midst of harshly contested political realignments in Eastern Europe and the former Soviet Union. Like a lot of people, I use these types of life course markers to think about the pattern and flow of my life, to capture the aspect of time in my life journey.

Since I was a child listening to my grandmother's stories about the challenges, joys, and dramatic as well as mundane events in her life, I have been captivated by people's stories. I have learned that a specific event can be understood only in the context of an ongoing life story. Social work has historically used the idea of person-in-environment to develop a holistic understanding of human behavior. This idea has become popular as well with most social and behavioral science disciplines. Recently, we have recognized the need to add the aspect of time to the person-environment construct, to capture the dynamic, changing nature of person-in-environment.

Organized around time, this book tries to help you understand the relationship between time and human behavior. The companion volume to this book, *Person and Environment,* analyzes relevant dimensions of person and environment and presents up-to-date reports on theory and research about each of these dimensions. The purpose of this volume is to show how these multiple dimensions of person and environment work together with dimensions of time to produce patterns in unique life course journeys.

## *Life Course Perspective*

My colleagues and I have chosen a life course perspective to capture the dynamic, changing nature of person-environment transactions. In the life course perspective, human behavior is not a linear march through time, nor is it simply played out in recurring cycles. Rather, the life course journey is a moving spiral, with both continuity and change, marked by both predictable and unpredictable twists and turns. It is influenced by changes in the physical and social environment, as well as by changes in the personal biological, psychological, and spiritual dimensions.

The life course perspective recognizes *patterns* in human behavior related to biological age, psychological age, and social age norms. We discuss theory and research about six age-graded periods of the life course, presenting both the continuity and the change in these patterns. The life course perspective also recognizes *diversity* in the life course related to historical time, gender, race, ethnicity, social class, and so forth, and we emphasize group-based sources of diversity in our discussion of age-graded periods. Finally, the life course perspective recognizes the *unique life stories* of individuals, the unique configuration of specific life events and person-environment transactions over time.

## General Knowledge and Unique Situations

The purpose of the social and behavioral sciences is to help us understand *general patterns* in person-environment transactions over time. The purpose of social work assessment is to understand *unique configurations* of person and environment dimensions at a given time. Those who practice social work must weave what they know about unique situations with general knowledge. To assist you in this process, we begin each chapter with a story or stories, which we then intertwine with contemporary theory and research. We also call attention to the successes and failures of theory and research to accommodate human diversity related to gender, race and ethnicity, culture, sexual orientation, and disability.

## Features of the Book

My colleagues and I wanted to write a book that gives you a state of the art knowledge base, but we also wanted you to find pleasure in your learning. We have tried to write as we teach, with enthusiasm for the content and a desire to connect with your process of learning. We have developed some special features that we hope will aid your learning process.

- *Visual Essays.* Each part of the book is introduced with a visual essay that makes use of photographs and other graphic materials to help you "see" how the dimensions of person and environment configure and reconfigure over time to produce both continuity and change in human behavior.

- *Reflections.* Each part of the book ends with a reflection on social work practice that chronicles the activities of one social worker and provides questions for you to consider how this social worker's practice reflects the content of preceding chapters.

- *Exhibits.* Much information in every chapter has been summarized in graphical or tabular form to help you understand and retain ideas.

- *Case Studies.* Each chapter in the book begins with one or more narratives so that you can put human faces on theory and research; these case studies help you weave unique, real-life situations with general knowledge. To assist you in recognizing the diversity of life course trajectories that you may encounter in your social work practice, we begin each of the life course chapters with three case studies.

- *Margin Notes.* Margin notes are used in Chapters 3-8 to help you recognize and think critically about the multiple dimensions of person and environment involved in human behavior across time and about their implications for a multidimensional approach to social work practice. We hope that the margin notes will help you to become a more active reader.

- *Implications for Social Work Practice.* Each chapter ends with a set of practice principles that will guide your use of general knowledge in social work practice.

## One Last Word

I hope that reading this book helps you understand the risk factors and protective factors involved in person-environment transactions during different age-graded periods. This book will, I trust, give you greater appreciation of the life stories in which specific life events are embedded. In addition, when you finish reading this book, I hope that you will have new ideas about how to reduce risk and increase protective factors during different age-graded periods and how to help clients find meaning and purpose in their own life stories.

You can help me in my learning process by letting me know what you liked or didn't like about the book.

*Elizabeth D. Hutchison*
School of Social Work
Virginia Commonwealth University
Richmond, Virginia 23284-2027
E-mail: ehutch@atlas.vcu.edu

# ACKNOWLEDGMENTS

This book and its companion volume have taken far longer to write than I had planned or others had counted on. It has often been a lonely journey, and yet I am indebted to so many people who have helped in so many ways to make the books a reality.

In the beginning, and through the entire journey, Steve Rutter, publisher and president of Pine Forge Press, was a constant presence. He has a vision of a new generation of social work textbooks, strong in both content and pedagogy and affordable to students. He has shepherded this project through its several stages and provided some of the ideas for the best features of the books. Jeff Edleson and Richard Tolman got me involved in this project and gave important feedback and encouragement at the various stages of development.

I am eternally grateful to the contributing authors, who came on board after the project was conceptualized, reinvigorated me with their enthusiasm, and reminded me of the synergy of collaborative efforts. They have responded in good humor to tight deadlines, requests for special features, and multiple reviews and requests for revisions.

In the later stages of this project, a whole host of people connected to Pine Forge Press became part of my life and helped me with the many processes and procedures that are involved in getting a project like this into print. Becky Smith amazed me! She took our early drafts, rough as they were and written in multiple voices, and helped us polish and bring coherence to them. She was demanding yet gentle-hearted in her feedback. She is really good at what she does! Peggy Tropp competently provided further editorial refinement. Anne Draus of Scratchgravel Publishing Services guided the production of the books. Anne kept me on track with gentle prompts, and she has taken the glitches and complications of this complex project in stride. First Sherith Pankratz and later Windy Just helped with the many details that were a mystery to me. Shelley Kowalski edited the visual essays.

Helpful comments and contributions were provided by the social work educators who reviewed drafts of the manuscript. They are:

Susan Fineran, Boston University
James Forte, Christopher Newport University
Maureen Connelly, Frostburg State University
Lois Cowles, Idaho State University
Kathryn Skinner, Marywood College
Cynthia Bishop, Meredith College
Anita Sharma, Northeast Louisiana University
Wayne Busby, Pittsburgh State University
Martin Bloom, University of Connecticut
Nancy Kropf, University of Georgia
James Taylor, University of Kansas
Michael Spencer, University of Michigan
David Lawson Burton, University of Michigan

David Pugh, Youngstown State University
James Wolk, Georgia State University
Alice Chornesky, New Mexico State University
William D. Eldridge, Ohio State University
William R. Downs, University of Northern Iowa
Carol H. Meyer, Columbia University
Nadine Medlin, Creighton University
Margaret Fontanesi, University of Arkansas, Fayetteville

Several students in the VCU School of Social Work have made contributions to the project at different stages. Susan Cummings and Sheila Crowley provided research assistance in the early conceptual phase of the project. Dan Arnold developed the web site resources. Jeremy Wenfro, a VCU art student, cheerfully and efficiently responded to our last-minute request for one graphic design.

I am also grateful to Dean Frank Baskind and my colleagues at the School of Social Work at VCU. They have tolerated my preoccupation, my whining, and my absences. They filled in for me while I was on scholarly leave to begin work on the book during the fall of 1994. They have given me support and encouragement and reined in their incredulity that this project was taking so long. I am particularly grateful for the support and insights of Stephen Gilson, Marcia Harrigan, Michael Sheridan, and Joe Walsh.

Special gratitude goes to my students, who have also been my teachers. They have added fun to my learning as well as to my teaching. Their contributions are embedded in the fabric of this book.

My deepest gratitude goes to my family, Hutch, Brad, and Abby. They have given me space to work, taken an interest in my project, supported me through the times of discouragement, and showered me with love. Each has added something to the project, and collaboratively they have reminded me that families develop together.

■     ■     ■

*Grateful acknowledgments are made to reprint the following:*

**Chapter 2:** Reprinted by permission. Hutchison, E., and L. Charlesworth. 1998. "Human Behavior in the Social Environment: The Role of Gender in the Expansion of Practice Knowledge." In *The Role of Gender in Practice Knowledge,* ed. J. Figueirra-McDonough, F. E. Netting, and A. Nichols-Casebolt. Pp. 41–92. New York: Garland.

**Exhibit 3.5:** From *Before We Are Born,* 5th ed. by K. L. Moore and T. V. N. Persaud. Copyright © 1998. Reprinted by permission of W. B. Saunders Company.

**Exhibit 7.3:** From *The Seasons of a Woman's Life* by Daniel J. Levinson and Judy D. Levinson. Copyright © 1996 by Daniel J. Levinson and Judy D. Levinson. Reprinted by permission of Alfred A. Knopf, Inc.

*Additional acknowledgments are made to reprint the following photographs:*

pages 6, 66, *Learning Spanish Grammer* © Joe Rodrigeuz/Black Star; page 6, *Domestic Violence* © Corbis Bettman; page 7, *Grace Thomas and Her Children* © Marc Pesetsky/Reuters Corbis-Bettman; page 7, *Brownie Troop Ceremony* © Emily Niebrand; page 8, *Line Up for Pork* © AP/Wide World Photos; pages 9, 289, *No Money* © AP/Wide World Photos; page 9, *Blind Man in Wheelchair* © Emily Niebrand; page 9, *Tired Diabetic* © Stacey Kowalski.

page 72, *Grandmother and Baby* © Greg Draus; page 73, *Anniversary 1* © Henry Kowalski; page 73, *Anniversary 2* © Henry Kowalski; page 73, *Anniversary 3* © Henry Kowalski; page 73, *Anniversary 4* © Henry Kowalski; page 74, *Wedding, Catholic* © Henry Kowalski; page 75, *Wedding, Mass* © Corbis-Bettmann; page 75, *Wedding, Jewish* © Corbis-Bettmann; page 75, *Hindu Wedding* © Corbis-Bettmann; page 75, *Gay Wedding* © Corbis-Bettmann; page 76, *New Mother* © Henry Kowalski; page 76, *Daughter as New Mother* © Henry Kowalski; page 77, *New Grandmother* © Henry Kowalski; page 77, *New Family* © Henry Kowalski.

# CONTRIBUTING AUTHORS

**Marian A. Aguilar,** M.S.W., Ph.D., is Associate Professor in the School of Social Work at the University of Texas at Austin. Her research and publications have focused on issues of diveristy, welfare, education, and health care delivery as they impact on women, persons with disabilities, older adults, and people of color. Her last two research grants were in the areas of diversity in adult protective services and an evaluation of managed care in Texas. She has taught courses in social policy, program evaluation, administration and planning, and psychosocial aspects of health and illness.

**Suzanne M. Baldwin,** B.S.N., R.N., M.S.W., L.C.S.W., is a doctoral candidate in the School of Social Work at Virginia Commonwealth University. She works as a clinical nurse specialist in newborn intensive care and as a clinical social worker in private practice with families. Her major areas of interest are medical social work and family systems. She has taught human behavior, practice, communications, and research courses at Old Dominion University and at the School of Social Work at Virginia Commonwealth University.

**Leanne Wood Charlesworth,** M.S.W., Ph.D., is a project director with the University of Maryland School of Social Work's welfare research group. She has held various child welfare positions. Her areas of interest include social welfare policy and poverty issues. She has taught human behavior and research at the School of Social Work at Virginia Commonwealth University.

**Marcia P. Harrigan,** M.S.W., Ph.D., is Associate Professor and Director of the M.S.W. Program in the School of Social Work at Virginia Commonwealth University. She has practiced in child welfare and juvenile justice. Her major areas of interest are family systems, family assessment, and multigenerational households. She has taught human behavior and practice courses.

**Susan Ainsley McCarter,** M.A., M.S.W., Ph.D., is an adjunct faculty member in the School of Social Work at Virginia Commonwealth University. She has worked as a juvenile probation officer; mental health counselor for children, adolescents, and families; AmeriCorps coordinator; mentor trainer; and mother. Her current research interest is minority overrepresentation in the juvenile justice system. She has taught human behavior, social policy, and sociology courses at both undergraduate and graduate levels.

**Matthias Naleppa,** M.S.W. equivalent (from the Catholic University of Applied Social Sciences in Munich, Germany), Ph.D., is Assistant Professor in the School of Social Work at Virginia Commonwealth University. His research focuses on social work with elderly clients, specifically on applying the task-centered model to case management and gerontological practice. He has taught courses in human behavior, social work practice, and research methodology at the University at Albany, Marywood University, and Virginia Commonwealth University.

**Pamela Viggiani,** M.S.W., Ph.D., is Assistant Professor in the Social Work Department at Rochester Institute of Technology. Her clinical and research interest is in school-based dropout prevention programs for at-risk elementary and middle school students. Dr. Vigianni directs the policy sequence in the Social Work Department. She also teaches human behavior and practice courses.

**Debra J. Woody,** Ph.D., L.M.S.W.-A.C.P., is Assistant Professor in the School of Social Work at the University of Texas at Arlington. Her most recent practice experience is in child and family practice. Her major areas of interest are child and family issues, particularly as they are influenced by race. She taught B.S.W. courses for several years at Baylor University. She currently teaches both undergraduate and graduate practice courses and graduate research courses.

# Dimensions of Human Behavior

*The Changing Life Course*

# PART I

# A Multidimensional Approach for Multifaceted Social Work

**C**onsider the following people:

- Caroline O'Malley is knocking at the door of a family reported to her agency for child abuse.
- Sylvia Smith and other members of her team at the rehabilitation hospital are meeting with the family of an 18-year-old man who is recovering from head injuries sustained in a motorcycle accident.
- Mark Adams is on the way to the county jail to assess the suicide risk of an inmate.
- Helen Moore is preparing a report for a legislative committee.
- Juanita Alvarez is talking with a homeless man about taking his psychotropic medications.
- Stan Weslowski is meeting with a couple who would like to adopt a child.
- Andrea Thomas is analyzing the results of a needs assessment recently conducted at the service center for older adults where she works.
- Anthony Pacino is wrapping up a meeting of a cancer support group.
- Sam Belick is writing a social history for tomorrow's team meeting at the high school where he works.
- Sarah Sahair has just begun a meeting of a recreational group of 9- and 10-year-old girls.
- Jane Kerr is facilitating the monthly meeting of an interagency coalition of service providers for substance-abusing women and their children.
- Ann Noles is planning a fund-raising project for the local Boys and Girls Clubs.
- Meg Hart is wrapping up her fourth counseling session with a lesbian couple.
- Chien Liu is meeting with a community group concerned about youth gang behavior in their neighborhood.
- Mary Wells is talking with one of her clients at a rape crisis center.

What do these people have in common? You have probably guessed that they are all social workers. They work in a variety of settings, and they are involved in a variety of activities, but they all are doing social work. Social work is, indeed, a multifaceted profession. And because it is multifaceted, social workers need a multidimensional understanding of human behavior. This book provides such an understanding.

The purpose of the two chapters in Part I is to introduce you to a multidimensional way of thinking about human behavior and to set the stage for subsequent discussion. In Chapter 1, you will be introduced to the multiple dimensions of person, environment, and time that will serve as the framework for the book. You will be given some tools to help you think critically about the multiple theories and varieties of research that make up our general knowledge of these dimensions of human behavior. And you will learn about the organization of the book. In Chapter 2, you will encounter eight theoretical perspectives that contribute to multidimensional understanding. You will learn about their central ideas and their scientific merits. Most important, you will consider the usefulness of these eight theoretical perspectives for social work. The reflection at the end of Part I illustrates the multifaceted nature of a day in the life of one social worker.

# Looking at a Complex World

**Consider a line.**

---

It is a single-dimensional representation of reality but still is useful.

It can give direction, like an arrow.

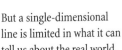

It can make connections between two items to show a relationship.

But a single-dimensional line is limited in what it can tell us about the real world. The real world is multi-dimensional. It has spatial and temporal dimensions. And within these dimensions, people live out very complex and dynamic lives.

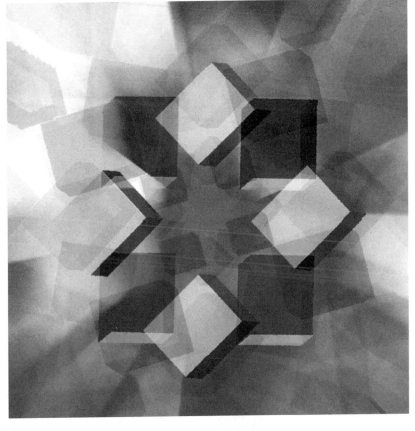

**Now consider a cube.**

It too is useful for describing and analyzing aspects of the world. It shows not only direction and relationship, as a line does, but also depth. But a cube too is limited in what it can tell us about the real world.

Consider how your image of the cube might change if you looked at it interacting with many other elements, as in a kaleidoscope. So it is with the world in which social workers function. This book urges you to look at the world as you might look at the ever-changing pattern in a kaleidoscope, appreciating its many elements and its complexity.

The multiple aspects of human behavior—person, environment, and time— will be explored throughout these pages. As you read, you will need to hold various dimensions of person, environment, and time in mind in order to develop a more complete picture of the world and of social work.

Furthermore, you will need to develop the ability to look at situations from as many different perspectives as possible. As a social worker, you will need to be able to look at each individual and situation from a variety of angles and positions.

Imagine that you have been called on to help a youngster having trouble adjusting to school. Naturally, you should look at the educational environment to understand the forces influencing the child.

But you can't stop there. You also need to look at the home environment. In this case, you might learn that the family is headed by a single mother who is over-coming domestic abuse and who has recently moved with her family into subsi-dized housing.

In looking for ways to assist the troubled child and her family, you might consult with social service agencies that have helped other children and families through difficult periods.

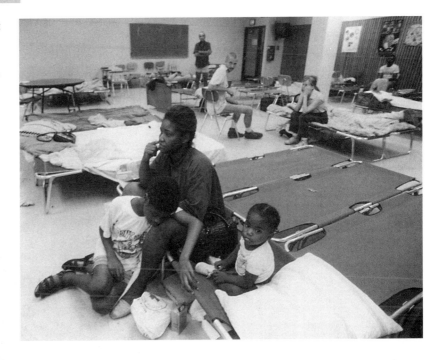

You might also need to help link the child and her family with other organizations outside the school setting, such as this Brownie troop, so she has positive interactions with other children and adults while trying to overcome her school difficulties.

Social workers generally encounter a great many other situations and settings. However, every case can be approached, as this one has been, from multiple perspectives.

As a social worker, you should also have a good grasp of general knowledge about human behavior and at the same time be able to apply that knowledge flexibly. General knowledge, which comes from both theory and research, helps social workers put their clients' lives into larger perspective. At the same time, all social workers must recognize that each individual responds to events in a unique way.

This line of people wrapping around the block is composed of people on welfare waiting for handouts of meat. Theory and research about social conditions and trends can give us a general perspective on the lives of these people.

However, only by discovering the unique details of their lives can we understand what brings individuals like these to us for help. Yes, they are part of a large group of poor people who share many traits. But each one has also experienced life in a unique way that no other person has experienced.

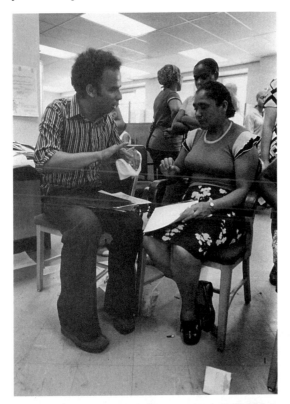

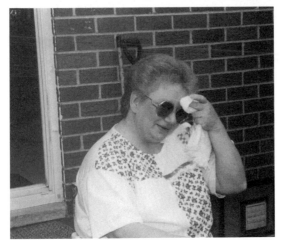

**General knowledge about human behavior and a good understanding of individuals' lives are the basic tools we need to do social work.**

# CHAPTER 1

# Aspects of Human Behavior: Person, Environment, Time

### SINA'S DETERMINATION TO SURVIVE

Sina is an attractive, soft-spoken, and gracious Cambodian-American woman who looks younger than her 44 years. She lives in the suburbs of a small Eastern city with her husband and four of her five children. If you speak with Sina, you will need to be very attentive and enunciate clearly, because Sina still struggles with the English language. You will be impressed with the sincerity of her efforts, however. If Sina gets to know you well, she may tell you some of her story, and you most likely will be struck by the matter-of-fact manner in which she recounts a story that to you probably seems quite remarkable.

Sina grew up in a suburb of Phnom Penh, Cambodia. Because there were so many children in the family into which she was born, Sina and her two younger sisters were sent to be raised by relatives who lived nearby and who could not have children of their own. Sina had a happy childhood with these relatives and thinks of them as her parents (therefore, I will refer to them as her parents). Sina's parents were merchants, and she worked in the store with them. Her marriage at the age of 16 was arranged. Both Sina and her husband completed the equivalent of our high school education and were considered, in Cambodia, to be quite well educated. Sina's husband worked as a mechanic until they left the Phnom Penh area.

When the Khmer Rouge soldiers came to the outskirts of Phnom Penh in April 1975, Sina had no idea that her pleasant life was about to be so radically changed. The soldiers spread the word that the Americans were planning to bomb Phnom Penh and that everyone had to leave the area for a little while. The whole city was quickly evacuated. Sina, who was pregnant, headed for the countryside with her husband, 4-year-old daughter, and very large extended families from both sides. In the countryside, people were instructed to build houses, which most of them did not know how to do. Very soon, it became apparent that all was not well. The soldiers became very dictatorial and were particularly harsh with people who appeared educated and otherwise demonstrated "Western ways." Sina and her family started trying to hide their "Western ways." They got rid of eyeglasses and books, changed their linguistic style to appear less educated, and tried to fake farming skills.

Things got worse. People, particularly men, began disappearing in the night, and gunshots were heard. Stories spread about terrible things happening. Rice began to disappear, and there was not enough to eat. The evacuees were forced to go to political meetings that lasted for hours. Fear was continual, but nighttime was the worst. That was when people disappeared and the gunshots were heard. The realization that they were prisoners came slowly. But the atrocities intensified, and soon it was not uncommon to witness people, even family members, being shot in front of you. People had to work in the rice fields all day, but they were not allowed to eat the rice. Many people were starving to death. Malaria and dysentery were common. Members of Sina's extended family held up as well as could be expected, but her husband's brothers disappeared and were believed to be dead, and his sisters became ill and died. Sina's baby was underweight and sick at delivery, and Sina was relieved to have enough milk to feed her. Starvation and fear were constant companions.

Sina and her family stayed in the camp for about three years. She became pregnant again. Her husband's parents died of starvation. One night, Sina said to her husband, "We have to escape." Her husband said, "No, I am afraid." Sina insisted that they were going, that she could take no more, and she knew that there had to be a better life for her children. Sina rounded up her parents and her sisters and told them that they were going. They too were afraid and tried to dissuade her. But Sina was resolved to go, and they left in the middle of the night—pregnant Sina, her husband and two daughters, her parents, and her two sisters. Some of them were without shoes. They were very anxious about the possibility of being apprehended by the soldiers as they fled, and there were land mines everywhere.

Leaving camp, they entered the jungle. They ate whatever they could find—Sina is very vague when she talks about what they ate—and were constantly afraid of being apprehended by soldiers or stepping on a land mine. Night was still the most frightening time. Sina's husband was always near tears. After a few days, they could only travel a few miles per day, because they were too weak to walk and some were sick with malaria and dysentery. Sina is not sure how long it took them to get to Thailand, but she estimates four or five months. They just kept moving, with no clear idea where they were headed. In Thailand, they stayed in a United Nations camp for about two years. It was months before they could take solid food, and it took them a long time to recover from the aftermath of starvation and trauma. Sina gave birth to her third child soon after reaching the camp, and a fourth child before they left the camp to come to the United States.

Sina and her family were sponsored as immigrants by a refugee resettlement organization. With the help of a sponsor and an agency social worker, they were settled into an apartment when they first arrived, and Sina and her hus-

**CASE STUDY**

discuss challenges the family was facing. Recently, she came to the agency to talk about her husband's constant sadness.

Sina's husband is still employed by the same construction company that hired him as a newly arrived refugee. At first, Sina worked as a hotel maid, but she now has a job as a case aide with a social service organization. When money is tight, she still works part-time as a maid. A fifth child was born after arriving in the United States, and all of the children have made good adjustments to their new environment. Sina and her husband put a high value on education, and the children have done well in school. The family's sponsor helped them to buy a house in the suburbs a few years ago.

Sina and members of her extended family report that they still have trouble being in the dark, and they get very anxious if the food supply runs low. Sina's husband seems very sad all the time, and he sometimes suggests that he should have stayed and died. Sina, however, thinks they had no choice but to leave, for the sake of the children, and she is matter-of-fact about their struggles. Sina is always motivated to learn something new. She has become a U.S. citizen and is putting great efforts into learning English. She has converted from Buddhism to Catholicism, but her husband has not. Sina and her husband sometimes have a great deal of tension between them because he thinks she is more assertive than women should be. Sina is not sure if this problem would have arisen between them if they had been able to continue with their lives in Cambodia. Sina is more comfortable in her current environment than her husband is, but she sometimes wonders why Americans are so brash, so loud, so direct, so demanding, and so lacking in humility.

## The Complexity of Human Behavior

As eventful as it has been, Sina's story is still unfolding. As a social worker, you will become a part of many unfolding life stories, and you will want to have a way of thinking about them. The purpose of this book is to provide a way for you to think about the nature and complexities of the people and situations that are at the center of social work practice. Three major aspects of this approach to human behavior are the person, the environment, and time.

If we focus on the *person*, we observe that Sina must have been blessed with a healthy biological constitution initially and must have been nurtured well in her youth. She was able to carry babies to term through starvation, illness, and a journey through a jungle. She was able to recover in the hospital camp when many others died of damaged bodies and/or broken spirits. She has emotional resilience and a belief in her own capabilities. Sina and her husband have both survived physically, but she has survived spiritually as well, with a zest for life and hope for the future that he lacks.

If we focus on the *environment*, we see many influences on Sina's story. Consider first the physical environment: Sina moved from a comfortable suburban environment into a very primitive rural prison camp. From there, she wandered in the jungle, with tigers and snakes as her fellow travelers and torrential rains, imagined soldiers, and land mines as foes. Her next stop was a hospital camp and, finally, an American city.

Sina's story has also been powerfully influenced by the geopolitical unrest of her early adulthood. Her relationships with social institutions have changed over time, and she has had to learn new rules based on her changing place in the social structure. Prior to evacuation, as an educated urban woman, she enjoyed high status and the respect that comes with it. In the prison camp, she had to learn to conceal that status and encountered greater powerlessness than she could have previously imagined. In the United States, she has often experienced the loss of status that comes from language barrier, regardless of one's educational background.

Culture, too, has been a powerful influence in Sina's story. She faced no stigma for being given to relatives at birth, because that was not an unusual custom in Cambodia where there was no birth control and extended families were close. Culture recommended what may appear to the reader to be an early marriage and that her partner would be chosen for her. Culture also held that women lack power and influence, and yet Sina assumed a powerful role in her family's escape from the prison camp. Culture accorded a high value to humility, indirect communication, and saving face. The suburban, modernized lifestyle in which Sina was reared contributed a value on education that was not shared with Cambodians who lived in rural areas. And now, Sina lives biculturally. She assists the social workers at her agency to understand the communication patterns of Cambodian clients, and yet she is often baffled by the communication patterns of her native-born American neighbors and coworkers. She is influenced by changing gender roles but is unhappy with the tension that such changes have produced in her marital relationship.

The momentous changes Sina encountered in the physical environment are paralleled by changes in community and organizational environments over time. Sina moved from a suburban community, where she was surrounded by extended family and long-term friends, to a prison camp, where fear was the driving force of relationships and loss of loved ones a common occurrence. Next she moved to a hospital camp, where recovery and taking note of losses took all the available energy. Finally, she moved to a city in the United States, where many people were willing to help but everything seemed strange and the language barrier was a serious impediment. Sina has found several organizations particularly helpful in mediating her struggles with resettlement: the refugee resettlement program that sponsored her family, the social service organization for which she works, the Catholic church of which she is a member, and the schools her children attend. Sina has drawn strength and courage from her associations with these organizations, and she differs from her husband in this regard.

A final dimension of the environment, family, is paramount to Sina. She was lucky that she did not have to leave many family members behind or see them die in the prison camp. Her husband was not so lucky. Sina's children are central to her life, and she suggests that they have motivated her to survive and reach beyond survival with hope. Sina and her husband are devoted to each other, but she is sorry about the tension in their relationship and her husband's enormous sadness. She is grateful, however, that her husband has not self-medicated his grief with alcohol as she has seen other Cambodian-American men do in her work.

If we now focus on the influence of *time*, we see that war and atrocity, escape, and resettlement have been powerful life events for Sina and her family. These events have left many trace effects in their current life. Experiences with past environments have left them with fear of the dark, panic regarding food shortages, and a preference for suburban environments. Both Sina and her husband have minor chronic medical problems from their years of hardship. Sina's husband has no surviving member of his family of origin, and his grief, and perhaps survivor's guilt, over the massive losses is severe. Language barrier is the most persistent reminder that this is not home. Luckily, Sina has managed to smuggle some personal documents and photographs out of Cambodia, and she uses these to invite fond memories of past joyful events, including her traditional Cambodian wedding. These memories give her pleasure, but Sina lives mostly in the present, while anticipating the future with confidence. To her husband, however, the past holds more positive meaning than either the present or future does.

Person, environment, and time interact dynamically. Relationships are reconfigured as the multiple influences on human behavior ebb and flow. The actions of one person can only be understood in relation to the actions of other people and in relation to ever-changing situations. Person and environment depend on each other for their definition; the same person in a different environment, or the same environment with a different person, most likely will yield different behaviors. In reality, of course, any configuration or situation involves multiple persons and multiple environments. We will be referring, at points, to this approach as a **transactional approach**, because that is the name used by other scholars who focus on changing relationships among inseparable aspects of a unity (Altman & Rogoff, 1987; Dewey & Bentley, 1949).

Sina's story provides a good illustration of the inseparability of person, environment, and time. What made her decide to attempt to escape from the prison camp? Was it something within her, something about her physical and social environment, or something about that time of her life? Or a combination of all three? What leads her, now, to reach out for help for her husband? It is impossible to focus on person, environment, and time independently; they are inseparable.

# A Multidimensional Approach

Thinking about human behavior as changing configurations of person and environment over time is a multidimensional approach. Such an approach is not new. Social work has historically recognized human behavior as an interaction of person with environment. The earliest social work practice book, *Social Diagnosis,* written by Mary Richmond in 1917, identified the social situation and the personality of the client as the dual focus of social work assessment. In the late 1960s, general systems theory and other related formulations were incorporated into the way social work scholars think about human behavior (Anderson & Carter, 1974; Bloom, 1984; Germain, 1973; Hartman, 1970; Hearn, 1958, 1969; Meyer, 1976; Pincus & Minahan, 1973; Siporin, 1975). These approaches—which have been called systems, ecological, ecosystem, and configural approaches—have helped social workers to understand the "pattern and flow" (Altman & Rogoff, 1987) of the processes and activities involved in the relationships between person and environment.

We need, of course, to move beyond general statements about the inseparability of person and environment and about changing configurations to bring these ideas alive in our day-to-day experiences as social workers and to understand how to talk with Sina about her concerns. A vast multidisciplinary literature, of both theory and research, is available to help us. The good news is that the multifaceted nature of this literature provides a broad knowledge base for the varied settings and roles involved in social work practice. The bad news is that this literature is highly fragmented. What we need is a structure for organizing our thinking about this multifaceted, fragmented literature.

The multidimensional approach provided in this book should help. This approach is built on the three major aspects of human behavior: person, environment, and time. Although in this book and in the companion volume we will focus on each of these aspects separately, keep in mind that no single aspect can be entirely understood without attention to the other aspects.

We can get a clearer picture of these three aspects if we think about the important dimensions of each—about what it is that we should study about person, about environment, and about time. Exhibit 1.1 provides a graphic overview of the dimensions of person, environment, and time discussed in this book.

Keep in mind that **dimension** refers to a feature that can be focused on separately but that cannot be understood without also considering other features. The dimensions identified in this book are usually studied as detached or semidetached realities, with one dimension characterized as causing or leading to another. However, I do not see dimensions as detached realities, and I am not presenting a causal model. I want instead to show how these dimensions work together, how they are embedded with each other, and how many possibilities are opened for social work

**EXHIBIT 1.1**

Person, Environment, and Time Dimensions

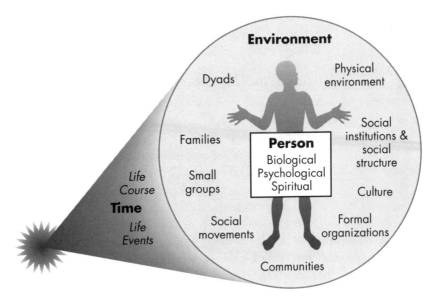

practice when we think about human behavior this way. I do think, however, that focusing on specific dimensions one at a time can clarify general, abstract statements about changing configurations of person and environment.

## Personal Dimensions

Any story could be told from the perspective of any person in the story. I have told a story from Sina's perspective, but this story could have been told from the perspectives of a variety of other persons: a Khmer Rouge soldier, Sina's husband, her mother, one of her children, a member of the sponsoring family, the social worker. You will want to recognize the multiple perspectives held by different persons involved in the stories of which you become a part in your social work activities.

You also will want tools for thinking about the various dimensions of the persons involved in these stories. Until recent years, social work scholars described the approach of social work as *psychosocial,* giving primacy to psychological dimensions of the person. Personality, ego states, emotion, and cognition are the important features of the person in this approach. Currently, however, the social work literature, like contemporary scholarship in other disciplines (for example, Johnson et al.,1990; Kaplan, Sadock, & Grebb, 1994; Longres, 1995; Saleeby, 1992), takes a **biopsychosocial approach**. In this approach, psychology cannot be separated from biology. Emotions and cognitions affect the health of the body, and are affected by it.

In recent years, social work scholars, as well as psychology scholars, have been debating whether spirituality should also be considered a personal dimension. Recent developments in neuroscience have delivered a near-fatal blow to the Cartesian dualism of mind/body and have generated new explorations of the unity of the biological, psychological, and spiritual dimensions of the person. For example, recent research has focused on the ways that emotions and thoughts, as well as spiritual states, influence the immune system (Maier, Watkins, & Fleshner, 1994; Moyers, 1993). Thus this book gives substantial coverage to all three of these dimensions.

## Environmental Dimensions

Social workers have always thought about the environment as multidimensional. As early as 1901, Mary Richmond presented a model of case coordination that took into account not only personal dimensions but also family, neighborhood, civic organizations, private charitable organizations, and public relief organizations (see Exhibit 1.2). Like contemporary social workers, Richmond saw the environment as multidimensional. Although social work scholars have continually revised their understanding of the multidimensional environment, Richmond's model is a forerunner of contemporary models.

Several models for classifying dimensions of the environment have been proposed more recently, six of which are summarized in Exhibit 1.3. Among social work scholars, Anderson and Carter (1974) made a historic contribution to systemic thinking about human behavior with the first edition of their *Human Behavior in the Social Evnironment: A Social Systems Approach,* one of the earliest textbooks on human behavior authored by social workers. Their classification of

**EXHIBIT 1.2**

Mary Richmond's 1901 Model of Case Coordination

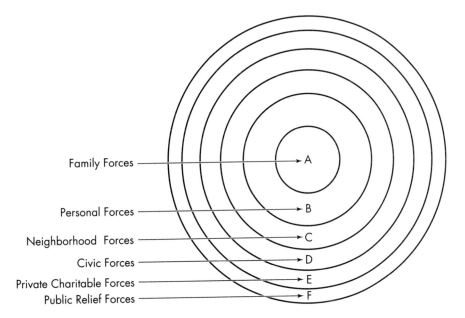

Family Forces      → A

Personal Forces      → B

Neighborhood  Forces      → C

Civic Forces      → D

Private Charitable Forces      → E

Public Relief Forces      → F

A. *Family Forces.*
    Capacity of each member for
    Affection.
    Training.
    Endeavor.
    Social development.

B. *Personal Forces.*
    Kindred.
    Friends.

C. *Neighborhood Forces.*
    Neighbors, landlords, tradesmen.
    Former and present employers.
    Clergymen, Sunday-school teachers,
        fellow church members.
    Doctors.
    Trade-unions, fraternal and benefit
        societies, social clubs,
        fellow-workmen.
    Libraries, educational clubs, classes,
        settlements, etc.
    Thrift agencies, savings-banks,
        stamp-savings, building and loan
        associations.

D. *Civic Forces.*
    School-teachers, truant officers.
    Police, police magistrates, probation
        officers, reformatories.

Health department, sanitary
    inspectors, factory inspectors.
Postmen.
Parks, baths, etc.

E. *Private Charitable Forces.*
    Charity organization society.
    Church of denomination to which
        family belongs.
    Benevolent individuals.
    National, special, and general relief
        societies.
    Charitable employment agencies and
        work-rooms.
    Fresh-air society, children's aid
        society, society for protection of
        children, children's homes, etc.
    District nurses, sick-diet kitchens,
        dispensaries, hospitals, etc.
    Society for suppression of vice,
        prisoner's aid society, etc.

F. *Public Relief Forces.*
    Almshouses.
    Outdoor poor department.
    Public hospitals and dispensaries.

*Source:* Richmond, 1901.

**EXHIBIT 1.3**
Models of
Environmental
Dimensions

| Field/Author | Proposed Dimensions | Definition of Dimension |
|---|---|---|
| *Psychology*<br>Bronfenbrenner (1989) | Microsystem | Face-to-face settings |
| | Mesosystem | Linkages between microsystems containing the focal person |
| | Exosystem | Linkages between two settings, one of which does not contain the focal person but influences her or him |
| | Macrosystem | Culture, subculture, or other broad social context |
| Ford & Lerner (1992) | Natural environments | Products of nature (rain, land, gravity, plants) |
| | Designed environments | Physical aspects constructed by humans |
| | Human environments | Personal interactions |
| | Sociocultural environments | Humanly created means for maintaining coherent, large social groups |
| *Social Work*<br>Anderson & Carter (1990) | Culture & society | Culture as way of life; society as group of people who have learned to live and work together |
| | Communities | Population whose members consciously identify with one another |
| | Organizations | Social system with purpose of achieving specific goals |
| | Groups | Patterns of association in which persons engage most of their "selves" from day to day |
| | Families | Social unit with primary responsibility for socialization |
| Bloom (1990) | Primary groups | Two or more persons with relatively persisting face-to-face communications |
| | Secondary groups | Larger organizations with specialized claim on certain parts of individual's interests and activities |
| | Sociocultural contexts | Ethnic heritage and societal order |
| | Physical environment & time | Natural and built environment; personal time and historical time |

*(continued)*

| Field/Author | Proposed Dimensions | Definition of Dimension |
|---|---|---|
| Carter & McGoldrick (1988b) | Nuclear family | Parents and children living together |
| | Extended family | Multigenerational family |
| | Community, work, friends | Sources of support and stress for families |
| | Social, cultural, political, economic | Gender, religion, ethnicity, social class |
| Schriver (1995) | Families | The intimate units where we carry out most of our lives |
| | Groups | Two or more individuals with shared purpose and common interaction |
| | Organizations | Collectivities of people working together to accomplish a goal or goals |
| | Communities | Collectivities of people with shared interests, regular interaction, and mutual identification |

environmental dimensions has had a significant impact on the way social workers think about the environment. Anderson and Carter divide the environment into five dimensions: culture and society, communities, organizations, groups, and families. Some recent models have added the physical environment (natural and designed environments) as a separate dimension. Failure to include the physical environment has most notably hampered social work's ability to respond to persons with disabilities.

In 1958, Herman Stein and Richard Cloward published an edited reader, *Social Perspectives on Behavior: A Reader in Social Science for Social Work and Related Professions*. In the preface, they commented that social work had failed, in the midst of its fascination with dynamic psychology, to keep abreast of developments in sociology, cultural anthropology, and social psychology. Unfortunately, social work continues to fall behind in its incorporation of the "social" in social work. To have an up-to-date understanding of the multidimensional environment, social workers need knowledge about eight dimensions of environment: the physical environment, social institutions and social structure, culture, formal organizations, communities, social movements, small groups, and families. We also need knowledge about dyadic relationships—relationships between two people, the most basic social relationships. Dyadic relationships receive attention throughout the book, and are the focus of the reflection at the end of Part II. Simultaneous consideration of multiple environmental dimensions provides new possibilities for action, perhaps even new or revised approaches to social work practice.

These dimensions are neither mutually exclusive nor hierarchically ordered. For example, family is sometimes referred to as a social institution; families can also be considered small groups or dyads; and family theorists write about family culture. Remember, dimensions are useful ways of thinking about person/environment configurations, but you should not think of them as detached realities.

## Time Dimensions

When I was a doctoral student in a social work practice course, Professor Max Siporin began his discussion about social work assessment with the comment "The date is the most important information on a written social work assessment." This was Siporin's way of acknowledging the importance of time in human behavior, of recognizing that person/environment transactions are ever-changing, dynamic, and flowing.

Carol Werner, Irwin Altman, and Diana Oxley's (1985) thinking about time is particularly useful for social workers. They suggest that we should think in terms of both linear time and cyclical time. **Linear time** is past, present, and future. People, environments, and the relationships between them have histories and futures, as well as a present, as seen in Sina's story. Some person/environment configurations put greater emphasis on the past, some on the present, and some on the future. Sometimes, the pace of change is more rapid than at other times; it is easy to imagine that the three years spent in the prison camps seemed much longer to Sina and her family than the preceding three years in their suburban home. Keep in mind, too, that social workers become part of changing, dynamic situations. In your transactions, remember that you as well as those with whom you interact bring the effects of the past to current transactions, and that the future for all of you will be affected by your current transactions. You should also remember that ways of thinking about human behavior are constantly changing because they are developing in changing configurations of person and environment. For this reason, this book will often tell you about the history of ideas as well as suggest some future possibilities.

Werner et al. (1985) also alert us to the effects of **cyclical time,** which is repetitive, recurring, spiraling. Cycles of behavior can recur in different patterns: daily, weekly, monthly, seasonally, annually, or in some other regular or partially regular pattern. As I work on this book in mid-July, I am cognizant that summer "vacation" is more than half over, and soon my time will be spent preparing lectures, grading papers, and making visits to field agencies, all activities that I do not engage in during the summer. I am also remembering the rhythm of the school semester: the intense activity to get the semester "up and rolling"; the "settling in time" when I think "I can handle this"; the accelerated pace beginning around mid-semester when I am determinedly focused on time management; and the hectic last weeks when, in spite of my best intentions, my health maintenance program is seriously compromised and I find myself wondering "How did I let this happen again?" This cycle has been repeating for almost twenty years, but it is never exactly the same. Stability, as well as change, comes with cyclical time.

There is also a temporal scope, or duration, to changing configurations. In linear time, the scope of some events is brief, such as a birthday party, an accident, loss of a job, winning the lottery, or a natural disaster. Werner et al. (1985) refer to these brief events as *incidents;* in this book, they will be called **life events.** Although life events are brief in scope, they may produce serious and long-lasting effects. Sina's remarkable story includes several of these transformational events, such as evacuation, escape, and resettlement.

Other events are long and complex transactions of people and environments. Werner et al. (1985) refer to these longer events as *stages;* it is the dimension of time that has been incorporated into life stage theories of human behavior. This book, however, uses a life course rather than life stage perspective. As explained in Chapter 2, life stage theories have been criticized for their overstatement of the consistency of the sequence of stages and of the timing of human behavior. In contrast, a **life course perspective** assumes that each person's life has a unique **trajectory**—a long-term pattern of stability and change—based on his/her own unique person/environment configurations over time, but that shared social and historical contexts produce some commonalities (George, 1993). A life course perspective is stagelike because it proposes that each person experiences a number of **transitions**, or changes in roles and statuses that represent a distinct departure from prior roles and statuses. These transitions may be unique, may be shared with a particular group of persons, or may be widely shared. A life course perspective also recognizes **life course markers** that are widely shared by particular **cohorts**—groups of persons who are of the same age group at the time of a particular social change within a given culture. But it also recognizes the influence of unexpected life events. Sina and her husband share much in common with other parents of adolescent and young adult offspring, but they have also experienced some life events that few of us share. In fact, even though they passed together through these events, it cannot be said that Sina and her husband have shared exactly the same life course.

## The General and the Unique

Let's assume that your field instructor has asked you to meet with Sina regarding her concerns about her husband. How will you know how to talk with her and what to talk with her about? What questions will you have before you get started? What do you want to know more about? Most likely, you want to know something about Sina's unique life story, and you must decide how much of that to learn from agency records and your field instructor and how much to wait and hear from Sina herself. But you will probably want to know some other, more general types of information that will not be in the agency record, and that you know your field instructor expects you to take some personal responsibility for learning. This general information might include aspects of Cambodian culture, family functioning, Buddhism and Catholicism, grief reactions, post–traumatic stress reactions, clinical depression, and cross-cultural communication.

Carol Meyer (1993) suggests that effective social work practice involves balancing an individualized (unique) assessment of the specific person(s) in a specific situation with general knowledge about human behavior:

> Practitioners of a profession must draw upon general knowledge about the class of clients
> of which the particular client may be a representative, and about the general nature of
> problems indicated in the case. The reliance upon general knowledge to help explain a
> unique case situation is one of the distinguishing features of a professionally educated vs. a
> volunteer or agency-trained social worker. (Meyer, 1993, p. 10)

Professional social workers weave idiosyncratic details of a client's story with general knowledge about patterns of relationships between persons and situations. Although Meyer writes about work with one particular client, her suggestions about general knowledge and unique situations could apply equally well to work with families, small groups, neighborhoods, and so on. You might want, for example, to form a mutual aid group of Cambodian men or develop an outreach program in a Cambodian neighborhood.

I want to emphasize two ideas about the relationship between general and unique knowledge: (1) It was Sina's unique story that suggested which general knowledge content was needed. (2) The general knowledge will suggest **hypotheses** to be explored and tested, not facts to be applied, in transactions with Sina (Schutt, 1996, p. 45). For example, your examination of general knowledge may lead you to hypothesize that Sina's husband understands the tenets of Buddhism to direct him to hold himself personally responsible for his own suffering. You may hypothesize that, like many Southeast Asians, he would find it disgraceful to engage in direct conversation about his emotions. You may have learned that although seeking help for physical problems was acceptable in Cambodia, there were no special professions for addressing emotional problems. This understanding may lead you to hypothesize that Sina's husband would be more comfortable talking about his situation in terms of its biological aspects instead of its emotional aspects. Some hypotheses will not be supported in this unique situation, but many hypotheses will prove to be useful. Ultimately, of course, you want to understand how Cambodian culture, family functioning, Buddhism and Catholicism, grief reactions, post–traumatic stress reactions, clinical depression, cross-cultural communication, and all the rest come together to form a whole in Sina's unfolding life story. That is a lot to think about, but such complexity is what makes social work such a demanding and exciting profession.

Today, the need to focus on "'diverse person(s) in diverse environments'" is more important than ever (Germain, 1994, p. 88). We are developing a heightened consciousness of human differences—gender differences, racial and ethnic differences, cultural differences, religious differences, differences in sexual orientation, differences in family forms, and so on—and the need to consider how they affect individuals. These differences among people are not new but simply newly recognized. Because of the globalization of cultures and economies, we are becoming a more diverse society all the time. We are experiencing a new tension to navigate the line between cultural sensitivity and stereotypical thinking about individuals. It is the intent of this book to capture the diversity of human experience in a manner that is respectful of all groups and conveys a positive value of human diversity. However, one of the challenges of diversity is the reality that power arrangements provide different opportunities for different groups. Maximizing the options for members of nondominant groups is part of social work's traditional mission, and it is important for social workers to understand power relations and processes of oppression.

Professional social workers must also struggle continuously with the tension between the general and the unique. The transactional, multidimensional approach presented in this book is well suited to this struggle. As suggested earlier, transactional approaches are interested both in unique events and in patterns across similar events (Altman & Rogoff, 1987). A multidimensional approach allows examination of an idiosyncratic event from several perspectives and opens the possibilities for considering the variety of factors that contribute to a particular transaction. Both the transactional and multidimensional approaches facilitate social work's emphasis on human diversity.

To assist you in moving between general knowledge and unique stories, each chapter in this book will begin, as this one did, with a story or stories. Each of these unique stories will suggest which general knowledge is needed. Then, throughout the chapter, the stories will be woven together with the relevant general knowledge. Keep in mind as you read that general knowledge is necessary, but you will not be an effective practitioner unless you take the time to learn about the unique life course of each person or collectivity you serve.

## General Knowledge: Theory and Research

General knowledge has recently come under attack for failure to recognize the uniqueness of persons and situations. Some would suggest that there can be no "general" knowledge because all situations are unique. I think you can see, however, that the details of Sina's unique story are inadequate for guiding you in thinking about how to talk with her and what to talk about. You also need some general knowledge about human behavior, which you can draw from two sources: theory and research.

Social workers use **theory** to help organize and make sense of the situations we encounter. Reid and Smith (1989, p. 45) suggest:

> Scratch any social worker and you will find a theoretician. Her own theoretical perspectives about people and practice may be informed by theories in print (or formal theories) but are put together in her own way with many modifications and additions growing out of her own professional and personal experience.

Thus, theory gives us a framework for interpreting person/environment transactions and planning interventions.

If you are to make good use of theory, you should know something about how it is constructed. **Concepts** are the building blocks of theory. They are symbols that allow us to communicate about the phenomena of interest. Culture, family functioning, Buddhism, grief reaction, post–traumatic stress disorder, clinical depression, and cross-cultural communication are all concepts relevant to Sina's story.

Theoretical concepts are put together to form **propositions** or assertions. For example, attachment theory asserts that loss of an attachment figure leads to a grief reaction. This proposition, which asserts a particular relationship among the concepts of loss, attachment figure, and grief, may help us understand the behavior of Sina's husband.

Social and behavioral science theories are based on **assumptions** about the nature of human social life. These theoretical assumptions have raised a number of controversies, three of which are worth introducing at this point (Burrell & Morgan, 1979; Martin & O'Connor, 1989; Monte, 1995):

- Do the dimensions of human behavior have an **objective reality** that exists outside of a person's consciousness, or is all reality based on personal perception (**subjective reality**)?

- Is human behavior determined by forces beyond the control of the person (**determinism**), or are persons free and proactive agents in the creation of their behavior (**voluntarism**)?

- Are the patterned interactions among people characterized by harmony, unity, and social cohesion or by conflict, domination, coercion, and exploitation?

The nature of these controversies will become more apparent to you in Chapter 2. The contributing authors and I will be taking a middle ground on all of them: We assume that reality has both objective and subjective aspects, that human behavior is partially constrained and partially free, and that social life is marked by both cohesion and conflict.

Theory is one source of general knowledge about human behavior. Research is the other. Rubin and Babbie (1993, p. xxv) remind us that "the practitioner who just conforms to ongoing practices without keeping abreast of the latest research in his or her field is not doing all possible to see that his or her clients get the best possible service." **Research** is typically viewed, in simple terms, as a problem-solving process, or a method of seeking answers to questions. The research process includes a careful, purposeful observation of events with the intent to note and record them in terms of their attributes and to look for patterns in those events.

Just as there are controversies about theoretical assumptions, there are also controversies about what constitutes appropriate research methods for understanding human behavior. Modern science is based on several assumptions, generally recognized as a **positivist perspective:** Findings of one study should be applicable to other groups; complex phenomena can be studied by reducing them to some component part; scientific methods are value-free. **Quantitative methods of research** are the preferred methods from the perspective of modern science. These methods use quantifiable measures of concepts, standardize the collection of data, attend only to preselected variables, and use statistical methods to look for patterns and associations. However, critics of these methods argue that quantitative methods cannot possibly capture the complex nature of social life. These critics suggest a need to replace existing methods with **qualitative methods of research,** providing "a firsthand, holistic understanding of phenomena of interest by means of a flexible strategy of problem formulation and data collection shaped as the investigation proceeds" (Reid & Smith, 1989, p. 87). Researchers using qualitative methods are more likely to present their findings in words than in numbers, and to attempt to capture the settings of behavior. They are likely to report the transactions of researcher and participant, as well as the values of the researcher, because they assume that value-free research is impossible. In this controversy, it is my position that there is no single research method that can adequately capture the whole, the complexity, of human behavior. Both quantitative and qualitative research methods have a place in a multidimensional approach.

## Critical Use of Theory and Research

Theories of and research about human behavior are nearly boundless and constantly growing. This book presents an up-to-date account of the current state of knowledge about human behavior, but quite possibly some of this knowledge will eventually be found mistaken. Thus, you are encouraged to be an active reader—reading with a sense of inquiry and curiosity, but also with a healthy skepticism. Eileen Gambrill (1990, p. 75) suggests that the active reader should

**EXHIBIT 1.4**

Questions Asked by
the Active Reader

1.  What is the evidence for this statement?
2.  Is this true for all people (for me, for my client, for other people I know)?
3.  How can I use this information in my practice?
4.  Is there anything left out of this argument?
5.  What is the main point of this section?
6.  Can I summarize the argument?
7   How does this relate to other evidence about this topic?

*Source:* Based on Gambrill, 1990, p. 75.

think about the questions listed in Exhibit 1.4. I hope that you will incorporate these questions into your reading of this book.

As you read this book and other sources of general knowledge, you will also want to begin to think critically about the theory and research that they present. Social and behavioral science scholars disagree about the criteria for evaluating theory and research. However, I recommend the criteria presented in Exhibit 1.5 because they are consistent with the transactional, multidimensional approach of this book.

The five criteria for evaluating a theory presented in Exhibit 1.5 are used in Chapter 2 to evaluate eight theoretical perspectives relevant to social work. Judging theory on the basis of coherence and conceptual clarity, testability, and compatibility raises little or no controversy in the social and behavioral science literature. However, the criterion of comprehensiveness is specifically related to the multidimensional approach of this book and would be challenged by many social scientists and social workers. And the criterion of significance for social work practice—relevant only to students of human behavior who are social workers—examines the utility of the theory for a profession that highly values social justice.

Exhibit 1.5 also presents six questions to ask when reading a research report. These criteria can be applied to either quantitative or qualitative research. Many research reports would be strengthened if their authors were to attend to these criteria.

## Theory and Research in a Multidimensional Approach

As you travel the journey on which this book takes you, you should have a clear understanding of the assumptions the contributing authors and I make about the role of theory and research in understanding human behavior. That understanding will assist you to be a critical reader of the book. I have written about some of these assumptions earlier in the chapter, but I summarize them for you here for emphasis.

Our assumptions about theory are as follows:

- Changing configurations of persons and environments may involve unique, unrepeatable events, but they also may involve consistencies and patterns of similar events. Therefore, general statements and theories are possible, but should not be expected to fit all situations or all aspects of a given situation.

**EXHIBIT 1.5**
Criteria for
Evaluating Theory
and Research

| **Criteria for Evaluating Theory** |
| --- |

*Coherence and conceptual clarity.* Are the concepts clearly defined and consistently used? Is the theory free of logical inconsistencies? Is it stated in the simplest possible way, without oversimplifying?

*Comprehensiveness.* Does the theory include multiple dimensions of persons, environments, and time? Does it account for things that other theories have overlooked or been unable to account for?

*Testability.* Can the concepts and propositions be expressed in language that makes them observable and accessible to corroboration or refutation by persons other than the theoretician?

*Compatibility with existing theory and research.* With which existing theories is this theory compatible? Incompatible? Is it incompatible with any theories that have received significant empirical validation?

*Significance of theory for social work practice.* Does the theory assist in the understanding of person and environment transactions over time? Can it accommodate uniqueness and diversity? Does it assist in understanding power arrangements and systems of oppression? Does it value human relationships and recognize the mutual dependence and obligation of persons and communities? Does it promote social justice? Does the theory suggest principles of action?

**Criteria for Evaluating Research**

*Multidimensionality.* Does the research include multiple dimensions of persons, environments, and time? If not, do the researchers acknowledge the omissions, connect the research to larger programs of research that include omitted dimensions, and/or recommend further research to include omitted dimensions?

*Acknowledgment of the influence of setting.* Does the researcher specify attributes of the setting of the research, acknowledge the possible contribution of the setting to research outcomes, and present the findings of similar research across a range of settings?

*Acknowledgment of differences in meaning.* Does the researcher specify the meanings of the research process to the research participants, and the contributions of these meanings to the research outcomes?

*Acknowledgment of the influence of the researcher.* Does the researcher specify the attributes of the researcher and the role of the researcher in the observed person/environment configurations? Does the researcher specify the possible contributions of the researcher to research outcomes?

*Specification of inferences.* Does the researcher specify how inferences are made, based on the data?

*Suitability of measures.* Does the researcher use measures that seem suited to, and sensitive to, the situation being researched?

■ Each situation allows examination from several perspectives, and using a variety of theoretical perspectives brings more dimensions of the situation into view. Different situations call for different combinations of theoretical concepts and propositions.

- Theories, like situations, are unfolding and should be viewed as tentative statements. Theoretical propositions serve as hypotheses to be tested, not as factual statements about the situation under examination.

- Given the complexity of human behavior, a given transaction is probably not predictable, but we do not rule out the possibility of prediction.

- Our goal as social workers should be to develop maximum understanding of situations in terms of whatever theoretical concepts and propositions apply. Multiple theoretical perspectives are necessary when taking a multidimensional approach to human behavior. This point will be the focus of Chapter 2.

- Social life is fraught with contradictions as well as consistencies, so it is acceptable to use multiple theoretical approaches that introduce contradictions. You will discover some contradictions in the theories discussed in Chapter 2.

Our assumptions about research include the following:

- Any setting is an acceptable research setting, but studying a variety of settings enhances the knowledge-building process.

- The researcher should always consider the contribution of the setting to the research findings.

- The characteristics, biases, and role of the researcher constitute aspects of the phenomenon under study and should be considered in interpretation of data. The meanings of the research activities to the participants are also important dimensions of the research situation and should be considered in interpreting the data.

- Standardized measures should be used only when they are suited to the situation under study.

- Understanding of human behavior may be advanced by both traditional and nontraditional methods of research.

- Research projects that exclude person, environment, or time dimensions may advance understanding of human behavior, but the researcher should recognize the omissions in interpretation of the data.

# Basic Concepts in the Life Course Perspective

This book is organized around one of the three aspects of human behavior: time. The first two aspects, person and environment, are covered in a companion volume titled *Dimensions of Human Behavior: Person and Environment*. The life course perspective that has been emerging over the last 30 years, across several disciplines, has proved to be a convenient way of understanding the relationship between time and human behavior. As Phyllis Moen (1995) explains, the life course perspective "attends to continuity and change in lives, looking at age-graded trajectories and transitions in social roles, relationships, and resources and documenting how these are shaped by social change" (p. 5). Thus it is well suited to understanding human behavior in a changing world and for people at different periods in their lives.

Glen Elder, Jr. (1994), a central figure in the development of the life course perspective, sees four dominant themes in the life course approach:

- *Interplay of human lives and historical time.* Persons born in different years face different historical worlds, with different options and constraints—especially in rapidly changing societies such as the United States at the end of the 20th century. Historical time may produce both cohort effects and period effects. **Cohort effects** are the effects of social change on a specific cohort. **Period effects** occur when the effects of social change are uniform across cohort groups.

- *Timing of lives.* Particular roles and behaviors are thought to be associated with particular age groups. Of course, it is not the passage of time itself that produces transitions; age-graded differences in roles and behaviors are the result of biological, psychological, and social processes. For this reason, age is often considered from each of the perspectives that make up the biopsychosocial approach to human behavior (e.g., Cavanaugh, 1993; Kimmel, 1990): **Biological age** indicates a person's level of biological development and physical health, as measured by the functioning of the various vital organ systems. **Psychological age** refers to the skills that people use to adapt to changing biological and environmental demands, skills such as intelligence, memory, emotions, and motivation. **Social age** refers to the age-graded roles and behaviors expected by society—in other words, the socially constructed meaning of various ages. The concept **age norms** is used to indicate the behaviors that are expected of people of a specific age in a given society at a particular point in time. Age norms may be informal expectations, or they may be encoded as formal age rules and laws. Life course scholars suggest that age norms vary not only across time and societies, but also by gender, race, ethnicity, and social class within a given time and society (Chudacoff, 1989; Kertzer, 1989). Although biological age and psychological age are recognized in the life course perspective, special emphasis is placed on social age.

- *Linked or interdependent lives.* The life course perspective emphasizes the interdependence of human lives and the ways in which both social control and social support occur in relationships and social networks of relationships. Particular attention has been paid to the family as the primary arena for experiencing and interpreting wider historical, cultural, and social phenomena. Family lives are thought to be linked across generations, with both opportunity and misfortune having an intergenerational impact. Elder (1992) comments that "each generation is bound to fateful decisions and events in the other's life course" (p. 1123).

- *Human agency in making choices.* The life course perspective recognizes both personal and environmental constraints on human behavior, but within those constraints, people are thought to shape their own life courses by making purposeful choices among options.

From the earliest empirical investigations by life course researchers, strong evidence has emerged of diversity in life course patterns. The sources of diversity are evident in Elder's four themes: First, differences can be expected between cohort groups. Second, age norms change with time and place; they also vary by gender, race, ethnicity, and social class. Third, the differing patterns of social networks in which persons are embedded produce differences in life course experiences. Fourth, human agency allows for extensive individual differences in life course trajectories. It is not surprising, given these possibilities for unique experience, that the stories of individuals vary so much.

Nevertheless, as I explained before, social workers need a framework of general knowledge for understanding unique stories, and for some time, age-graded stages have provided that framework (Germain, 1994). There is good reason to continue to do so. Chudacoff's (1989) historical analysis suggests that age became an increasingly dominant feature of the organization of U.S. society during the 20th century. Recent research indicates that age continues to be a dominant feature, and there is a great deal of agreement among the members of any society about age norms (e.g., Lawrence, 1996; Riley, 1994; Settersten & Hagestad, 1996). On the other hand, this same research suggests that there have been recent changes in some age norms in our society and that we are becoming increasingly flexible in our thinking about them, reporting greater ranges of acceptable ages for specific role transitions. Thus, we should recognize the influence of age norms, while also acknowledging the diversity of life course trajectories that arise from historical time, gender, race, ethnicity, social class, social networks, and personal agency.

# Organization of the Book

The next chapter provides a foundation for thinking critically about life course theory and research. It is followed by a reflection that demonstrates the multifaceted nature of social work. Part II includes six chapters that analyze well-accepted periods of the life course: conception, pregnancy, and birth; infancy and early childhood; middle childhood; adolescence; adulthood; and late adulthood. Finally at the end of Part II, a reflection demonstrates a community prevention project based on a life course perspective.

Focusing on time dimensions to explain human behavior is a convenient approach, but it is risky. I do not wish to reinforce any tendency to think about person, environment, and time as distinct and separate aspects of human behavior. Remember, no single dimension of human behavior can be understood without attention to the other dimensions. Understanding of the unity of persons, environments, and time will be aided by frequent references to all three aspects of human behavior throughout this book, highlighted with margin notes asking you to consider a specific dimension.

## IMPLICATIONS FOR SOCIAL WORK PRACTICE

The multidimensional approach outlined in this chapter suggests several principles for social work assessment and intervention, for both prevention and remediation services:

- In the assessment process, collect information about all of the critical dimensions of the changing configuration of person and environment.

- In the assessment process, attempt to see the situation from a variety of perspectives. Use multiple data sources, including the person(s), significant others, and direct observations.

- Allow people to tell their own stories, and pay attention to how they describe the pattern and flow of their person/environment configurations.

- Use the multidimensional data base to develop a dynamic picture of the person-environment configuration.

- Link intervention strategies to the dimensions of the assessment.

- In general, expect more effective outcomes from interventions that are multidimensional, because the situation itself is multidimensional.

- Allow the unique stories of people and situations to direct the choice of theory and research to be used.

- Use general knowledge to suggest tentative hypotheses to be explored in the unique situation.

- Think of social work practice as a continuous, dialectical movement between unique knowledge and general knowledge.

- In the assessment process, recognize the interplay of human lives and historical time; the biological, psychological, and social ages of clients; the interdependence of human lives; and the ways that individuals shape their own life courses.

## MAIN POINTS

1. This book provides a way of thinking about human behavior in terms of changing configurations of persons and environments. Its approach is transactional and multidimensional.

2. Although person, environment, and time are inseparable, we can focus on them separately by thinking about the relevant dimensions of each.

3. A dimension is a feature of person, environment, or time that can be focused on separately, but that cannot be understood without also considering other relevant features.

4. Relevant personal dimensions include the biological, the psychological, and the spiritual.

sions have been studied separately, but they are neither mutually exclusive nor hierarchically ordered.

6. Two dimensions of time, based on temporal scope, are life events and life course.

7. The transactional approach presented in this book is interested in both unique events and patterns across similar events. Such an approach facilitates social work's emphasis on human diversity.

8. Special attention should be paid to power relations and processes of oppression.

9. General knowledge, as well as knowledge about the unique situation, is necessary for effective social work practice.

10. General knowledge about human behavior comes from two sources: theory and research.

11. Theory can be evaluated according to the following five criteria: coherence and conceptual clarity, comprehensiveness, testability, compatibility with existing theory and research, and significance for social work practice.

12. The transactional approach suggests that research should be evaluated according to the following criteria: inclusion of multiple dimensions of persons, environments, and time; specification of the attributes of the research setting; specification of the meaning of the research to participants; specification of the attributes and role of the researcher; specification of how inferences are made; and suitability of the measures to the situation.

13. Contemporary social and behavioral science is marked by controversies about theoretical assumptions and research methods: objective versus subjective reality, determinism versus voluntarism, cohesion versus conflict. The multidimensional perspective presented in this book takes a middle ground on these controversies.

14. A multidimensional approach to human behavior requires multiple theoretical perspectives.

15. A life course perspective is well suited for understanding human behavior in a changing world and for people at different periods in their lives.

## KEY TERMS

age norm
assumption
biological age
biopsychosocial approach
cohort
cohort effect

concept
cyclical time
determinism
dimension
hypothesis
life course marker

life course perspective

life event

linear time

objective reality

period effect

positivist perspective

proposition

psychological age

qualitative method of research

quantitative method of research

research

social age

subjective reality

theory

trajectory

transactional approach

transition

voluntarism

## WORLD WIDE WEB RESOURCES

Each chapter of this textbook will contain a list of Internet resources and Web sites that may be useful to the reader in his or her search for further information. Each site listing will include the address and a brief description of the contents of the site. The reader should be aware that the information contained in Web sites may not be truthful or reliable and should be confirmed before being used as a reference. The reader should also be aware that Internet addresses, or URLs, are constantly changing; therefore, the addresses listed may no longer be active or accurate. Many of the Internet sites listed in each chapter contain links to other Internet sites containing more information on the topic. The reader may use these links for further investigation.

Information not included in the WWW Resources sections of each chapter can be found by using one of the many Internet search engines provided free of charge on the Internet. These search engines enable you to search using keywords or phrases, or you can use the search engines' topical listings. You should use several search engines when researching a topic, as each will retrieve different Internet sites.

YAHOO

**http:// www.yahoo.com**

EXCITE

**http:// www.excite.com**

HOTBOT

**http:// www.hotbot.com**

LYCOS

**http:// www.lycos.com**

Many Internet sites provide statistical data that are very useful for research. The majority are government sites; therefore, the addresses will be more reliable, and the information provided can be deemed more trustworthy.

U.S. Census Bureau Official Statistics

**http://www.census.gov/**

Social Statistics Briefing Room

**http://www.whitehouse.gov/fsbr/ssbr.html**

White House site contains current federal statistics on crime, demographics, health, education, and economics.

National Center for Health Statistics

**http://cdc.gov/nchswww/default.htm**

Health statistics from the Centers for Disease Control on topics such as life expectancy, the uninsured population, and disabilities.

Statistical Resources on the Web

**http://www.lib.umich.edu/libhome/Documents.center/stats.html**

Hosted by the University of Michigan, this site provides links to various statistical information on the Internet, including such topics as housing, demographics, and sociology.

World Wide Web Resources for Social Workers

**http://pages.nyu.edu/~gh5/gh-w3-f.htm**

Written and maintained by Professor Gary Holden of New York University's School of Social Work, this site contains links to many federal and state Internet sites as well as journals, assessment and measurement tools, and sites pertaining to client issues.

## CHAPTER 2

# Theoretical Perspectives on Human Behavior

*Elizabeth D. Hutchison, Virginia Commonwealth University, and Leanne Wood Charlesworth, University of Maryland*

### INTERGENERATIONAL STRESSES IN THE CLARK FAMILY

You have been asked to investigate the possibility that Martha Clark's family caregivers are emotionally and physically abusing her, as well as neglecting her. Martha Clark is an 81-year-old widow who has lived with her 58-year-old son, Al, and his wife, Betty, since moving from her one-story apartment in a senior housing project when her husband died. Mrs. Clark never held a job outside the home, and her current income consists of the $400 per month she receives from Social Security. She has no savings. Mrs. Clark has arthritis that limits her mobility, making it difficult for her to walk the stairs from the main floor of Al and Betty's home to her bedroom, and the only bathroom, on the second floor. Mrs. Clark also has heart disease and diabetes. She has been challenged by periodic episodes of depression throughout adulthood, and she has been despondent since her husband died two years ago.

Nine months ago, Al Clark was laid off from the plant where he had worked for the past 15 years. He had a massive heart attack six months ago, and he remains very fearful of having a second heart attack. Betty Clark works an 8:30-to-4:30 shift at the factory where she has worked on and off for 30 years. Currently, there is a rumor that the company is planning to relocate the factory outside the United States. Al and Betty Clark have two young adult children, both of whom live out of town. Their son, father of two children, was recently divorced; their daughter is pregnant with her third child. Both children are struggling financially, and their son often turns to Al and Betty with his grief about the divorce.

Before she leaves for work every morning, Betty prepares breakfast for Al and Martha. Most mornings, Martha does not come down until it's almost time for Betty to leave for work, and then Martha only picks at her food. Al has become concerned that Martha usually eats no lunch, and he admits that on several occasions he has lost his temper, screamed at his mother, and even hit her a few times. He feels angry, frustrated, and a failure for losing his temper, but he doesn't know how to get his mother to eat. He also discovered recently that she has not been taking her medication for depression. When he discovered that, he berated Martha, screaming that she is "just a useless old woman."

Since Al's heart attack, money has been tight. The family car needed an expensive repair, and the hot water heater had to be replaced. Martha's medications are not covered by Medicare, and for the past two weeks Al and Betty have not renewed some of her prescriptions, hoping each week that the money situation will be better next week. Al and Betty often have harsh words about the money problems.

Martha Clark reports that Al and Betty are doing a good job caring for her. She says that she has lived too long anyway, and that Al is right: she is a use-

**CASE STUDY**

less old woman. The doctor tells her that walking would be good for both her arthritis and her heart disease, but she spends most of her time sitting in a chair in her bedroom. She says she does not eat because she has no appetite.

# Multiple Perspectives for a Multidimensional Approach

The unfolding story of Martha Clark, her son, and her daughter-in-law is certainly unique in the way particular persons and environments are interacting over time. As a social worker, you need to understand these details about the situation of the Clark family. However, if you are to be helpful in improving the situation, you also need some general knowledge that will assist you in thinking about its unique elements. As suggested in Chapter 1, the range of general knowledge offered by a multitheoretical approach is necessary when taking a multidimensional approach to human behavior. The purpose of this chapter is to introduce you to eight theoretical perspectives that are particularly useful for thinking about changing configurations of persons and environments: systems perspective, conflict perspective, rational choice perspective, social constructionist perspective, psychodynamic perspective, developmental perspective, social behavioral perspective, and humanistic perspective.

As Exhibit 2.1 demonstrates, you will find these eight perspectives threaded throughout the discussions in Part II of this book and in the companion volume, *Dimensions of Human Behavior: Person and Environment.* In *Person and Environment,* margin notes are used to help you recognize ideas from specific perspectives. The margin notes in this book are questions intended to help you think critically about the implications of the dimensions in the practice of social work. Our purpose here is to introduce the central ideas of the eight perspectives and to analyze their scientific merit, as well as their significance for social work practice. The five criteria for critical understanding of theory, identified in Chapter 1, provide the framework for the discussion of perspectives in this chapter: coherence and conceptual clarity, comprehensiveness, testability, compatibility with existing theory and research, and significance for social work practice.

Four of the perspectives introduced in this chapter are based in sociology, four are based in psychology, and several have interdisciplinary roots. Carel Germain (1994), in her historical overview, suggests that social work professionals began with a preference for sociological knowledge, moved over time to a preference for psychological knowledge, and have recently come to seek knowledge of both environmental and personal factors. This recent trend is consistent with the multidimensional, transactional approach of this book. Overall, however, the eight perspectives described here do not adequately embrace the biological and spiritual dimensions, and you will find few traces of them in the chapters on the biological person and the spiritual person.

As noted in Chapter 1, diversity is a major theme of this book. In earlier versions of the eight perspectives, few, if any, met Germain's criterion for attention to diverse persons in diverse environments. Each of the perspectives has continued to evolve, however, and the current trend is to reconstruct the perspectives to better accommodate diversity. Recent theorizing also suggests that the boundaries between perspectives are blurring, consistent with George Ritzer's (1992)

**EXHIBIT 2.1**

Chapters Drawing on Each Theoretical Perspective

| Theoretical Perspective | Chapters in *Dimensions of Human Behavior: Person and Environment* | Chapters in *Dimensions of Human Behavior: The Changing Life Course* |
|---|---|---|
| **Sociology-Based Perspectives** | | |
| Systems Perspective | 3 The Biological Person<br>5 The Psychological Person: Stress, Coping, and Adaptation<br>6 The Spiritual Person<br>7 The Physical Environment<br>8 Social Institutions and Social Structure<br>9 Culture<br>10 Formal Organizations<br>11 Communities<br>13 Small Groups<br>14 Families | 3 Conception, Pregnancy, and Birth<br>4 Infancy and Early Childhood<br>5 Middle Childhood<br>6 Adolescence<br>7 Adulthood<br>8 Late Adulthood |
| Conflict Perspective | 3 The Biological Person<br>5 The Psychological Person: Stress, Coping, and Adaptation<br>6 The Spiritual Person<br>7 The Physical Environment<br>8 Social Institutions and Social Structure<br>9 Culture<br>10 Formal Organizations<br>11 Communities<br>12 Social Movements<br>14 Families | 3 Conception, Pregnancy, and Birth<br>4 Infancy and Early Childhood<br>5 Middle Childhood<br>6 Adolescence<br>7 Adulthood |
| Rational Choice Perspective | 8 Social Institutions and Social Structure<br>10 Formal Organizations<br>12 Social Movements<br>13 Small Groups | 3 Conception, Pregnancy, and Birth<br>4 Infancy and Early Childhood<br>5 Middle Childhood<br>6 Adolescence<br>7 Adulthood<br>8 Late Adulthood |
| Social Constructionist Perspective | 3 The Biological Person<br>4 The Psychological Person: Cognition, Emotion, and Self<br>5 The Psychological Person: Stress, Coping, and Adaptation<br>7 The Physical Environment<br>8 Social Institutions and Social Structure<br>9 Culture<br>10 Formal Organizations<br>11 Communities<br>12 Social Movements<br>13 Small Groups<br>14 Families | 3 Conception, Pregnancy, and Birth<br>4 Infancy and Early Childhood<br>5 Middle Childhood<br>6 Adolescence<br>7 Adulthood<br>8 Late Adulthood |

(continued)

**EXHIBIT 2.1**

Chapters Drawing on Each Theoretical Perspective *(continued)*

| Theoretical Perspective | Chapters in *Dimensions of Human Behavior: Person and Environment* | | Chapters in *Dimensions of Human Behavior: The Changing Life Course* | |
|---|---|---|---|---|
| *Psychology-Based Perspectives.* | | | | |
| Psychodynamic Perspective | 4 | The Psychological Person: Cognition, Emotion, and Self | 3 | Conception, Pregnancy, and Birth |
| | 5 | The Psychological Person: Stress, Coping, and Adaptation | 4 | Infancy and Early Childhood |
| | 6 | The Spiritual Person | 5 | Middle Childhood |
| | 7 | The Physical Environment | 6 | Adolescence |
| | 9 | Culture | 7 | Adulthood |
| | 12 | Social Movements | 8 | Late Adulthood |
| | 13 | Small Groups | | |
| | 14 | Families | | |
| Developmental Perspective | 3 | The Biological Person | 3 | Conception, Pregnancy, and Birth |
| | 4 | The Psychological Person: Cognition, Emotion, and Self | 4 | Infancy and Early Childhood |
| | 5 | The Psychological Person: Stress, Coping, and Adaptation | 5 | Middle Childhood |
| | 6 | The Spiritual Person | 6 | Adolescence |
| | 7 | The Physical Environment | 7 | Adulthood |
| | 12 | Social Movements | 8 | Late Adulthood |
| | 13 | Small Groups | | |
| | 14 | Families | | |
| Social Behavioral Perspective | 4 | The Psychological Person: Cognition, Emotion, and Self | 3 | Conception, Pregnancy, and Birth |
| | 6 | The Spiritual Person | 4 | Infancy and Early Childhood |
| | 7 | The Physical Environment | 5 | Middle Childhood |
| | 8 | Social Institutions and Social Structure | 6 | Adolescence |
| | 9 | Culture | 7 | Adulthood |
| | 13 | Small Groups | 8 | Late Adulthood |
| | 14 | Families | | |
| Humanistic Perspective | 3 | The Biological Person | 4 | Infancy and Early Childhood |
| | 4 | The Psychological Person: Cognition, Emotion, and Self | 5 | Middle Childhood |
| | 6 | The Spiritual Person | 6 | Adolescence |
| | 8 | Social Institutions and Social Structure | 7 | Adulthood |
| | 9 | Culture | 8 | Late Adulthood |
| | 10 | Formal Organizations | | |
| | 13 | Small Groups | | |
| | 14 | Families | | |

prediction that the 1990s would be an era of theoretical synthesizing. As you read about each of the perspectives, think not only about how it can be applied in social work practice but also how well it represents all the complexities of human behavior.

# The Systems Perspective

When you read the story at the beginning of this chapter, you probably first thought of it as a story about a family system—a story about Martha Clark, her son Al, and her daughter-in-law Betty—rather than "Martha Clark's story." You probably noted how Martha's, Al's, and Betty's lives are interrelated, how they influence one another's behavior, and what impact each of them has on the overall well-being of the family. You may be thinking that Al's treatment of Martha contributes to her despondence, and that her despondent behaviors are feeding his sense of failure and frustration. You also may note that this family, like other families, has a **boundary** indicating who is in and who is out, and you may be wondering if the boundary around this family is as closed as it appears, with minimal input from friends, extended family, neighborhood, church, and so on. You may also have noted the influence of larger systems on this family: the insecurity of the labor market, the limitations of the health care delivery system, historical gender roles that influenced Martha to confine her work history to the home.

You can see, in Exhibit 2.2, how these observations about Martha, Al, and Betty fit with the central ideas of the **systems perspective**. The systems perspective sees human behavior as the outcome of reciprocal interactions of persons operating within organized and integrated social systems. Its roots are very interdisciplinary. During the 1940s and 1950s, a variety of disciplines—including mathematics, physics, engineering, biology, psychology, cultural anthropology, economics, and sociology—began looking at phenomena as the outcome of interactions within and among systems. Mathematicians and engineers used the new ideas about system **feedback mechanisms**—the processes by which information about past behaviors in a system are fed back into the system in a circular manner—to develop military technology for World War II; scientists at the Bell Laboratories used the same ideas to develop transistors and other communication technology (Becvar & Becvar, 1996). Later, George Engel (1977) used the same ideas to develop a biopsychosocial model of disease.

Social workers were attracted to the systems perspective in the 1960s, as they shifted from a psychiatric model to a model more inclusive of environment. Social work has drawn most heavily on the work of sociologists Talcott Parsons and Robert Merton, psychologists Kurt Lewin and Uri Bronfenbrenner, and biologist Ludwig von Bertalanffy. With the possible exception of the developmental perspective, the systems perspective thus has the greatest potential of the perspectives discussed in this chapter to accommodate the biological person. In addition, systems theorists recognize—even if they do not always make clear—the social, cultural, eco-

**EXHIBIT 2.2**

Central Ideas of the Systems Perspective

- Systems are made up of interrelated members (parts) that constitute an ordered whole.
- Each part of the system impacts all other parts, and the system as a whole.
- All systems are subsystems of other larger systems.
- Systems maintain boundaries that give them their identities.
- Systems tend toward homeostasis, or equilibrium.

nomic, and political environments of human behavior. They acknowledge the role of external influences and demands in creating and maintaining patterns of interaction within the system.

Thus, the systems perspective is much like the transactional approach of this book. However, early systems theory saw persons and environments as separate but interrelated, whereas a transactional approach emphasizes the inseparability of persons and environments. Nor did early theorizing in the systems perspective deal with the time dimension—the focus was always on the present. But recent formulations have attempted to add a time dimension to accommodate both past and future influences on human behavior (see Bronfenbrenner, 1989; Ford & Lerner, 1992; Hannerz, 1992; Wachs, 1992).

The social workers who first adopted the systems perspective were heavily influenced by **functionalist sociology,** which was the dominant sociological theory during the 1940s and 1950s. In functionalism, social systems are thought to remain in a relatively stable state. Each part of the system serves an essential function in maintaining the system, and the functions of the various parts are coordinated to produce a well-functioning whole. The biggest problem with this perspective is that it tends to assume that interactions take place within a **closed system,** isolated from exchanges with other systems and thus unable to receive needed resources. An **open system,** as Exhibit 2.3 illustrates, is more likely to receive resources from external systems. Actually, there is no such thing as a totally closed system, because it could not survive without some external resources, but much of social science research is based on a closed-system model and does not account for intersystem exchanges.

Functionalist sociology also assumes that social systems are held together by social consensus and shared values. The focus is on maintenance of the "normal" or "healthy" state of affairs, known as homeostasis or equilibrium, a state that all members work hard to maintain and restore. What is good for the system is considered good for each of the parts, and conflict and change are seen as threats to be overcome (Wallace & Wolf, 1995). This emphasis on system equilibrium and on the necessity of traditional roles to hold systems together has led many to

**EXHIBIT 2.3**
Closed and Open
Systems

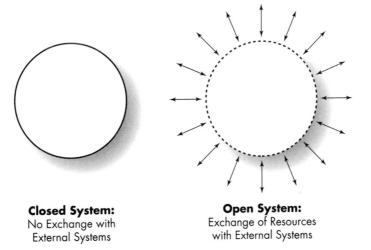

**Closed System:**
No Exchange with
External Systems

**Open System:**
Exchange of Resources
with External Systems

criticize the systems perspective in the functionalist tradition as socially conservative (Cohen, 1968; Gouldner, 1970). Contemporary systems theory, however, has begun to recognize power and oppression, and recent social work textbooks written from the systems perspective recognize both conflict and cooperation, stability and change, as inherent in system interactions (see Longres, 1995; Martin & O'Connor, 1989).

Now let's look at how the systems perspective can help us analyze the problems in the Clark family. Consider the roles played by each person and the stresses the family has faced as a result of role transitions over the past two years. **Role** refers to the usual behaviors of persons occupying a particular social position. Martha Clark went from being wife and co-manager of her own home to a less well defined role in the home of Al and Betty. Al has seen his relationship with his mother change toward a caregiver role, has lost his role as worker, and has taken on a "sick" role. We might anticipate that Betty is experiencing role overload as she becomes the only wage earner, maintains the role of primary housekeeper, and takes on new caregiver roles with both her mother-in-law and her husband.

In the systems perspective, the structure of roles is an important mechanism for maintaining system balance. You can understand why this might be if you think for a moment about the sometimes rocky transitions in roles across the life course—from infancy, through childhood, adolescence, adulthood, and late adulthood. At each passage, the individual has to redefine her or his relationships with others in the environment.

The conceptualization of role incorporates several key concepts (Davis, 1986; Germain, 1994; Longres, 1995):

- **Expected role.** The set of behaviors that others expect of persons in a particular social position. Much of the stress in the Clark family stems from changing abilities to fulfill expected roles. Al, for example, feels the pressure of expectations that he will fill the breadwinner role.

- **Enacted role.** The way in which a specific person in a particular position actually behaves. Al is struggling with the caregiver role, and the community questions how well he is performing, or enacting, that role.

- **Role overload.** A set of roles that, taken together, are too demanding. As suggested earlier, we can well imagine that Betty may be currently experiencing role overload. This is a hypothesis that you will want to explore.

- **Role ambiguity.** Unclear expectations for successful performance of a given role. You will want to explore the possibility that both Martha and Al are facing some role ambiguity. Martha may not be clear what her role should be in Al and Betty's house, and Al may have lots of questions about the role of heart patient.

- **Role conflict.** Incompatible expectations for the various roles a person holds, or competing expectations for performance in a particular role. Betty, like many employed caregivers, may be experiencing conflict between work and family roles.

Although popular, the systems perspective is often criticized as vague and somewhat ambiguous. Early theorists rarely applied their work to the empirical world, and many concepts were not clearly defined for research or practice purposes. However, this aspect of the systems perspective has been strengthened in recent years; systems concepts have been applied in research on social support and on the relationship between socioeconomic stressors and social and individual problems (see Garbarino, 1976, 1977; Garbarino & Sherman, 1980; Gelles, 1992; Zuravin, 1986, 1989). We agree with Germain (1994) that the systems perspective is more useful for understanding human behavior than for directing social work interventions, but several social work practice textbooks were based on the systems perspective in the 1970s and 1980s (see Germain & Gitterman, 1980; Meyer, 1983; Pincus & Minahan, 1973; Siporin, 1975). Its value is that, like the transactional approach in this book, the systems perspective suggests that we should widen the scope of assessment and intervention (Allen-Meares & Lane, 1987) and expect better outcomes from multidimensional interventions (Ford & Lerner, 1992).

# The Conflict Perspective

In your case assessment with the Clark family, you have probably observed that Martha Clark is highly dependent on Al and Betty. Thus, another way of looking at her situation is to suggest that her lack of power in the family contributes to her problems. In a larger sense, Martha is a member of a class of people—old, poor, frail, single women—who hold little power in society. You may also note that Al and Betty, while holding more power in the family than Martha, hold little power in the labor market; they are vulnerable to the economic interests of other, more dominant, groups. You could be thinking in a new way about recent political debates about health care funding now that you have recognized the financial strain this family faces and its inability to pay for Martha Clark's medications. You may also note the authority associated with your role as protective investigator, and you wonder how Martha, Al, and Betty will react to your power. Compare these observations with the central ideas of the conflict perspective, presented in Exhibit 2.4.

The **conflict perspective** has emerged over and over again in history, drawing attention to conflict, dominance, and oppression in social life (Collins, 1994). The conflict perspective typically looks for sources of conflict, and causes of human behavior, in the economic and political arenas. In sociology, the conflict perspective has two traditions: a utopian tradition that foresees a society in which there is no longer a basis for social conflict, and a second tradition that sees conflict as inevitable in social life (Wallace & Wolf, 1995).

**EXHIBIT 2.4**

Central Ideas of the Conflict Perspective

- Groups and individuals try to advance their own interests over the interests of others.
- Power is unequally divided, and some social groups dominate others.
- Social order is based on the manipulation and control of nondominant groups by dominant groups.
- Lack of open conflict is a sign of exploitation.
- Social change is driven by conflict, with periods of change interrupting long periods of stability.

The roots of contemporary conflict theory are usually traced to the works of Karl Marx and his collaborator Friedrich Engels, and to the works of Max Weber. Marx (1887/1967) and Engels (1884/1970) focused on economic structures, but Weber (1904–1905/1958) criticized this singular emphasis in favor of a multidimensional perspective on social class. Contemporary conflict theory tends to favor Weber's multidimensional perspective, calling attention to a confluence of social, economic, and political structures in the creation of inequality (Collins, 1994; Ritzer, 1992; Wallace & Wolf, 1995). As you have probably noted, Weber's perspective is also more consistent with the multidimensional approach of this book.

Power relationships are the focus of the conflict perspective. Some theorists in the conflict tradition limit their focus to the large-scale structure of power relationships, but many theorists also look at the reactions and adaptations of individual members of nondominant groups. Habermas (1984, 1987) and other **critical theorists** are interested in the connections between culture, social structure, and personality, paying particular attention to the role of individual perception. Coser (1956) proposes a **pluralistic theory of social conflict,** which recognizes that more than one social conflict is going on at all times, and that individuals hold cross-cutting and overlapping memberships in status groups. Thus, it seeks to understand life experience by looking at simultaneous memberships—for example, a white, Italian-American, Protestant, heterosexual, male semiskilled worker, or a black, African-American, Catholic, lesbian, female professional worker. Social conflict exists between economic groups, racial groups, ethnic groups, religious groups, age groups, and gender groups.

Conflict theory has developed, in the main, through attempts to codify persistent themes in history (Collins, 1990). The preferred research method is empirical historical research that looks at large-scale patterns of history (see Mann, 1986; McCarthy & Zald, 1977; Skocpol, 1979; Wallerstein, 1974–1989). As with other methods of research, critics have attacked some interpretations of historical data from the conflict perspective, but the historical analyses of Mann, Skocpol, and Wallerstein are some of the most influential works in contemporary sociology. In addition to historical analysis, conflict theorists have used experimental methods to study reactions to coercive power (see Willer, 1987) and naturalistic inquiry to study social ranking through interaction rituals (Collins, 1981). Contemporary conflict theorists are also drawing on network analysis, which plots the relationships among a group of people, and are finding support for their propositions about power and domination (see Burt, 1983).

Concepts of power and social conflict came into social work in the 1960s (Germain, 1994). These concepts have great value for understanding community, group, and family relationships, as well as the power differential between social worker and client. The conflict perspective, as it currently exists, however, is weak in suggesting principles of action beyond assessment. Randall Collins, a conflict theorist, suggests that "where conflict theory is weak is in explaining what will happen after the revolution, or after a successful movement has won some power" (Collins, 1994, p. 178). The conflict perspective is nonetheless crucial to social work because it shines a spotlight on how domination and oppression might be affecting human behavior, because it illuminates processes by which people become estranged and discouraged, and because it encourages social workers to consider the meaning of their power relationships with clients, particularly nonvoluntary clients (Cingolani, 1984). Social movement theories (see Chapter 12), which are based in the conflict perspective, have some implications for mobilization of oppressed groups, but the conflict perspective, in general, provides little in the way of policy direction. It is stronger in helping us to understand how the Clark family came to be discouraged than in guiding policies that might prevent or alleviate such situations.

# The Rational Choice Perspective

Another way to think about the Clark family is to focus on the costs and benefits that each of them derives from interacting with the others. You might suggest that Martha Clark receives the benefit of having most of her basic needs met, but endures the cost of feeling that she has nothing to offer in exchange, as well as the blows to body and spirit delivered by her son. She seems to think that the care she is receiving is as good as she deserves, and probably sees no better alternative. Al Clark benefits from the household management that Betty provides but has recently endured the cost of feeling that his contributions, economic and otherwise, are not equal to hers, as well as the cost of feeling inadequate in his ability to meet his mother's needs. Now he must endure the embarrassment of an adult protective investigation. By virtue of the greater resources she brings to exchanges, Betty Clark holds a power position in the family, but she endures the cost of inadequate support from her husband and mother-in-law. Exhibit 2.5 reveals a fit between these observations about the Clark family and the central ideas of the rational choice perspective.

The **rational choice perspective** sees human behavior as based on self-interest and rational choices about effective ways to accomplish goals. The perspective is interdisciplinary, with strong roots in utilitarian philosophy, economics, and social behaviorism. Social workers are most familiar with social exchange theory in sociology, rational choice models of organizations, public choice theory in political science, and the emerging social network theory. As Collins (1994) notes, the rational choice perspective is a very old tradition in social thought, but the roots of contemporary sociological theories of rational choice are generally traced to Claude Levi-Strauss, George Homans, and Peter Blau. Other theorists making major contributions include John Thibaut and Harold Kelley, James March and Herbert Simon, Michael Hechter, James Coleman, James Buchanan, Richard Emerson, and Karen Cook.

**Social exchange theory** starts with the premise that social behavior is based on the desire to maximize benefits and minimize costs. In the early development of social exchange theory, Homans (1958) insisted that behavior can be understood at the psychological level, denying the

**EXHIBIT 2.5**

Central Ideas of the Rational Choice Perspective

- People are rational and goal-directed.
- Social exchange is based on self-interest, with actors trying to maximize rewards and minimize costs.
- Reciprocity of exchange is essential to social life.
- Power comes from unequal resources in an exchange.

relevance of the cultural and social environments. Homans was particularly forceful in attacking the Parsonian view that individuals are influenced in their behavior by role expectations that emanate from sociocultural systems. History, to Homans, was important only because the history of rewards for past behavior informs an actor about what is in his or her best interest. More recent formulations of social exchange theory have moved from this position toward a greater emphasis on the social, economic, political, and historical contexts of social exchanges (see Levi, Cook, O'Brien, & Faye, 1990). These formulations would emphasize how the Clark family conflicts are influenced by the structure of the labor market and political decisions about health care. Beginning with the work of Peter Blau (1964), social exchange theorists and researchers have taken a strong interest in how power is negotiated at all levels, from interactions between two people to Realpolitik among nations. Particularly noteworthy in this regard is Emerson's (1972a, 1972b) power-dependency theory and Karen Cook's (1987) exchange network theory.

Some feminists have criticized exchange theory on the grounds that its emphasis on rational calculation of personal advantage is a male attitude and does not represent the female perspective (Collins, 1994). This criticism might be shared by ethnic groups who are more collectivist, and less individualist, than white Anglo-Saxon Protestant Americans. In fact, Homans developed his American version of exchange theory partially in reaction to Levi-Strauss's French collectivist version, which argued that social exchange is driven by collective, cultural, symbolic forces and not based simply on self-interest (Ekeh, 1974). Recently, Karen Cook and her colleagues (Cook, O'Brien, & Kollock, 1990) have undertaken a synthesis of social exchange and symbolic interaction theories (see the discussion of the social constructionist perspective), recognizing the possibility that different people hold different definitions of positive outcomes in social exchange.

Thibaut and Kelley's (Kelley & Thibaut, 1978; Thibaut & Kelley, 1959) concepts of comparison level and comparison level alternatives are also useful in accommodating diversity of experience. **Comparison level,** a standard for evaluating the rewards and costs of a given relationship, is based on what the evaluator feels he or she deserves. Martha Clark's suggestion that she is receiving good care may well be based on such a standard; she may well believe that a woman in her situation deserves no better care. **Comparison level alternative** is the lowest level of outcomes a person will accept in light of alternative opportunities. Martha Clark might find her current situation less acceptable if she had another son or daughter who was in a position to provide a better quality of life.

As the rational choice perspective has developed, two conceptual puzzles have emerged, one at the individual level and one at the collective level. At the individual level, the individual's capacity to process information and make rational decisions is limited. At the collective level, how is collective action possible if each actor maximizes rewards and minimizes costs? To their credit, recent theorists have embraced these puzzles. Recent developments in the rational choice perspective emphasize the limits to rational choice in social life (see Cook et al., 1990; Levi et al., 1990; March & Simon, 1958). James Coleman (1990) is particularly noted for his attempts to employ rational choice theory to activate collective action for the purpose of social justice.

The rational choice perspective has stimulated empirical research at several levels of analysis, with mixed results. Cognitive psychologists Daniel Kahneman and Amos Tversky (1982,

1984) dealt a blow to the rational choice perspective in the 1980s. They reported research findings that individual choices and decisions are often inconsistent with assumed rationality and that, indeed, situations are often too complicated for individuals to ascertain what is the most rational choice. On the other hand, more than modest support for the perspective has been found in research on dyads, families, and labor markets (see Adams & Jacobsen, 1964; Becker, 1981; Blood & Wolfe, 1960; Burgess & Nielsen, 1974; Carter & Glick, 1976). Collins (1988) suggests that a serious problem for the rational choice perspective is the lack of a common metric for calculating the costs and benefits derived from social exchange. Contemporary theorists acknowledge the inherent imprecision of this metric and suggest that the rational choice perspective must find a way to incorporate both what people value and the context of social exchange (see Cook et al., 1990).

Some versions of rational choice theory serve as little more than a defense of the rationality of the marketplace of social exchange, suggesting a noninterventionist approach. In other words, if all social exchanges are based on rational choices, then who are we to interfere with this process? This stance, of course, is inconsistent with the purposes of social work.

Other versions of rational choice theory emphasize the ways in which patterns of exchange lead to social inequalities and social injustices. Some theorists in this tradition have begun to propose solutions for creating social solidarity while recognizing the self-interestedness that is characteristic of Western, industrialized societies. These attempts have led Collins (1994) to suggest that, out of all current social theories, contemporary rational choice theories have the greatest chance of informing social policy. One of the most promising approaches is that of Coleman (1990), who explores possible incentives to encourage actors to behave in ways more beneficial to others. For example, Coleman has recommended financial incentives for providing nurturant care to children and adolescents at risk of becoming an economic drain on society—incentives that increase with the potential hazard to society. He has also proposed lifting the legal immunity of members of corporate boards to encourage them to act in a more prosocial manner.

Theorists in the rational choice tradition are also advancing **social network theory,** which actually has intellectual roots in the systems perspective. Still in the early stages of development, social network theory already provides useful tools for person/environment assessments and holds great promise for the future (Specht, 1986). Social workers make use of social network theory at the micro level, to assess and enhance the social support networks of individual clients and families (see Collins & Pancoast, 1976; Tracy & Whittaker, 1990). Social work administrators and planners use social network theory to understand and enhance the exchange of resources in networks of social service providers (see Streeter & Gillespie, 1992).

Social networks are typically presented visually as **sociograms,** which illustrate the relations among network members (see Hartman, 1978, 1995; Meyer, 1993). Members of the network—individuals, groups, or organizations—are represented as points, and lines are drawn between pairs of points to demonstrate a relationship between them. Arrows are often used to show the flow of exchanges in a relationship. These graphic displays illuminate such issues as network size, density of relationships, strength of relationships, reciprocity of relationships, and access to power and influence. Sociograms are usually called **ecomaps** in the social work literature. An ecomap of the Clark family is presented in Exhibit 2.6.

**EXHIBIT 2.6**

Ecomap of the Clark
Family

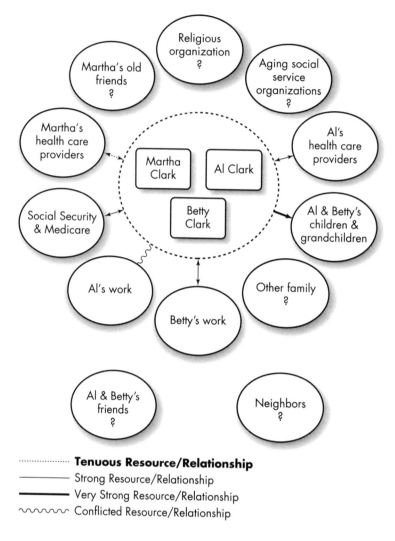

............... **Tenuous Resource/Relationship**
——————   Strong Resource/Relationship
——————   Very Strong Resource/Relationship
〜〜〜〜〜   Conflicted Resource/Relationship

# The Social Constructionist Perspective

Both Martha Clark and her son sometimes think of her as a "useless old woman." You may be thinking that this idea could be contributing to Martha's growing despondency and passive approach to life, and to her son's impatient treatment of her. Their current interactions help to reinforce this idea. It is likely, however, that both Martha and her son entered the current situation with a shared understanding about "useless old women." This is an understanding that may have been developed and sustained across generations in their family, but it also clearly reflects traditional images of old women in the popular culture. You may also be wondering what kinds of ideas Martha, Al, and Betty have about gender roles and about heart disease, and how their cur-

**EXHIBIT 2.7**

Central Ideas
of the Social
Constructionist
Perspective

- Actors are free, active, and creative.
- Social reality is created when actors, in social interaction, develop a common understanding of their world.
- Social interaction is grounded in language customs, as well as cultural and historical contexts.
- People can modify meanings in the process of interaction.
- Society consists of social processes, not social structures.

rent interactions are affected by these ideas. By considering these issues, you have begun to explore the central ideas of the social constructionist perspective (see Exhibit 2.7).

To understand human behavior, the **social constructionist perspective** focuses on "actors, the way in which they construct social reality, and the action that results from such construction" (Ritzer, 1992, p. 176). The intellectual roots of the social constructionist perspective are usually traced to the German philosopher Edmund Husserl, as well as to the philosophical pragmatism of John Dewey and early theorists in the symbolic interaction tradition including Charles Horton Cooley, W. I. Thomas, and George Herbert Mead. More recent theorists include Herbert Blumer, Erving Goffman, Alfred Schutz, Harold Garfinkel, Peter Berger, and Thomas Luckmann. Collins (1994) suggests that social constructionist theorizing is the type of sociology that American sociologists do best.

To the social constructionist, there is no singular objective reality, only the shared subjective realities that are created as people interact. Constructionists emphasize the existence of multiple social and cultural realities, developed in changing configurations of persons and environments. The sociopolitical environment and history of any situation play an important role in understanding human behavior, particularly if these are significant to the individual. However, social constructionists disagree about how constraining the environment is. The dominant position is probably the one represented by Schutz's (1932/1967) **phenomenological sociology**. While arguing that people shape social reality, Schutz also suggests that individuals and groups are constrained by the preexisting social and cultural structures created by their predecessors. Schutz does not provide theoretical tools for understanding social institutions and their links to individual constructions of reality, however.

In his 1975 presidential address to the American Sociological Association, Lewis Coser attacked ethnomethodology, another theory in the social constructionist tradition, for ignoring "institutional factors in general, and the centrality of power in social interaction in particular" (Coser, 1975, p. 696). In a similar vein, Wallace and Wolf (1995) and Ritzer (1992) have suggested that symbolic interactionism, ethnomethodology, and phenomenological sociology all lack the theoretical tools necessary for the analysis of power relationships. Middleton (1989) has suggested that many contemporary postmodern versions of social constructionism, by ignoring power while focusing on multiple voices and multiple meanings in the construction of reality, reduce oppression to difference. These critics suggest that some actors have greater power than others to privilege their own constructions of reality and to disadvantage the constructions of other actors.

This criticism cannot be leveled at all versions of social constructionism, however. Social work scholars have been particularly attracted to those versions of the social constructionist perspective that have incorporated pieces of the conflict tradition (Laird, 1994; Saleeby, 1994; Witkin & Gottschalk, 1988), particularly to the early work of Michel Foucault (1969) on the relationship between power and knowledge. They propose that in contemporary society, minority or "local" knowledges are denied credibility in majority-dominated social arenas and suggest that social work practitioners can bring credibility to minority viewpoints by allowing oppressed individuals and groups to tell their own stories.

Social constructionism, particularly the original phenomenological and symbolic interactional concepts, is criticized at times as vague and difficult to operationalize for empirical research. However, many social constructionist proponents have challenged this criticism and offered alternative criteria for evaluating theory (see Witkin & Gottschalk, 1988), as well as an alternative research methodology, **constructivist research** (Lincoln & Guba, 1985), that is sensitive to the context of the research, seeks the views of key parties, and takes into account the interactions involved in the research process (Sherman & Reid, 1994). Sociologists in the conflict and rational choice traditions have begun to incorporate social constructionist ideas and now use a mix of qualitative and quantitative research methodologies to accommodate both objective and subjective reality (see Collins, 1990; Cook et al., 1990).

Cynthia Franklin (1995) suggests that the emphasis on social context is the reason that social constructionism is often pointed to as an important theory for social work practice (see Imre, 1984; Rodwell, 1987; Saleeby, 1994; Weick, 1994). Social constructionism gives new meaning to the old social work adage "Begin where the client is." The social work relationship begins with developing an understanding of how the client views the situation and what the client would like to have happen. The current interest in narrative and storytelling therapies is based on the social constructionist perspective. In addition to this attention to the client's construction of reality, the social worker should engage the client in thinking about the social, cultural, and historical environments in which this version of reality was constructed. As Laird (1994) and Saleeby (1994) suggest, such conversations with members of oppressed groups may lead to empowerment through restorying. In your work with the Clark family, you might want to test this hypothesis by inviting Martha Clark to tell her story about how she came to see herself as "just a useless old woman." In the process, she might realize that another interpretation of her status is possible. At the level of groups and organizations, the social constructionist perspective recommends getting discordant groups to engage in sincere discussion of their disparate constructions of reality and to negotiate lines of actions acceptable to all (Fox & Miller, 1995) (see Chapter 10 for further discussion).

# The Psychodynamic Perspective

Martha Clark's despondence, her loss of confidence and hope are apparent—and easy to understand. Think about the losses she has recently experienced: loss of husband, loss of home, loss of privacy, loss of income, and loss of health. You may begin to wonder, given her long-term struggle with depression, about the possibility of early experiences with loss, deprivation, or

**EXHIBIT 2.8**

Central Ideas of the
Psychodynamic
Perspective

- Emotions have a central place in human behavior.

- Unconscious, as well as conscious, mental activity serves as the motivating force in human behavior.

- Early childhood experiences are central in the patterning of an individual's emotions, and therefore, central to problems of living throughout life.

- Individuals may become overwhelmed by internal and/or external demands.

- Individuals frequently use ego defense mechanisms to avoid becoming overwhelmed by internal and/or external demands.

trauma. You may also note her son's anger and frustration. Think about the losses he too has recently experienced: loss of father, loss of job, loss of income, loss of privacy, and loss of health. You also may wonder if he has a residue of anger toward his mother, perhaps related to childhood deprivation that he experienced during her episodes of depression. Is it possible that his label of "useless old woman" is a projection of his own sense of uselessness? As you explore the Clark family's situation from the psychodynamic perspective (see Exhibit 2.8), these and other possibilities emerge.

The **psychodynamic perspective** is concerned with how internal processes such as needs, drives, and emotions motivate human behavior. The perspective has evolved over the years, moving from the classical psychodynamic emphasis on innate drives and unconscious processes toward greater emphasis on the adaptive capacities of individuals and their interactions with the environment. The origins of all psychodynamic theories are in the work of Sigmund Freud; other prominent theorists in the evolving psychodynamic perspective include Anna Freud, Melanie Klein, Margaret Mahler, Karen Horney, Heinz Hartmann, Robert W. White, Donald Winnicott, Otto Kernberg, Heinz Kohut, and Erik Erikson. More recent formulations of the perspective include ego psychology and object relations theories.

In general, the psychodynamic perspective takes account of the environments of behavior only in the sense that these environments are conceptualized as presenting conflicts with which the individual must struggle. Recent formulations put greater emphasis on human behavior as a response to challenges in the environment than was found in classical theory, but theoretical propositions about internal processes continue to predominate. When environmental forces are considered, they include only passing mention of social forces beyond the family. Social, economic, political, and historical environments of human behavior are probably implied in ego psychology, but they are not explicated. This failure to expand the view of social beyond the family has led to accusations that psychodynamic theories are "mother blaming" and "family blaming" (Luepnitz, 1988).

Theorists in the psychodynamic tradition search for universal laws of behavior and their applicability to unique individuals. Thus, diversity of experience at the group level has been quite neglected in this tradition. Moreover, in the main, "universal" laws have been developed through analysis of heterosexual men of white, Anglo-Saxon, middle-class culture.

Feminists, as well as members of racial and ethnic minority groups, have criticized the psychodynamic bias toward thinking of people as autonomous individuals (Berzoff, 1989; Bricker-Jenkins, Hooyman, & Gottlieb, 1991; Gilligan, 1982; Ho, 1992; Sue & Sue, 1990). These critics suggest that viewing this standard as "normal" makes the connectedness found among many women and members of racial and ethnic minority groups seem pathological. Overemphasis on autonomy may also lead us to think of Martha Clark's growing dependence in pathological terms.

Psychodynamic theories are strong in their recognition of power dynamics in parent/child relationships, and in exploration of the life worlds of children. They are weak in looking at power issues in other relationships, however, including gender relationships. Early on, Freud recognized gender differences, even gender inequality, but attributed them to moral deficits within women.

Erik Erikson's theory, which has been widely used in social work curricula, has a somewhat greater emphasis on social forces. However, Erikson's work has been criticized for its lack of attention to the life worlds of women, racial minorities, and sexual minorities (Berzoff, 1989; Chestang, 1972; Kravetz, 1982; Kropf & Greene, 1994; Schwartz, 1973; Wesley, 1975). Chestang (1972) has asserted that Erikson's theory does not take into account the persistently hostile environments in which minority group members interact, or the extraordinary coping strategies needed to negotiate those environments.

Criticisms that the psychodynamic perspective lacks logical consistency and empirical support are directed primarily at Freud's original concepts and propositions, which were not measurable and not entirely consistent. Ego psychology and object relations theorists strengthened the logical consistency of the psychodynamic perspective by expanding and clarifying definitions of major concepts, and later psychodynamic theorists translated Freud's ideas into more measurable terms. Consequently, much empirical work has been based on the psychodynamic perspective. Contradictions in the research findings may be due in large part to the use of different definitions and measures. Some concepts, such as mastery or competence, have strong empirical support, but this support has been generated primarily by other schools of thought, such as developmental psychology and Albert Bandura's social behaviorism.

Most versions of the psychodynamic perspective have included clinical theory as well as human behavior theory. Differences of opinion about principles of practice reflect the theoretical evolution that has occurred. Practice principles common to all versions of the psychodynamic perspective include the centrality of the professional/client relationship, the curative value of expressing emotional conflicts and understanding past events, and the goals of self-awareness and self-control. Thus, you would be interested in having both Martha and Al discuss their past, as well as present, emotional conflicts. In contrast to the classical psychodynamic approach, recent formulations include directive as well as nondirective intervention, short-term as well as long-term intervention, and environmental manipulations—such as locating a day-care program for Martha—as well as intrapsychic manipulations such as emotional catharsis. Ego psychology has also been used to develop principles for prevention activities in addition to principles of remediation (Goldstein, 1984, 1986). In general, however, the psychodynamic perspective does not suggest practice principles at the level of communities, organizations, and social institutions. Thus, it would not help you to think about how to influence public policy to secure coverage for Martha Clark's medications.

# The Developmental Perspective

Another way to think about the story of the Clark family is to view their situation in terms of the developmental tasks they face. You might note that Martha Clark is entering late old age and struggling with the chronic illnesses and losses that people in this life stage frequently experience. She must make peace with the life that she has lived and find purpose to continue to live. You might also note that Al and Betty are part of the "sandwich generation," which must take on caregiving responsibilities for the older generation while also continuing to provide support to the generation behind them. They may be plagued with fears about their own vulnerability to the aging process. These observations are consistent with the central ideas of the developmental perspective, summarized in Exhibit 2.9.

The focus of the **developmental perspective** is on how human behavior changes and stays the same across the life cycle. The study of life cycle development is rooted in Freud's (1905/1953) theory of psychosexual stages of childhood development, but Erikson (1963) has been the most influential developmental theorist to date because his model of development includes adult, as well as child, stages of development. Other early developmental theorists include Margaret Mahler, Harry Stack Sullivan, and Jean Piaget. More recent developmental theorists include Daniel Levinson, George Vaillant, Roger Gould, Lawrence Kohlberg, Robert Havighurst, Barbara Newman, and Philip Newman. Bernice Neugarten (1979) was one of the first developmental theorists to study women as well as men. In the past several decades, sociologists have applied the developmental perspective to the study of family life stages (Carter & McGoldrick, 1988a; Duvall, 1962).

A frequent criticism of the developmental perspective is that it fails to take account of the social, economic, political, and historical environments of human behavior. Although some theorists conceptualize stages of development as biopsychosocial phenomena and recognize the way social forces affect individual development, most, including Erikson, see the stages as universal. All traditional developmental theorists ignore economic and political forces. The failure of developmental theories to deal with historical time has prompted researchers of adult behavior to point out the cohort effects on human behavior that arise when groups of persons born in the same historical time share cultural influences and historical events at the same period in their lives.

These criticisms have helped to stimulate development of the life course perspective in sociology. This perspective conceptualizes the life course as a social, rather than psychological,

**EXHIBIT 2.9**

Central Ideas of the Developmental Perspective

- Human development occurs in clearly defined stages.
- Each stage of life is qualitatively different from all other stages.
- Stages of development are sequential, with each stage building on earlier stages.
- Stages of development are universal.
- All environments provide the support necessary for development.

phenomenon that is nonetheless unique for each individual, with some common life course markers, or transitions, related to shared social and historical contexts (George, 1993). The life course perspective would suggest that Martha Clark's beliefs about what it means to be "old" or to be female have been influenced by the historical time in which she has lived and are probably shared by many other women her age. The evolving life course model respects the idea of role transition that is so central to the developmental perspective, but it also recognizes the multiplicity of interacting factors that contribute to diversity in the timing and experience of these transitions.

The traditional developmental perspective does not take account of power relationships, with the possible exception of power dynamics in the parent/child relationship. Moreover, traditional developmental models are based on the average white, middle-class, heterosexual, Anglo-Saxon male and ignore the life worlds of members of nondominant groups. In response to these limitations, several women have developed life cycle models for women (Gilligan, 1982; Jordan, 1992; Weenolsen, 1988). Daniel Levinson's (1996) recent study of women's lives, which includes a sample of women diversified by race and social class, acknowledges the impact of gender power differentials. Proponents of the family life cycle perspective have begun to respond with discussion of gender in the family life cycle. They are also presenting models of the family life cycle for gay and lesbian couples and for poor and minority families (Colon, 1980; Falicov & Karrer, 1980; Fulmer, 1988; Hines, 1988; McGoldrick, 1988; McWhirter & Mattison, 1984; Slater, 1995). Some of these discussions give explicit consideration to the impact of oppression, but others do not.

Classical developmental theory's notion of life stages is internally consistent, and many of Erikson's ideas have been employed and verified in empirical research. One example is Marcia's (1993) study of identity development, which supports Erikson's propositions about the development of identity in adolescence. As noted previously, however, much of developmental research has been based on white, heterosexual, middle-class males. Another concern is that by defining normal as average, developmental research fails to capture the life worlds of groups who deviate even moderately from the average, or even to capture the broad range of behavior considered normal. Thus, the consistency of and empirical support for the developmental perspective are based to some extent on statistical masking of diversity.

Through some lenses, the developmental perspective can be viewed as optimistic. Most people face life crises and challenges at some point, and many people have been reassured to hear that their struggle is "typical." Because the developmental perspective sees individuals as having the possibility to rework their inner experiences, as well as their family relationships, clients may be assisted in finding new strategies for getting their lives back "on course." For example, Al Clark could explore new roles that would make him feel more productive.

Erikson's model has often been used for assessment purposes in social work practice, and in a positive sense, the model can aid indirectly in the identification of potential personal and social developmental resources. Traditional developmental theories should be applied, however, only with recognition of the ethnocentrism expressed in them. They suggest, for example, that there is one right way to raise a child, one "appropriate" type of relationship with the family of origin, and one "healthy" way to develop intimate relationships in adulthood. Although it is harder to extrapolate practice principles from the more complex, emerging life course perspective, it seems more promising for understanding diverse persons in diverse environments. It suggests that individuals must always be assessed within familial, cultural, and historical contexts.

# The Social Behavioral Perspective

In your assessment of Martha Clark, you may think that she has developed feelings of incompetence, which may have some relationship to her episodes of depression. Perhaps Martha's prior experiences reinforced a sense of incompetence rather than competence. Perhaps certain aspects of her current environment further reinforce this belief. For example, when she moved from a one-story apartment in senior housing to the two-story home of Al and Betty, certain aspects of the new physical environment, such as stairs, complicated her ability to do things for herself. You may also want to learn more about her son's aggressive behavior. When did it begin? How often does it happen? In which kinds of situations and environments? Is he imitating behavior that he saw modeled in his parents' home? Viewing the Clark family's situation from the social behavioral perspective (see Exhibit 2.10) leads you to pursue such questions in your assessment.

As you probably recall from a course in psychology, theories in the **social behavioral perspective** suggest that human behavior is learned as individuals interact with their environments. But behaviorists disagree among themselves about the processes by which behavior is learned. This book presents a very inclusive view of behaviorism, including both the "hard" behaviorism of classical and operant conditioning and the "soft" behaviorism of cognitive social learning theory. **Classical conditioning theory**, which sees behavior as the result of associating a conditioned stimulus with an unconditioned stimulus, can be traced to the Russian physiologist Ivan Pavlov. **Operant conditioning theory**, which sees behavior as the result of reinforcement, is built on the work of two American psychologists, John B. Watson and B. F. Skinner. **Cognitive social learning theory**, with Albert Bandura as its chief contemporary proponent, suggests that behavior is also learned by imitation and through cognitive processes.

Although contemporary proponents of the social behavioral perspective generally recognize that cognition exists, a major split has developed over the role of cognition in human behavior.

**EXHIBIT 2.10**

Central Ideas of the Social Behavioral Perspective

- Human behavior is learned when individuals interact with the environment.
- Similar learning processes taking place in different environments produce differences in human behavior.
- Human behavior is learned by association of environmental stimuli.
- Human behavior is learned by reinforcement.
- Human behavior is learned by imitation.
- Human behavior is influenced by personal expectations and meanings.

The central question is whether thoughts are antecedents or results of behavior—the independent or dependent variable. "Hard" behaviorism, when it recognizes cognition at all, sees it as a result, not a cause, of behavior; "soft" behaviorism, however, sees cognition as both result and cause of behavior. In short, "hard" behaviorism sees human behavior as totally determined by environment; "soft" behaviorism sees human behavior as resulting from the reciprocal interaction of person and environment.

Differences in behavior, in the social behavioral perspective, occur when the same learning processes occur in different environments. The theory does not allow for variations in learning processes based on biology. Typically, the social behavioral perspective searches for the *one* environmental factor, or contingency, that has reinforced *one* specific behavior. Thus, a proponent of this perspective might attribute Martha Clark's current depression to her son's abusive behavior and ignore both her previous episodes and the multiple losses that she has faced since her husband's death. The identified contingency is usually in the micro system (such as the family), or sometimes in the meso system (for example, a school classroom), but these systems are not typically put in social, economic, political, or historical contexts. One exception is Albert Bandura's cognitive social learning theory, which acknowledges broad systemic influences on the development of gender roles. Social work scholars applying behavioral principles have also made notable efforts in recent years to incorporate a broader view of the environments of human behavior (Berlin, 1983; Gambrill, 1987; Reid, 1985).

Bruce Thyer (1994) suggests that "behavior social work practice is embedded in traditional social work values of respect for individuals, maximizing client autonomy, and working toward the elimination of racism, discrimination, and social injustice" (p. 136). "Hard" behaviorism provides few theoretical tools for understanding or changing power relationships, however. Operant behavioral theory recommends rewards over punishment, but it does not account for the coercion and oppression inherent in power relationships at every system level. It is quite possible, therefore, for the professional behavior modifier to be in service to oppressive forces.

In contrast, Bandura (1986) writes specifically about power as related to gender roles. He also presents the concepts of **self-efficacy**, by which he means a sense of personal competence, and **efficacy expectation**, by which he means an expectation that one can personally accomplish a goal (Bandura, 1977, 1986). Persons in nondominant positions are seen as particularly vulnerable to **learned helplessness** (see Mikulincer, 1994; Seligman, 1992), in which a person's prior experience with environmental forces has led to low self-efficacy and efficacy expectation. You may find the concepts of self-efficacy and learned helplessness particularly useful in thinking about both Martha's and Al's situations. Both have experienced some defeats and changes in their physical functioning that may be leading them to expect less of themselves and to resist measures that might improve their functioning.

Social behavioral concepts are easily measured for empirical investigation because theorizing has been based, in very large part, on laboratory research. This characteristic is also a drawback of the social behavioral perspective, however, because laboratory experiments by design eliminate much of the complexity of person/environment configurations. Overall, the social behavioral perspective sacrifices multidimensional understanding to gain logical consistency. Christopher Monte (1995) suggests that all versions of the social behavioral perspective have had their "share of confirmations and disconfirmations" (p. 769). In general, however, it seems fair to say that there is a relatively high degree of empirical support for the propositions of both "hard" and "soft" behaviorism (see Thyer, 1991).

A major strength of the social behavioral perspective is the ease with which principles of behavior modification can be extrapolated, and it is probably a rare person who has not used social behavioral principles of action at some point. Social workers and psychologists, primarily, have used social behavioral methods to modify atypical behavior of individuals. But these methods have not been used effectively to produce social reform. Richard Stuart (1989) reminds us that behavior modification was once a "social movement" that appealed to young social reformers who were more interested in changing social conditions that produce atypical behaviors than in changing systems for managing atypical behavior. Skinner's *Walden Two* was the impetus for attempts by these young reformers to build nonpunitive communities, which represented significant modification of social conditions (see Kinkade, 1973; Wheeler, 1973).

# The Humanistic Perspective

In a sense, Martha Clark has shown a lot of strength to persevere through all of the losses she has experienced over the past two years, even though many of her attempts to cope are not working well for her. You could reason that biology and social circumstances constrain her behavioral choices to some degree but that Martha is making choices and is capable of rethinking those choices. However, your reflections about her situation may be very different from her own, and thus your overarching concern is to get a chance to meet with Martha and hear more about how she sees her situation. Similarly, you applaud Al and Betty's commitment to their mother's care, even though some of their attempts to cope are not currently working well for them. You reason that social circumstances serve as constraints to Al's behavior, but you also think that he has made conscious choices and is capable of reworking those choices. The same can be said for Betty. You are eager to hear how both Al and Betty see their current situation. Your thoughts and planned course of action at this point reflect the humanistic perspective, summarized in Exhibit 2.11.

The humanistic perspective is often called the third force of psychology, because it was developed in reaction to the determinism found in early versions of both the psychodynamic and behavioral perspectives (Monte, 1995). We are using the term **humanistic perspective** to

**EXHIBIT 2.11**
Central Ideas of the Humanistic Perspective

- Humans are "spiritual, rational, purposeful, and autonomous" (Monte, 1995, p. 665).
- Human behavior can be understood only from the vantage point of the phenomenal self—from the internal frame of reference of the individual.
- People make psychologically destructive demands on each other, and attempts to meet those demands produce anxiety.
- Human behavior is driven by a desire for growth and competence, and by a need for love and acceptance.

include humanistic psychology and existential psychology, both of which emphasize the individual's freedom of action. The term also includes the existential sociology tradition, which counters the structural determinism found in some sociological theories and presents as a dominant theme the idea that people are simultaneously free and constrained, both active and passive agents.

Like social constructionism, the humanistic perspective is often traced to the German phenomenological philosopher Edmund Husserl (Krill, 1986). It is also influenced by a host of existential philosophers, beginning with Soren Kierkegaard and including Freidrich Nietzche, Martin Heidegger, Jean-Paul Sartre, Albert Camus, Simone de Beauvoir, Martin Buber, and Paul Tillich. Other early contributors to existential psychology include Viktor Frankl, Rollo May, Carl Jung, R. D. Laing, Karen Horney, and Erich Fromm. Perhaps the most influential contributions to humanistic psychology were made by Carl Rogers (1951) and Abraham Maslow (1962). Carl Rogers began his professional career at the Rochester Child Guidance Center, where he worked with social workers who had been trained at the Philadelphia School of Social Work. He has acknowledged the influence of Otto Rank, Jessie Taft, and the social workers at the Rochester agency on his thinking about the importance of responding to client feelings (Hart, 1970).

The internal life of the individual is the focus of the humanistic perspective and, as might be expected, most theorists in the tradition give limited attention to the environments of human behavior. Taking the lead from existential philosophers, R. D. Laing sees humans as interrelated with their worlds and frowns on the word *environment* because it implies a fragmented person. In discussions of human behavior, however, Laing (1967, 1969) emphasizes the insane situations in which human behavior is enacted. Erich Fromm was heavily influenced by Karl Marx and is much more inclusive of environment than other theorists in the humanistic perspective, emphasizing industrialization, Protestant reformation, capitalism, and technological revolution as alienating contexts against which humans search for meaning (Fromm, 1941). Although existential sociologists emphasize the importance of feelings and emotions, they also focus on the problematic nature of social life under modernization (see Fontana, 1984). A dehumanizing world is implicit in the works of Maslow and Rogers, but neither theorist focuses on the environments of human behavior, nor do they acknowledge that some environments are more dehumanizing than others.

The humanistic perspective, with its almost singular consideration of an internal frame of reference, devotes more attention to individual differences than to differences between groups. The works of Fromm and Horney are striking exceptions to this statement. Karen Horney identified culturally based gender differences at a time when psychology either ignored gender or took a "biology as destiny" approach. She also lost favor among other psychodynamic theorists by reworking Freud's conceptualization of the Oedipus conflict and of feminine psychology to produce a more gender-sensitive perspective (Horney, 1939, 1967).

The humanistic perspective, with its emphasis on search for meaning, is the only perspective presented in this chapter to explicitly recognize the role of spirituality in human behavior.

In general, far too little attention is given in the humanistic tradition to the processes by which institutional oppression influences the **phenomenal self**—the individual's subjectively felt and interpreted experience of "who I am." Like the social constructionist perspective, however, the humanistic perspective is sometimes quite strong in giving voice to experiences of members of nondominant groups. With the emphasis on the phenomenal self, members of nondominant groups are more likely to have preferential input into the telling of their own stories. Your intention to hear and honor the stories of Martha, Al, and Betty may be a novel experience for each of them, and you may, indeed, hear very different stories than you expect to hear. Fromm and Maccoby (1970) illustrate this emphasis in their identification of the different life worlds of members of groups of different socioeconomic statuses in a Mexican village. Most significantly, Rogers developed his respect for the personal self, and consequently his client-centered approach to therapy, when he realized that his perception of the life worlds of his low-income clients in the Child Guidance Clinic were very different from their own perceptions (Hart, 1970).

Theories in the humanistic perspective are often criticized for being vague and highly abstract, with concepts such as "being" and "phenomenal self." Indeed, theorists in the humanistic perspective, in general, have not been afraid to sacrifice coherence to gain what they see as a more complete understanding of human behavior. As might be expected, empirically minded scholars have not been attracted to the humanistic perspective, and consequently there is little empirical literature to support the perspective. A notable exception is the clinical side of Rogers's theory. Rogers began a rigorous program of empirical investigation of the therapeutic process, and such research has provided strong empirical support for his conceptualization of the necessary conditions for the therapeutic relationship: warmth, empathy, and genuineness (Monte, 1995).

If the social constructionist perspective gives new meaning to the old social work adage "Begin where the client is," it is social work's historical involvement in the development of the humanistic perspective that gave original meaning to the adage. The humanistic perspective suggests that social workers begin by developing an understanding of how the client views the situation and, with its emphasis on the individual drive for growth and competence, recommends a "strengths" rather than "pathology" approach to practice. From this perspective, then, you might note the strong commitment to helping one another displayed by the Clark family, which might be the basis for successful intervention. At the organizational level, the humanistic perspective has been used by organizational theorists, such as Douglas McGregor (1960), to prescribe administrative actions that focus on employee well-being as the best route to organizational efficiency and effectiveness. Conflict theorists have criticized the organizational humanists, however, for their failure to take account of the ways in which organizations are instruments of domination (Hearn & Parkin, 1993).

## The Merits of Multiple Perspectives

You can see that each of these perspectives puts a different lens on the unfolding story of the Clark family. But do these different ways of thinking make you more effective when you meet with clients like the Clarks? We think so. It was suggested in Chapter 1 that each situation can be examined from several perspectives, and that using a variety of perspectives brings more dimensions of the situation into view. Eileen Gambrill (1990) has suggested that all of us, whether new or experienced social workers, have biases that predispose us to do too little thinking, rather than too much, about the practice situations we confront. We are, she suggests, particularly proned to ignore information that is contrary to our hypotheses about situations. Consequently, we tend to end our search for understanding prematurely. One step we can take to prevent this premature closure is to think about practice situations from multiple theoretical perspectives.

The fields of psychology and sociology offer a variety of patterned ways of thinking about changing person/environment configurations, ways that have been worked out over time to assist in understanding human behavior. They are tools that can help us make sense of the situations we encounter. We do not mean to suggest that all eight of the perspectives discussed in this chapter will be equally useful, or even useful at all, in all situations. But each of these perspectives will be useful in some situations that you encounter as a social worker, and therefore should be in your general knowledge base. We hope that over time you will begin to use these multiple perspectives in an integrated fashion so that you can see the many dimensions, the contradictions as well as the consistencies, in stories like the Clark family's. We remind you, again, however, to use general knowledge only to generate hypotheses to be tested in specific situations.

## IMPLICATIONS FOR SOCIAL WORK PRACTICE

The eight perspectives on human behavior discussed in this chapter suggest a variety of principles for social work assessment and intervention:

- In assessment, consider any recent role transitions, as well as role ambiguity, role overload, and role conflict. Assist families and groups to renegotiate unsatisfactory role structures. Develop networks of support for persons experiencing challenging role transitions.

- In assessment, consider power arrangements and forces of oppression, and the alienation that emanates from them. Assist in the development of advocacy efforts to challenge patterns of dominance, when possible. Be aware of the power dynamics in your relationships with clients; when working with nonvoluntary clients, speak directly about the limits and uses of your power.

- In assessment, consider the patterns of exchange in the social support networks of individual clients, families, and organizations, using sociograms (ecomaps) for network mapping when useful. Assist individuals, families, and organizations to renegotiate unsatisfactory patterns of exchange, when possible. Consider how social policy can increase the rewards for prosocial behavior.

- Begin your work by understanding how clients view their situations. Engage clients in thinking about the environments in which these constructions of situations have developed. When working in situations characterized by differences in belief systems, assist members to engage in sincere discussions and to negotiate lines of actions.

- Assist clients to express emotional conflicts and to understand how these are related to past events, when appropriate. Assist clients to develop self-awareness and self-control, where needed. Assist clients to locate and use needed environmental resources.

- In assessment, consider the familial, cultural, and historical contexts in the timing and experience of developmental transitions.

- In assessment, consider the variety of learning processes by which behavior is learned. Be sensitive to the possibility of learned helplessness when clients lack motivation for change. Consider issues of social justice and fairness before engaging in behavior modification.

- Be aware of the potential for significant differences between your assessment of the situation and the client's own assessment. Focus on strengths rather than pathology.

## MAIN POINTS

1. Both sociological and psychological theories are needed for considering changing configurations of persons and environments.

2. Four sociological perspectives (systems, conflict, rational choice, and social constructionist) and four psychological perspectives (psychodynamic, developmental, social behavioral, and humanistic) can help social workers bring different dimensions of person/environment configurations into view.

3. The systems perspective sees human behavior as the outcome of reciprocal interactions of persons operating within organized and integrated social systems.

4. The conflict perspective draws attention to conflict, dominance, and oppression in social life.

5. The rational choice perspective sees human behavior as based on self-interest and rational choices about effective goal accomplishment.

6. The social constructionist perspective recognizes no objective reality, only the shared subjective realities that are created as people interact. The social constructionist thus sees multiple social and cultural realities.

7. The psychodynamic perspective is concerned with how internal processes such as needs, drives, and emotions motivate human behavior.

8. The developmental perspective focuses on how behavior changes and stays the same across the life cycle.

9. Theories in the social behavioral perspective suggest that human behavior is learned as individuals interact with their environments.

10. The humanistic perspective emphasizes freedom of action, while recognizing that people are both free and constrained. It focuses on strengths rather than pathologies.

11. Using multiple perspectives for thinking about changing person/environment configurations can help us avoid a premature end to our search for understanding.

*Know*

## KEY TERMS

boundary

classical conditioning theory

closed system

cognitive social learning theory

comparison level

comparison level alternative

conflict perspective

constructivist research

critical theorists

developmental perspective

ecomaps

efficacy expectation

enacted role

expected role

feedback mechanisms

functionalist sociology

humanistic perspective

learned helplessness

open system

operant conditioning theory

phenomenal self

phenomenological sociology

pluralistic theory of social conflict

psychodynamic perspective

rational choice perspective

role

role ambiguity

role conflict

role overload

self-efficacy

social behavioral perspective

social constructionist perspective

social exchange theory

social network theory

sociograms

systems perspective

## WORLD WIDE WEB RESOURCES

Humanistic Psychology

**http://www.ahpweb.org/aboutahp/whatis.html**

Web site maintained by the Association of Humanistic Psychology containing the history of humanistic psychology, information on Carl Rogers, the humanistic view of human behavior, methods of inquiry, and humanistic psychotherapies.

Types of Theories

**http://www.grohol.com/therapy.htm**

Site run by Dr. John Grohol, Psy.D., listing four major schools of theory and therapy: psychodynamic, cognitive-behavioral, humanistic, and eclectic.

William Alanson White Institute

**http://wawhite.org/**

The William Alanson White Institute of Psychiatry, Psychoanalysis, and Psychology was co-founded by Harry Stack Sullivan and Erich Fromm. This site contains contemporary psychoanalysis journal articles, definition and description of psychoanalysis, issues of transference/countertransference, and links to other psychoanalytic sites.

Randall Collins – Conflict Theory

**http://www.runet.edu/~Iridener/courses/COLLINR1.HTML**

Site maintained by Larry Ridener, professor of sociology at Radford University. Contains an excerpt from Randall Collins, *Conflict of Sociology* (New York: Academic Press, 1974), pp. 56–61. Discussion of the basics of conflict theory.

APA Online

**http://www.psych.org/**

The American Psychiatric Association site contains information on policy advocacy, clinical resources, research resources, current news, and education.

## A Day in the Life of a School Social Worker: One Person's Multifaceted Social Work Practice

Mary Gay Hutcherson has worked in a variety of social work settings, including a state psychiatric hospital, protective services, hospitals, and the Red Cross. Currently, she works in the Social Work Department of a suburban school system. She loves this position because of the variety of roles she gets to play in the course of a day. Mary Gay provides social work services to three schools—two elementary schools and one high school. We are going to follow her through a typical day's work at the high school.

*Early morning.* Mary Gay arrives at the high school, as usual, at about 7:00 A.M. She feeds the fish in her office and goes immediately to meet with one of the special education teachers, to touch base about a student with whom they have both been working.

Earlier in the week, the student had reported to the teacher that his mother had been behaving very strangely for a few weeks—laughing to herself all day, not paying bills, and quitting her job. There was no food in the house, and his mother was not providing care to his younger siblings. The teacher had called Mary Gay to discuss this situation, because she knew that Mary Gay had met with the mother. Mary Gay was concerned and thought that she should go to the home to assess the situation. Because the student knew the teacher well and trusted her, Mary Gay asked the teacher to join her on the home visit.

When they arrived at the home, they found the situation very much as the student had described it. After assessing the situation, Mary Gay returned to her office and called the crisis unit at the county mental health center. She also placed a call to child protective services because of her concern about the care of the children. The crisis worker agreed to see the client if she could be brought to the crisis center. Mary Gay contacted the police department to request assistance in transporting the mother to the crisis center; she met them at the home and persuaded the mother to go for the assessment. The crisis worker recommended that the mother needed to be hospitalized. Mary Gay consulted with the child protection agency to discuss arrangements for the care of the children, and called relatives in another state to let them know what was happening with the family.

This morning, Mary Gay is checking with the teacher to get a report on how the student is coping with this family crisis. She learns that the student and his siblings are being well cared for and seem to be coping adequately with the situation.

Mary Gay goes back to her office and checks her phone messages. She has a message to call Ms. C at home. Mary Gay is well acquainted with Ms. C, because she has been working with her and her daughter, Jan, for several weeks. Jan, a ninth-grader, has a seizure disorder and severe migraine headaches. She has been refusing to come to school because she does not want the other students to see her while she is having a seizure. She gets very anxious in the mornings when it is about time for the school bus, and anxiety exacerbates both the seizure disorder and the migraines.

Mary Gay has been working with Jan to help her learn to use relaxation exercises before getting on the school bus. She has been working with Ms. C about making firmer demands that Jan get on the school bus in the mornings. She has been collaborating with teachers and other school personnel to help them be more supportive of Jan's efforts to be in school. She has asked some of Jan's teachers to reach out to her. She has also been trying to get Jan involved in the after-school Bible Study Group, where she might make connections with other students with similar interests. She has referred Jan to the school psychologist to have the necessary testing completed to qualify Jan for special education services.

This morning, Ms. C is distressed. Jan was scheduled to meet with the psychologist this morning, but she did not want to come to school. She was afraid that the meeting with the psychologist would upset her and precipitate a seizure. Ms. C also reports that her employer has given her a warning that she must become more consistent in arriving at work punctually. She is "at her wit's end" with trying to get Jan on the school bus in the mornings. Mary Gay and Ms. C problem-solve how Ms. C can talk with her employer about her situation. They agree that a top priority is to get Jan tested, so that she will be eligible to have a special education plan developed. Mary Gay tells Ms. C that she will see what she can do to facilitate that.

Mary Gay goes to the office of the school psychologist and discusses Jan's situation. She requests that the psychologist go to Jan's home to do the testing. The psychologist, who has never done testing away from the office and is reluctant to do so now, gets called away to a meeting. Mary Gay resolves to take this issue up later.

*Midmorning.* Mary Gay leaves the school and drives to the nearby shopping mall, where she and prevention staff from the county mental health center are presenting a two-hour parent training program, "Love and Logic." Attendance is good today—15 parents present—and the parents are receptive.

*Early afternoon.* When Mary Gay arrives back at school, she has a few minutes to finish writing a social history report for tomorrow's meeting of the Special Education Eligibility Team. Then she goes across the hall to attend today's meeting to review three applications. After this meeting, Mary Gay has a few minutes to talk with the psychologist about Jan's evaluation and to return phone calls.

Then she moves on to a meeting with the Student Assistance Team. This team reviews referrals from teachers and parents that involve a variety of student problems. Recently it seems that most of the situations are drug-related, and Mary Gay suggests that the Student

Assistance Team invite a substance abuse consultant from the county mental health center to meet with them. Other team members like this idea, and Mary Gay volunteers to make the call.

*Midafternoon.* A teacher from one of the elementary schools calls to consult with Mary Gay about a potential child abuse situation. Mary Gay concludes that the situation needs to be reported and calls a social worker at protective services because the teacher is uncomfortable about making the call herself.

Mary Gay meets for a few minutes with the social work student for whom she is serving as field instructor, to review the social history report that the student will be presenting at tomorrow's Special Education Eligibility Team meeting. Mary Gay is pleased with the progress the student is making and tells her so.

*Late afternoon.* Mary Gay makes two home visits to meet with families of students who have been referred for special education eligibility screening. Both students are thought to have undiagnosed learning disabilities. Mary Gay sees these meetings with families as the core of her job as a school social worker. In addition to obtaining social history data, her goal is to get the family "on board" as active members of the team. She wants to understand how the family feels about learning disabilities, and she wants to make sure that they understand the process of eligibility screening, what to expect at the team meeting, and the criteria used for diagnosing a learning disability. She prefers to have these conversations in the families' homes—on their turf—to get a better understanding of the family's needs and strengths and to allow the family the opportunity to be interviewed in the comfort of familiar surroundings.

In her second visit today, Mary Gay learns that the single mother is facing severe financial problems. As she problem-solves with the mother, she realizes that this family does not qualify for the free lunch program because the mother is employed. She reminds herself to check with the school principal about the possibility of waiving this policy, which is detrimental to families like this one.

*Evening.* After a quick dinner, Mary Gay is off to the weekly meeting of the Organization for Sexual Minority Youth. Mary Gay was instrumental in forming this group a few years ago when she became aware that these youth were frequent targets of hate crimes. The purpose of the group is twofold: to be supportive to gay and lesbian youth, and to work with the community to develop better understanding of issues facing these youth. Although this is not an official part of Mary Gay's work as a school social worker, she sees it as a part of her professional obligation to actively promote social justice.

## Something to Think About

I continue to be impressed with the multifaceted nature of social work practice and challenged by the demands of such work. In the beginning, of course, the demands seemed overwhelming—just as they did when I was first learning to play the piano and to play basketball. The following questions should help you think about your own process of learning to do social work:

- How does this day in the life of Mary Gay Hutcherson fit with the understanding you had about what social work is when you decided you wanted to be a social worker? How is it similar, and how is it different?

- What about the way your family and friends understand social work? Which of Mary Gay's activities fit with their picture of social work? Given this day in Mary Gay's life, how would you answer when Aunt Louise asks "What is social work, anyway?"

- How does this day fit with your experiences, to date, as a social work student? How is it similar, and how is it different?

- As you follow Mary Gay through the day, think about what general information she needs for each of the activities in which she engages. What have you learned already—from experience and education—in each of these knowledge areas? What else do you need to learn to be able to step into Mary Gay's shoes?

- What dimensions of person and environment seem to be important to Mary Gay's work on this particular day? Do the same dimensions seem important across the different activities of the day, or do you find yourself thinking more about specific dimensions during specific episodes?

- How might you draw on specific theoretical perspectives to assist in any of the social work roles played by Mary Gay on this day?

# PART II

## The Changing Life Course

**"H**ow old are you?" You have probably been asked that question many times, and no doubt you find yourself curious about the age of new acquaintances. We are an age-conscious society, and our speech abounds with expressions related to age: "terrible twos," "sweet 16," "life begins at 40," "senior discounts." Age is also a prominent attribute in contemporary efforts by social scientists to bring order and predictability to our understanding of human behavior. Thus, we all associate particular roles and behaviors with particular age groups.

Part II is organized around six age-graded periods of the life course: Conception, Pregnancy, and Birth; Infancy and Early Childhood; Middle Childhood; Adolescence; Adulthood; Late Adulthood. To capture some of the diversity of life course trajectories, each chapter in Part II begins with three stories.

The purpose of Part II is to explore the life events associated with various ages. Keep in mind as you read, however, that within this framework we will find much diversity. Different cohorts will experience each period of life differently from other cohorts. The same is true for people of different genders, races, cultural backgrounds, and so on. And each individual is unique. This discussion of age-graded periods demonstrates the complex interplay of multiple dimensions of person and environment in life course trajectories.

# Tracking Time

**The expression "the march of time" conjures an image
of a simple progression through the years.**

But time is not just linear. It is also cyclical. Just consider the way the four seasons return, one after another, year after year. Lives, too, are both linear and cyclical.

As time passes, we progressively age, and we move from one life situation to another. But culture and tradition give us opportunities—such as birthday celebrations and family gatherings at holidays—to repeatedly honor significant elements of our lives.

Consider the dual nature of time in this couple's anniversary photographs, which span 30 years. We see the linear progression of time in the environmental and biological changes affecting the couple. But we also see the cyclical nature of the life course in the fact that this couple took time every year to celebrate their marriage.

**Cyclical celebrations like birthdays and wedding anniversaries are cultural markers drawing attention to significant relationships and important aspects of life.**

Some cultural markers are not cyclical, however. They mark special events that might occur only once (or a limited number of times) in a person's life. Consider occasions like the first day of school, the loss of the last baby tooth, the first romantic kiss, the birth of a child, the first gray hair, and a retirement party after a long career. Events like these mark our place along the life course.

A wedding is one such event. To a certain extent, it marks the transition from carefree youth to responsible adulthood. It also marks a change in family affiliations. Instead of "belonging" to their family of birth, the newlyweds simultaneously form their own family and extend their family circle to include their in-laws.

Most of us participate in such life events, but the particular form they take is specific to our era, culture, and social setting and uniquely shaped by who we are.

For example, although the wedding tradition has a long history in many cultures, not all cultures celebrate weddings in the same way. Nor do all individuals in a culture observe life events in exactly the same way. Note the similarities and differences in these wedding pictures, all from the United States: a mass wedding in Harlem, a Jewish wedding, a Hindu wedding, and a gay wedding.

Just as life events take shape from our lives, our lives take shape with each new life event. Life events give us roles—such as spouse or parent—and those roles change over time.

The newlywed becomes a mother, taking on new responsibilities and new relationships with the people in her world.

One day the newlywed's child becomes a mother herself.

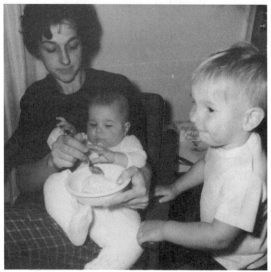

And in the process, her mother gains a new role: grandmother.

Eventually the grandson grows up and shifts into the role of father. But the way he plays that role reflects his own era, personality, and life situation, not those of his grandmother.

As social workers, our job is to pay attention to a client's place in the life course and the way that life events may be affecting the client. But we must not forget that each person experiences the life course in a unique manner, influenced by the multiple dimensions of person and of environment.

# CHAPTER 3

# Conception, Pregnancy, and Birth

*Marcia Harrigan and Suzanne Baldwin, Virginia Commonwealth University*

## A CHANGE OF PLANS FOR TAHESHA GIBBON

For as long as 15-year-old Tahesha can remember, her mother has told her that she would be the first in the family to go to college. Tahesha's mother had once planned to live out this dream herself, but the dream began to fade when Tahesha was born. Her mother was 13 years old at the time. Over and over, Tahesha's mother has told her about the reality that displaced the dream: years of poverty and struggle, multiple pregnancies, spontaneous abortion, and four children ages 15, 14, 9, and 6, the last born with sickle-cell anemia. Diagnosed with acquired immune deficiency syndrome (AIDS) four years ago, Tahesha's mom now increasingly focuses on Tahesha's future—as a college-educated woman and the family caretaker. "Don't play the fool, Tahesha. Get you an education, a steady pay job, one that makes the rent and the doctor . . . then have your babies."

Tonight Tahesha lies in her own bed, listening to the sounds of her brothers who share the room next to hers. Outside, tires screech. She holds her breath, and then quickly lets it out when she does not hear metal crashing. Then, she hears the familiar "pop"—perhaps a gunshot. Tahesha feels relieved that everyone is in bed and out of the line of any stray bullet.

Tahesha closes her eyes, trying to recapture how she felt that night over a month ago. She wanted to say "No, I don't do that," but it did not seem to fit the occasion. She had already declined the heroin that many of her friends used as a buffer against the strain of living in a violence-infested neighborhood. But Tahesha remembers saying yes to some wine, thinking a little would not hurt; maybe it would even offer some relief from her constant feelings of dread and anxious anticipation of more "bad news." But the wine only led to other things: "Come on, Tahesha, you'll like it. Ain't nothing you ever felt. Don't deny me my manhood, girl. Heck, there's nothin' to worry for . . . this is God's gift. . . ." God. Comfort. Hope. But in the end what she felt was not the promise she had felt a few years ago, singing in the choir, listening to the preacher talk about the promised land and better times. "Is there any more wine?" Tahesha remembers asking, while thinking it was not really her voice giving in to the moment. She had made a request. Or was it a choice? Are they the same? What "choice" did she have? Why did she think she was so different from her friends, who laughed and seemed to enjoy the moment?

Now, six weeks later, Tahesha feels nauseous for the second morning in a row. A missed period: pregnant. What will her mother say? Tahesha cringes to think that her life goals may have been sacrificed for an hour spent pursuing peace and pleasure—a high price for any 15-year-old girl. Yet, maybe her mother would be proud. Tahesha recalls how her mother had responded to her aunt's first pregnancy: "You're no woman until you have that first one."

A few days later, Tahesha drops by the community center—where, until two years ago, she was an active member of your after-school program—and shares her confusion with you.

## THE RANDOLPHS' PREMATURE BIRTH

The movement of her growing infant drew Karen into an entrancing world of hope and fantasy. For eight weeks Bob had been watching Karen's abdomen rise and fall to the rhythm of their son's gymnastics. Although they were only six months into the pregnancy, the colors for the nursery had been selected and a baby shower was being planned. Already her changing figure was eliciting comments from her coworkers in the office where she worked part-time as a secretary. With weeks of nausea and fatigue behind her, a general sense of well-being pervaded Karen's mind and body.

Then, with dawn hours away, Karen woke to cramping and blood. With 14 more weeks before her delivery date, Karen was seized with fear. Wishing that Bob was not 1500 miles away, Karen fervently prayed for herself and her baby. The ambulance ride to the hospital became a blur of pain mixed with feelings of unreality. When she arrived in the labor and delivery suite, masked individuals in scrubs took control of her body while demanding answers to a seemingly endless number of questions. Karen knew everything would be fine if only she could feel her son kick. Why didn't he kick?

As the pediatrician spoke of the risks of early delivery, the torrent of words and images threatened to engulf her. Suddenly, the doctors were telling her to push her son into the world—her fragile son who was too small and vulnerable to come out of his cocoon so soon. Then the pain stopped. Oblivious to the relief, Karen listened for her baby's cry. It didn't come. Just a few hours earlier, she had fallen asleep while her baby danced inside her. Now there was only emptiness. Her arms ached for the weight of her infant, and her heart broke with her failure as a parent.

In the newborn intensive care nursery, a flurry of activity revolved around baby boy Randolph. Born weighing only 1 pound 3 ounces, this tiny red baby's immature systems were unprepared for the demands of the extrauterine world. Rapidly he was connected to a ventilator; intravenous lines were placed in his umbilicus and arm; and monitor leads were placed on all available surfaces. Nameless to his caregivers, the baby his parents had already named Joseph was now the recipient of some of the most advanced technological interventions available in modern medicine.

About an hour after giving birth, Karen saw Joseph for the first time. Lying on a stretcher, she counted 10 miniature toes and fingers. Through a film of tears, trying to find resemblance to Bob or herself in this tiny form, Karen's breathing synchronized to Joseph's as she willed him to keep fighting.

Alone in her room, she was flooded with fear, grief, and guilt. What had she done wrong? Could Joseph's premature birth have been caused by paint fumes from decorating his room?

Karen greeted Bob's arrival the next day with mixed feelings. Although she told herself she was being unreasonable, she was angry that he had not been available during the past day. Simultaneously, she was grateful to see him. She was not left to face her feelings alone.

Thirteen days after his arrival, Joseph took his first breath by himself. His hoarse, faint cry provoked both ecstasy and terror in his parents. Off the ventilator, he would periodically miss a breath, which would lead to a decreased heart rate, then monitors flashing and beeping. Throughout the next 10 weeks, Joseph's struggle to survive led Karen and Bob on the most exhilarating yet terrifying roller-coaster ride of their lives. Shattered hopes were mended, only to be reshattered with the next telephone call. Each visit to Joseph was followed by the long trip home to the empty nursery.

The close relationship that Karen and Bob had previously experienced began to fray. Karen was remote during their times alone. They had unaccustomed arguments and little time or energy for intimacy. Bob's attempt to concentrate on his job had limited success, although his job was more important than ever as the medical bills continued to accumulate.

As the weeks passed and Joseph's survival seemed assured, the medical staff continued to equivocate about possible long-term problems. Attempting to focus on the present, slowly Bob and Karen learned to recognize Joseph's preference for gentle stroking during waking periods and to anticipate his angry crying when procedures were performed.

Great joy and equally intense anxiety pervaded Joseph's homecoming day. After spending 53 days in the newborn intensive care unit (NICU) and still weighing only 4 pounds 13 ounces, Joseph was handed to his parents. With more questions than answers about their son's future and their abilities to take care of him, Bob and Karen took their baby to his new home.

As the NICU social worker, your major goal is to support these individuals as a family unit facing this challenging transition to parenthood. In the past 53 days, you have helped Bob and Karen get their questions answered, understand the unfamiliar medical language of the health care providers, and understand and cope with the strong emotions they are experiencing.

### THE GEREKES' LATE-LIFE PREGNANCY

Thirty-one years ago, at age 44, Hazel Gereke gave birth to her fifth child, Terry. At the time of his birth, Terry's siblings ranged in age from 2 to 25, and his father was 48. The following interview tells their story:

Q: It's been 31 years, but what do you remember about your pregnancy with Terry?

A: Well, I menstruated regularly and had long, heavy bleeding. It lasted two to three weeks every month, so I went to the doctor. He said I was four and one-half months pregnant! I cried . . . I was too far along to do anything. You see, back then you had to have three doctors go before the hospital board to say the pregnancy jeopardized the mother's health. Well, my doctor was Catholic, so I knew that would not happen.

Q: Do you remember how Mr. Gereke reacted to this pregnancy?

A: I can remember exactly what he said like it was yesterday: "Hazel, we'll love it!"

Q: What was the rest of the pregnancy like?

A: Horrible! Right after I found out, in October, Grandma and Grandpa moved in to live with us, and in November, Ann, our oldest child, got married! I wasn't feeling the best in the world. I would wake up at 3:00 A.M. with pains in my hand, elbows, and arm . . . I walked the floor. I had carpel tunnel, but at the time I thought it was the pregnancy. In December, I had false labor and was due in January. Terry was born on February 7, 1966.

Q: What was Terry's pregnancy like compared to the other four?

A: Ann's was normal; she was born in 1941 at home, with a doctor and a nurse who came with gas, oxygen, and a birthing table. John was more diffi-cult; I had a prolapsed uterus and difficult delivery. He was premature and blue at birth. Gail, I carried breech, but she was turned in labor. You could tell by her black and blue nose, mouth, chin, and forehead! But everything was OK. Mike was normal. I had no morning sickness but a long delivery. Terry I don't remember because I was put under when I went into the delivery room. They said the delivery was hard due to my age.

Q: What do you remember right after Terry's birth?

A: I bottle-fed him but had difficulty, so the nurse taught me how. The doctor said, "He might be a little slow."

Q: When and how did you find out that Terry had Down's syndrome?

A: I first heard "Down's" when I enrolled him in school and saw on the record "Down's child"! I went right away to the doctor, who said the test would cost $75. Well, I said, "there's no need for a test—it won't change what he is." He wasn't that bad. After his first birthday, he sat, began to walk, and said "Mama," "Daddy," "bye-bye," and "eat"—about 7 to 10 words. He was beginning to dress and potty train. At birth the nurses said, "You won't have any problem training this one; when he's wet, he screams!" But when he was 15 to 18 months old he had terrible seizures . . . all summer. He left the table, walked into the living room, and we heard a terrible sound. He had fallen backwards and hit his head on the table. He was limp. They put him on dilantin and phenobarbital and kept increasing it. He became a vegetable. I gradually withdrew him from his medication . . . boy, was the doctor upset when he found that out, but Terry was doing better!

Q: What impact do you remember Terry's difficulties having on the rest of the family?

A: Gail and Mike were still at home. Gail said, "He doesn't look good—he looks funny." I took Terry to the mirror to teach him his eyes, ears, and mouth like I had the others. "Look at the pretty baby!" I said. He hung his head . . . he never looked in the mirror again. He was down about himself; he knew he was different. I worried that Mike was teased by the other kids when the bus came for Terry—they called it "the dummy bus." I always knew who had compassion because if they did, Terry stayed around. Otherwise, he went to his room.

Five years ago, the Gerekes followed advice they had received and arranged for Terry to go to a group home, but no one in the family felt comfortable about this plan. The day he was to move into the group home, Hazel Gereke learned that Terry would be sharing a room with five other adult males, and she refused to let him live there. After two more years at home, at age 29, Terry moved to a different group home. Now, he visits his parents every Saturday and helps his father mow the grass, but he is always eager to return to the group home.

When asked if she thinks anything should have happened differently over the years, Hazel reluctantly but honestly replies that "the pregnancy should have been stopped." When asked, "What has Terry contributed to your family?" she replies, "He has kept the family together and taught us not to take things for granted."

Although the Gerekes did not have contact with a social worker when they first encountered their late-life pregnancy, Hazel Gereke has reminded us about the ambivalences and ambiguities that social workers need to keep in mind when working with issues of problem pregnancies.

# Sociocultural Organization of Childbearing

These three stories tell us that conception, pregnancy, and birth are experienced in different ways by different people. But they do not tell us about all the possible variations, which reflect the complex interplay of person, environment, and time. The biological processes vary little for the vast majority of women and their families, but researchers continue to study the psychological, social, and spiritual dimensions of childbearing. This chapter presents a multidimensional overview of current knowledge about conception, pregnancy, and childbirth, gleaned from the literatures of anthropology, genetics, medicine, nursing, psychology, social work, and sociology.

*In what other ways might the cultural dimension affect the childbearing experience?*

As you read, keep in mind that all elements of childbearing have deep meaning for a society. Procreation allows a culture to persist, as children are raised to follow the ways of their predecessors. Procreation may also allow a culture to expand if the birthrate exceeds the rate at which the society loses members. Thus, as Valsiner (1989a) reminds us, "human procreation is socially organized in all its aspects. In any cultural group around the world, society regulates the conditions under which a woman is to become pregnant, how she and her husband should conduct themselves during the pregnancy, how labor and delivery take place, and how the newborn child is introduced into society" (p. 117).

In the United States, the social meaning of childbearing has changed rather dramatically over the past 20 years, in several ways (Carter & McGoldrick, 1989; Chadiha & Danziger, 1995; Danziger & Danziger, 1993; Ellman & Taggart, 1993; Furstenberg, 1994; Moss, 1987; Skolnick & Skolnick, 1996):

- Smaller desired family size
- Decreased gender role stereotyping for parents
- More available and accessible reproductive options
- Greater sexual freedom
- Increased incidence of pregnancy among single women of all ages
- Increased contraception and family planning
- More delayed marriage and childbirth
- Increased diversity in family values and sexual mores
- Increased recognition of the role of fathers beyond their genetic contributions
- Continued high priority on childbearing
- Increased prevalence and acceptance of elected childlessness

These trends have prompted considerable debate over how our society should define *family*. Less than 50 percent of family households today comprise married couples and their children. Some people have voiced dismay, decrying the demise of the nuclear family structure and "family values." Others have noted that we are simply witnessing what family historians call family pluralism, or recognition of many viable types of family structures. As Hareven (1982, p. 463) notes, such pluralism is nothing new:

> Many different family forms have been in existence all along, but they have been less visible. The more recent forms of alternative life styles have now become a part of the official fiber of society, because they are now being tolerated much more than in the past.

In short, what we are witnessing is not a fragmentation of traditional family patterns, but, rather, the emergence of a pluralism in family ways.

We take the position that the definition of *family* must reflect this pluralism. Yet unresolved moral, political, and economic issues abound (Stacey, 1996). These debates influence what family research is funded (Udry, 1993); how abortion and family policy is constructed (Figueira-McDonough, 1990), particularly at the national level; and who gets access to such family resources as birth control pills and prenatal care.

## Conception and Pregnancy

The three stories at the beginning of the chapter remind us that the emotional reaction to conception may vary widely. The Randolphs' conception brought joy, in contrast to Tahesha Gibbon's initial dismay followed by rising hopefulness; Mr. Gereke voiced confidence in contrast to his wife's apprehension. The conception experience is influenced by many factors: the mother's age, health, marital status, social status, cultural expectations, peer expectations, school or employment circumstances, and prior experiences with conception and childbearing, as well as the interplay of these factors with those of other people significant to the mother.

The conception experience may also be influenced by organized religion. Church policies reflect different views about the purpose of human sexual expression: pleasure, procreation, or perhaps both. Many mainstream religions, in their denominational policy statements, specify acceptable sexual behaviors (Bullis & Harrigan, 1992). Unwanted conception may be seen as an act of carelessness, promiscuity, or merely God's will—perhaps even punishment for wrongdoing. These beliefs are usually strongly held and have become powerful fodder for numerous social, political, and religious debates related to conception.

Even the mechanisms of conception are socially constructed. Some traditional cultures, such as the Telefomin of New Guinea, believe that repeated intercourse is necessary to conceive, but forbid intercourse after conception so that multiple births will not occur. In contrast, the Dusan of Borneo believe that conception occurs when the body heat created between males and females causes the woman's blood to boil, forming the child drop by drop; consequently, intercourse must occur throughout pregnancy for the child to develop fully (Valsiner, 1989). In the United States, conception is believed to be a complex biological event.

Just as the experience of conception has varied over time and across cultures, so has the experience of pregnancy. It too is influenced by religious orientations, social customs, changing values, economics, and even political ideologies. For example, societal expectations of pregnant women in the United States have changed, from simply waiting for birth to actively seeking to maintain the mother's—and hence the baby's—health, preparing for the birth process, and sometimes even trying to influence the baby's cognitive and emotional development while it is in the womb.

## Birth

Throughout history, families and particularly women have passed on to young girls the traditions of childbirth practices. These traditions have been shaped by cultural and institutional changes, however.

*Place of Childbirth.* Until the early 20th century, when physician training was formalized, most births were at home, with a midwife (a trained birthing specialist) attending and the family intimately involved. The move to hospitals formalized the birthing process, and more women were subjected to episiotomies (incisions to enlarge the opening for the baby during birth), enemas, and anesthesia in a male-dominated arena (Ashford, LeCroy, & Lortie, 1997). The feminist movement inspired a return to natural birthing practices, as women advocated for less invasive deliveries in more friendly environments (Riedmann, 1996a). Their advocacy has led to the reemergence of midwives, but with advanced education and training (Bain, Gau, & Reed, 1995).

Hazel Gereke's first child was born at home, but her later children were born in a hospital. Today, only 1 percent of all U.S. births occur in the home. Because 5 to 10 percent of all low-risk pregnancies result in complications, most medical professionals prefer an environment equipped for emergencies. **Birthing centers,** a more recent development, are located close to major hospitals but feature comfortably decorated rooms and allow participation of extended family members, including siblings. One measure of the success of these centers is the large discrepancy in rates of birth by Cesarean section: only 4.4 percent of women in birthing centers, compared to approximately 20 percent for women in major hospitals (Novak & Broom, 1995; Riedmann, 1996a). These data are hard to interpret, however, because women with the greatest potential for at-risk births are encouraged to have hospital delivery.

How does childbirth education assist the social worker in helping the biological person?

*Childbirth Education.* Childbirth education was not formalized until the early 1900s, when the Red Cross set up hygiene and health care classes as a public health initiative. Dr. Grantley Dick-Read's book *Childbirth without Fear,* published in 1944, was summarily rejected, as was the idea that women who were educated about birth would have less fear and therefore less need for pain medication. Not until the 1950s did the idea of childbirth education gain credibility. A French obstetrician, Dr. Fernand Lamaze, learned of Russian attempts to use hypnosis to reduce childbirth pain. His book *Painless Childbirth* (1958) has become the foundation for contemporary childbirth education. It instructs women, and more recently fathers and significant others, about female anatomy, the physiology of pregnancy, and relaxation techniques based on hypnosis (Novak & Broom, 1995; Sroufe, Cooper, & DeHart, 1996). Outcome studies have shown that childbirth classes do indeed result in decreased pain and anxiety (Dickason, Schult, & Silverman, 1990), shorter labor, decreased use of forceps, improved infant outcome, and an overall positive experience (Reidmann, 1996b).

The need for childbirth classes cuts across demographic lines in theory but, in many cases, not in practice. Studies show that better-educated women of higher socioeconomic status are more likely to participate in childbirth classes (Grossman, Fitzsimmons, Larsen-Alexander, Sachs, & Harter, 1990; Reidmann, 1996a). The Maternity Care Access Act of 1989 created a means-tested program called First Steps to provide parenting and childbirth classes to women who previously could not afford them (Rabkin, Balassone, & Bell, 1995).

*Hospital Stay.* We are in the midst of a changing philosophy, replacing a view of the incipient mother as "ill" with a view that giving birth is a normal life transition. We are also living in an era that values cost-effective, innovative, comprehensive health services. All promote family contact during birth—hence the rise of birthing centers.

Forty years ago, women remained hospitalized for 7 to 10 days following birth. Recently, controversial managed-care policies have pushed for women with uncomplicated deliveries to be discharged within 24 hours. However, both mother and infant undergo rapid transitions during the period following delivery. The infant must adjust to a new environment, learn to nurse, and begin the process of **bonding**—development of a close emotional attachment—with parents. Life-threatening problems, such as heart problems or infections, may not be detected until the second or third day of life. In response, some birthing facilities send a nurse to visit the home for the first few days after discharge to assess the mother and the infant for any problems. These home visitors also provide education and emotional support.

*Breastfeeding.*    Throughout history, most infants have been breastfed. However, alternatives to breastfeeding by the mother have always existed. Archeological records from 2000 B.C. show that at least some infants had a wet nurse (a woman employed to breastfeed someone else's infant) or were fed animal milks (Coates, 1993). Following the Second World War, breastfeeding ceased to be the primary nutritional source for infants because of the promotion of manufactured formula in industrialized and nonindustrialized countries. Since the 1980s, cultural attitudes have shifted again in favor of breastfeeding.

Today, the typical profile of a nursing mother in the United States is an "older Caucasian woman of higher social class; they are more affluent, have more years of formal education, are non-smokers, have attended childbirth classes, have more social support" (Coates, 1993, p. 18). The greatest decline in breastfeeding has been among young, unmarried, African American women of lower income. They are less likely to have education regarding the benefits of breastfeeding and the flexibility in the workplace to pump and store milk (Fletcher, 1994; Grossman et al., 1990). In an attempt to address these racial and economic differences, in the late 1980s the federally subsidized **Women, Infants, and Children (WIC) program** expanded food benefits from 6 to 12 months for breastfeeding mothers (Coates, 1993).

How else might the environmental dimensions of families and peers influence childbearing?

Cultural norms also influence breastfeeding. In European American and Mexican American families, the mother seeks the opinion of the baby's father and maternal and paternal grandparents, whereas in African American families the maternal grandmother and peers are most influential in the decision to breastfeed (Baranowski, 1983). Korean mothers-in-law care for the new mother and are a powerful influence in choices about breastfeeding. In Saudi Arabia, a woman may breastfeed her infant openly and receive no notice, although otherwise she is fully veiled. In France, topless swimming is culturally acceptable, but breastfeeding in public is not (Riordan, 1993a).

Studies have demonstrated that the breastfeeding decision is typically made in the first trimester of pregnancy and is most influenced by the father's support (Aberman & Kirchoff, 1985; Kaufman & Hall, 1989). The length of time a child is nursed is proportional to the number of persons supporting the decision (Cronenwett & Reinhardt, 1987; Walker, 1992). Women decide to nurse primarily for infant health benefits, which include increased immunity—which begins in the third trimester—to viruses such as mumps, chicken pox, and influenza (Riordan, 1993b); sterile milk always at the correct temperature; lower but higher-quality protein content; well-absorbed fat content (Fletcher, 1994); more efficient vitamin and mineral balance; and a 50 percent decrease in the rate of infant hospitalizations and illness such as gastrointestinal illness and ear infections (Chen, Yu, & Li, 1988; Howie, Forsyth, Ogston, Clark, & Florey, 1990). Postpartum maternal benefits of breastfeeding include increased calorie consumption without weight gain; the release of the hormone oxytocin, causing uterine contractions; reduced uterine bleeding; and lower cost.

Mothers also choose to bottle-feed for a variety of reasons, including convenience and flexibility of scheduling (Aberman & Kirchoff, 1985)—particularly important to women who work outside the home (Frederick & Auerbach, 1985). Employer support for nursing mothers, such as on-site day care, is most likely to be available in large corporations and is seldom available to lower-income working women—a discrepancy that contributes to class differences between those who breastfeed and those who do not. Contraindications to breastfeeding are few, but they include maternal medical conditions such as untreated tuberculosis, leukemia, breast cancer diagnosed during lactation, drug abuse, and sexually transmitted diseases (STDs) or human immunodeficiency virus (HIV) (Dickason, Silverman, & Kaplan, 1998).

# Control over Conception and Pregnancy

The desire to plan the timing of childbearing is an ancient one, as is the desire to stimulate pregnancy in the event of infertility. Contraception and induced abortion have probably always existed in every culture. Effective solutions for infertility are more recent. But it is important to remember that not all methods of controlling conception and pregnancy are equally acceptable to all people. Cultural and religious beliefs, as well as personal circumstances, make some people more accepting of some methods than others.

## *Contraception*

The range of birth control options available today provides women and men the ability to plan pregnancy and birth more than ever before. Perhaps that is why U.S. birthrates declined in 1995 for the fifth consecutive year (National Center for Health Services [NCHS], 1997) and why other societies offering ready access to birth control have had similar declines.

Each birth control option needs to be considered in light of its cost, failure rate, potential health risks, and probability of use, given the user's sociocultural circumstances.

- *Breastfeeding.* Women who are breastfeeding are less likely to conceive than other women are. It is estimated that if breastfeeding were stopped and not replaced with other contraceptives, the fertility rate would increase by 12 percent (Thapa, Short, & Potts, 1988). Breastfeeding is not recommended as a reliable contraceptive method, however.

- *Coitus interruptus.* Premature withdrawal of the penis from the vagina, before ejaculation, is probably the oldest form of birth control. However, the failure rate is approximately 19 percent, and coitus interruptus offers no protection from STDs and HIV (Hatecher et al., 1994).

- *Periodic abstinence.* "Natural family planning" or the "rhythm method" involves daily tracking of changes in the woman's body associated with the menstrual cycle and an avoidance of intercourse during fertile periods.

- *Barrier methods.* The condom (for men) and the diaphragm, cervical cap, and vaginal sponge (for women) provide increased protection against STDs but still have fairly high failure rates: approximately 12 percent for condoms and 18–36 percent for female barrier methods. Spermicides, acting as chemical barriers, have a high failure rate (21 percent) and provide minimal protection against STDs and HIV.

- *Oral contraceptives.* The introduction of "birth control pills" in the United States in 1960 precipitated major changes in reproduction. With a failure rate of only about 1 to 3 percent, they revolutionized family planning. The results of recent studies have raised concerns about long-term problems associated with "the pill," especially among women who smoke, but this continues to be one of the most popular forms of birth control. Recently, Mifepristone (RU 486), a "morning after" contraceptive, was developed in Europe and introduced in the United States, but it remains controversial because some people believe it essentially aborts an embryo.

- *Intermuscular injections.* In 1992, the introduction in the United States of Depo-Medroxy-progesterone acetate (Depo-Provera), a drug used for many years in Europe, allowed women protection against pregnancy for three months.

- *Intrauterine devices.* The use of IUDs has been marked by controversy and legal disputes for a number of years. They were introduced in the early 1900s, but high rates of infection and tissue damage discouraged their use until the 1960s. Most manufacturers discontinued production in the 1980s following expensive legal settlements. Currently, detailed consent forms are required for their use.

- *Voluntary surgical sterilization.* Sterilization is considered effective but permanent. However, recent advances in microsurgery have increased the success rates for reversal procedures. Informed consent is required prior to surgical sterilization.

## Medical Abortion

Abortion may be the most politicized, hotly debated social issue related to pregnancy today. But it was not always so controversial. Prior to the mid-1800s, abortion was practiced in the United States but was not considered a crime if performed before the fetus quickened (or showed signs of life). After 1860, however, physicians advocated banning abortion because of maternal harm caused by the use of dangerous poisons and practices (Figueira-McDonough, 1990). Legislators also wanted to see growth in the U.S. population. By 1900, all states had legislation prohibiting abortion except in extreme circumstances, typically medically related. Over the years, moral issues increasingly became the basis for debate.

Which social institutions and social structures are involved in the childbearing experience?

Despite laws controlling abortion, it has remained an option for those with the economic means. Poor women have been the ones whose access to abortion services is limited. Hazel Gereke recounted that as late as 1966 legal abortion had to be "medically related," which did not cover the difficulty of another child for older parents or the difficulty of raising a child with Down's syndrome. Hazel's situation was also influenced by the moral or religious stance of the physician and perhaps the hospital.

In 1973, in ***Roe v. Wade,*** the U.S. Supreme Court legalized abortion in the first trimester and left it to the discretion of the woman and her physician. However, the Supreme Court ruled in

1989, in ***Webster* v. *Reproductive Health Services,*** that Medicaid could no longer fund abortions and that much of the decision making related to abortion should return to the states. Today, states vary considerably in who has access to abortion, when, how, and at what cost. In some states, new rules are effectively decreasing access, particularly for poor and minority populations. Some poor African American women have no greater access to abortion now than they did more than 100 years ago (Ross, 1992). It is unlikely that Tahesha would have access to a legal and safe abortion if she were interested in that option.

Today, approximately half of all unintended pregnancies in the United States end in abortion. During the first trimester and until **fetal viability** (the point at which the baby could survive outside the womb) in the second trimester, a pregnant woman can choose an abortion. Approximately 88 percent of abortions are performed during the first 12 weeks of pregnancy (National Center for Health Services, 1997). Recent controversy regarding procedures for terminating a pregnancy after fetal viability have raised ethical and legal dilemmas that are being addressed in the legal system, by most religions, and in other parts of the culture. Opinion polls continually reveal, however, that like Hazel Gereke, the majority of Americans favor abortion as an option under specified conditions (Cook, Jelen, & Wilcox, 1992; Figueria-McDonough, 1990). Still, in 1994, the national ratio of abortions to live births (321 to 1000) was lower than in any other year since 1976.

Abortion procedures fall into three categories:

1. *Menstrual regulation.* The hormone prostaglandin is given to the woman within six to seven weeks after the last period to stimulate shedding of the uterine lining and, with it, the embryo. It accounts for only 0.5 percent of abortions and is associated with such complications as threatened spontaneous ("natural") abortions and **ectopic pregnancy** (implantation of the embryo outside the uterus).

2. *Instrumental evacuations.* One of two types of instruments is used in 98.9 percent of all abortions. The standard first-trimester **vacuum curettage** is the one most frequently performed in an outpatient clinic. A suction device is threaded through the cervix to remove the contents of the uterus. It is fairly safe, but because it is invasive, it introduces greater risks than the use of prostaglandin. The second-trimester **curettage abortion** requires even greater dilatation of the cervix to allow passage of a surgical instrument used to scrape the walls of the uterus. If cutterage abortion is performed on an outpatient basis, a second visit is required. With both types of instrumental evacuation, the woman faces risks of bleeding, infection, and subsequent infertility.

3. **Amnioinfusion.** In the second trimester, a saline solution can be infused into the uterus to end the pregnancy. Amnioinfusion is used in only 0.4 percent of abortions and requires the greatest medical expertise and follow-up care.

How can social workers assist the psychological person in cases of abortion?

Regardless of the timing or type of abortion, all women should be carefully counseled before and after the procedure. Unplanned pregnancies typically create considerable psychological stress, and social workers can help pregnant women consider all alternatives to an unwanted pregnancy—including abortion—consistent with the client's personal value and belief system. Following an abortion, most women experience only mild feelings of guilt, sadness, or regret that abate fairly soon, followed by relief that the crisis is resolved (David, 1996). Nevertheless, some women have a more severe response and may require ongoing counseling (Erikson, 1993; Speckland, 1993). Counseling is also particularly important from a prevention perspective, because women receiving counseling following a first abortion have been found to practice contraception with greater frequency and success (David, 1996).

## Infertility Treatment

Children in most segments of today's society are taught that one of their major goals in life should be to become a parent. Thus, **infertility,** the inability to create a viable embryo, is often a life crisis. In one study, 50 percent of women and 15 percent of men experiencing infertility reported that it was the most upsetting experience in their lives (Collins, Freeman, Boxer, & Tureck, 1992). It combines threats to sexuality, self-esteem, and the marital relationship with perceived failure to meet societal expectations and with social isolation from family and friends (Keye, 1995). Couples struggling to conceive report higher rates of marital dissatisfaction because of the need to have sex on schedule, the specific details of techniques meant to increase fertility, and the pain that may accompany sexual intercourse (Keye, 1995).

The causes of infertility are many. New studies demonstrate a possible link between fertility and the reaction to stress created by infertility itself. Conditions that affect male erectile function or ejaculation impair both male fertility and female receptivity. An alarming increase in STDs has contributed to rising infertility rates. Pelvic adhesions and endometriosis (abnormal growth of the uterine lining) in the female reproductive system also decrease conception rates.

In the past, infertile couples could keep trying and hope for the best, but medical technology has given today's couples a variety of options, summarized in Exhibit 3.1.

**EXHIBIT 3.1**

Causes and Cures for Infertility

| Male Infertility | | Female Infertility | |
|---|---|---|---|
| **Problem** | **Treatment** | **Problem** | **Treatment** |
| Low sperm count | Change of environment; antibiotics; surgery; hormonal therapy; artificial insemination | Vaginal structural problem | Surgery |
| | | Abnormal cervical mucus | Hormonal therapy |
| | | Abnormal absence of ovulation | Antibiotics for infection; hormonal therapy |
| Physical defect affecting transport of sperm | Microsurgery | Blocked or scarred fallopian tubes | Surgery; in vitro fertilization |
| Genetic disorder | Artificial insemination | Uterine lining unfavorable to implantation | Hormone therapy; antibiotics; surgery |

*Source:* Based on Milunsky, 1987.

The use of **replacement hormonal therapy (RHT),** which restores key hormones to normal levels, often mitigates infertility problems that are due to hormonal deficiency. The resultant pregnancy rate is variable, ranging from 20 to 90 percent (Dickason, Silverman, & Kaplan, 1998). The risk of multiple births with RHT can be as high as 30 percent, however, depending on the medication regime selected (Dickason, Schult, & Silverman, 1990).

If the problem is male infertility (diagnosed by a sperm analysis), the preferred method is artificial insemination, using fresh or frozen donor sperm. The success rate is as high as 90 percent. Ethical and legal questions have been raised, however, regarding the legal status of the sperm donor (what parental rights does he have?) and the psychosocial impact on the mother. Sperm donors are routinely screened for genetic defects and physical suitability, but psychological screening remains controversial—in large part because it is nonstandardized and thus easily misinterpreted.

The birth of the first "test tube baby" in 1978, demonstrating the first of many **assisted reproductive technologies (ART),** initiated a new era in infertility management and research. By the time a couple considers the use of ART, they have often struggled for a long time, emotionally and physically, with infertility and may be desperate. But the high cost and limited success rates deter some prospective candidates. Some ART centers require a psychological evaluation of the couple to assess competency to parent, although studies have demonstrated that those couples seeking ART are generally psychologically healthy and that in any case they tend to minimize problems when applying for ART (Keye, 1995).

The most common types of ART are the following:

- **In vitro fertilization (IVF)** has a success rate of only 15 to 20 percent and costs between $2,000 and $10,000 per attempt. In this procedure, ova are surgically removed during ovulation, mixed with donor sperm, then inserted into the uterus after fertilization and the beginning of cell division.

- **Gamete intra–fallopian tube transfer (GIFT)** has a success rate of 35 to 40 percent. GIFT uses the same procedure as IVF, except that the fertilized ova are surgically returned to the woman's fallopian tubes. Like IVF, this technique requires daily participation. It also entails an increased risk for ectopic pregnancy, multiple births, and surgical complications.

- **Intrauterine insemination (IUI)** is a very costly procedure that may take several attempts over a six- to nine-month period before pregnancy occurs (Dickason, Silverman, & Kaplan, 1998). IUI involves bypassing the cervix (usually altered by antibodies or infection) and surgically implanting the ovum and spermatazoa into the uterus.

All of these procedures may use donated ova, but that practice has raised further legal and ethical questions, especially regarding parental rights and responsibilities. Psychological and emotional issues may also arise, related to the introduction of third-party genetic material, secrecy, and confidentiality.

Although ART was originally limited to married couples, unattached females in increasing numbers are using this method of conception. Their reasons include unsuccessful relationships with men in the past, prior abuse, or a lesbian lifestyle. Women well beyond traditional childbearing age have also begun to use ART. This trend has raised moral and ethical questions in some segments of society: How well can a single mother, a lesbian mother, or an older mother raise a child?

Adoption is one last alternative for the infertile couple. That is the option chosen by Robert Johnson and Cindy Marsh in Chapter 7. It is not much less daunting than infertility treatment, however. A time-consuming multiphase evaluation, which includes a home study, is required before finalization of custody. The idea of parenting an infant with an unknown genetic heritage may also be a challenge for some persons, particularly because an increasing number of problems previously thought to be environmentally induced are being linked—at least in part—to genetics. On the positive side, however, some individuals and couples prefer adoption to the demands and uncertainties of ART. Some adoptive parents are also committed to giving a home to children in need of care.

# Reproductive Genetics

Recognition of the need for genetics knowledge is not new to social work. In fact, Mary Richmond (1917) advocated that a social worker "get the facts of heredity" in the face of marriage between close relatives, miscarriage, tuberculosis, alcoholism, mental disorder, nervousness, epilepsy, cancer, deformities or abnormalities, or an exceptional ability.

*Why is social work central to the application of knowledge about genetics?*

Almost 50 years later, Watson and Clark first described the mechanisms of genetic inheritance. But it was not until 1970 that our knowledge of genetics began to explode. This knowledge altered social work practice in many areas, primarily in working with persons of reproductive age. The interdisciplinary field of genetics acknowledges social work as one of its essential disciplines, and thus social workers should have at least a rudimentary understanding of genetics (Garver, 1995; Rauch, 1988; Reed, 1996).

Chromosomes and genes are the essential components of this process. Genetic instructions are coded in **chromosomes** found in each cell; **genes** are segments of DNA carried by the chromosomes that contain the codes that produce particular traits and dispositions. Each mature **germ cell**—ovum or sperm—contains 23 chromosomes, half of the set of 46 present in each parent's cells. As you can see in Exhibit 3.2, when the sperm penetrates the ovum (**fertilization**), the parents' chromosomes combine to make a total of 46 chromosomes arrayed in 23 pairs. Each chromosome may have as many as 20,000 genes, with an average of 3,000–5,000 genes per chromosome. The genes constitute a "map" to guide the protein and enzyme reactions for every subsequent cell in the developing person and across the life span. Thus, every physical trait and many behavioral traits are influenced by the combined genes from the ovum and sperm. Every person has a unique **genotype,** or array of genes, unless the person is an identical twin. Yet the environment may influence how each gene pilots the growth of cells. The result is a **phenotype** (observable trait) that differs somewhat from the genotype. Thus, even identical twins are unique. On initial observation, you may not be able to distinguish between identical twins, but if you look closely enough, you will probably find some variation, such as differences in the size of an ear, hair thickness, or temperament.

A chromosome and its pair have the same types of genes at the same location. The exception is the last pair of chromosomes, the **sex chromosomes**, which, among other things, determine

**EXHIBIT 3.2**

Gene Cell Division,
Fertilization, and
Chromosome Pairs

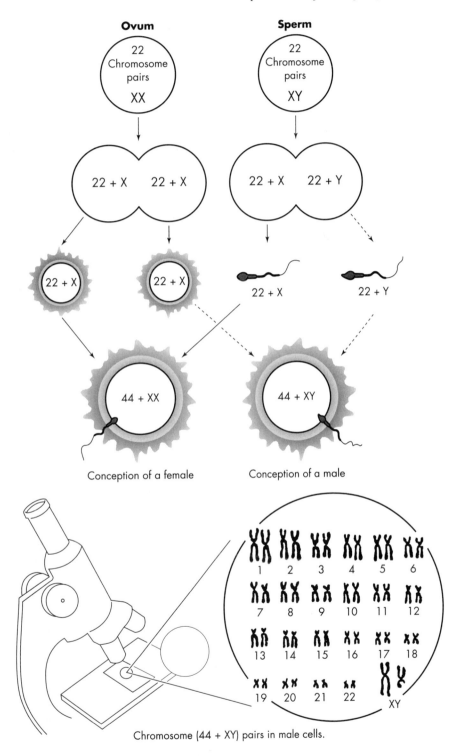

Conception of a female

Conception of a male

Chromosome (44 + XY) pairs in male cells.

sex. The ovum can contribute only an X chromosome to the 23rd pair, but the sperm can contribute either an X or a Y and therefore determines the sex of the developing person. A person with XX sex chromosomes is female; a person with XY sex chromosomes is male (see Exhibit 3.2).

Genes that do not have a counterpart on the other sex chromosome create **sex-linked traits.** A gene for red/green color blindness, for example, is carried only on the X chromosome. When an X chromosome that carries this gene is paired with a Y chromosome, which could not carry the gene, red/green color blindness is manifested. So, almost all red/green color blindness is found in males. This gene for color blindness does not manifest if paired with an X chromosome, unless it is inherited from both parents, which is rare. However, if a woman inherits the gene from either parent, she can unknowingly pass it on to her sons.

Whether genes express certain traits depends on their being either dominant or recessive. Traits governed by **recessive genes** (for example, hemophilia, baldness, thin lips) will only be expressed if the responsible gene is present on each chromosome of the relevant pair. In contrast, traits governed by **dominant genes** (normal blood clotting, curly hair, thick lips) will be expressed if one or both paired chromosomes have the gene. When the genes on a chromosome pair give competing, yet controlling, messages, they are called **interactive genes**, meaning that both messages may be followed to varying degrees. Hair, eye, and skin color often depend on such interactivity. For example, a light-skinned person with red hair and hazel eyes may mate with a person having dark skin, brown hair, and blue eyes and produce a child with a dark complexion, red hair, and blue eyes.

Although Mary Richmond in 1917 noted that many physical traits, medical problems, and mental health problems have a genetic basis, only recently has technology allowed us to identify the specific genes governing these traits. As of August 30, 1998, a total of 6,736 genes had been mapped on the chromosomes (Online Mendelian Inheritance in Man, 1998), and the mapping of new genes is proceeding at a phenomenal rate. Our understanding of physical and psychological traits heretofore attributed to factors other than genetics, such as the environment, are therefore advancing rapidly as well (Takahashi & Turnbull, 1994).

Our rapidly increasing ability to read a person's genetic code and understand the impact it could have on the person's life has led to the relatively new discipline of **genetic counseling,** which provides information and advice to guide decisions of persons concerned about hereditary abnormalities. Social workers, with their biopsychosocial perspective, are well positioned to provide such services (Bishop, 1993; Schild & Black, 1984; Takahashi & Turnbull, 1994).

A major concern of genetic counseling is whether all genetic information should be shared with a client. Some information may only cause distress, because the technology for altering genes is in its infancy and applicable to only a few situations. But recent advances allow for earlier diagnosis and give some clients more decision options. Today, for example, a late-life pregnancy such as Hazel Gereke's could be evaluated genetically using amniocentesis or chorion villi testing. Such evaluation could lead to decisions ranging from abortion to preparation for parenting a child with a disability. However, these options typically are laced with economic, political, legal, ethical, moral, and religious considerations (Andrews, 1994; Chadwick, Levitt, & Shickle, 1997).

Ethical issues related to genetic engineering have an impact not only at the individual and family levels but also at the societal level. For example, when we are able to manipulate genes at will, we will need to be on guard against genetic elitism. It is one thing to use genetic engineering to eliminate such inherited diseases as sickle-cell anemia, but quite another to use it to select the sex, body type, or coloring of a child. We are living in a time of tremendous ethical complexity, involving the interplay of new reproductive technologies; changing family structures, values, and mores; political and religious debate; and economic considerations. This ethical complexity extends to issues of social justice: As increasing numbers of persons gain the ability to control conception, plan pregnancy, and control pregnancy outcomes, we need to protect the interests of those who lack the knowledge and other resources to do so.

# Normal Fetal Development

The 40 weeks of **gestation,** during which the fertilized ovum becomes a fully developed infant, are a remarkable time. **Gestational age** is calculated from the date of the woman's last menstrual period, a fairly easy time for the woman to identify. In contrast, **fertilization age** is measured from the time of fertilization, approximately 14 days after the last menstrual period. The average pregnancy lasts 280 days when calculated from gestational age and 266 from the time of fertilization. Conventionally, the gestation period is organized by trimesters of about three months each. This is a convenient system, but note that these divisions are not supported by clearly demarcated events.

## *First Trimester*

In some ways, the first 12 weeks of pregnancy are the most remarkable. In an amazingly short time, sperm and ovum unite and are transformed into a being with identifiable body parts. The mother's body also undergoes dramatic changes.

***Fertilization and the Embryonic Period.*** Sexual intercourse results in the release of an average of 200 to 300 million sperm. Their life span is relatively short, and their journey through the female reproductive tract is fraught with hazards. Thus, only about 1 or 2 in 1000 of the original sperm reach the fallopian tubes, which lead from the ovaries to the uterus. Typically, only one sperm penetrates the ripened ovum, triggering a biochemical reaction that prevents entry of any other sperm. The **zygote** (fertilized egg) continues to divide and begins about a seven-day journey to the uterus.

Following implantation in the uterine wall, the zygote matures into an **embryo.** The placenta, which acts like a filter between the mother and the growing embryo, also forms. The umbilical cord connects the fetus to the placenta. Oxygen, water, and glucose, as well as many drugs, viruses, bacteria, vitamins, and hormones, pass through the placenta to the embryo. Amniotic fluid in the uterus protects the embryo throughout the pregnancy.

By the third week, tissue begins differentiating into organs. During this period, the embryo is vulnerable to **teratogens**—substances that may harm the developing organism—but most women do not know they are pregnant. Exhibit 3.3 shows how some relatively common drugs may affect the earliest stage of fetal development.

**EXHIBIT 3.3**

Potential Teratogens
during the First
Trimester

| Substance | Effects on Fetal Development |
|---|---|
| Acetaminophen (Tylenol) | None |
| Amphetamines | Cardiac defects, cleft palate |
| Antacids | Increase of anomalies |
| Antianxiety medications | Increase in anomalies |
| Antihistamines | None |
| Barbiturates | Increase of anomalies |
| Gentamycin (antibiotic) | Eighth cranial nerve damage |
| Glucocorticoids (steroids) | Cleft palate, cardiac defects |
| Haloperidol | Limb malformations |
| Insulin | Skeletal malformations |
| Lithium | Goiter, eye anomalies, cleft palate |
| LSD | Chromosomal abnormalities |
| Penicillins | None |
| Phenobarbital | Multiple anomalies |
| Podophyllin (in laxatives) | Multiple anomalies |
| Tetracycline (antibiotic) | Inhibition of bone growth, discoloration of teeth |
| Tricyclic antidepressants | Central nervous system and limb malformations |

*The Fetal Period.*   By the eighth week, the embryo is mature enough to be called a **fetus** (meaning "young one") (Novak & Broom, 1995) and, as we see in Tahesha's story, the mother is experiencing signs of her pregnancy. Usually the mother has now missed one menstrual period, but if her cycle was irregular, this may not be a reliable sign. Approximately 50 percent of women experience nausea and vomiting ("morning sickness") during the first trimester. A few experience vomiting so severe that it causes dehydration and metabolic changes requiring hospitalization. **Multigravidas,** women who have had a previous pregnancy, often recognize the signs of excessive fatigue and soreness in their breasts as a sign of pregnancy.

Between the 8th and 12th week, the fetal heart rate can be heard using a Doppler device. At 12 weeks, the gender of the fetus can be detected, and the face is fully formed. The fetus is moving within the mother, but it is still too early for her to feel the movement.

Newly pregnant women often feel ambivalence. Because of hormonal changes, they may experience mood swings and become less outgoing. Concerns about the changes in their bodies, finances, the impact on their life goals, lifestyle adjustments, and other interpersonal interactions may cause anxiety. Often the father experiences similar ambivalence, and he may be distressed by his partner's mood swings. Parents who have previously miscarried may have a heightened concern for the well-being of this fetus.

What aspects of the psychological person are involved in the first trimester of pregnancy?

## Second Trimester

By the 16th week, the fetus is approximately 19 centimeters (7.5 inches) long and weighs 100 grams (3.3 ounces). The second trimester is generally a period of contentment and planning for most women, as it seems to have been for Karen Randolph. For problem pregnancies, or in troubled environments, quite the opposite may occur. However, the fatigue, nausea and vomiting, and mood swings that often accompany the first few weeks usually disappear in the second trimester.

Hearing the heartbeat and seeing the fetus via ultrasound often bring the reality of the pregnancy home. As seen in the story of the Randolphs, **quickening**—the experience of feeling fetal movement—usually occurs around this time, further validating the personhood of the fetus. **Fetal differentiation,** whereby the mother separates the individuality of the fetus from her own personhood, is usually completed by the end of this trimester. Many fathers, too, begin to relate to the fetus as a developing offspring.

Some fathers enjoy the changing shape of the woman's body, but others may struggle with the changes. Unless there are specific contraindications, sexual relations may continue throughout the pregnancy, and some men find the second trimester a period of great sexual satisfaction. Often during the second trimester the pregnant woman also experiences a return of her prepregnancy level of sexual desire.

## Third Trimester

By 24 weeks, the fetus is considered viable in many hospitals. However, the parents may be less confident. Karen Randolph, for instance, was not prepared for the birth of her son, Joseph, who at 26 weeks' gestation struggled to survive. Clearly, mothers are usually not psychologically prepared for delivery so early in the third trimester, and the risks to newborns are very great if birth occurs prior to the 26th week of pregnancy.

The tasks of the fetus during the third trimester are to gain weight and mature in preparation for delivery. As delivery nears, the increased weight of the fetus can cause discomfort for the mother, and often she looks forward to delivery with increasing anticipation. Completion of preparations for the new arrival consume much of her attention.

## Labor and Delivery of the Neonate

Predicting when labor will begin is impossible. However, one indication of imminent labor is **lightening** (the descent of the fetus into the mother's pelvis). For a **primipara**—a first-time mother—lightening occurs approximately two weeks before delivery. For a multipara—a mother who has previously given birth—lightening typically occurs at the beginning of labor. Often the mother experiences **Braxton-Hicks contractions**, brief contractions that prepare the mother and fetus for labor—what Hazel Gereke referred to as "false labor." Usually, true labor begins with a show, or release of the mucous plug that covered the cervical opening.

Labor is divided into three stages:

1. In the first stage, the cervix thins and dilates. The amniotic fluid is usually released during this stage ("water breaking"), and the mother feels regular contractions that intensify in frequency and strength as labor progresses. Many factors determine the length of this stage, including **gravidity** (number of pregnancies this mother has experienced), the weight of the fetus, the anatomy of the mother, the strength of the contractions, and the relaxation of the mother in the process. Despite the stories that abound, most mothers have plenty of

time to prepare for the upcoming birth. Near the end of this phase, "transition" occurs, marked by a significant increase in the intensity and frequency of the contractions and heightened emotionalism. The head crowns (is visible at the vulva) at the end of this stage.

2. The second stage is delivery, when the **neonate** (newborn) is expelled from the mother. If the newborn is born breech (feet or buttocks first) or is transverse (positioned horizontally in the birth canal) and cannot be turned prior to birth, the mother may require a Cesarean section.

3. Typically, within one hour after delivery, the placenta, the remaining amniotic fluid, and the membrane that separated the fetus from the uterine wall are delivered with a few contractions. If the newborn breastfeeds immediately, the hormone oxytocin is released to stimulate these contractions.

Following birth, the neonate undergoes rapid physiological changes, particularly in its respiratory and cardiac systems. Prior to birth, oxygen is delivered to the fetus through the umbilical vein, and carbon dioxide is eliminated by the two umbilical arteries. Although the fetus begins to breathe prior to birth, breathing serves no purpose until after delivery. The neonate's first breath, typically in the form of a cry, creates tremendous pressure within the lungs, which clears amniotic fluid and triggers the opening and closing of several shunts and vessels in the heart. The blood flow is rerouted to the lungs.

Many factors, such as maternal exposure to narcotics during pregnancy or labor, can adversely affect the neonate's attempts to breathe—as can prematurity, congenital anomalies, and neonatal infections. Drugs and other interventions may be administered to maintain adequate respiration. To measure the neonate's adjustment to extrauterine life, **Apgar scores**—rather simple measurements of physiological health—are assessed at 1, 5, and 10 minutes after birth. Apgar scores determine the need for resuscitation and indicate the effectiveness of resuscitation efforts and long-term problems that might arise. The other immediate challenge to the newborn is to establish a stable temperature. Inadequately maintained body temperature creates neonatal stress and thus increased respiratory and cardiac effort, which can result in respiratory failure. Close monitoring of the neonate during the first four hours after birth is critical to detect any such problems in adapting to extrauterine life.

# Pregnancy and the Life Course

As the three stories at the beginning of the chapter indicate, pregnancy is a period of transition. Each family member faces changes in role identification and prescribed tasks.

Regardless of her age or number of previous births, the pregnant woman must complete four different developmental tasks:

- Provide safety for herself and the infant throughout pregnancy, labor, and delivery
- Help people in her social support system to accept this event
- Bond with her unborn infant
- Come to terms with the inequality inherent in a mother/neonate relationship (Rubin, 1995)

Although these tasks were the same for Tahesha Gibbon, Karen Randolph, and Hazel Gereke, each had very different resources for negotiating the tasks. To some extent, those resources were specific to their position in the life course. Remember, however, that the tasks are the same regardless of maternal age.

## Teen Pregnancy

Tahesha Gibbon represents a well-known situation in the United States. Each year, 1 out of 10 American females between the ages of 15 and 19 becomes pregnant. One-fourth of African American women have had their first baby before the age of 19 (Chadiha & Danziger, 1995). In 1995, adolescents accounted for 26 percent of all abortions, 15 percent of all births, and approximately 46 percent of all infants born to single mothers. Less than 10 percent of infants of single mothers are placed for adoption (Novak & Broom, 1995).

One study showed that twice as many teens coerced into sex or raped experienced teenage pregnancy compared to their nonabused peers (Kenney, Reinholtz, & Angelini, 1997). A boyfriend was identified as the perpetrator in almost 30 percent of these rapes. Approximately 5 percent of all rapes result in pregnancy regardless of age (Holmes, Resnick, Kilpatrick, & Best, 1996).

Teenage mothers are considered at high risk medically and psychologically. At greatest risk are teens who experience pregnancy as a result of rape or sexual abuse. But pregnant adolescents in general have a higher incidence of toxemia (pregnancy-induced high blood pressure) and anemia than adult women, and their neonates are at greater risk for low birth weight, prematurity, and infant mortality than neonates born to adult women. Pregnant adolescents are also at greater risk for physical assault during pregnancy. One study indicated that 40 percent of teens had been physically hit during their pregnancy, and 8 percent had suffered sexual assault (Berenson, San Miguel, & Wilkinson, 1992). This violence places mother and fetus at higher risk for complications.

The rate of prematurity and low birth weight among African American adolescents is twice as high as the rate for Hispanic and European American adolescents, primarily because of differences in access to, and use of, prenatal services (DuPlessis, Bell, & Richards, 1997). Limited financial resources, inadequate and fragmented facilities often found in poverty-stricken communities, and the normal adolescent avoidance of problems frequently contribute to a delayed diagnosis of pregnancy for these young women. Of course, delayed diagnosis hampers timely prenatal care (Osofsky, Osofsky, & Diamond, 1988) and limits pregnancy options.

The experience of pregnancy varies somewhat with stage of adolescence:

*Young adolescents, ages 12 to 14.* Pregnancy rates for this group are increasing as the age of first menstruation decreases. It is not uncommon for girls as young as 10 years old to ovulate. At the same time, the interval between the onset of menstruation and the completion of the educational process has lengthened, increasing the possibility of disrupting pregnant teens' education and thus condemning them to a lifetime of poverty. The increase of pregnancies in this age group can be attributed in part to increased rates of child sexual abuse (National Center for Child Abuse and Neglect, 1995). Longstanding incest can result in pregnancy as the teen becomes fertile. Long-term commitment and financial support from the father of the pregnant teen's child are unusual, and the young adolescent mother is often isolated and impoverished. Furthermore, premature birth is 3.4 times more common for young adolescents than for nonadolescent women, possibly because of the difficulty of meeting the nutritional demands of both the growing fetus and the growing adolescent (DuPlessis, Bell, & Richards, 1997).

*Middle adolescents, 15 to 17 years old.* Young women at this age have completed most of their physical growth but are still emotionally immature. They may engage in sexual activity as a sign of independence, to maintain status in their peer group (which appears to be part of the story for Tahesha), as an attempt to master self-identity, or as experimentation with new behaviors. The sense of invulnerability that permeates adolescence often provides a false sense of security.

*Late adolescents, ages 18 to 20 years.* Late adolescents who become pregnant tend to be more mature than younger teens and often have a positive relationship with the infant's father. They are more focused on the future and may have more social supports. However, if the teen's education is disrupted, the pregnancy may be viewed as a major impediment to achieving career goals.

One significant feature of teen pregnancy is the extent to which the adolescent mother connects with other family members. From a family system's perspective, the pregnant teen may be repeating her mother's behaviors, as seen in Tahesha's story. Research also suggests that younger sisters of pregnant teens, compared to younger sisters without a pregnant older sister, show more acceptance of at-risk behaviors for pregnancy, engage in more problem behaviors, and have more interaction with the older sibling's social network (East, 1996; East & Shi, 1997). The family's response to the pregnancy and the teen mother's emotional stability will significantly influence her parenting behaviors. Positive role modeling of family dynamics and social support are especially important.

The role and needs of the adolescent father have been woefully neglected in the research on adolescent pregnancy. Teen fathers who remain involved with the mother and infant provide a significant source of support for both (Osofsky, Hann, & Peebles, 1993). Pregnant adolescents who maintain a relationship with the baby's father seek prenatal care earlier than teens who terminate the relationship (Moss, 1987). For these reasons, many programs targeting teen mothers provide services to engage teen fathers.

## *Early Adulthood Pregnancy*

Physiologically, the young woman in her 20s and 30s is at the optimal age for pregnancy. Psychologically, young adults are involved in establishing life goals, and these often involve parenthood. Thus, pregnancy during this period of the life course is a normative event in most cultures.

Research suggests that even during the prime childbearing years, women who have appropriate social support are healthier psychologically and physically during their pregnancies. Their infants are six times less likely to experience pathology, and they have more positive developmental outcomes, compared to women who lack social support (Hogoel, Van-Raalte, Kalekin-Fishman, & Shlfroni, 1995; Oakley, Hickey, Rojan, & Rigby, 1996).

*[margin note:]* How does the small group, an environmental dimension, affect teen pregnancy?

*[margin note:]* How does the family dimension affect social work practice with a pregnant teenager?

## *Delayed Pregnancy*

How has the cultural
dimension changed
attitudes toward
delayed pregnancy?

An increasing number of women are delaying childbirth until their late 30s and 40s. Many have been struggling with infertility for several years (Berryman & Wendridge, 1991). Other women have purposefully delayed childbearing until their careers are established, or they are choosing to have children with a new partner. Some single women, driven by the ticking of the "biological clock," choose to go ahead and have a child on their own, often using artificial insemination.

Unlike Hazel Gereke, who 30 years ago unexpectedly became pregnant in later life, many women today intentionally become pregnant later in the childbearing cycle. They are often less traditional than their peers, have a more autonomous personality, and are more likely to have younger partners (Berryman & Wendridge, 1991).

Women who conceive after 35 may have more difficulty adjusting to the pregnancy during the first trimester than do their younger cohorts, but by the third trimester there is no difference in acceptance (Berryman & Wendridge, 1996). Preexisting medical conditions, such as diabetes or hypertension, may increase the risks of pregnancy, and older women, like Hazel Gereke, face the increased risk of giving birth to an infant with Down's syndrome. Older women have higher incidences of complications during labor and delivery and an increased rate of Cesarean births. With appropriate physical care, however, most women can successfully negotiate most of the hazards of later-life pregnancy.

In some cases, "elderly gravidas"—the medical term for pregnant women over 35—may be embarrassed by their pregnancy and resent the disruption of their established routine. They may be concerned about care for the child as they age, leading to increased stress. Older children may also have difficulty accepting the mother's pregnancy and the arrival of a new sibling. However, older women also feel more self-confident in their mothering role (Pridham & Chang, 1992), and increasing numbers of women are choosing to have a child after age 35, despite the greater risks.

# Social Work and Problems of Childbearing

Conception, pregnancy, and birth occur within diverse family contexts and are affected by economic, political, and social forces. Social workers, with their understanding of changing configurations of person and environment, are well equipped to address the needs of all persons of reproductive age. Although most pregnancies result in favorable outcomes, for those that do not, social workers can play an important role. Moreover, many negative outcomes can be prevented through prenatal care, childbirth education, new medical technologies, and genetic counseling. The social worker who participates in these interventions requires knowledge of, and collaboration with, a range of other professionals.

## *Problem Pregnancies*

In some sense, each of the pregnancies described at the beginning of this chapter (Tahesha's, Karen's, and Hazel's) is a problem pregnancy. Pregnancy can become problematic for a variety of reasons. Three types of problem pregnancies are discussed here: undesired pregnancy, ectopic pregnancy, and miscarriage and stillbirth.

*Undesired Pregnancy.*   Pregnancies that are unplanned are a problem because they are associated with increased stress. They carry a higher risk for inadequate prenatal care, health problems late in the pregnancy and right after birth, and significant postnatal problems. Some data indicate that women who are unhappy about their pregnancy during the first trimester may experience up to two times greater neonatal mortality than women who are accepting of their pregnancy (Bustan, 1994). Women who experience unplanned pregnancies are more likely to have been influenced by their partner's choice of birth control and more likely to have used unreliable methods of birth control compared to women who do not become pregnant (Rosenfeld & Everett, 1996). Social workers can use this knowledge to target at-risk teens, provide essential information, link teens to reproductive resources, and assist in problem solving about other reproductive concerns.

*Ectopic Pregnancy.*   An ectopic pregnancy occurs if the zygote implants outside the uterus, usually in the fallopian tubes. Previous ectopic pregnancies, pelvic infections (such as chlamydia or gonorrhea), and endometriosis increase the risk. Ectopic pregnancy can cause a life-threatening emergency—when the tube ruptures—and contribute to infertility.

Ectopic implantation occurs in 1 in 60 pregnancies, with higher rates among women in poverty. At the end of the 19th century, the mortality rate from ectopic pregnancy was close to 50 percent; it is now less than 5 in 10,000 cases (.05 percent), thanks to sophisticated medical detection and intervention (Stock, 1990). However, despite advances, ectopic pregnancy has been the second leading cause of maternal mortality in the United States since 1982 (Dickason, Shult, & Silverman, 1990).

*Miscarriage and Stillbirth.*   Miscarriage is the naturally occurring loss of a fetus prior to 20 weeks' gestation—a spontaneous abortion. Approximately 10 to 15 percent of all pregnancies end in spontaneous abortion, without a discernible cause and often unrecognized by the mother. An estimated 50 percent of threatened spontaneous abortions become complete abortions. If the abortion is incomplete, any placenta or fetus that is not expelled must be surgically removed (Novak & Broom, 1995) or the mother risks hemorrhage and infection.

In late pregnancy, if the fetus does not breathe or exhibit a heartbeat, or if the umbilical cord stops pulsating, the birth is considered a **stillbirth** or **intrauterine fetal death (IUFD).** Stillbirths account for up to 50 percent of perinatal mortality (death of the baby just before, during, or just after birth) (Dickason, Schult, & Silverman, 1990). Stillbirths are caused by numerous maternal problems and fetal conditions. In cases of stillbirth, labor generally proceeds immediately and is allowed to occur naturally. But the pregnancy may continue for several days following cessation of movement, and in extreme cases surgery may be needed to end the pregnancy. Stillbirth frequently occurs without explanation, typically resulting in great stress and anguish for parents, who blame themselves and struggle with unresolved guilt. Social workers can help parents to understand and cope with the strong emotions they are experiencing.

## At-Risk Newborns

Not all pregnancies proceed smoothly and end in routine deliveries. The newborn may face a variety of risks related to genetics, pregnancy complications, and birth complications.

*Prematurity and Low Birth Weight.*　　A radical shift has occurred in our culture over the past 20 years: The desire for a positive pregnancy outcome has been replaced by the assumption that the pregnancy will be flawless and the baby will be perfect (Forrest, 1993; McCarton, 1986). But alarming statistics debunk this myth. The United States ranks 22nd in infant mortality among industrialized nations (Wegman, 1992). The rate of **low birth weight (LBW)** infants—infants weighing less than 2500 grams (5 pounds 8 ounces) at birth—has changed little over the past 30 years and may in fact be increasing. More LBW infants were born in 1995 (7.3 percent of all births) than in each of the previous 20 years. The rate for LBW infants born to African American women remains almost twice as high, at 13.1 percent (NCHS, 1997; Zahr, Parker, & Cole, 1992). The overall rate of **premature birth** (less than 37 weeks' gestation) has also remained high (11.0 percent of all births are premature), but the rate for European American women is rising while the rate for African Americans is at its lowest level since the mid-1980s.

The survival rates of premature infants have improved, due largely to explosive growth in the field of neonatal medicine and the establishment of regional newborn intensive care units. However, approximately 50 percent of infants weighing less than 1500 grams (3.3 pounds) still have moderate to severe developmental delays, and 33 percent require frequent hospitalizations during their first years of life (Koeske & Koeske, 1992; Wittenberg, 1990). Thus, the Randolphs have reason to wonder what the future holds for their baby.

The major correlates of prematurity include maternal age, race or ethnicity, health, and behaviors. Among pregnant women, African Americans are more likely than European Americans to be unmarried, have less education, and be younger. African Americans also have higher rates of hypertension, anemia, and low-level lead exposure, indicating that their general health status may be suboptimal (Kleinman, Fingerhut, & Prager, 1991; NCHS, 1993a).

The greatest risk factor for LBW and infant mortality is smoking (NCHS, 1997). Almost 20 percent of low birth weight births (48,000 neonates a year) are attributed to maternal smoking. It is estimated that 10 percent of fetal and neonatal deaths could be prevented if pregnant women did not smoke (Kleinman & Madans, 1985). The third trimester is the period of rapid fetal weight gain, and because smoking reduces the amount of oxygen and the flow of nutrients to the fetus, smoking during this time is especially harmful. However, cessation of smoking at any time during the pregnancy will have a positive effect (Wilner, Secker-Walker, & Flynn, 1987).

Other risk factors for prematurity and LBW include alcohol use and other drug use. The mother's adequate nutrition prior to conception, as well as during pregnancy, is another important factor in fetal health. Women with total weight gains during pregnancy of less than 22 pounds are two to three times more likely to deliver LBW infants than women who gain more weight (Kramer, Coates, Michoud, & Hamilton, 1994; Kramer, McLean, Eason, & Usher, 1992).

How is the psychological dimension a factor in dealing with low birth weight babies?

A variety of neurological, developmental, and physical health problems are related to LBW. Less than 5 percent of infants of normal birth weight are affected by cerebral palsy, hydrocephalus and microcephaly (disorders of the cranium), blindness, deafness, and seizures, whereas approximately 20 percent of infants under 2.2 pounds demonstrate impairment (Hack, Breslau, & Aram, 1992; McCormick, Brooks-Gunn, Workman-Daniels, Turner, & Peckman, 1993). On the average, LBW children score significantly lower than children of normal birth weight on intelligence tests; have decreased fine and gross motor coordination; have impaired perceptual-motor skills; and demonstrate increased difficulties in language, nonverbal reasoning, and problem solving (Hack, Breslau, & Aram, 1992; Hack, Taylor, Klein, & Eiben, 1994; McDermott, Cokert, &

McKeown, 1993; Peterson, Greisen, & Kovacs, 1994; Teplin, Burchinal, Johnson-Martin, Humphrey, & Kraybill, 1991). Very low birth weight neonates (VLBW) such as Joseph Randolph run an even greater risk of problems associated with prematurity.

*Newborn Intensive Care.*   As the Randolphs know all too well, parents' expectations for a healthy newborn are shattered when their child is admitted to a newborn intensive care unit (NICU). Their fear and anxiety often make it hard for them to attach to their newborn. Klaus and Kennel (1982) define attachment as "a unique relationship between two people that is specific and endures through time." About 90 percent of mothers and 80 percent of fathers report that they develop an attachment to the infant during the third trimester of pregnancy. But when an infant is premature, the parents have not had the same opportunity. In addition, the fear that a sickly newborn may die inhibits some parents from risking attachment. Others are consumed with guilt at their baby's condition and believe that they will only harm the newborn by their presence. Karen and Bob Randolph had to work hard to contain their anxiety about Joseph's frailties.

How have formal organizations changed to keep up with growing numbers of at-risk neonates?

Outcome studies indicate that early disruption in bonding may have a more significant long-term impact than the infant's actual medical condition (Wittenberg, 1990). The response has been a movement toward family-centered NICU environments, which are structured to promote interaction between the infant and the parents, siblings, and others in the family's support system. Ample opportunity to interact with Joseph facilitated Karen and Bob Randolph's attempts to bond with him.

Understanding the psychological stresses confronting the family with a baby in the NICU is the basis for social work interventions. As the Randolphs' story suggests, deciding whether to invest in the newborn and risk great loss or to withdraw in an effort to protect oneself against pain causes continuing tension. Witnessing the suffering and death of other neonates is traumatizing as well (Yu, Jamieson, & Asbury, 1981). Social workers can help parents understand and cope with this stress.

**Neonatology**, the care of critically ill newborns, has only recently been recognized as a medical specialty. It is a much-needed specialty, however. Neonatal mortality accounts for 67 percent of all infant deaths. LBW, acute breathing problems, congenital anomalies, and infections account for half of all neonatal deaths (The Robert Wood Foundation, 1991). Since the advent of the NICU in the 1970s, the survival rate of critically ill neonates has continued to increase. In 1970, an infant weighing 1500 grams (3.3 pounds) had a 50 percent chance of survival; by 1990, a 700-gram (1.5-pound) infant had a 50 percent chance of survival (Glass, 1994). It is highly unlikely that Joseph Randolph would have survived in 1970.

Social workers in a NICU must negotiate a complex technological environment requiring specialized skill and knowledge while attempting to respond with compassion, understanding, and appropriate advocacy. It helps to remember that the effort could affect a neonate's life course.

*Major Congenital Anomalies.*   The number of neonates born with anomalies due to genetics and exposure to teratogens during their development does not reflect the number of abnormal embryos. Fewer than half of all fertilized ova result in a live birth; the rest are spontaneously aborted. The probability that a fertilized ovum with a genetic anomaly will abort spontaneously ranges from 80 to 90 percent (Opitz, 1996). Thus, overall, only 2 to 4 percent of all surviving newborns have a birth defect. Social workers need to be mindful of the low probability that a child will be born with a genetic disorder or congenital anomaly when responding to parental fears.

Preventing, diagnosing, and predicting the outcome of genetic disorders is very difficult because of the complexities of genetic processes:

- **Variable expressivity**. Genes manifest differently in different people. For example, persons with cystic fibrosis, caused by a recessive gene, display wide variability in the severity of symptoms. The expression of the disorder appears to be influenced by the interplay of psychological, social, political, economic, and other environmental factors. The effects can be exacerbated by maternal substance abuse, inadequate maternal nutrition, and birth trauma. Children with cystic fibrosis born into poverty may not have benefited from early diagnosis, may live in an inner city that exposes them to increased levels of pollution, or may lack adequate home medical care because the primary caregiver is also responsible for meeting the family's economic needs.

- **Genetic heterogeneity**. The same characteristic may be a consequence of one of a number of genetic anomalies. For example, neural tube defects may result either from gene mutations or from exposure to specific teratogens.

- **Pleiotropy principle**. The same gene may influence seemingly unrelated systems (Rauch, 1988). Hair color, for example, is typically linked to a particular skin color (such as blonde hair with light complexion, black hair with olive complexion).

Genetic disorders fall into four categories, summarized in Exhibit 3.4 (Opitz, 1996; Rauch, 1988; Reed, 1996; Vekemans, 1996):

1. *Inheritance of a single abnormal gene*. An inherited anomaly in a single gene may lead to a serious disorder. The gene may be recessive, meaning that both parents must pass it along, or it may be dominant, in which case only one parent must have the gene. A third possibility is that the disorder is sex-linked, meaning that it is passed along by either the father or the mother.

2. *Multifactorial inheritance*. Some genetic traits, such as height and intelligence, are influenced by environmental factors such as nutrition. Their expression varies because they are controlled by multiple genes. Multifactorial inheritance is implicated in traits that predispose a person to mental illnesses, such as depression. However, these traits are merely predisposing factors, creating what is called **genetic liability**. Siblings born with the same genetic traits may thus vary in the likelihood of developing a specific genetically based disorder, such as alcoholism or mental illness (Takahashi & Turnbull, 1994; Rauch, 1988).

3. *Chromosomal aberration*. Some genetic abnormalities are not hereditary but rather are caused by a genetic mishap during development of the ovum or sperm cells. Sometimes the cells end up missing chromosomes or having too many. When the ovum or sperm cell has fewer than 23 chromosomes, the probability of conception and survival is minimal. But in the presence of too many chromosomes in the ovum or the sperm, various anomalies occur.

**EXHIBIT 3.4**

Four Categories of
Genetic Anomalies

| **Inheritance of Single Abnormal Gene** | | |
| --- | --- | --- |
| *Recessive* | *Dominant* | *Sex-Linked* |
| Sickle-cell anemia<br>Tay-Sachs disease<br>Cystic fibrosis | Neurofibromatosis<br>Huntington's disease | Hemophilia<br>Duchenne's<br>muscular dystrophy |

| **Multifactorial Inheritance** | | |
| --- | --- | --- |
| Possible mental illness | Alcoholism | |

| **Chromosomal Aberration** | | |
| --- | --- | --- |
| Down's syndrome<br>(additional 21st chromosome) | Turner's syndrome (x) | Klinefelter's<br>syndrome (xxy) |

| **Exposure to Teratogens** | | | |
| --- | --- | --- | --- |
| *Radiation* | *Infections* | *Maternal Metabolic Imbalance* | *Drugs and Environmental Chemicals* |
| Neural tube defects | Rubella: deafness, glaucoma | Diabetes: neural tube defects | Alcohol: mental retardation |
| | Syphilis: neurological, ocular, and skeletal defects | Folic acid deficiency: brain and neural tube defects | Heroin: attention deficit disorder |
| | | Hyperthermia (at 14–28 days): neural tube defects | Amphetamines: urogenital defects |

Down's syndrome, or trisomy 21, the most common chromosomal aberration, is the presence of 47 chromosomes—specifically, an extra chromosome in the 21st pair. Its prevalence is 1 in 600–1000 live births overall, but, as seen in the Hazel Gereke's story, it increases to 1 in 350 for women over age 35 (Vekemans, 1996). Other chromosome anomalies include Turner's syndrome (a single sex chromosome, X) and Klinefelter's syndrome (an extra sex chromosome, XXY).

4. *Exposure to teratogens.* A teratogen is "any agent or factor [not hereditary] that when present during prenatal life produces a permanent alteration in form or function" (Shepard, 1995). Teratogens can be divided into four categories: radiation, infections, maternal metabolic imbalance, and drugs and environmental chemicals. In the Randolph story, Karen wondered if Joseph's premature birth was a result of prenatal exposure to paint fumes. It may have been, depending on what specific chemicals were involved, when exposure occurred, and to what degree. Parents who, like the Randolphs, are experiencing considerable guilt over their possible responsibility for their baby's problems may take comfort from the knowledge that the

**EXHIBIT 3.5**

Sensitive Periods in Prenatal Development

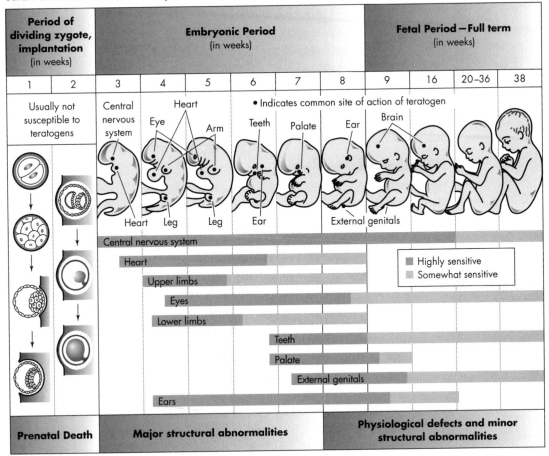

*Source:* Moore & Persaud, 1993.

impact of exposure to teratogens can vary greatly. Much depends on the timing of exposure. The various organ systems have different critical or **sensitive periods,** summarized in Exhibit 3.5.

Parents who have reason to fear these congenital anomalies often opt for diagnosis during pregnancy. **Amniocentesis** is the extraction of amniotic fluid for chromosomal analysis; it involves inserting a hollow needle through the abdominal wall during the second trimester. **Chorion villi testing (CVT)** involves the cervical insertion of a catheter into the uterus to obtain a sample of the developing placenta; it can be done as early as eight weeks but carries a slightly higher risk of spontaneous abortion (miscarriage). A more frequent procedure is **ultrasonography** (ultrasound), which produces a visual image of the developing fetus.

If an anomaly is detected, the decisions that need to be made are not easy ones. The possibility of false readings on these tests makes the decisions even more complicated. Should the fetus be aborted? Should fetal surgery—a surgical specialty still in the early stages of development—be undertaken? Could **gene replacement therapy**—still a costly experimental procedure—prevent an anomaly or limit its manifestation? Do the parents have the financial and psychological means to care for a neonate with a disability? This was a question that the Gereke's asked of themselves. What is the potential impact on the marriage and extended family system? Nonurgent decisions should be postponed until parents have an opportunity to adjust to the crisis and acquire the necessary information (Fost, 1981). The multidimensional perspective of social workers can contribute to a more holistic understanding of a client's situation, leading to appropriate and effective interventions when genetic anomalies are likely to, or do, occur.

## Special Parent Populations

Social workers should recognize the risks involved in the configurations of person and environment for some special parent populations. Four of these special populations are discussed here.

**Pregnant Substance Abusers.**    Our knowledge of the developmental impact of maternal use of illegal and legal substances is rapidly increasing. The good news is that health care professionals are increasingly able to avoid prescribing legal drugs that might harm the developing fetus, once pregnancy is confirmed. The bad news is that too many pregnant women are still harming their babies through use of illegal drugs or abuse of legal substances. And, unfortunately, many women do not know they are pregnant during the first trimester, a period when the fetus is very vulnerable to teratogens. Although it is difficult to obtain reliable statistics, it is estimated that between 10 and 15 percent of pregnant women use illicit drugs (Chasnoff, Landress, & Barrett, 1990; NCHS, 1997). Moreover, approximately 14 percent of pregnant women use two or more teratogenic substances (NCHS, 1997). These women have a higher incidence of miscarriages, prematurity, and LBW, as well as sexually transmitted disease, tuberculosis, and AIDS, than other pregnant women. Furthermore, the neonate is 46 times more likely to die in the first month of life if exposed prenatally to substances like alcohol, tobacco, and illegal drugs (Larson, 1995). **Fetal alcohol syndrome (FAS)**, a complex of anomalies, is the leading cause of mental retardation worldwide (Abel & Sokol, 1987; Beckman & Brent, 1994; Light, Irvine, & Kjerulf, 1996). Possible effects of commonly abused legal and illegal substances are presented in Exhibit 3.6.

Interestingly, some individuals appear to be "resistant" to teratogens like alcohol. According to Opitz (1996, p. 23), "there is virtually no such thing as an absolute teratogen, i.e. an exogenous agent that causes defects in 100 percent of offspring; even in chronically alcoholic women apparently only 40 percent of offspring are visibly affected." Still, teratogenic substances should be avoided during pregnancy to increase the chances of a healthy outcome. Social workers are collaborating with other professionals to provide public education to women in the childbearing years about the teratogenic effects of alcohol, tobacco, and other drugs.

**Mothers with Eating Disorders.**    During the past 15 years, there has been a striking increase in eating disorders, primarily anorexia nervosa (self-imposed starvation) and bulimia (binging and purging), among American teenagers and women (Pirke, Dogs, Fichter, & Tuschil, 1988).

**EXHIBIT 3.6**

Commonly Abused
Drugs and Fetal
Effects

| | Alcohol | Cocaine | Amphetamines | Cigarettes | Heroin |
|---|---|---|---|---|---|
| Abortion | x | x | x | | x |
| Stillbirth | x | x | x | | x |
| Prematurity | x | x | x | x | x |
| Intrauterine growth retardation | x | x | x | x | x |
| Respiratory distress | x | x | | | x |
| Withdrawal | x | x | x | | x |
| Fine motor problems | x | | | | x |
| Malformations | x | x | x | | x |
| Developmental delays | x | x | x | | x |

Since eating disorders frequently result in menstrual disorders, reduced sex drive, and infertility, pregnancy is frequently overlooked in this population (Bonne, Rubinoff, & Berry, 1996). Apparently, however, some women first develop eating disorders during pregnancy, perhaps in response to their weight gain and change in shape (Fahy, 1991).

An eating disorder is likely to result in poor pregnancy outcomes, such as infants **small for gestational age (SGA),** LBW, and increased neonatal mortality (Bakan, Birmingham, & Goldner, 1991; Pomeroy & Mitchell, 1989). Premature delivery occurs at twice the expected rate, and perinatal mortality is six times the expected rate. The length of time the mother is able to breastfeed her infant has not been found to be affected by eating disorders, however (Brinch, Isager, & Tolstrup, 1988). Social workers who work regularly with women with eating disorders or with pregnant women need to be knowledgeable about the possibilities for poor pregnancy outcomes in pregnant women with eating disorders.

*Lesbian Mothers.* In recent years, the number of lesbians who are or who desire to be mothers has increased, but these women continue to face many obstacles and dilemmas (Gartrell et al., 1996). More than one-third of lesbians are estimated to be mothers, and it is reasonable to assume that more would choose motherhood if the larger society offered greater support.

Despite increased availability of alternative fertilization methods, many health care providers remain insensitive to issues of conception, pregnancy, and birth with lesbian women. Lesbian women may lack family support and friends, and birthing facilities may not allow female partners to be involved with the birth process. In addition, employers may limit access to, or reluctantly provide, resources such as medical benefits for pregnancy and birth.

Conception, pregnancy, and birth demand role realignments for heterosexual couples and create stress. These same dynamics occur in lesbian couples but may be exacerbated by the lack of societal recognition of and support for lesbian relationships.

Studies of lesbian mothers report that all respondents sought prenatal care and that 89 to 100 percent attended childbirth education classes (Gartrell et al., 1996; Harvey, Carr, & Bernheime, 1989). Using this information, what social work services would you anticipate that lesbian mothers might need to successfully navigate the transition to parenthood?

***Mothers and Fathers with Disabilities.*** People with physical or mental disabilities tend to be perceived as "asexual," and thus conception, pregnancy, and birth are not considered relevant issues for them (Cole & Cole, 1993; Sawin, 1998). This is not the case. For one thing, not all disabilities negatively affect reproduction. For example, 75 percent of women with rheumatoid arthritis experience remission of disease during pregnancy (Connie, 1988; Corbin, 1987). Other interesting data come from a four-year national study funded by the National Institutes of Health, which compared 506 women with physical disabilities to 444 women without a disability. Women with disabilities reported a 32 percent marriage rate, compared to 36 percent of nondisabled women. For women living with partners, 71 percent of those with disabilities were sexually active at the time of the study, compared to 96 percent of nondisabled women. Birthrates were 38 percent for women with disabilities and 51 percent for nondisabled women (Nosek, 1995).

There is a remarkable difference between the two populations in the use of contraception, however, because women with disabilities have more limited options. For example, the use of barrier methods may be compromised by limited use of hands. Overall, women with disabilities were less likely to use oral contraception, possibly because their access to it was limited. Tubal ligation and partner vasectomy did not differ between the groups, but women with disabilities were much more likely to have had a hysterectomy (22% versus 12%), the most invasive and risky surgical sterilization option (Nosek, 1995).

Perhaps one of the most striking findings of the study was that 10 percent of women with disabilities reported abuse—such as coerced sterilization—by health care providers, compared to only 3 percent of nondisabled women. Additionally, for the women who had access to medical care, 37 percent of women with disabilities perceived their physician as uninformed about the effect of their disability on reproductive health (Nosek, 1995).

Despite public distaste for the practice, some persons with disabilities continue to be targets of involuntary sterilization (Rock, 1996; Smith & Polloway, 1993; Waxman, 1994). Professionals do not agree about how to handle the reproductive rights of individuals with severe inheritable disorders or with limited capacity to care for a child (Brantlinger, 1992). Many do agree, however, that physical, environmental, interpersonal, informational, and policy barriers leave people with disabilities disenfranchised from both the reproductive health system and other reproductive options.

As society slowly begins to recognize persons with disabilities as full members of society, some of the negative implications of conception, pregnancy, and birth with this population may be dispelled. Meanwhile, however, social workers, who have traditionally been a voice for this population, must not let that voice be lost at this stage of the life course.

## IMPLICATIONS FOR SOCIAL WORK PRACTICE

Social workers practicing with persons at the stage of life concerned with conception, pregnancy, and birth should follow these principles:

- Apply a multidimensional perspective so you can respond to the complex interplay of biopsychosocial and spiritual factors related to conception, pregnancy, and birth.

- Continuously update your knowledge of the physiological process of pregnancy, labor, and delivery.

- When working with any client of childbearing age, always consider the possibility of conception, pregnancy, and birth, their potential outcomes, and their impact on the changing person/environment configuration.

- In all assessments, consider a client's religious/spiritual beliefs and basic genetic history.

- Identify the needs of vulnerable or at-risk groups, and work to provide services for them. For example, structure birth education classes to include not only family but family-like persons, and provide interpreters for the hearing impaired.

- Actively pursue information about particular disabilities and their impact on conception, pregnancy, and birth.

- Acquire and apply skills in advocacy, education about reproductive options, consumer guidance in accessing services, and case management.

- Assume a proactive stance when working with at-risk populations to limit undesirable reproductive outcomes and to help meet their reproductive needs. At-risk groups include adolescents, low-income women, women involved with substance abuse, women with eating disorders, and women with disabilities who lack access to financial, physical, psychological, and social services.

- Ensure prenatal services, particularly for at-risk populations.

- Identify supportive family patterns unique to various racial, ethnic, and cultural groups to ensure sensitive and effective interventions.

- Assist parents faced with a potential genetic anomaly to gain access to genetic screenings, prenatal diagnosis, postnatal diagnosis, treatment, and genetic counseling.

- Involve parents in decision making to the greatest extent possible by delaying nonurgent decisions until parents have had a chance to adjust to any crisis and acquire the necessary information to make an informed decision.

- Establish collaborative relationships with other professionals to enhance and guide assessment and intervention.
- Identify and use existing programs that provide education and prenatal services to women, such as the WIC program, particularly for those most at risk of undesirable outcomes.

## MAIN POINTS

1. Conception, pregnancy, and birth should be viewed as normative life transitions that require family or family-like supportive relationships to maximize favorable outcomes.

2. Conception, pregnancy, and birth are influenced by changing family structures and gender roles.

3. Variations in human behavior at this life stage relate to social class, race and ethnicity, and religion, and their interplay must be considered in assessment and intervention.

4. Women who are poor or lack social support—and therefore experience greater stress than other women—are most at risk for poor pregnancy outcomes.

5. Research increasingly indicates that father involvement has a positive effect on pregnancy and childbirth.

6. Disrupted parent/infant bonding may have long-term negative consequences.

7. Prenatal care, including childbirth education, ensures the most positive pregnancy outcome possible. Universal access to prenatal care should be a social work priority.

8. Adjustment to parenthood is influenced by the type and structure of reproductive services, such as "rooming in," involvement of significant others, and support for breastfeeding.

9. Five primary categories of contraception provide options that potentially can meet the needs of everyone of reproductive age.

10. About one-half of unintended pregnancies result in elected abortion, which usually occurs in the first trimester of pregnancy.

11. Infertility is a major life crisis, but many new interventions provide options and hope to most persons wanting to conceive a child.

12. About 10 percent of all female adolescents become pregnant. They are at risk because they may lack the necessary education, emotional stamina, social support, economic means, and social skills to carry a fetus to term and successfully care for the child.

13. Changing norms and family structures are major factors in the increase in delayed pregnancy, which carries more risk than pregnancy in early adulthood.

14. Since there is an estimated 80–90 percent chance that a fertilized ovum with a genetic anomaly will abort spontaneously, 94–96 percent of all live births result in a normal neonate.

15. Genetic disorders may result from genetic inheritance (single gene or multifactorial), chromosomal aberrations, or exposure to teratogens.

16. Exposure to teratogens may have a differential impact on pregnancy outcome depending on the type and amount of substance and the time of pregnancy exposure.

17. The incidence of low birth weight infants continues to be high, particularly for neonates born to poor and minority women and those exposed to teratogens such as nicotine, illegal drugs, and alcohol.

## KEY TERMS

amniocentesis

amnioinfusion

Apgar score

assisted reproductive technologies (ART)

barrier methods

birthing center

bonding

Braxton-Hicks contractions

chorion villi testing (CVT)

chromosomes

curettage abortion

dominant genes

ectopic pregnancy

embryo

fertilization

fertilization age

fetal alcohol syndrome (FAS)

fetal differentiation

fetal viability

fetus

gamete intra–fallopian tube transfer (GIFT)

gene

gene replacement therapy

genetic counseling

genetic heterogeneity

genetic liability

genotype

germ cell

gestation

gestational age

gravidity

infertility

interactive genes

intrauterine fetal death (IUFD)

intrauterine insemination (IUI)

in vitro fertilization (IVF)

lightening

low birth weight (LBW)

multifactorial inheritance

multigravida

neonate

neonatology

phenotype

pleiotropy principle

premature birth

primipara

quickening

recessive genes

replacement hormonal therapy (RHT)
*Roe* v. *Wade*
sensitive period
sex chromosome
sex-linked trait
small for gestational age (SGA)
stillbirth
teratogen

ultrasonography (ultrasound)
vacuum curettage
variable expressivity
*Webster* v. *Reproductive Health Services*
Women, Infants, and Children (WIC)
   program
zygote

## WORLD WIDE WEB RESOURCES

Information About Pregnancy

**http://www.thebabiesplanet.com/bbpregna.htm**

Site presented by The Last Planet Internet Services. Contains links to various sites concerning
pregnancy and childbirth.

Pregnancy and Childbirth

**http://www.luhs.org/frames/health/preg/index.htm**

Site maintained by the Loyola University Health System. Contains information on pregnancy
and childbirth from fetal development, to danger signs, to morning sickness, and postpartum depression.

Childbirth.org

**http://www.childbirth.org/**

Award-winning site maintained by Robin Elise Weiss. Contains information on birth plans, cesareans, complications, episiotomies, feeding, fertility, health, and labor. Also contains a section of frequently asked questions (FAQ) and a chat room.

Infertility Center

**http://www.womens-health.com/InfertilityCenter/**

Site presented by Women's Health Interactive and the National Council on Women's Health. Contains information on human reproduction, assessment of pregnancy factors, infertility evaluations and treatments, emotional aspects of infertility, and a FAQ section.

Planned Parenthood

**http://www.plannedparenthood.org/textdefault.htm**

Official site of the Planned Parenthood Federation of America, Inc. Contains information about Planned Parenthood, health and pregnancy, birth control, abortion, sexually transmitted diseases, pro-choice advocacy, and a guide for parents.

Human Genome Project

**http://www.er.doe.gov**

Site of the federal program that is sequencing all of the genes present in human DNA.

## CHAPTER 4

# Infancy and Early Childhood

*Debra J. Woody, University of Texas at Arlington*

### DEMARCUS'S VIOLENT NEIGHBORHOOD

Ynecka Green is a 17-year-old African American single parent who needs help overcoming depression and anxiety. She has told you that she still cries each night about the death of both of her brothers in unrelated shootings. She always felt that her older brother, Marcus, would probably die at a young age because he had long been involved in "questionable" activities. He had skipped school since fifth grade and had "hung out" with several convicted felons. At the time of his death, he was awaiting trial for a burglary in which a store attendant had been killed. Even so, it came as a great shock to Ynecka and her parents when he was killed outside his parents' home in what appeared to be a drive-by shooting.

On the other hand, Robert, Ynecka's younger brother, had been a good student. He was on the honor roll and was very excited about beginning junior high in the fall. He looked forward to all the additional activities junior high would offer—band, art classes, and the opportunity to participate in the science fair. But his good grades and good behavior had not saved him either. The Green family had teased Robert about his "nosiness" and had warned him on several occasions that his curiosity would one day get him in trouble. And then he too was gunned down in front of his parents' home when he happened upon an unrelated shooting. "If only he had not looked up and been able to identify the shooter, maybe then his life would have been spared," Ynecka had thought to herself many times.

Robert had been on his way to escaping from their drug-infested, high-crime neighborhood. Ynecka had been secretly hoping that once he made his way out, he would help her, and she too would have a better life. But she also loved her younger brother very much. Robert made her feel special because he spent many hours telling her great stories about African kings and queens and had once saved his allowance to buy her a plastic tiara.

Ynecka's heart has literally ached since Robert's death a year ago. The only thing that has kept her going is the birth of her child, Demarcus, six months ago. Ynecka has admitted to you, though, that she felt a sense of panic when she found out the baby was a boy. How would she be able to save him from the perils that had taken the lives of her brothers? Her fears have become barely controllable over the past month because she has noted the same "nosy" personality in her son that she saw in her brother Robert. When placed on his tummy, Demarcus lifts his head in an attempt to see his environment. Ynecka becomes even more anxious when Demarcus lifts his head while riding in his stroller. She fears that he too will eventually be a witness to the "wrong" event.

**CASE STUDIES**

### CARETAKING DECISIONS FOR JESSICA, ALEXIA, AND STEVEN JR.

Melanie Schmidt is a 33-year-old European American female. She has been married to Steve for eight years. They have three children: 4-year-old Jessica, 2-year-old Alexia, and 5-month-old Steven Jr. The Schmidts met in college. They were both business majors, but Melanie was the better student. Steve has confided to you that he would not have passed several classes had it not been for Melanie's help. Immediately after college, they were both able to find employment with major companies. Melanie was able to advance quickly up the corporate ladder. Although she worked long hours, she was happy and enjoyed every aspect of her job.

When Melanie and Steve decided to have children, Melanie suggested that she quit her job and become a full-time, stay-at-home mother. After all, her mother had not worked when Melanie was growing up, and the idea that "real" mothers stay home with their children was ingrained in her. Although she felt ambivalent about abandoning her career, Melanie looked forward to the birth of her first child and fantasized about how wonderful it would be at home with her new baby.

Even though Steve wanted to be supportive of Melanie's decision, he was quite worried about how they would get along financially after Melanie was no longer employed—especially since Melanie's salary was almost twice his. However, Steve's mother had also stayed home with him and his siblings, and he understood and supported Melanie's desire to stay home after the children were born.

It had been a rough four years. Although they had enough money to cover the basics, "extras" were nonexistent. This had been a difficult adjustment for Melanie; she had never had to consider money before. Steve and Melanie began to argue frequently about money, mainly about Melanie's spending. Steve often felt guilty about not earning enough money for Melanie and the children to have the items they desired. When the opportunity presented itself, Steve took a new job at a higher salary, but it required longer working hours, including most weekends, and traveling, sometimes for three months at a time.

When Melanie sought your services at the Community Mental Health Service Agency, she described herself as "overwhelmed" and the children as "difficult to manage." She described Alexia as "out of control" and Steven Jr. as "crying all the time." Jessica, the "good child," often helps by comforting Steven Jr. when Melanie can no longer tolerate his crying. Melanie has reluctantly admitted to you that most of the time she feels angry and frustrated about Steve's blooming career while she is stuck at home with the children. She envies the fact that Steve is able to travel and that he often travels out of the country. Melanie describes herself as spending most of her day yelling at the children and looking forward to the times the children either nap or attend play group.

When asked about returning to work, Melanie states that she really wants to do so but feels she would be a "bad" mother if she put the children in day care. She describes conversations with other mothers in her children's play group in which they talk about being "true" mothers compared to those women who let day-care centers raise their children. When Melanie tried to discuss her feelings with her own mother, she was warned that the children might become "juvenile delinquents." Melanie's mother solemnly predicted that the children would feel abandoned, become detached, and resent her working outside the home.

## TAYLOR'S DISRUPTED DEVELOPMENT

Cynthia Lewis lets you know that she is very proud of the progress Taylor has made in the past four years. Cynthia became Taylor's foster mother when Taylor was only 3 months old. When she first came to live with Cynthia, Taylor spent all her waking and sleeping hours in the fetal position. Cynthia describes having to teach Taylor how to eat by physically closing Taylor's lips around the bottle nipple and moving Taylor's jaws and lips in the sucking motion.

Before she came to live with Cynthia, Taylor had been left in her crib most of the day. The only nourishment she had been given was soda, fed to her through a straw several times daily by an older sibling. In addition to eating problems, Taylor had many bedsores as a result of spending most of her hours in the crib.

Even with Cynthia's attentive care, Taylor is still behind in most developmental areas. At age 4, she weighs only 20 pounds and has the overall appearance of an 18-month-old. Although she can walk, her movements are clumsy, resulting in frequent falls. She likes to scribble, but still has difficulty stacking blocks and often becomes frustrated. Cynthia provides solid food for Taylor, which Taylor feeds to herself, but Cynthia describes Taylor as being a "picky" eater who often has to be coaxed. Taylor attends a Parent's Day Out program twice a week. She seems to enjoy attending the program but prefers solitary play. Taylor's vocabulary consists of about 25 words, but she most often uses sounds instead of words to communicate and sometimes has difficulty understanding what is being said to or asked of her.

What worries Cynthia most is the "empty" look she observes in Taylor's eyes, as if Taylor is looking right through her. Cynthia has spent many hours holding, caressing, and stroking Taylor. In the beginning, Taylor would become annoyed with Cynthia's nurturing and would cry when picked up. However, Taylor now seems to cry less, and Cynthia describes cuddling as a source of enjoyment for both of them. Every now and then, Cynthia tells you, she observes Taylor staring at her in a way that indicates that Taylor does on occasion "connect" with her.

# Healthy Development in Infancy and Early Childhood

In all three of these stories, we can identify factors that may have a negative effect on the children's development. But to understand the consequences of such factors, we must first understand how healthy growth and development occur. Therefore, this section describes what is traditionally referred to as "normal" development in children 6 and younger. But because *normal* is a relative term with some judgmental overtones, the term *healthy* will be used instead.

Social workers employed in schools, hospitals, community mental health centers, and other public settings are often approached by parents and teachers with questions about development in young children. To assess whether any of the children they bring to your attention require intervention, you must be able to distinguish between healthy and problematic development in three areas: physical, cognitive, and emotional development. As you will see, young children go through a multitude of changes in all three areas simultaneously. Inadequate development in any one of them—or in multiple areas—may have long-lasting consequences for the individual. Keep in mind, however, that what is considered to be healthy is relative to environment and culture. Valsiner (1989b, p. 163) argues that "all of the environment into which the newborn is born and in which the infant develops is culturally structured." Therefore, all aspects of development must be considered in a cultural context.

## *Physical Development*

Newborns are dependent on others for basic physical needs. They must be fed, cleaned, and kept safe and comfortable. But within the first six years, children develop the physical coordination to perform these functions for themselves—with guidance from caregivers, of course.

**How might variations in the biological person in infancy affect later psychosocial adjustment?**

With adequate nourishment and care, the physical growth of the infant is quite predictable. Most newborns weigh between 5 and 10 pounds at birth and are between 15 and 25 inches long. Infants double their weight by age 4 months. By age 2, most toddlers are quadruple their original weight and are double their original height (inches long). It is important to note that Taylor, the foster child you read about, has just now, at age 4, quadrupled her birth weight. After age 2, physical growth slows significantly. Between ages 2 and 6, the average child gains only 4 to 5 pounds per year and grows about 3 inches per year. Thus, the average 6-year-old weighs 40 to 50 pounds and measures between 40 and 50 inches in height. These changes in size are accompanied by the development of reflexes, motor skills, and neurological processing power.

*Reflexes.*    Although dependent on others, newborns are equipped from the start with tools for survival called **reflexes.** Reflexes aid the infant in adapting to the environment outside the womb.

Newborns have two critical reflexes:

- *Rooting reflex.* When you gently stroke an infant's cheek or the corner of its mouth with a finger, the infant will turn its head in the direction of the touch and open its mouth in an attempt to suck the finger. This reflex aids in feeding, because it guides the infant to the nipple.

- *Sucking reflex.* When a nipple or some other "suckable" object is presented to the infant, the infant sucks it. This reflex is another important tool for feeding.

These two reflexes are of great importance. Taylor did not have well-developed rooting and sucking reflexes and thus had to learn how to take in nourishment. Imagine the time and effort Cynthia required for feeding her foster child. Many infants would probably perish if they did not have the rooting and sucking reflexes.

Reflexes disappear at identified times during infancy. Both the rooting reflex and the sucking reflex disappear between 2 and 4 months (Sroufe, Cooper, & DeHart, 1996). By this time, the infant has mastered the voluntary act of sucking and is therefore no longer in need of the reflexive response. Several other infant reflexes are listed in Exhibit 4.1. Some of these reflexes appear to have little use now but probably had some specific survival purposes in earlier times.

Reflexes are important in the evaluation of neurological functioning. The absence of reflexes can indicate a serious developmental disorder. Taylor's poorly developed reflexes may be a sign of serious developmental problems.

*Motor Skills.*    The infant advances from reflex functioning to motor functioning. The development of **motor skills**—the ability to manipulate—occurs in a more or less orderly, logical sequence. It begins with simple actions such as lifting the chin and progresses to more complex acts such as walking, running, and throwing. Infants usually crawl before they walk.

Motor development is somewhat predictable, in that children tend to reach milestones at about the same age. Typical ages for some significant developmental milestones are listed in Exhibit 4.2. Remember, however, that development of motor skills varies from child to child. Many parents, for example, become concerned if their child has not attempted to walk unassisted by age 1. However, some children walk alone at age 9 months; others do not even attempt to walk until 15 months. Although there is variation in the ages at which children accomplish specific developmental milestones, Taylor's development of walking skills at age 4 falls outside the range for healthy development.

The development of motor skills (and most other types of skills, for that matter) is a continuous process. It progresses from broad capacities to more specific refined abilities. For example, preschoolers initially can scribble only unrecognizable figures on paper. Later, they are able to draw identifiable shapes, such as circles and squares.

**EXHIBIT 4.1**
Infant Reflexes

| Reflex | Description | Visible |
|---|---|---|
| Sucking | The infant instinctively sucks any object of appropriate size that is presented to it. | First 2–4 months |
| Rooting | The head turns in the direction of a stimulus when the cheek is touched. The infant's mouth opens in an attempt to suck. | First 3 months |
| Moro/Startle | The arms thrust outward when the infant is released in midair, as if attempting to regain support. | First 5 months |
| Swimming | When placed face down in water, the infant makes paddling, swimlike motions. | First 3 months |
| Stepping | When the infant is held in an upright position with the feet placed on a firm surface, the infant moves the feet in a walking motion. | First 3 months |
| Blinking | The eyes blink in response to light, air, and other stimuli. | Lifetime |
| Grasping | The infant grasps objects placed in its hand. | First 4 months |
| Babinski | The toes spread when the soles of the feet are stroked. | First year |

**EXHIBIT 4.2**
Selected Milestones in Physical Development

| Milestone | Age of Onset |
|---|---|
| Sits unassisted | 8 to 12 months |
| Crawls | 10 to 12 months |
| Pulls to standing position | 8 to 10 months |
| Walks independently | 18 months |
| Feeds self with fingers | 8 to 10 months |
| Uses spoon proficiently | 12 to 18 months |
| Waves "bye-bye" | 8 to 10 months |
| Drinks from a cup | 10 to 12 months |
| Scribbles with crayon | 12 to 18 months |
| Walks and runs well | 2 to 3 years |
| Enjoys looking at books | 2 to 3 years |
| Rides a tricycle | 3 to 5 years |
| Skips and jumps | 4 to 5 years |
| Dresses and undresses self | 4 to 5 years |
| Roller-skates and jumps rope | 5 to 6 years |

In what other ways does the environmental dimension of family influence childrearing?

Parents are usually only minimally impatient with their child's motor development. However, toilet training (potty training) is often a source of stress and uncertainty for new parents. Until recently, many child development experts recommended that babies be potty trained during the first year of life. Consequently, many parents exercised strong measures, including scolding and punishment, to ensure timely toilet training. Even now, many grandparents proudly report that they tied their infants to the potty chair at times of predicted elimination (after eating, for example) until the child was able to master the skill. T. Berry Brazelton (1983), one of America's best-known pediatricians, endeavored to change this perspective and abolish the use of scolding and punishment during the potty training process. He continues to promote the second year of life, during the "lull time" after standing and walking have been accomplished, as a more appropriate time for potty training to begin. Brazelton proposes that only then is the infant physiologically and psychologically ready to master this skill. By age 3, most children have mastered toilet training, but even 5-year-olds are still prone to soiling accidents.

How else might culture affect infant development?

Culture and ethnicity appear to influence motor development in young children. For example, African American and Hispanic children may develop motor skills at a faster rate than do European American children of the same age. The most extensive research in this area was conducted by Bartz and Levine (1978). They compared African American, Hispanic, and European American families of similar socioeconomic status. They concluded that the African American and Hispanic children in their study did have more advanced motor skills than their European American counterparts. They attributed these differences to different parental expectations. African American and Hispanic parents expected their children to become more independent earlier. They therefore encouraged skills that lead to independence, such as walking, self-feeding, and potty training.

***The Growing Brain.***   Discussing physical development in young children without discussing the brain is irresponsible, given the wealth of findings from recent neurological research. The brain is 25 percent of its adult weight at birth, 70 percent by the end of the first year, and 80 percent by the end of the second year. In short, the brain develops most rapidly in the first two years of life. Any future brain growth and functioning greatly depends on healthy brain development during these first two years.

Two factors determine how the brain develops: genetics and environment (Stepp-Gilbert, 1988). Genetics appears to determine some basic structures and functioning, but environmental factors are highly influential. The environmental factors thought to influence brain development during this time are family environment, parent/child relationships (Healy, 1995), and sensory stimulation (Stepp-Gilbert, 1988). Taylor's first three months, spent in a crib with minimal nurturance and sensory stimulation, did not give her brain a healthy start.

Several types of sensory stimulation are needed (see Exhibit 4.3). The more the brain is stimulated by input from sensory receptors, the better the quality of brain development. Stepp-Gilbert (1988) contends that preschoolers must be allowed opportunities for play and for other activities that promote the development of gross and fine motor skills. Talking and reading to infants also stimulates brain growth. The fact that these sorts of early childhood experiences are crucial to brain development not only points up the importance of the caregiver role but also suggests that we need effective early intervention programs to find children who are not getting adequate stimulation and then enrich their environments.

**EXHIBIT 4.3**

Sensory Stimuli That Facilitate Brain Growth and Development

| Type of Stimulation | Definition | Example |
|---|---|---|
| Vestibular stimulation | Any activity that involves the child with movement | Rocking in rocking chair, swinging, bouncing, rolling |
| Tactile stimulation | Appropriate and frequent touching | Carrying infant in Snugli, letting infant sleep next to parents, breastfeeding and bottle feeding next to chest, massaging |
| Proprioceptive stimulation | Any activity that stimulates physical development and strengthens muscles | Encouraging infant exercise, push and pull activities, outdoor activities involving full body movements |

*Source:* Stepp-Gilbert, 1988.

## Cognitive Development

Is the psychological person formed in infancy?

As the brain develops, so does its ability to process and store information and to solve problems. These abilities are known as **cognition.** When we talk about how fast a child is learning, we are talking about cognitive development. A central element of cognition is language, which facilitates both thinking and communicating. Exhibit 4.4 lists some milestones in cognitive development.

***Piaget's Stages of Cognitive Development.*** To assess children's cognitive progress, many people use the concepts developed by the best-known cognitive development theorist, Jean Piaget (1952). Piaget believed that cognitive development occurs in successive stages, determined

**EXHIBIT 4.4**

Selected Milestones in Cognitive Development

| Milestone | Age at Onset |
|---|---|
| Coos responsively | Birth to 3 months |
| Smiles responsively | 3 to 4 months |
| Smiles at self in mirror | 3 to 4 months |
| Laughs out loud | 3 to 4 months |
| Plays peek-a-boo | 3 to 4 months |
| Shows displeasure | 5 to 6 months |
| Babbles | 6 to 8 months |
| Understands simple commands | 12 months |
| Follows directions | 2 years |
| Puts 2 to 3 words together | 2 years |
| Uses sentences | 2 to 3 years |

by the age of the child. His overall contention was that as a child grows and develops, cognition changes not only in quantity but also in quality.

Piaget used the metaphor of a slow-motion movie to explain his theory:

1. **Sensorimotor stage** (ages 0 to 2 years). Infants at this stage of development can look at only one frame of the movie at a time. When the next picture appears on the screen, infants focus on it and cannot go back to the previous frame.

2. **Preoperational stage** (ages 2 to 7). Preschool children and children in the early grades can remember (recall) the sequence of the pictures in the movie. They also develop **symbolic functioning**—the ability to use symbols to represent what is not present. However, they do not necessarily understand what has happened in the movie or how the pictures fit together.

3. **Concrete operations stage** (ages 7 to 11). Not until this stage can children run the pictures in the movie backward and forward to better understand how they blend to form a specific meaning.

4. **Formal operations stage** (ages 11 and beyond). Children gain the capacity to apply logic to various situations and to use symbols to solve problems. Adding to Piaget's metaphor, Edwards (1992) describes formal operations as the ability not only to understand the observed movie but also to add or change characters and create an additional plot or a staging plan.

The first two of Piaget's stages apply to infants and young children. In the sensorimotor stage, infants respond to immediate stimuli—what they see, hear, taste, touch, and smell—and learning takes place through the senses and motor activities. According to Piaget, the mastery of **object permanence** is also a significant task during this stage. Piaget contended that around 9 months of age, toddlers develop the ability to understand that an object or a person exists even when not in their immediate surroundings. In other words, children become aware that a favored toy or favored person exists even when not seen.

The second stage of cognitive development, also relevant to early childhood, is the preoperational period. It is in turn divided into two substages:

1. *Preconceptual stage* (ages 2 to 4). The most important aspect of the preoperational stage is the development of symbolic representation, which occurs in the preconceptual stage. Through play, children learn to use symbols and actively engage in what Piaget labeled deferred imitation. **Deferred imitation** refers to the child's ability to view an image and then, significantly later, recall and imitate the image. For example, a preschooler who looks at Super Friends on television may later use a sheet as a cape (an example of symbolic play) and leap off the fireplace as if flying like the Super Friends did in the cartoon.

2. *Intuitive stage* (ages 4 to 7). During the second part of the preoperational stage, children use language to represent objects. During the preconceptual stage, any object with long ears may be called "bunny." However, during the intuitive stage, children begin to understand that the term *bunny* represents the entire animal, not just a property of it. Consider the preschoolers' use of classification skills. They are able to classify objects, but based on only one attribute at a time. For example, given a set of stuffed animals of various sizes and colors, the pre-

schooler will group the animals either by color or by size. In contrast, an older child who has reached the intuitive stage may sort them by both size and color.

Preschool children also engage in what Piaget termed **transductive reasoning**. The best explanation of this term is an illustration. Imagine that 5-year-old Sam immediately smells chicken when he enters his grandmother's home. He comments that she must be having a party and asks who is coming over for dinner. When the grandmother replies that no one is coming over and that a party is not planned, Sam shakes his head in disbelief and states that he will just wait to see when the guests arrive. In this example, through the process of transductive reasoning, Sam recalls that the last time his grandmother cooked chicken was for a party. Because grandmother is cooking chicken again, Sam thinks another party is going to occur.

One last related preoperational concept described by Piaget is **egocentrism**. According to Piaget, preschoolers perceive reality only from their own experience and believe themselves to be at the center of existence. They are unable to recognize the possibility of other perspectives on a situation. For example, a 3-year-old who stands between you and the television to watch a program believes that you can see the television because she can.

Piaget is considered the pioneer of cognitive development theory. One of his most significant insights is that children are not simply miniature adults but rather that they advance in cognitive abilities as they advance in age. This understanding is the foundation on which our formal educational curriculum is planned.

As much as Piaget's work has been praised, however, it has also been questioned and criticized. Piaget constructed his theory based on his observations of his own three children. Thus, one question has been how objective he was and whether his concepts can really be generalized to all children. Also, Piaget suggested that his developmental model describes the "average" child, but he did not define or describe what he meant by "average." Finally, Piaget did not address the influence of environmental factors—such as culture, family, and significant relationships and friendships—on cognitive development.

Findings from more recent research have also called into question some aspects of Piaget's theory. For example, researchers examining preschool children's ability to understand others' feelings concluded that many preschoolers do demonstrate empathy, depending on their family's empathy skills (Dunn, Brown, Slomkowski, Telsa, & Youngblade, 1991). Some social scientists have inferred from this finding that preschool children are not as egocentric as Piaget described (Zastrow & Kirst-Ashman, 1997). In addition, Piaget described young children as being incapable of object permanence until at least 9 months of age. In a study of infants, Baillargeon (1987) observed infants as young as $3^1/2$ and $4^1/2$ months of age who were already proficient at object permanence. Findings like these suggest using Piaget's model with caution. It remains, however, our most useful overall view of how cognition develops.

*Language Skills.*   Language is included under cognitive development because it is the mechanism by which cognitive interpretations are communicated to others. Note that for language to exist, children must be able to "organize" their experiences (Hopper & Naremore, 1978).

There has been a long-standing debate about how language is acquired. How much of language ability is a result of genetic processes, and how much of it is learned? Is Taylor's delay in

language development, for example, the result of being left unattended for most of her first three months or the result of some biological malfunction? Skinner (1957) argued that children learn language by imitating what they hear in the environment and then being reinforced. When children utter sounds heard in their environment, he contended, parents respond in a manner (smiling, laughing, clapping) that encourages young children to repeat the sound. As children grow older, they are often corrected by caregivers and preschool teachers for the misuse of words or phases. At the other end of the spectrum, Chomsky (1968) contended that language ability is primarily a function of genetics. Although somewhat influenced by the environment, children develop language skills as long as the appropriate genetic material is in place.

Some scholars assert that both perspectives have merit. Hopper and Naremore (1978) suggest that language development is best thought of as "innate-learned." They propose that the ability to develop language skills is genetic, but this ability must be activated and cultivated by forces in the environment. Research seems to support this premise. In studies of healthy infants, researchers have found that language development is influenced more by biological factors during the first two years of life and more by environmental factors during the third year (Molfese, Holcomb, & Helwig, 1994). Studies involving preterm infants also support the interaction of biological and environmental factors (Beckwith, 1984). Neonatal medical problems were found to have some influence on cognitive development, including language development; however, the development of cognitive skills was more influenced by the amount of maternal attention the children received.

"Developmental niche" is another environmental factor considered important in the development of language skills (Harkness, 1990). From observation of their environment—physical and social surroundings, child-rearing customs, and caregiver personality—children learn a set of regulations or rules for communication that shape their developing language skills. Children have an innate capacity for language, but the structuring of the environment through culture is what allows language development to occur.

## Emotional Development

The key concern for Melanie's children—Jessica, Alexia, and Steven Jr.—is their emotional development. Specifically, Melanie wonders if they will grow into happy, loving, well-adjusted people if she puts them into day care and pursues her career. Young children do face important developmental tasks in the emotional arena, some of which are listed in Exhibit 4.5. This section addresses these tasks, drawing on Erikson's theory of psychosocial development.

### Erikson's Theory of Psychosocial Development.

Erikson's (1950) theory is organized around eight consecutive, age-defined stages of emotional development. Each stage requires the mastery of a developmental task. Mastery at each stage depends on mastery in the previous stages. If the "task facilitating factors" for a stage are absent, the individual will become "stuck" in that stage of development.

The following three stages are relevant to children 6 and younger (additional stages are discussed in Chapters 5, 6, and 7):

**EXHIBIT 4.5**

Selected Milestones in Emotional Development

| Milestone | Age at Onset |
|---|---|
| Recognizes family members | 3 to 4 months |
| Clings to parental figure | 5 to 6 months |
| Expresses joy | 7 to 9 months |
| Forms gender identity | 2 to 2½ years |
| Develops friendships | 3 to 5 years |

1. *Trust versus mistrust* (birth to age 1½). The overall task of this stage is for infants to develop a sense that their needs will be met by the outside world and that the outside world is an "OK" place to be. In addition, the infant develops an emotional bond with an adult, which Erikson believes becomes the foundation for being able to form intimate, loving relationships in the future. Erikson argues the need for one, consistent mother figure. The most important factor facilitating growth in this stage is consistency in having physical and emotional needs met: being fed when hungry, being kept warm and dry, and being allowed undisturbed sleep. In addition, the infant has to be protected from injury, disease, and so on, and receive adequate stimulation. Infants who develop mistrust at this stage become suspicious of the world and withdraw, react with rage, and have deep-seated feelings of dependency. These infants lack drive, hope, and motivation for continued growth. They cannot trust their environment and are unable to form intimate relationships with others. Let's look at the children you met at the beginning of the chapter. Demarcus's needs seem to be adequately met, but he appears to be receiving messages from Ynecka that the outside world is not a safe place. Steven Jr. also appears to have most of his needs adequately met, but his sense of safety and security may be hampered by Melanie's moodiness. Taylor's world was not a nurturing, secure place during her first three months, but Cynthia has provided trustworthy care since then.

2. *Autonomy versus shame and doubt* (ages 1½ to 3). A child with autonomy has a growing sense of self-awareness and begins to strive for independence and self-control. These children feel proud that they can perform tasks and exercise control over bodily functions. They relate well with close people in the environment and begin to exercise self-control in response to parental limits. To develop autonomy, children need firm limits that still allow them the freedom to explore their environment. They also need an environment rich with stimulating and interesting objects and with opportunities for freedom of choice. Adults must accept the child's bodily functions as normal and good and offer praise and encouragement to enhance the child's mastery of self-control. At the other end of the spectrum are children who doubt themselves. They fear a loss of love and are overly concerned about their parents' approval. These children are ashamed of their abilities and develop an "unhealthy" kind of self-consciousness. We would expect that Alexia Schmidt is engaged in a struggle for mastery, but Melanie describes her as "out of control." Melanie's support is essential if Alexia is to learn to trust her own competence.

Why should social workers be concerned about the influence of small groups during early childhood?

3. *Initiative versus guilt* (ages 3 to 6). Children in this stage get satisfaction from completing tasks. They develop imagination and fantasies and can handle guilt about their fantasies. At the beginning of this stage, children's focus is on family relationships. They learn what roles are appropriate for various family members, and they accept parental limits. In addition, they develop gender identity through identification with the parent of the same sex. Jessica Schmidt demonstrates identification with her mother when she comforts her baby brother. By the end of this stage, the child's focus turns to friendships outside the family. Children engage in cooperative play and enjoy both sharing and competing with peers. Age and sex boundaries must be appropriately defined at this stage, and parents must be secure enough to set limits and resist the child's possessiveness. Children must also have the opportunity to establish peer relationships outside the family. The Parent's Day Out program provides a valuable opportunity for Taylor to establish peer relationships, and the play group serves the same purpose for the Schmidt children. Children who become stuck in this stage are plagued with guilt about their goals and fantasies. They become confused about their gender identity and about family roles. These children are overly anxious and self-centered.

From Erikson's perspective, Taylor's story illustrates what happens when physical and emotional needs go unmet in the first months of life. Taylor became stuck in the trust versus mistrust stage. Her ability to form relationships with others is severely impaired, and her initial response has been to withdraw. Given Taylor's negative experiences at such a young age, can she ever really connect with her foster mother? Will Taylor ever be able to "trust" and feel the world is a good pace to be?

Erikson does not address whether tasks that should be mastered in one stage can be mastered at a later stage if the needed task facilitating factors—such as a dependable nurturing caregiver—are introduced. Given that Taylor was deprived of factors needed to develop trust for the first three months, does she still have the potential to develop trust if these factors are introduced in her fourth month of life? At what point is it too late? Critics also question his emphasis on the process of individualization, through which children develop a strong identity separate from that of their family. Many believe this to be an American, Western value and therefore not applicable to collectivistic societies, or collectivistic subcultures within American society.

How do the biological and the psychological dimensions interact to produce temperament?

*Temperament.*   Another way to look at emotional development is by evaluating **temperament**—the individual's innate disposition. The best-known study of temperament in infants and young children was conducted by Thomas, Chess, and Birch (1968, 1970). They studied nine components of temperament, which they described as appearing shortly after birth: activity level, regularity of biological functions, initial reaction to any new stimulus, adaptability, intensity of reaction, level of stimulation needed to evoke a discernible response, quality of mood, distractibility, and attention span or persistence. From their observations, Thomas et al. identified three types of temperament: easy, difficult, and slow to warm up. Thomas and his colleagues believed that a child's temperament is set, or remains unchanged, throughout life. They cautioned, however, that a difficult temperament is not indicative of future childhood behavior problems, as one might logically assume.

More significant than an infant's temperament type is the "goodness of fit" between the infant and those in the child's environment (Thomas & Chess, 1986). In other words, how well the child's temperament matches with the expectations, temperament, and needs of those in the child's environment (parents, caregivers, siblings) is crucial to the infant's emotional development. For example, there appears to be a "good fit" between Cynthia Lewis and Taylor. In addition to meeting Taylor's basic needs, Cynthia responds effectively to what can be described as Taylor's "slow to warm up" to "difficult" temperament. Although Taylor sometimes becomes irritated with Cynthia's nurturing style, Cynthia is unaffected by Taylor's rebuffs and accommodates her need for "space" while maintaining a patient, affectionate stance. The good fit between Cynthia and Taylor will help Taylor develop toward healthy functioning. Thomas and Chess suggest that, regardless of a child's temperament, caregivers and others in the child's environment can learn, like Cynthia, to "work with" a child's temperament.

More recent research, investigating temperament as a predictor of preschool behavior problems, yielded a surprising result (Oberklaid, Sanson, Pedlow, & Prior, 1993). Investigators found that the parent's perception of the preschool child's temperament had more influence on the development of behavior problems than did the child's actual temperament. Children who were perceived by their caregivers as having a "difficult" temperament were twice as likely to develop a behavior problem during the preschool years, regardless of their empirically measured temperament type. You may see Demarcus's curiosity as a healthy trait, but if Ynecka perceives it as difficult, behavior problems may develop.

Studies like these call into question whether temperament is genetically determined or environmentally induced. In a study of temperament among twins and among adopted siblings, investigators found that genetics contributed more than environment to temperament development (Braungart, Plomin, DeFries, & Fulker, 1992). The twins' temperaments were more alike than were those of the adopted siblings. The researchers concluded that environment contributes very little to temperament. However, deVries and Sameroff (1984) studied temperament among infants from three distinct East African societies. They concluded that factors in the infant's environment—such as child-rearing practices, level of social change or modernization, maternal attitudes, ecological setting, and specific early life events—have more influence on temperament development. We could infer from this study that temperament is "neutral" and then molded and shaped by parental characteristics and expectations (Oberklaid et al., 1993). As with other aspects of personality, however, perhaps children are born with a genetic predisposition to a temperament type that is then significantly influenced by environmental factors.

***Attachment.*** Another key component of emotional development is **attachment**—the ability to form emotional bonds with other people. Many child development scholars have suggested that attachment is one of the most important issues in infant development, mainly because attachment is the foundation for emotional development and a predictor of later functioning. Note that this view of attachment is similar to Erikson's first stage of psychosocial development.

The two most popular theories of attachment were developed by Bowlby (1969) and Ainsworth and colleagues (Ainsworth, Blehar, Waters, & Wall, 1978). Bowlby initially studied attachment in animals and developed a theory of human attachment from these studies. According to Bowlby's theory, attachment is natural, a result of the infant's instinct for survival and consequent need to be protected. Attachment between infant and mother ensures that the infant will be adequately nurtured and protected from attack or, in the case of human infants, from a harsh environment. The infant is innately programmed to emit stimuli (smiling, clinging, and so on) to which the mother responds. This exchange between infant and mother creates a bond of attachment. The infant initiates the attachment process, but later the mother's behavior is what strengthens the bond. Bowlby contends that infants can demonstrate attachment behavior to others; however, attachment to the mother occurs earlier than attachment to others and is stronger and more consistent. Melanie Schmidt fears a disruption in her attachment relationships with her children if she returns to work.

Bowlby hypothesized that attachment advances through four stages: preattachment, attachment in the making, clear-cut attachment, and goal corrected attachment. This process begins in the first month of life, with the infant's ability to discriminate the mother's voice. Attachment becomes fully developed during the second year of life, when the mother and infant develop a partnership. During this later phase of attachment, the child is able to manipulate the mother into desired outcomes, but the child also has the capacity to understand the mother's point of view. The term *partnership* indicates that the mother and the child reach a mutually acceptable compromise.

One of the most widely used methods to investigate infant attachment, known as the strange situation procedure, was developed by Ainsworth and colleagues. The Ainsworth group believed that you could assess the level of infant attachment to the mother through the infant's response to a series of "strange" episodes. Basically, the child is exposed over a period of 25 minutes to eight constructed episodes involving separation and reunion with the mother. The amount of child attachment to the mother is measured by how the child responds to the mother following the "distressing" separation.

Ainsworth and her colleagues identified three types of attachment:

1. *Secure attachment.* The child uses the mother as a home base and feels comfortable leaving this base to explore the playroom. The child returns to the mother every so often to ensure that she is still present. When the mother leaves the room (act of separation), the securely attached child will cry and seek comfort from the mother when she returns. But this child is easily reassured and soothed by the mother's return.

2. *Anxious attachment.* The child is reluctant to explore the playroom and clings to the mother. When the mother leaves the room, the child cries for a long time. When the mother returns, this child seeks solace from the mother but continues to cry and may swat at or pull away from the mother. Ainsworth and colleagues described these infants as somewhat insecure and doubted that their mothers would ever be able to provide the security and safety they need.

3. *Avoidant attachment.* Some infants seem indifferent to the presence of their mother. Whether the mother is present or absent from the room, these children's responses are the same.

Recent scholars have added a fourth possible response, known as the insecure disorganized/disoriented response (Main & Hesse, 1990). These children display contradictory behavior: They attempt physical closeness, but retreat with acts of avoidance. These infants typically have mothers who either have a history of abusive behavior or continue to struggle with a traumatic experience in their own lives. As a result, these infants become confused in the "strange" situation. They fear the unknown figure and seek solace from the mother, but retreat because they are also fearful of the mother.

According to attachment theory, children whose mothers are consistently present and responsive to their needs and whose mothers exhibit a warm, caring relationship develop an appropriate attachment. The implication is that infants and young children need their mother as the sole caregiver for healthy development. This assumption probably seemed unquestionable when these theories were constructed. However, over the past 20 to 30 years, more women have entered the workforce. About 57 percent of women with children ages 6 and under work outside the home, and 53 percent of women with children age 1 year and younger work outside of the home (Reskin & Padavic, 1994; U.S. Department of Labor, 1988). Thus, many more children experience alternative forms of child care, including day care.

The effect day care has on the development of attachment in young children continues to be a hotly debated topic. Some argue that day care has a negative effect on infant attachment and increases the risk of the infant's developing insecure and avoidant forms of attachment (see, for example, Belsky, 1987; Belsky & Braungart, 1991). The risks are especially high if the infant attends day care during the first year of life. Others argue that day care does not have a negative effect on infant and early childhood attachment (Griffith, 1996).

The question of how day care attendance affects attachment is probably not as simplistic as either side contends. Many factors appear to be associated with the development of attachment for children in day care. The overriding factor is the quality of the relationship between the infant and the parents, regardless of the child's care arrangements. For example, mothers who have a positive attitude toward their infant, are emotionally available to their infant, and encourage age-appropriate levels of independence produce infants with secure attachment (Clarke-Stewart, 1988).

Other investigations suggest that the amount of involvement by the father and the quality of the marital relationship between the mother and father are also relevant to the development of secure infant attachment. Infants with fathers who are significantly involved in their nurturing and care and whose parents have a stable and loving marriage tend to develop secure attachment, even if they spend a significant portion of the day in child care (Schachere, 1990).

What formal organizations other than day care might affect young children?

Even the skeptics concede that perhaps the true impact of day care on child development has to do with the quality of day care. Quality day care can foster many positive skills in young children; it can promote social competence, a positive sense of identity, trust in others, and enriched academic skills (Dodge, 1995). An extensive study by Griffith (1996), which compared children ages 3, 4, and 5, found that attendance in quality day-care programs promoted higher levels of "prosociability." Children who had been in day care the longest were found to be most sensitive to the needs of others, including their peers, and were the most giving, cooperative, and helpful. The National Research Council (1990) has identified three factors essential to quality day care, described in Exhibit 4.6.

One final note on the issue of attachment: The manner in which infant attachment is measured raises some concerns. Most studies of attachment have used the Ainsworth group's

**EXHIBIT 4.6**

Essential Features of
Quality Day Care

| Staff/child ratio | One staff member for every 3 infants, for every 4 toddlers, and for every 8 preschoolers |
|---|---|
| Group/age ratio | No larger than 6 infants, 8 toddlers, and 16 preschoolers per group |
| Staff training | Well-defined curriculum focused on child development theory and age-appropriate child-care techniques. |

*Source:* Adapted from National Research Council, 1990. See also Bredekamp, 1992; Dodge, 1995.

strange situation method. However, this measure may not yield valid results with some groups or under certain conditions. For example, Clarke-Stewart (1989) suggests that the avoidant pattern of attachment some investigators have noted among children in day care may not indicate lack of attachment, as some have concluded. These children may be securely attached but seem indifferent to the exit and return of the mother simply because they have become accustomed to routine separations and reunions with their mother.

The appropriateness of using the strange situation method with certain ethnic groups has also been questioned (Fracasso, Busch-Rossnagel, & Fisher, 1994; Jackson, 1993). Researchers evaluating attachment in Puerto Rican and Dominican infants (Fracasso et al., 1994) and African American infants (Jackson, 1993) have concluded that the pattern of attachment in these ethnic groups is different from that identified in studies of European American infants and is thus often mislabeled. For example, Jackson observes that multiple caregiving is tradition in the African American community. Many extended-family members (both blood and nonblood relations) participate in the rearing of children—for a number of reasons, including accommodation of parents' unconventional work schedules, for both single and married parents. This multiple caregiving arrangement encourages African American infants to befriend "strangers" introduced to them by their mothers. As a result, African American children often are more independent and do not experience the same level of anxiety that European American children experience when left by their mother. As occurs with children in day care, the "apathy" of African American children toward the mother may be not be apathy at all, but rather an indication of their comfort with the exit and return of the mother. In other words, they have adapted to the multiple caregiver arrangement. Interestingly, this tradition of shared child rearing echoes the African proverb "It takes a village to raise a child," which has become a popular adage in the United States. Also, it should be noted that the extended kinship network has been found to be a strength of African American families (Hill, 1972; Logan, Freeman, & McRoy, 1990).

## The Role of Play

Play is essential to all three aspects of development. Through play, children develop the motor skills essential for physical development, learn the problem-solving skills and communication skills fundamental to cognitive development, and express the feelings and gain the self-confidence needed for emotional growth. Essentially, play is what young children are all about; it is their work.

**EXHIBIT 4.7**
Types of Play
Observed in Young
Children

| | |
|---|---|
| Solitary play | Most characteristic of 2- and 3-year-olds. Children engaged in this type of play keep to themselves, often with some sort of toy or toy substitute, even in the presence of other children. |
| Parallel play | Characteristic of 2- and 3-year-olds. Young children continue to play by themselves, but in the proximity of another child. Although the children may play with similar objects, they are autonomous of each other. |
| Associative play | Characteristic of 3- and 4-year-olds. The focus of play is the interaction as opposed to the actual activity of play. Two or more children play with similar objects in the same proximity and may even follow each other around the playground. These children talk to each other about their toys but make no attempt to play with the objects together. |
| Cooperative play | Characteristic of children 4 to 5. These children play with each other and usually have an identified goal to the play—for example, to get the ball in the goal. |

*Source:* Adapted from Parten, 1932.

How might play
activities differ
among children
from different
cultures?

Play may be one of the few elements in the development of young children that is universal regardless of culture. Comparing children from six different countries with significantly different cultures, Whiting and Whiting (1975) found that all preschool children constructed spontaneous play activities. Even preschoolers in cultures that require young children to work or complete chores included play in their work activities. Some suggest that the act of play is almost automatic, driven by physiological functions (Gandelman, 1992; Panksepp, 1986).

Preschoolers engage in four types of play (Parten, 1932), summarized in Exhibit 4.7. Parten asserted that children progress through the levels of play as they mature. The implication is that the last levels of play, which involve social interaction, are more mature levels of play. If so, one cannot help wondering what effect the popularity of computer and video games, which promote solitary play, will have on children's development. However, Rubin (1982), in his investigation of "nonsocial" play among 4-year-olds, concluded that even children who spend large amounts of time in nonsocial play develop normal social, cognitive, and interpersonal skills. Is one level of play, then, really more "mature" than another?

## Developmental Disruptions

Most developmental problems in infants and preschoolers are more accurately described as **developmental delays,** offering the hope that early intervention, or even natural processes, will mitigate the long-term effects. In contrast, developmental problems in school-age children are typically labeled disabilities and classified into groups, such as mental retardation, learning disabilities, and motor impairment (Zipper & Simeonsson, 1997).

The most pressing concern in this area is the difficulty of accurately assessing developmental delays in children under age 6. Zipper and Simeonsson (1997) provide several explanations for this difficulty. For one, growth and development among young children varies. Although we have loose guidelines for healthy development in infants and preschoolers, development varies by individual child. Children walk, master potty training, understand abstract concepts, speak in sentences, and learn to play with others at different ages. It is therefore difficult to assess whether a particular child has a case of delayed development—and if so, which faculties are delayed.

The other reason that accurate assessment of developmental difficulties in infants and preschool children is hard is that although many physical and cognitive disabilities have been found to be genetic in nature, and others to be associated with environmental factors, the cause of most disabilities is unknown. Zipper and Simeonsson (1997) note, for example, that mental retardation has 350 known causes, yet the cause of most identified cases of mental retardation is unknown. Anticipating what the risk factors might be for a particular child and how they might influence developmental delays is therefore difficult. It is hard for us to know what mix of biological, psychological, and social factors are responsible for Taylor's delayed development—or to know exactly what the future holds for her.

Many young children with emotional and behavioral problems are also inaccurately assessed and misdiagnosed. After interviewing professionals who work with children 6 and under, Schmitz and Hilton (1996) compiled a list of traits observed in young children that are indicative of emotional and behavioral problems: extreme aggressive behavior, difficulty with change, invasion of others' personal space, compulsive or impulsive behavior, low ability to trust others, lack of empathy or remorse, and cruelty to animals. Parents and teachers often handle these behaviors with firmer limits and more discipline. However, environmental risk factors, such as emotional abuse or neglect and domestic violence, may be the actual cause. Freeman and Dyer (1993) contend that misdiagnosis often occurs because young children are assessed independently of their environment and the complexity of their problems is misunderstood.

Given the difficulty of accurate assessment, assessment in young children should include many disciplines, to gain as broad an understanding as possible (Zipper & Simeonsson, 1997). Assessment and service delivery should also be culturally relevant (Parette, 1995). In other words, culture and other related issues—such as family interaction patterns and stress, the social environment, ethnicity, acculturation, social influences, and developmental expectations—should all be considered when evaluating a child's developmental abilities.

For those children who have been labeled developmentally delayed, the main focus has been on programs that promote social skill development. Do these programs work? And under what conditions do they work? In one such program, two types of preschool classrooms were evaluated (Roberts, Burchinal, & Bailey, 1994). In one classroom, developmentally delayed preschool children were matched with nondelayed children of the same age; in another classroom, some of the "normal" children were the same age as the developmentally delayed children, and some were older. Social exchange between the children with disabilities and those without disabilities was greater in the mixed-aged classroom. In another study, Lewis (1994) evaluated the usefulness of providing social skills training to children with mild developmental disabilities. In a preschool setting, developmentally delayed children were put in situations requiring social interaction and were praised for successful interaction. Lewis found this method to be effective in increasing social interaction among the preschool children.

# Risks to Healthy Development

You have probably already surmised what some of the environmental factors are that inhibit healthy growth and development in young children. This section addresses a few of those factors that social workers are especially likely to encounter: poverty, ineffective discipline, divorce, and violence (including child abuse).

## *Poverty*

How can social workers help children overcome the influence of an inequitable social structure?

In recent years, the greatest increase in poverty in the United States has been among families with young children (Schmitz & Hilton, 1996). About 24 million children live in poverty, a tremendous increase from the 1980s—including one out of four children ages 6 and younger (McWhirter, McWhirter, McWhirter, & McWhirter, 1993). About 27 percent of children younger than 3 live in poverty (Schmitz & Hilton, 1996). The upsurge of female-headed households is a major factor in the increase of children living in poverty (Canino & Spurlock, 1994; Duncan, 1991; McWhirter et al., 1993). Other contributors have been a significant decrease in the real incomes of families, growing inequality in income distribution, stagnant wages for young workers, high unemployment among minority men, and a decrease in cash benefits available to young families (Duncan, 1991). Finally an African American child is three times more likely than a European American child to live in poverty, and a Hispanic child is twice as likely (McWhitrter et al., 1993).

Although some young children who live in poverty flourish, poverty presents considerable risks to children's growth and development. (That risk continues into middle childhood, as Chapter 5 explains.) Children living in poverty often suffer the consequences of poor nutrition and inadequate health care. Many of these children do not receive proper immunizations, and many minor illnesses go untreated, increasing the potential for serious health problems. This phenomenon is particularly disturbing because many of these minor illnesses are easily treated. Most childhood ear infections, for example, are easily treated with antibiotics; left untreated, they can result in hearing loss.

What other aspects of the physical environment might be risks to the development of children?

In addition to inadequate health care and nutrition, children living in poverty often experience overcrowded living conditions. Overcrowding restricts opportunities for play and thus, because most learning and development in young children takes place in the context of play, restricts healthy development. Widmayer, Peterson, and Larner (1990) studied development among 12-month-old Haitian American children. They found that the poorer children experienced more overcrowded conditions than those not living in poverty and consequently had less play time, fewer toys, a smaller number of safe areas to play, and less private time with parents. The living conditions of the children who were poor were associated with delayed motor development and lower cognitive functioning.

Other researchers have found that children who live in poverty are at high risk for low self-esteem, school failure, peer conflict, depression, and childhood psychological disorders (McLoyd & Wilson, 1991; McWhirter et al., 1993). These problems are primarily the outcome of living in a violent setting or in deteriorated housing and of the instability that results from frequent changes in residence and schools (McLoyd & Wilson, 1991).

Children are affected not only by the direct consequences of poverty but also by indirect factors, such as family stress, parental depression, and inadequate or nonsupportive parenting (Kirby & Fraser, 1997; McLoyd & Wilson, 1991). Ynecka Green's depression and anxiety will affect her relationship with Demarcus.

Most disturbing is the link between poverty and **infant mortality**—the death of a child before its first birthday. Infant mortality rates in the United States are high compared to other industrialized nations (National Center for Health Statistics [NCHS], 1990). Within the United States, mortality rates for infants are higher among the poor, and the rate among African Americans is twice that of European Americans (Frank, Strobino, Salkever, & Jackson, 1992; Klerman, 1991; NCHS, 1990). As discussed in Chapter 3, low birth weight as a result of inadequate prenatal care is the primary factor that contributes to the high infant mortality rate (Frank et al., 1992; Halpern, 1992; Klerman, 1991).

Interestingly, the infant mortality rate for Hispanic women is lower than that of European American women (NCHS, 1990), even though inadequate prenatal care is prominent among Hispanic women. This fact suggests that differences in prenatal care explain only part of the disparity in infant mortality rates. The mother's diet and social support network have been suggested as other factors that may affect infant mortality rates (NCHS, 1990). Comparing data on Hispanic women and women of other racial/ethnic groups, Rogers (1989) found lower rates of alcohol and tobacco use among Hispanic women and the presence of stronger family, cultural, and social ties. These findings suggest that social support may offset the consequences of inadequate prenatal care.

*How might the support of small groups be used to lower prenatal risks among non-Hispanic women?*

## Ineffective Discipline

In his guidebook for parenting, Moyer (1974, p. 40) declares, "Under no circumstances should you ever punish your child!!" Moyer's argument is that punishment is completely different from discipline. Punishment implies an attempt to get even with the child, whereas **discipline** involves helping the child overcome a problem.

Parents often struggle with how forceful to be in response to undesired behavior. Because parents are not formally trained in parenting skills in the United States, the type of discipline they use, and under what circumstances, is often molded by how they were disciplined as children and by cultural and societal norms. However, research suggests that parenting styles are not permanent (Hemenway, Solnick, & Carter, 1994). Even those adults who experienced the most punitive type of correction as children were able to escape the "transgenerational cycle" of punitive child-rearing practices.

Extensive research by Baumrind (1971) led her to propose three parenting styles: authoritarian, authoritative, and permissive (see Exhibit 4.8). The **authoritative parenting** style is considered the most desirable approach to discipline and behavior management. Baumrind sug-

| Parenting Style | Description | Type of Discipline |
|---|---|---|
| Authoritarian | Parents who use this type of parenting are rigid and controlling. Rules are narrow and specific, with little room for negotiation, and children are expected to follow the rules without explanation. | Cold and harsh. Physical force. No explanation of rules provided. |
| Authoritative | These parents are more flexible than authoritarian parents. Their rules are more reasonable, and they leave opportunities for compromise and negotiation. | Warm and nurturing. Positive reinforcement. Set firm limits and provide rationale behind rules and decisions. |
| Permissive | The parents' rules are unclear, and children are left to make their own decisions. | Warm and friendly toward their children. No direction given. |

*Source:* Adapted from Baumrind, 1971.

gests that children reared from the authoritative perspective are energetic, competent, and more socially adept than others. Children reared from the **permissive parenting** orientation are said to be cheerful but demonstrate little if any impulse control. In addition, these children are overly dependent and have low levels of self-reliance. Children reared under an **authoritarian parenting** style become hostile and moody and have difficulty managing stress. Others argue that discipline that is punitive in nature, especially spanking, is associated with increased levels of aggression in children (Carey, 1994; Welsh, 1985).

Some parenting styles are prescribed by the community and the culture. For example, West Indian and Puerto Rican communities typically use physical punishment as a discipline technique (Canino & Spurlock, 1994).

Also, some differences in parenting styles are a product of the socioeconomic environment in which they occur. Low-income parents are often more authoritarian than other parents, exercising rigid, controlling techniques (Maccoby, 1980). This practice, however, may seem more legitimate in context. Parents usually respond with discipline to three types of situations: physical danger, their children's expression of psychobiological drives such as sex and aggression, and their children's socializing inside and outside of the family (Epstein, Bishop, Ruan, Miller, & Keitner, 1993). Logically, dangerous situations require more rigid and uncompromising forms of discipline. A middle-income mother who professes to be radically opposed to physical punishment may admit that she spanked her child once for running out of a store into a busy parking lot. Low-income parents are likely to be confronted with many dangerous situations involving their children. In neighborhoods where violence is a part of everyday life, as it is in the neighborhood where Demarcus lives, rules become a matter of protection, and adherence to the rules is a survival tactic. Physical punishment for disobeying the rules is not necessarily the best or only solution. But for many low-income parents, harsh punishment may be less an issue of control or "bad parenting" than an effort to cope with a desperate situation.

## Divorce

The divorce rate has quadrupled over the past 20 years, and 14 million children are now being raised by one parent, usually the mother (McWhirter et al., 1993). These single-parent families often live in poverty, and as you have already seen, poverty often has a negative effect on children's development.

What signs might indicate that the dimension of family is harming a child of divorce?

Regardless of family income level, many children suffer when their parents divorce. It has been suggested, however, that the negative effects children experience may actually be the result of parents' responses to divorce rather than of the divorce itself (Brown, Eichenberger, Portes, & Christensen, 1991). In fact, parental coping and adjustment may be solely responsible for the negative adjustment of children after a divorce (Kurtz, 1995).

One significant parental issue is the relationship that the parents maintain during and after the divorce. With minimal conflict between the parents about custody, visitation, and child-rearing issues, and with parents' positive attitude toward each other, children experience fewer negative consequences (Wallerstein & Kelly, 1980). Unfortunately, many children become wedged in the middle of a war, trying to avoid or defuse raging anger and disagreement between the two parents.

Many divorced parents also have difficulty maintaining effective levels of parenting. Consequently, children often experience inconsistent discipline and a decrease in attention and nurturing. For example, divorced mothers of toddlers provide less stimulation and support to their children, a consequence of the mothers' dissatisfaction with and concern about their own lives (Poehlmann & Fiese, 1994). This lack of stimulation and support has a negative effect on the toddlers' cognitive development.

Preschool children are more vulnerable than older children to emotional and psychological consequences during separation and divorce (Wallerstein, Corbin, & Lewis, 1988; Wallerstein & Blakeslee, 1989; Wallerstein & Corbin, 1991). One reason may be that preschool children have difficulty understanding divorce and often believe that the absent parent is no longer a member of the family and will never be seen again. In addition, because of preschool children's egocentrism, they often feel that the divorce is a result of their behavior and experience the absent parent's leaving as a rejection of them.

The "good news/bad news" is that children's adaptation to divorce is not necessarily permanent. Wallerstein and Blakeslee (1989) found that many children who initially were negatively affected by their parents' divorce were well adjusted when evaluated 10 years later. Conversely, however, many children who initially seemed to adjust well to their parents' divorce were not as well adjusted 10 years later.

To successfully adjust to their parents' divorce, children must accomplish six tasks (Wallerstein, 1983):

1. Come to accept that their parents are divorced and that their access to at least one parent will change.

2. Disengage from their parents' conflict and get on with their own "work" (school, play, friends, and so on).

3. Cope with such losses as moving, losing income, and losing a parent.

4. Acknowledge and resolve their feelings of anger at themselves or at one or both parents.

5. Accept that the divorce is permanent.

6. Realize that just because their parents' marriage failed does not mean they are incapable of healthy relationships with others—in other words, that their parents' divorce does not preclude a successful marriage for them.

Task 6 is the most important, and the child's ability to accomplish it depends on successful resolution of the other five tasks. Obviously, most preschool children are not capable of resolving all these tasks, but they can begin working toward resolution during the preschool years.

## Violence

Many parents complain that keeping violence away from children requires tremendous work even in the best of circumstances. Children witness violence on television and hear about it through many other sources. In the worst of circumstances, young children not only are exposed to violence but become victims of it as well. This section discusses three types of violence experienced by many young children: community violence, domestic violence, and child abuse.

*What other sorts of community environments might negatively affect children?*

***Community Violence.***    In some neighborhoods, like the one where Demarcus lives, acts of violence are so common that the communities are labeled "war zones." However, like Ynecka Green, most residents prefer not to be combatants. When surveyed, mothers in a Chicago housing project ranked neighborhood violence as their number one concern and as the condition that most negatively affects the quality of their life and the lives of their children (Dubrow & Garbarino, 1989). Unfortunately, neighborhood violence has become a major health issue for children (Pennekamp, 1995).

I recently had the opportunity to observe the effects of community violence "up close," when I took my daughter to get her hair braided. A friend had referred me to an acquaintance, who lived in a housing project. Because the hair-braiding procedure takes several hours, my daughter and I were in the home for an extended period. While we were there, the news was released that Tupac Shakur (a popular rap singer) had died from gunshot injuries received earlier. An impromptu gathering of friends and relatives of the woman who was doing the braiding ensued. Ten men and women in their early 20s, along with their young children, gathered to discuss the shooting and to pay tribute to Tupac, who had been one of their favorite artists. As Tupac's music played in the background, I was struck by several themes:

■ Many in the room told of a close relative who had died as a result of neighborhood violence. I noticed on the wall of the apartment three framed programs from funerals of young men. I later learned that these dead men were a brother and two cousins of the woman who lived in the apartment. All three had been killed in separate violent incidents in their neighborhood.

- A sense of hopelessness permeated the conversation. The men especially had little hope of a future, and most thought they would be dead by age 40. Clinicians who work with young children living in neighborhoods in which violence is prevalent relate similar comments from children (National Center for Clinical Infant Programs, 1992). When asked if he had decided what he wanted to be when he grew up, one child is quoted as saying, "Why should I? I might not grow up" (p. 25).

- Perhaps related to the sense of hopelessness was an "embracing" of violence. I observed that during lighter moments in the conversation, the guests would chuckle about physical confrontations between common acquaintances.

Ironically, as my daughter and I were about to leave, gunshots sounded and the evening get-together was temporarily interrupted. Everyone, including the children, ran out of the apartment to see what had happened. For me, the significance of the evening was summarized in one of the last comments I heard before leaving. One of the men stated, "If all that money didn't save Tupac, what chance do we have?"

These sorts of conditions are not favorable for adequate child development (Dubrow & Garbarino, 1989). Investigations into the effects of living in violent neighborhoods support this claim. Children who grow up in a violent environment are reported to demonstrate low self-esteem, deficient social skills, and difficulty coping with and managing conflict (MacLennan, 1994). When my daughter and I visited the housing project, for example, we witnessed a 3-year-old telling her mother to "shut up." The mother and child then began hitting each other. Yes, some of this behavior is a result of parenting style, but one cannot help wondering about the influence of living in a violent community.

For many children living in violent neighborhoods, the death of a close friend or family member is commonplace. My husband, who is also a social worker, was employed at a community child guidance center. He reported that appointments were often canceled so the parents could attend funerals. Freeman, Shaffer, and Smith (1996) studied young children whose older siblings had been victims of homicide. The surviving siblings showed symptoms of depression, anxiety, psychosocial impairment, and post–traumatic stress disorder. These symptoms are similar to those observed in preschool children in situations of political and military violence—for example, in Palestinian children in the occupied West Bank (Baker, 1990) and in children in South African townships (Magwaza, Kilian, Peterson, & Pillay, 1993). Perhaps the label "war zone" is an appropriate one for violent communities. Demarcus is spending his infancy in a "war zone," being parented by a young mother who has lost two siblings to homicide.

***Domestic Violence.***   Domestic violence may take the form of verbal, psychological, or physical abuse, although physical abuse is the form most often implied. It is estimated that more than 3 million children per year witness their mothers being assaulted by their fathers (Silvern & Kaersvang, 1989). The number of children who witness domestic violence is even higher when instances of abuse by stepfathers, boyfriends, and other male liaisons are included.

Preschool children respond in a number of ways during violent episodes (Smith, O'Connor, & Berthelsen, 1996). Some children display fright—that is, they cry and scream. Others attempt to stop the violence by ordering the abuser to stop, by physically placing themselves between the mother and the abuser, or by hitting the abuser. Many children attempt to flee by retreating to a different room, turning up the volume on the TV, or trying to ignore the violence.

The effects of domestic violence on children's development are well documented. Distress, problems with adjustment, characteristics of trauma, and increased behavior problems have all been observed in children exposed to domestic violence (Hughes, 1988; Perloff & Buckner, 1996; Shepard, 1992; Silvern & Kaersvang, 1989). In addition, these children develop either aggressive behaviors or passive responses, both of which make them potential targets for abuse as teens and adults (Suh & Abel, 1990; Tutty & Wagar, 1994).

Preschool children are more vulnerable than older children to the effects of living with domestic violence (O'Keefe, 1994; Smith et al., 1996). Younger children simply have fewer internal resources to help them cope with the experience. In addition, older children have friendships outside the family for support, whereas younger children rely primarily on the family. Many parents who are victims of domestic violence become emotionally unavailable to their young children. Battered mothers, for example, often become depressed and preoccupied with the abuse and their personal safety, leaving little time and energy for the attention and nurturing needed by young children. Another reason that preschool children are more vulnerable to the effects of domestic violence is that children between the ages of 3 and 6 lack the skills to verbalize their feelings and thoughts. As a result, thoughts and feelings about the violence get trapped inside and continually infringe upon the child's thoughts and emotions. Finally, because of their egocentrism, preschool children often blame themselves for the domestic abuse.

Despite these common negative effects, domestic violence does not always affect children's long-term development. In research conducted by Smith et al. (1996), one-third of the children seemed unaffected by the domestic violence they witnessed at home; these children were well adjusted and showed no signs of distress, anxiety, or behavior problems. Two factors have been suggested to buffer the effect that domestic violence has on children (O'Keefe, 1994):

- *Amount of domestic violence witnessed by the child.* The more violent episodes children witness, the more likely they are to develop problematic behavior.

- *Relationship between the child and the mother, assuming the mother is the victim.* If the mother/child relationship remains stable and secure, the probability of the child's developing behavioral difficulties decreases significantly—even when the amount of violence witnessed by the child is relatively high.

Interestingly, O'Keefe (1994) found that the father/child relationship was not related to the effect of domestic abuse on the child's emotional or psychological development. O'Keefe suggests that either the father figure in many of these cases is not the biological father or the mother/child attachment is more significant for younger children.

***Child Abuse.*** A child is abused every two minutes in the United States (McWhirter et al., 1993). Child abuse may take the form of verbal, emotional, physical, or sexual abuse, or child neglect. Taylor was the victim of severe child neglect during the critical first three months of her life. Child abuse creates risks to all aspects of growth and development, as shown Exhibit 4.9.

Veltkamp and Miller (1994) have identified some effects of abuse and neglect that apply particularly to preschool children. Abused or neglected preschoolers are often withdrawn,

**EXHIBIT 4.9**

Some Potential
Effects of Child
Abuse on Growth
and Development

| Physical Impairments | Cognitive Impairments | Emotional Impairments |
| --- | --- | --- |
| *Physical Abuse and Neglect* | | |
| Burns, scars, fractures, broken bones, damage to vital organs and limbs | Delayed cognitive skills | Negative self-concept |
| Malnourishment | Delayed language skills | Increased aggressiveness |
| Physical exposure | Mental retardation | Poor peer relations |
| Poor skin hygiene | Failure-to-thrive syndrome | Poor impulse control |
| Poor (if any) medical care | Delayed reality testing | |
| Poor (if any) dental care | Overall disruption of thought processes | |
| Serious medical problems | | |
| Serious dental problems | | |
| Death | | |
| | | |
| *Sexual Abuse* | | |
| Trauma to mouth, anus, vaginal area | Hyperactivity | Overly adaptive behavior |
| Genital and rectal pain | Bizarre sexual behavior | Overly compliant behavior |
| Genital and rectal bleeding | | Habit disorders (nail biting) |
| Genital and rectal tearing | | Sleep disturbances |
| Sexually transmitted disease | | Night terrors |
| Pregnancy | | Self-mutilation |
| | | |
| *Psychological/Emotional Abuse* | | |
| | Pessimistic view of life | Alienation |
| | Anxiety and fear | Intimacy problems |
| | Distorted perception of world | Low self-esteem |
| | Deficits in moral development | Depression |

*Source:* Adapted from Drisko, 1992. See also Veltkamp & Miller, 1994.

fatigued, immobile, and lacking in age-appropriate curiosity. They are often overly dependent on others and excessively concerned about parental needs, at the expense of their own needs. These preschoolers are also leery of physical contact and are excessively self-controlled.

Although child abuse and neglect occur across gender, ethnic, and socioeconomic divisions, some of these factors present a higher risk than others. Poverty and the lack of economic resources are correlated with abuse, especially physical abuse and neglect. In addition, family isolation and lack of a support system, parental drug and alcohol abuse, lack of knowledge regarding child rearing, and parental difficulty in expressing feelings are all related to child abuse (Gelles, 1989; Veltkamp & Miller, 1994; Wolfner & Gelles, 1993). An association has also been noted between abuse of preschool children and the overload of responsibilities that women often encounter. Mothers who work outside the home and are also responsible for most or all of the domestic responsibilities, and mothers with unemployed husbands, are more prone to abuse their young children than other groups of mothers are (Gelles & Hargreaves, 1981).

There is also a high correlation between domestic violence and child abuse. Results from one study indicated that men who physically abuse their spouses are also more likely to abuse their children (Ross, 1996).

## Social Work Interventions: Promoting Resilience

Many young children experience healthy growth and development despite the presence of risk factors. They are said to have **resilience**. (For more on this concept, see Chapter 5.) Several factors have been identified as mediating between the risks children experience and their growth and development (Kirby & Fraser, 1997; Werner, 1984; Werner & Smith, 1982). Kirby and Fraser (1997) refer to these factors as "protective," in that they shield the child from the consequences of potential hazards. Following are some methods that social workers can use to promote resilience in young children.

*Advocacy for Social Equity.*   For healthy growth and development, infants and young children need the opportunity to explore and play, as well as good nutrition and adequate health care. Poverty is one of the conditions that tends to impede their developmental potential. One traditional mission for the social work profession has been the elimination of poverty through direct services to poor families, political and social action, and the promotion of social and economic justice.

As welfare reform continues, social workers must address the availability, affordability, and quality of services for poor families, guided by the understanding of the effect of poverty on families and children. Social workers can also help by creating neighborhood-based programs that reduce class conflict, counter feelings of alienation, localize control of social institutions, create jobs and reverse neighborhood economic decline, and improve human services (Halpern, 1993).

What sorts of behavior might alert social workers to psychological problems in young children?

*Alleviation of Emotional and Behavioral Problems.*   Providing opportunity for young children also means alleviating, and if possible eliminating, problematic emotional and behavioral symptoms through therapeutic services to young children. The risks to healthy development have increased for children of all socioeconomic levels over the past decade, and the needs of younger children have grown and have become more complex (Schmitz & Hilton, 1996). The result has been an increase in the number of emotional and behavioral problems observed in children 6 and younger. In their review of the literature, Schmitz and Hilton (1996) found that older children and adolescents with behavior disorders first exhibited problems at a very young age.

Children under 6, however, are often excluded from therapeutic services because of their age. Many assume these children are too young to benefit from therapeutic intervention because they lack the verbal skills to participate in a therapeutic process and because the "real" problem is with the parents. Parents have described their futile attempts to solicit therapeutic services for their young children who exhibit emotional and behavioral problems. They are usually turned away with the recommendation that they consider a parenting class. Even when a traumatic event, such as the murder of an older sibling, occurs, younger children are unlikely to receive any type of mental health services (Freeman et al., 1996). In fact, younger children of battered women are often referred to as "the forgotten victims" (Grusznski, Brink, & Edleson, 1988).

Given these findings and the fact that younger children respond more quickly than older ones to treatment, it seems therapeutically and financially wise to target this age group for therapeutic services. The idea of providing services at an earlier age is supported by an evaluation of a child abuse prevention program providing the same type of intervention to children of various ages (Dhooper & Schneider, 1995). The researchers found a correlation between age and therapeutic gain. The younger the child, the more was gained from the intervention experience. Some have also suggested that services must begin with younger children to break the transgenerational cycle of disruptive behavior often associated with such risk factors as poverty and violence (Frey, 1989). Alternative forms of intervention—such as play, drawings, and storybooks, where children act out feelings and problems—have been successful in alleviating symptomatic behavior in younger children (Magwaza et al., 1993; Tutty & Wagar, 1994).

***Risk Prevention.***    Logically, if the occurrence of a risk factor could be prevented, children would have a greater opportunity for healthy development. Prevention occurs through community outreach and education. Examples are community-based prenatal outreach programs, federally funded family planning programs, and groups focused on parenting skills for expectant parents.

One innovative program was a parent education group for parents of preschoolers in a housing project (Dubrow & Garbarino, 1989). The group focused on helping the parents understand the effects of neighborhood violence on young children. Parents were advised about how to recognize signs of distress and when to seek services for their children. A group like this one could be beneficial to Ynecka Green, Demarcus's mother. This type of experience would provide a place for her to express her grief and to gain survival skills. She would then have more freedom to encourage and support Demarcus's development.

Why does community building help children?

***Community Support.***    Social workers can facilitate informal helping and mutual aid at the community level. The challenge is to create more comprehensive programs and to develop better collaboration among existing services. One suggestion has been "one-stop shopping" (National Commission to Prevent Infant Mortality, 1992), which involves shortening application forms, creating one application form for multiple services, expediting eligibility, maintaining the case manager model, and creating interagency partnerships. One attempt at providing more comprehensive services for children was a day-care program set up for children, ages newborn to 5, of migrant workers (Achata, 1993). In addition to regular day-care services, the program provided extended meal service and immunizations, thus increasing the number of children with up-to-date vaccinations.

***Day Care Advocacy.***    A large percentage of women with children under 6 work full-time outside the home. The question of whether or not their children should attend day care is futile; large numbers of them do. The primary focus has to be on the quality of day care, with particular emphasis on training for child-care providers. These adults must be trained to provide the care and support that preschool children require. One analysis of the social work literature suggests that social work as a profession is not involved enough in child-care systems on either a local or national level (Frankel, 1991). Social workers could provide more services at day-care sites and advocate for more affordable, quality day-care services.

***Promotion of Effective Parenting.***    At one level, promoting effective parenting means helping to eliminate such risk factors to healthy development as poverty and domestic abuse. But social workers can often help a great deal at the individual level by promoting positive parent/child relationships. This approach fits well with the social work concept of the person in the environment: The parent is the most important component of young children's environments. Social workers must continue to provide services to parents from this perspective, which often means helping parents diminish their own level of stress in order to meet the needs of their children. In addition, helping parents work toward fulfillment of their own needs will help them be more effective parents. Social workers must also understand the significance of both mothers and fathers in the development of children.

Jessica, Alexia, and Steven Jr.'s story is a classic example. Like many parents, Melanie Schmidt has played the dutiful mother role at the expense of her own needs. Giving Melanie the opportunity to articulate her ambivalence, promoting a more realistic understanding of her children's needs, and enabling her to explore options will empower her to make a decision responsive to her needs and the needs of her children. At the same time, Steven Schmidt could be encouraged to consider a career move that would give him more time with the family.

***Promotion of Self-Efficacy and Self-Esteem.***    Social workers can promote the healthy development of young children by helping create opportunities for them to increase self-efficacy and self-esteem. For example, groups in which young children learn and demonstrate problem-solving and safety skills have been effective in helping them anticipate potential violence and practice potential responses (Grusznski et al., 1988; Tutty & Wagar, 1994). Such groups help children gain more feelings of control.

The common threads in all these interventions are opportunity and resilience. Young children need the opportunity for growth, health, and achievement. But we need to recognize that a large percentage of young children today face risks to healthy development. As social workers, we must be prepared to help them develop the resilience they need to overcome those risks.

## IMPLICATIONS FOR SOCIAL WORK PRACTICE

In summary, social work practice with young children has several implications:

- Become well acquainted with theories and empirical research about growth and development among young children.

- Continue to promote the elimination of poverty and the advancement of social justice.
- Collaborate with other professionals in the creation of laws, interventions, and programs that assist in the elimination of violence.
- Create and support easy access to services for young children and their parents.
- Advocate for more affordable, quality day care.
- Assess younger children in the context of their environment.
- Become familiar with the physical and emotional signs of child abuse.
- Directly engage younger children in an age-appropriate intervention process.
- Provide support to parents and help facilitate positive parent/child relationships.
- Encourage and engage both mothers and fathers in the intervention process.
- Provide opportunities for children to increase self-efficacy and self-esteem.
- Help parents understand the potential effects of negative environmental factors on their children.

## MAIN POINTS

1. Healthy development is in many ways defined by the environment and culture in which the child is raised. In addition, although growth and development in young children have some predictability and logic, the timing and expression of many developmental skills vary from child to child.

2. Physical growth, reflexes, and motor development are all relevant aspects of physical development in young children.

3. According to Piaget, as infants mature, they become capable of increased and more complex cognitive abilities. Infants begin in the sensorimotor stage of development—responding to what they hear, see, taste, touch, smell, and feel—and progress to the preoperational period as preschoolers become capable of cognitive recall and symbolic functioning.

4. Some suggest that language is learned; others suggest language is a result of genetic processes. Research indicates that language is a result of both genetics and environmental factors.

5. Erikson describes three stages of psychosocial development relevant to early childhood, each with its own central task: trust versus mistrust (birth to age $1^1/_2$); autonomy versus shame and doubt ($1^1/_2$ to 3 years); and initiative versus guilt (ages 3 to 6).

6. Emotional development proceeds more smoothly if the temperament of the child and the temperament of the parents are a good fit.

7. Levels of infant/mother attachment are most often measured by the strange situation procedure, developed by Ainsworth and her colleagues. They identified four types of attachment: secure attachment, anxious attachment, avoidant attachment, and disorganized attachment. One hotly debated issue has been the effect of day care on mother/child attachment. The quality of day care is more important than the simple fact that it is used. Some scholars question the use of the strange situation procedure with children who have been in day care and with some ethnic groups.

8. Regardless of country of residence or culture, all preschool children engage in spontaneous play.

9. In younger children, physical and cognitive developmental delays and emotional and psychological problems are often misdiagnosed.

10. Researchers have found that children who live in poor economic conditions are at high risk for low self-esteem, school failure, peer conflict, and childhood clinical disorders. In addition to prenatal care, diet and social support are thought to influence infant mortality rates in the United States.

11. Three types of parenting styles have been described: authoritarian, authoritative, and permissive. Parenting styles are prescribed to some extent by the community and culture in which the parent resides. However, authoritarian and permissive styles often lead to emotional and behavioral problems.

12. Preschool children are more vulnerable to the emotional and psychological consequences of divorce than older children, because of the preschool child's limited ability to understand the concept of divorce.

13. Mothers living in a housing project ranked neighborhood violence as the number one condition that most negatively affects the quality of their children's lives. Young children exposed to community violence often demonstrate low self-esteem, have deficient social skills, and have difficulty coping with and managing conflict.

14. Distress, problems with adjustment, characteristics of trauma, and increased behavior problems have all been observed in children exposed to domestic violence.

15. Abused and neglected preschoolers are often withdrawn, fatigued, immobile, and lacking in age-appropriate curiosity.

16. Many professionals assume that children age 6 and under are too young to benefit from mental health services. However, children under 6 can benefit from age-appropriate mental health interventions.

17. Social workers can help young children by promoting opportunities for growth and development, providing social support, and encouraging the presence of a supportive adult, positive parent/child relationships, and child self-efficacy and self-esteem.

## KEY TERMS

attachment
authoritarian parenting
authoritative parenting
cognition
concrete operations stage
deferred imitation
developmental delay
discipline
egocentrism
formal operations stage
infant mortality

motor skills
object permanence
permissive parenting
preoperational stage
reflex
resilience
sensorimotor stage
symbolic functioning
temperament
transductive reasoning

## WORLD WIDE WEB RESOURCES

Jean Piaget
**http://snycorva.cortland.edu/~ANDERSMD/piaget/PIAGET.HTML**
Site maintained by the State University of New York–Cortland. Contains the history of Piaget, stages of development, experiments, discussions, intelligence, and a reference section.

Erik Erikson's Eight Stages
**http://syncorva.cortland.edu/~ANDERSMD/ERIK/welcome.HTML**
Site maintained by the State University of New York–Cortland. Contains the eight stages of psychosocial development, a summary of stages, biography, critiques and controversies, references, and links to other pertinent Internet sites.

National Center for Children in Poverty (NCCP)
**http://cpmcnet.columbia.edu/dept/nccp/**
The NCCP is part of Columbia University's Columbia-Presbyterian Medical Center. The NCCP's mission is to "identify and promote strategies that reduce the incidence of young child poverty in the United States." Contains news releases, facts, state and local information, information on child care and welfare reform, and a research forum.

Divorce & Your Children
**http://parent.net/resources/divorce.html**
Site written and maintained by Ken Giddens, part of Parent News. Contains links to various Internet sites concerning divorce and its impact on children.

# CHAPTER 5

# Middle Childhood

*Leanne Wood Charlesworth, University of Maryland,*
*and Pamela Viggiani, Rochester Institute of Technology*

### MALIK'S HIGH SPIRITS

Malik is a 12-year-old African American boy living in an impoverished central city. A student in the sixth grade at a private Catholic school (St. Joseph's Academy), Malik is an enthusiastic participant in extracurricular activities. Although Malik's teachers generally view him as a good student, he is at times disruptive in the classroom and has had several run-ins with the school disciplinarians over fights with peers. Most of these incidents have been minor, but on a few occasions Malik's mother, Shirley, has had to visit the school for conferences with the principal. St. Joseph's principal responds quickly to incidents between students because he worries that, in his school's violence-ridden community, even small conflicts could quickly escalate.

Shirley tells you that she considers herself a strict mother. Malik has always been a "handful," in need of clear rules and structure. In fact, Shirley decided to enroll Malik in St. Joseph's because she felt the teachers in the public school did not demand his respect. The extra cost of the private school has been a significant burden on the family's finances, but she fears that without strict discipline in the school environment, Malik's disruptive tendencies may turn into a serious behavior problem. Even though Malik has had his share of trouble at St. Joseph's, Shirley is satisfied with the school and its approach to discipline.

Lately, Shirley says, she feels she never has a moment to spend alone with Malik. Malik's extracurricular activities, especially sports, occupy every weekday evening. However, Malik is proud of his accomplishments and physical talents, so Shirley tries to be supportive. On the weekends, he is typically at a friend's house or visiting his father, who lives about 30 miles away. Malik seems to thrive on the busy lifestyle, but Shirley worries that he devotes too little time to the family and schoolwork. At times, she also worries that he does not have enough adult African American role models. Many of the teachers at St. Joseph's are European American, but most of Malik's friends are African American.

Ron, Malik's stepfather, seems content with Malik's busy social life. When Malik was younger and Ron and Shirley's marriage was relatively new, Ron says he resented the time Shirley spent with Malik. Ron felt that Shirley put Malik's needs before his own and often failed to consult him on important decisions. He was particularly upset when Shirley made the decision to transfer Malik to St. Joseph's without consulting him. Ron thought Malik viewed the transfer to St. Joseph's as a reward when, in Ron's view, Malik needed punishment instead of praise.

### RHODA'S LACK OF SELF-ESTEEM

Rhoda, a 10-year-old fourth grade student, attends a rural elementary school. Rhoda lives with her grandmother in a one-bedroom apartment on a country road half a mile away from the small town where her school is located. Rhoda doesn't know her mother or father because they died in a car accident when she was an infant.

Rhoda, who is about five feet tall and weighs approximately 160 pounds, is very sensitive about her weight and tries to hide her body under baggy sweaters and her winter coat. Rhoda's grandmother, Elaine, has difficulty getting Rhoda to shower on a regular basis. Rather than arguing, Elaine allows Rhoda to skip showering most nights. As a result, Rhoda's hair is rather greasy, her fingernails often have dirt under them, and she has strong body odor. Elaine insists that Rhoda shower when she notices that Rhoda smells bad, but Rhoda recently commented that she'd prefer not to shower at all.

Elaine is a loving caregiver, but she readily admits that she has a hard time asserting authority over Rhoda. She and Rhoda struggle over school attendance. Often when Elaine wakes her in the morning, Rhoda complains of a headache; Elaine usually lets her stay home. Some days, Rhoda leaves the apartment for school on time but does not actually make it to school. She wanders around the small town and often finds herself playing video games in the town pizza shop for hours. By the time she notices how much time has passed, it seems too late to go to school, so she doesn't go at all. When Rhoda does make it to school, she frequently calls her grandmother and asks to come home because she doesn't feel well. On these occasions, Elaine often feels sympathetic and calls on a friend who has a car to pick Rhoda up from school.

Rhoda is open about her dislike of school, telling you bluntly that she hates her teacher because the teacher picks on her when she tries to answer questions and can't get them right. Rhoda also says that she hates all of her classmates. She says they are mean, they call her names, and they refuse to sit by her in class. Things are especially bad in gym class. Rhoda despises Ms. Phyniss, the gym teacher. Rhoda has been placed on detention for the past several weeks because she refuses to change for gym. Recently, Ms. Phyniss sent a note home to Elaine explaining that Rhoda will fail gym for the year if she continues to refuse to change for class. Rhoda cannot afford to fail gym since she is also failing math and English.

When you ask Rhoda about any positive feelings toward school, she shrugs her shoulders at first. Finally, after a long pause, she reports "loving" the school nurse, Ms. Joy. Ms. Joy always greets Rhoda with a smile when she comes to the nurse's office and listens to Rhoda when she talks about her various ailments. Rhoda visits the nurse almost every day she is at school. Rhoda also eventually mentions that she likes another fourth grader, Jane, who is often in the nurse's office when Rhoda comes to visit. Jane is a very shy, timid fourth grader. She likes to talk with Rhoda about video games and favorite television shows when they are both in the nurse's office.

In general, Rhoda seems to be a very isolated, often unhappy fourth grader with few friends. She is not doing well academically and does not like the way she looks. She doesn't have many hobbies, but she does like watching television, playing video games, and eating ice cream. When you talk with her, she tells you that she is not treated fairly at school, and she insists that everyone at school hates her. Rhoda adds that she "hates them back." But once Rhoda admitted to you that she sometimes wishes she could make a few more friends and that she would like to do a little better in school.

### JUAN'S UNSETTLED LIFE

This year has been full of change for Juan, a 7-year-old with large brown eyes. Juan is in first grade at Williamson Elementary School and has two younger half siblings of whom he speaks fondly. Juan's mother and father had a brief relationship and never married. Until recently, Juan lived with his mother, Silvia, and his two siblings in a small apartment near his school, which is located in an economically impoverished section of a medium-sized city. Although many think of the neighborhood as "rough," Juan speaks of his home in a warm and protective tone.

Throughout most of his life, Juan has had little contact with his father, Carlos, visiting him only occasionally on weekends. Juan and both of his parents are bilingual, but Juan knows little about his Mexican roots. Even though Silvia is more comfortable speaking Spanish, she has never wanted her children to feel "different." As a result, she has always told Juan that he is an "American" and that he should tell people he is an American when asked about his background. Carlos and Silvia have had several arguments about this issue. Carlos, who is very proud of his Mexican heritage, would like Juan to feel equally proud of his country and family. During his occasional weekends with Juan, Carlos has always enjoyed telling stories about their extended family and his childhood in rural Mexico.

A few weeks ago, Juan and his siblings were removed from Silvia by child protective services after she was arrested late one Saturday night outside a bar for assault and disorderly conduct. The details of the case are unclear, but Juan tells you a police officer came to the home and woke him and his siblings. Juan cannot describe anything else about the night very clearly except that it was after this night that he began to live with Carlos. Juan is aware of tension between his parents, and he knows that they have been going to court lately. When you ask Juan about his living situation or about either of his parents, he usually grows quiet and avoids eye contact.

Since moving in with Carlos, Juan has continued to attend Williamson Elementary. Carlos and his current girlfriend, Melissa, drop Juan off at school each morning on their way to work. After-school arrangements have been difficult. Carlos has attempted to enroll Juan in after-school activities, but they are available only one day per week. Sometimes, Carlos brings Juan to work with him; on occasion, he drives Juan to a baby-sitter's house in Carlos and Melissa's neighborhood and then returns to work.

Juan's teacher, Mrs. Lawrence, has observed Juan's situation with concern. Mrs. Lawrence is an enthusiastic teacher who cares about her students and often worries about the numerous stressors they face. She has taken a particular interest in Juan because this is his second time in first grade. Despite her best efforts, Juan seems to make little progress with reading and basic math, and she fears the possibility of another grade retention. Although he is often quiet and at times appears withdrawn, he is a pleasant child, and most of his classmates are fond of him. Mrs. Lawrence tells you that, throughout the early part of the school year, Juan frequently seemed exhausted during the day and often used to talk about baby-sitting for his younger siblings.

Since gaining temporary custody of Juan, Carlos has had several conferences with Mrs. Lawrence and has requested updates on Juan's school progress. Although Carlos and Melissa believe that Juan's skills are improving, Mrs. Lawrence has just told Carlos that she is considering referring Juan for a learning disability screening. In the meantime, it appears that Juan may return to his mother's custody. Juan expresses no strong preference for either his mother or his father but frequently mentions that he misses his younger siblings. In addition, Silvia has told you and everyone else involved with the case that Carlos never showed any interest in Juan before now and that his current concern will fade once he realizes the work involved in being a father. She also says that Carlos has a history of substance abuse problems.

# Cognitive, Moral, and Spiritual Development in Middle Childhood

Middle childhood, traditionally perceived as a relatively uneventful phase of development, is increasingly recognized as an exciting and challenging time in every child's life. However, the age range classified as middle childhood is subject to debate—encompassing ages 5 to 11 for some (Sroufe, Cooper, & DeHart, 1996), 6 to 12 for others (Green, 1994)—and it is increasingly encroached upon by adolescence. Images of middle childhood usually include children like Malik, healthy and curious, making new friends and learning new things. But middle childhood is filled with both opportunities and challenges. For some children, like Juan and Rhoda, it is a period of particular vulnerability.

When Juan, Malik, and Rhoda first entered school, their readiness to confront the challenges and opportunities that school presents was shaped by prior experiences. Malik, for example, seems to have entered school prepared for and excited about the various experiences associated with kindergarten. For Malik, as for most children, the acquisition of cognitive abilities that occurs early in middle childhood has allowed him to communicate thoughts with increasing complexity. As cognitive skills develop, the ability to understand people and situations in the surrounding environment matures (Green, 1994).

Several developmental theorists, including those listed in Exhibit 5.1, have described the developments and tasks associated with middle childhood. According to these theorists, reasoning

**EXHIBIT 5.1**

Phases and Tasks of Middle Childhood

| Theorist | Phase or Task | Description |
|---|---|---|
| Freud (1938/1973) | Latency | Sexual instincts become less dominant; superego develops further. |
| Erikson (1950) | Industry versus inferiority | Capacity to cooperate develops; result is sense of either mastery or incompetence. |
| Piaget (1936/1952) | Concrete operational | Reasoning becomes more logical but remains at concrete level; principle of conservation is learned. |
| Piaget (1932/1965) | Moral realism and autonomous morality | Conception of morality changes from absolute and external to relative and internal. |
| Kohlberg (1969) | Preconventional and conventional morality | Reasoning based on punishment and reward is replaced by reasoning based on formal law and external opinion. |
| Selman (1976) | Self-reflective perspective taking | Ability develops to view own actions, thoughts, and emotions from another's perspective. |

in middle childhood becomes more logical, the child's sense of morality expands and develops into a more internally based system, and the ability to understand the perspectives of others emerges.

Perhaps the most central developmental task of this period is the acquisition of feelings of **self-competence**. The child strives to recognize and value personal accomplishments and achievements. The experiences of middle childhood foster or thwart the child's attempts to acquire an enhanced sense of **mastery** and self-efficacy. Family and community support further enhances the child's growing sense of competence; lack of such support undermines this sense. The child's definitions of accomplishment vary greatly according to interpretations in the surrounding environment.

As Malik, Rhoda, and Juan move through middle childhood, they gain an increasing awareness of how they fit into the network of relationships in their surrounding environment. This growing awareness surfaces in the questions they ask about those affecting their lives (Green, 1994). Simultaneously, family and peers have a significant impact on children's development during this period.

Children experience this phase of life differently based on their personality differences and differences in the surrounding environment, such as family structure, socioeconomic status, and culture. In each social setting, a particular child's personality and learning style may be valued or devalued, problematic or nonproblematic (Green, 1994). Thus Rhoda, Juan, and Malik, although they are moving through the same developmental period and facing many common tasks, will experience these tasks differently and will emerge into adolescence as unique individuals.

As the three children increasingly view their lives as part of the network of lives within their environment, communities have the potential to provide important support and structure. Today, however, many communities provide as many challenges as opportunities for development. Garbarino (1995) has labeled communities in which challenges outweigh opportunities as "socially toxic," by which he means that "the social world of children, the social context in which they grow up, has become poisonous to their development" (p. 4). In contrast, within a socially supportive environment, children have access to peers and adults who can lead them toward more developed thinking. This development occurs in part through the modeling of **prosocial behavior**, which injects moral reasoning and social sensitivity into the child's traditional manner of reasoning and behaving. Thus, cognitive and moral development is a social issue. The failure of adults to take on moral and spiritual mentoring roles contributes significantly to the development of socially toxic environments.

This concept is not unique to Garbarino. Vygotsky (1986) refers to this type of moral mentoring as taking place in the **zone of proximal development**—the theoretical space between the child's current developmental level and the child's potential level if given access to appropriate models and developmental experiences in the social environment. Thus, children do not develop in isolation. Instead, the child's competence alone interacts dynamically with the child's competence in the company of others. The result is developmental progress.

The link between actions and mastery, competence and self-esteem, is strengthened when the child's struggles and accomplishments are recognized. Thus, Shirley's pride in Malik is essential to his growing sense of self-esteem, and Rhoda's inability to establish areas in which she can demonstrate mastery threatens her developing sense of self.

How can social workers improve the environmental dimension of community for children?

# Formal Schooling

How does formal
schooling shape
behavior?

During middle childhood, school becomes the primary context for complex developmental challenges and opportunities. The current importance of formal schooling in middle childhood cannot be overstated. Children entering school must learn to navigate a new environment quite different from the family. In school, they are evaluated on the basis of how well they perform tasks; people outside the family—teachers and peers—begin shaping the child's personality, dreams, and aspirations (Zastrow & Kirst-Ashman, 1997). At the same time, the school environment may serve as an important resource for middle childhood cognitive, emotional, and physical tasks. Schools offer a great deal of academic and social knowledge, through both teachers and peers (Kail & Cavanaugh, 1996).

Success in the school environment, then, is very important to the development of self-esteem. Malik, for instance, finds his school activities generally rewarding. Students like Juan, however, face considerable challenges in the school setting. Juan is not meeting the cognitive challenges that school demands of him. His inability to read or do basic math frustrates both Juan and his teacher and places him at risk of grade retention. Juan's lack of progress thus threatens the development of positive self-regard and the achievement of cognitive tasks. Fortunately, if Juan's parents and teachers take action, they may help him overcome his developmental challenges.

Rhoda, like Juan, is challenged by school. Her inability to fit in with her peers compounds her academic difficulty. Rhoda's school experience is so threatening and unpleasant that she has begun to withdraw from the process, but her withdrawal represents a serious threat to her continued cognitive, emotional, and social development. Attention to Rhoda's social concerns may help prevent her complete withdrawal from school while providing her with the supports needed to gain crucial skills.

## *History and Current Trends in Schooling*

Today, the role of school in the life of a child like Rhoda is not disputed. Although all parents now expect the school to play a fundamental role in the development of their children, they have not always felt this way. Our current conception of formal schooling—that is, public education—is only about 150 years old. It was conceived of by a new country eager to educate its citizens to participate fully in a democratic society (Constable, 1996).

Mirroring political ideals of the new United States, public education in the 19th century was intended to be an equalizer, enabling individuals from a variety of economic backgrounds to become righteous and economically successful citizens. Public schools were to be free and open to all. Instead, however, they reflected traditional public ambiguity toward poverty and diversity, and they embodied particular value systems and excluded certain groups. For instance, the first schools were "primarily agrarian . . . Protestant-Republican, and thus virtually guaranteed the exclusion of certain ethnic and religious groups" (Allen-Meares, Washington, & Walsh, 1996, p. 57). The first public schools were, in effect, open to European American males only, and throughout their history, public schools have often either excluded or marginalized members of nondominant groups.

Over time, however, the public schools gradually reflected changes occurring in other public institutions. They began to accept females, immigrants, African Americans, and other historically excluded groups. In most parts of the country, however, members of these groups did not receive equal treatment, and they were forced to attend segregated and inferior schools throughout most of the 20th century. However, various court rulings, most prominently the 1954 *Brown v. Board of Education* decision (347 U.S. 483), made equal, integrated education the right of all American citizens. Throughout the past few decades, the courts have continued to assert democratic ideology and have opposed school segregation (Constable, 1996).

What can social workers do to help disadvantaged children overcome inequitable social institutions?

Despite these court rulings and democratic ideals, public schooling continues to mirror the social systems with which it interacts, and thus often falls short. In particular, racial and ethnic minorities and poor children still suffer in inferior schools that frequently do not provide enough books, supplies, or teachers, or curricula challenging enough to facilitate success in American society (Kozol, 1991). The juxtaposition of inner-city and suburban schools points to increasing division between the "haves" and the "have-nots."

Schools in economically impoverished areas simultaneously suffer from a lack of funding and an increasing number of educational challenges as the needs of their students grow more and more complex. Students in late-20th-century America have overwhelming psychosocial needs, which schools are asked to address. Social ills such as poverty, changing family structures (dual-income and single-parent families) that decrease parents' involvement, lack of access to health and social services, and lack of high-quality, appropriate day care have forced schools to broaden their array of health and social services. Today, schools give increasing attention to the diverse needs that their students present, striving toward the provision of holistic services to all students (Dryfoos, 1994).

## *Physical and Symbolic Organization of the School*

The structure of American schools plays an important role in shaping the experience of the children who attend them. Physical layout and functional systems create and maintain a symbolic structure for administrators, teachers, students, and families. The school's combined symbolic and physical structures both reflect and help maintain the hierarchal nature of public education as well as the status quo within the larger society.

What is the message children might absorb from the physical layout of schools?

***Physical Structure.*** Most American school buildings follow the same general physical layout. Administrators have a suite of private offices with a common reception area and a secretary. These offices are walled off and often located in a wing separate from classrooms. Classrooms in schools are designed for one teacher and approximately 25 to 30 students. They often contain desks that face the front of the room, thereby facilitating a lecture model of teaching (Swap, 1993). The front of the classroom has a chalkboard on which assignments are written and rules posted. The school day is structured into 40- to 50-minute periods, announced by the ringing of bells. With the exception of schools with extended day programs, the school day begins between 7:00 and 9:00 in the morning and rarely ends later than 3:00 in the afternoon.

The rigid physical structure of American schools is thought to contribute to the learning of essential academic course material (Oakes & Lipton, 1990). Yet research suggests that the academic progress of many students is not well served by a rigid school structure. For example, sitting at desks and learning through the lecture format is not an appropriate way for most children to learn (Roueche & Baker, 1986).

Controversy over the structure most conducive to learning has prompted the development of a variety of alternative, model, and demonstration schools. These schools offer a variety of classroom settings, feature open floor plans, and provide a flexible approach to teaching and learning (Barr & Parrett, 1995). Although the traditional school structure prevails, interest is growing in the development of innovative structures and systems that are as attentive to developmental needs and as supportive of learning as possible.

*Symbolic Structure.*    Upon entering a school, children—and their parents—may find the physical layout confusing and intimidating. Authoritarian communication systems and closed classrooms may act as a hindrance to open communication. The physical setting may act as a subtle barrier that prohibits meaningful dialogue between students and teachers, teachers and administrators, and parents and school personnel. Moreover, the school's structure typically delineates its members' roles. The most striking physical illustration of such delineation is the position of teacher at the head of the classroom and students in small desks facing him or her. This physical organization of the classroom reinforces the passive learner role (Swap, 1993).

When parents, teachers, or students attempt to create new roles within traditional school systems, they often do not receive an encouraging response. Parents who come into school and request atypical services for their children are often quickly labeled "a problem" by school personnel. Personnel may then ignore the parents' requests or refuse to see them. In the school system's perspective, these parents have failed to adhere to their traditional role as supporter of the school's decisions for their child. Parents who wish to participate in their child's education are encouraged to do so in prescribed ways, such as helping with homework and attending parent-teacher meetings.

Thus, the traditional school system often fails to accommodate students like Rhoda, who have special concerns. At this point in her childhood, for example, Rhoda might benefit from an alternative to the traditional gym class. Rhoda's current gym class, rather than facilitating her social and physical development, instead highlights her weight and social insecurities. Adults and a physical education system that address Rhoda's insecurities while empowering her to work toward a healthy weight would support, rather than thwart, healthy development.

Another problematic aspect of the American public educational structure is "the practice of dividing students into instructional groups on the criterion of assumed similarity in ability or attainment" (Oakes, 1985, p. ix). This practice, frequently referred to as **tracking**, divides students into college-bound and non-college-bound classes, accelerated and nonaccelerated classes, and regular and special education classes. This division of students into groups based on perceived or demonstrated ability may ease teaching challenges and benefit accelerated students, but it disadvantages students with special needs.

In addition, division of students is most often based on standardized tests, which research suggests may be culturally and class biased. Students may also be divided based on school personnel reports. Such reports are often subjective and may inadvertently be based on assessments of students' dress, language, and behavior (Oakes, 1985; Oakes & Lipton, 1992). Throughout the history of public schooling, most counselors and teachers have belonged to dominant groups, and consciously or unconsciously, they may have awarded privilege and preference to learning styles, language, and dress that they find familiar.

In short, tracking has traditionally served as a two-tiered system of inequality. Special education, non-college-bound, and nonaccelerated classes have been disproportionately populated by minority and poor students. These classes too often prepare students to work only in low-skilled, low-paying jobs. Conversely, regular education, college bound, and accelerated classes have been disproportionately white and middle-class. These classes typically prepare their members for college and leadership roles. Thus, the traditional structure of public education has often both reflected and supported ethnic and class divisions within American society (Oakes, 1985; Oakes & Lipton, 1992; Winters, 1993).

For an example of the dangers of tracking, consider Malik. His behavior puts him at high risk for placement in a special education class for emotionally disturbed children, even though his behavior may be a normal part of his developmental process. Currently, his fairly infrequent aggressive behavior is dealt with by school personnel swiftly, which may prevent an escalation of the problem. However, because he is African American and living in a poor, inner-city neighborhood, the professionals making decisions at his school and in his community may begin to interpret his behavior as serious and threatening. Thus, Malik faces an increased risk of placement outside of the "regular" track. However, his generally prosocial personality and his mother's attentiveness may provide the buffers necessary to avoid such placement.

## *Formal Schooling and Cognitive Development*

Public education plays a major role in the cognitive development of American children, if only because children attend school throughout the formative years of such development. In Piaget's (1936/1952) terms, children start school during the second stage (preoperational thought) and finish school when they are completing the fourth and final stage of cognitive development (formal operations). (See Chapter 4 for a discussion of Piaget's stages of cognitive development.) Schoolchildren rapidly develop conceptual thought, the ability to categorize complicated systems of objects, and the ability to solve problems (Allen-Meares, 1995). Schools typically try to ensure that students achieve their potential and acquire the cognitive skills that play an important role in economic and social success within the larger society.

*How does good cognitive development contribute to the overall health of the psychological person?*

Students in middle childhood, however, have individual cognitive styles. As a result, they benefit from diverse educational materials and varied activities that appeal to visual, auditory, and experiential learning styles. Such activities can include group work, student presentations, field trips, audiovisual presentations, written and oral skill activities, discussion, and lectures (Roueche & Baker, 1986).

According to Roueche and Baker (1986), traditional American schooling has four major shortcomings:

1. It does not typically put enough time into schooling students to increase their cognitive functioning.

2. It does not ask the students to think enough.

3. It provides too few substantive courses.

4. It often encourages ineffective teaching methods.

However, many schools are working toward changes in these four areas. Teachers are encouraged to use a variety of teaching methods, and recent federal and state initiatives seek to add substance to classes. And the Roueche and Baker study suggests that many teachers are effective. They encourage active student involvement, give a great deal of feedback to their students, contact students outside of class, and have a flexible teaching approach and student-centered style.

Under what circumstances might a small homogeneous group also benefit young clients?

Studies of **heterogeneous grouping**—the educational practice of grouping students with a variety of different skill levels in the same classroom—show that peer interaction often fosters cognitive development as well (Oakes, 1985; Oakes & Lipton, 1990, 1992). Grouping peers in small heterogeneous groups to complete a variety of activities has resulted in positive gains for both high- and low-achieving students (Oakes, 1985; Viggiani, 1996). Students learn from one another and are highly influenced by their peers. Structured peer group activities thus take advantage of the natural tendency of children to learn from their peers. Juan, who is having a difficult time with many aspects of school, may benefit from working within a small, heterogeneous group of peers. Students with more academic skill may model proper school behavior and effective methods of mastering academic material for Juan. Furthermore, this teaching method may help Juan strengthen peer friendships, an important source of support as he confronts family disruption and conflict.

## Formal Schooling and Physical Development

How might social workers address challenges to the biological person during middle childhood?

Middle childhood marks the beginning of many physical changes, a stage that leads from **prepubescence** (the period prior to commencement of the physiological processes and changes associated with puberty) to **pubescence** (the period during which the child begins to experience diverse and gradual physical processes associated with puberty). Because puberty is a process rather than an event, pubescence can be thought of as the initial stages of the process, with the changes associated with adolescence corresponding to the latter stages of the process. In middle childhood, especially the latter part, boys and girls vary greatly in stature, weight, and sexual development. Although estimates of the age at which puberty commences diverge widely, a recent study found that some girls may begin puberty as early as 8 years of age, with African American girls developing sooner than European American girls by one to two years (Peck, 1997). Because physical development is outwardly visible, it affects the way a child is both viewed and treated by peers and teachers.

Girls and boys who develop early are often treated as if they are older than their peers. Adults often give these children more responsibility, perhaps more than is ideal for their cognitive and emotional developmental stage. Early puberty may also result in higher expectations for mature behavior and understanding of academic material. Some students may thrive on these heightened expectations, but others may feel unable to meet the expectations and thus defeated. Adults who place more responsibility on physically mature students may also neglect or expect less from students who are physically immature. Because physical development is not necessarily consistent with cognitive development, however, adults should focus on children's actual ability level as represented by the successful completion of tasks.

Physical development can also affect children's peer relationships. School-age children constantly compare themselves to others, and physical differences are often the topic of discussion. Whereas late developers may feel inferior about their size or lack of sexual development, early developers may feel awkward and out of place among their peers. Most children worry about being "normal." They want to be sure that they are "on track" in their development. Reassurance by adults that physical development varies among people and that all development is "normal" is therefore crucial.

Girls who develop early are often faced with unwanted sexual attention from both peers and adults. Breast and hip development often bring unwanted harassment and advances. Young girls may not understand their own bodies yet, so unwanted sexual attention is often a cause of great confusion and concern. Counseling on self-protection and individual rights may be beneficial for these girls, and schools committed to the safety of their students must diligently educate staff and students about sexual harassment and sexual abuse.

Physical differences of any sort are often noticed by children. Thus, students who are overweight, underweight, very tall, or very short are often excluded from peer groups and exposed to harassment and name-calling. Students who have physical or developmental disabilities are at particular risk for being singled out by their peers. Teacher leadership aimed at educating children about disability issues and encouraging the support and acceptance of peers with disabilities may help to minimize negative attitudes and incidents (Ware, 1995).

Students with disabilities and others who feel misunderstood by their peers are particularly likely to feel alone, afraid, and isolated in the school setting. Students who are socially excluded by their peers often do not like school and dread going to class. Some students who are teased on a regular basis may simply skip school in order to avoid unpleasant experiences. Teachers, parents, and other school personnel who pay special attention to, and intervene with, students in this situation may prevent the escalation of such problems. Rhoda's case is a good example. The fact that Rhoda is obese is apparent to her classmates and may cause them to tease her. But Rhoda's teacher and grandmother can be instrumental in helping both Rhoda and her peers come to terms with physical difference. Furthermore, considering Rhoda's concerns about her appearance, she may benefit from counseling regarding her weight. Good nutrition and a healthy level of exercise may help to improve Rhoda's appearance and, with it, her self-esteem.

## Formal Schooling and Self-Evaluation

As children move through the middle years, they become increasingly aware that they are evaluated on the basis of what they are able to do. In turn, they begin to evaluate themselves based on treatment by teachers and peers and on self-assessments of what they can and cannot do (Harter, 1988). Rhoda is beginning to develop a negative evaluation of herself because of her peers' reactions to her weight and hygiene. Her negative self-evaluation is further fueled by lack of academic success.

How can social workers help children who can't adjust to schools' formal system of evaluation?

Formal schooling is significant in middle childhood in large part because children typically move from the safety and support of home and day-care environments to the pressures of a system that closely monitors accomplishments. Sensitive to peer and teacher evaluation, children self-evaluate their abilities and competency based on how those in their new environment view them (Barr & Parrett, 1995). Specifically, children evaluate themselves based on their performance in school tasks and on their ability to interact successfully with their peers (Zastrow & Kirst-Ashman, 1997).

Children develop their sense of self-worth through the amount of positive regard they feel from people around them. School-age children consistently rate parents, classmates, friends, and teachers as the most important influences in their lives (Harter, 1988). Thus, children are likely to evaluate themselves in a positive manner if they receive encouraging feedback in both their academic and social environments.

Schools can help children develop a positive self-evaluation by providing a variety of activities that allow children with different strengths to succeed. For example, schools that assess children in many areas, including physical ability, social ability, academic ability, artistic ability, and musical ability, may help children who have a deficit in one area to experience success in another realm. Children can also be encouraged to evaluate themselves positively by school initiatives that promote skill development. For instance, one-on-one tutoring programs, after-school reading programs, and after-school sports programs can build on children's abilities and help them develop or maintain self-confidence (Barr & Parrett, 1995). Conversely, schools can contribute to the development of a negative self-evaluation by judging students based on only one ability or skill, such as academics or physical ability.

## The Effects of Race, Ethnicity, Gender, and Class

Schools are microcosms of the larger American society and mirror its institutional structures. Thus, schools often uphold racism, classism, and sexism (Bowles & Gintis, 1976; Keating, 1994; Ogbu, 1994). Unequal treatment of members of nondominant groups reflects and maintains the status quo both in schools and in the larger society and has an impact on individual development (Bowles & Gintis, 1976; Kozol, 1991). Students belonging to nondominant groups are often viewed as inherently less capable and thus fail to receive the cognitive stimulation needed for optimal growth and development. During all phases of childhood, children benefit from equal treatment and attention.

*How might early discrimination affect later interactions with social institutions?*

**Institutional discrimination**—systemic denial of access to assets, economic opportunities, associations, and organizations based upon minority status—has traditionally occurred in a variety of ways within schools. For example, girls have a history of disadvantage in the school environment (Gilligan, 1982). Textbooks and literature used in schools were rarely authored by women and generally minimized women's perspectives, including little mention of women's contributions to history. Girls have been less likely to receive positive teacher attention and feedback; moreover, girls have traditionally been either excluded or discouraged from pursuing courses or career tracks in mathematics, the sciences, or athletics. Finally, female students, particularly adolescents, have traditionally suffered from unwanted sexual advances by both peers and teachers (Sadker, Sadker, Fox, & Salata, 1994).

Recently, however, many school systems have recognized their historically unequal treatment of students and taken steps to reduce discrimination. One approach is **mainstreaming**, the practice of placing all children who could be assigned to special education classrooms into regular education classrooms (Slee, 1995). Heterogenous grouping, discussed earlier, prevents students of different races, socioeconomic classes, and genders from being separated and

**EXHIBIT 5.2**

Common
Characteristics
of Full-Service
Schools and
School-Linked
and School-Based
Services

- Commitment to providing access to all necessary services for school-age children and their families at the school or some other neighborhood facility.
- Provision of physical and mental health, job development, and child-care services, among others.
- Extensive collaboration among service providers.
- Preventative services focused on community development and family support.
- Commitment to new, flexible, empowering ways for schools and communities to work together.

*Source:* Adapted from Adler, 1993.

treated in an unequal manner. Schools have also begun to include in their curricula academic content that reflects the diversity of their students. More literature and history lessons represent females and minorities who have contributed to American life. Different approaches to teaching academic content are used in hopes of accommodating a variety of learning styles and social backgrounds. Teachers, students, and other school personnel receive training on diversity. And sexual harassment policies have slowly been implemented and enforced in public schools.

Schools located in areas with high rates of poverty have also been targeted for extra attention. **Full-service schools** attempt to provide school-based or school-linked health and social services for schoolchildren and their families (Dryfoos, 1994). Similarly, school-based family resource centers attempt to provide children, families, and communities with needed supports. Exhibit 5.2 outlines several common characteristics of school-based services. The move toward providing more holistic services illustrates public education's continuing effort to meet the ideal of equal and comprehensive education, allowing all Americans the opportunity to achieve economic and social success.

## Home and School

How can social workers help children negotiate the different cultures of home and school?

The link between school and home is important even in affluent neighborhoods, because school and home are the two major spheres in which children exist. The more similar these two environments are, the more successful the child will be at school and at home. Students who experience vastly different cultures at home and in school are likely to have difficulty accommodating the two worlds.

A great deal of learning goes on before a child enters school. By the time Malik, Juan, and Rhoda began school, they had acquired routines and habits and had developed cognitive, social, and physical skills (Kellaghan, Sloane, Alvarez, & Bloom, 1993). School is merely the next step in the educational process. The more similarity that exists between the school and the child's routines and habits, the more likely it is that the child will adapt and thrive in the school environment (Ryan & Adams, 1995).

The transition is relatively easy for middle-class students, because schools present a mainstream, or middle-class, model for behavior and learning. As middle-class parents interact with their children, they model and promote the behavior acceptable in school. Children are taught the necessities of social interaction, such as saying "thank you" and "please" (Comer, 1994). Middle-class parents also teach their children the rules of the classroom, such as "sit in your chair" and "wait to speak until you are acknowledged." Children from such backgrounds are often well prepared for the school environment because, quite simply, they understand the rules; as a result, the school is accepting of them. Further, the school environment helps reinforce rules and skills taught in the home environment, just as the home environment helps reinforce rules and skills taught in the school environment. Current research indicates that this type of home-school continuity often predicts school success (Ameta & Sherrard, 1995; Comer, 1994; Epstein & Lee, 1995; Kellaghan et al., 1993; Ryan & Adams, 1995).

In contrast, when the home and school environments differ greatly in rules, social norms, and expectations, children experience a discontinuity between home and school. Children with a minority background may not know mainstream speech patterns and may not have been exposed to school materials such as scissors and crayons. These children, although possessing skills and curiosity, are often viewed as "dumb" or "bad" by the school (Comer, 1994). Children viewed in this manner may feel inferior and either act out or disengage from the school process (Finn, 1989). Because the school environment does not support the home environment and the home environment does not support the school environment, these children face an increased risk of poor school outcomes.

Schools that recognize the contribution of home to school success actively seek parental involvement. Parents can help establish the motivation for learning and provide learning opportunities within the home environment (Constable & Walberg, 1996). Children whose parents are involved in their education typically succeed academically (Kurtz, 1988; Kurtz & Barth, 1989).

Poor communication among parents, children, and schools may short-circuit parental involvement. Traditionally, schools have asked parents only to participate in Parent Teacher Association meetings, to attend parent-teacher meetings, to act as helpers in the classroom, and to review notes and written communication sent home via the schoolchild. This sort of parental participation does not always facilitate open communication. However, schools can establish meaningful two-way communication with parents by reaching out to them, involving them as partners in decision making and school governance, treating parents (and their children) with respect, providing support and coordination to implement and sustain parental involvement, and connecting parents with resources (Comer, 1980; Dupper & Poertner, 1997; Kellaghan et al., 1993; Swap, 1993).

One successful method for facilitating open and constructive communication is the use of **collaborative teams** in problem solving. Bailey-Dempsey (1993) found that involving parents, teachers, students, and other school personnel on collaborative, goal-oriented teams was successful in resolving school problems and promoting school success among children at risk for school failure. In Juan's case for example, cooperation among the social worker, teacher, and parents (if they can overcome their hostilities) may be the most effective way to determine the cause of his difficulties in school and forge effective remedies.

Juan's case points to another way that home and school can cooperate. His parents would undoubtedly appreciate quality, affordable before- and after-school care—as would many of today's working parents. It has long been recognized that quality child care is closely linked with children's social, cognitive, and language development (Helburn & Howes, 1996). But such child-care facilities are few and far between. Some school districts have been able to implement be-fore- and after-school programs through a mixture of parental fees and local, state, federal, and private dollars (Zigler & Finn-Stevenson, 1995). Most schools, however, have not been able to se-cure the necessary funding and have also had difficulty altering their schedules and structures to accommodate such changes.

# Social Development in the Peer Group

What signs might indicate that a child is having trouble with small groups of peers?

Schools certainly play a large role in children's lives. Nearly as influential during middle child-hood are **peer groups**—collections of children with unique values and goals (Hartup, 1983). As children progress through middle childhood, peers have an increasingly important impact on such everyday matters as social behavior, activities, and dress. By this phase of development, a desire for group belongingness is especially strong. Within peer groups, children first learn about the functioning of social organizations and develop their skills in communication and so-cial interaction. Whereas individual friendships facilitate the development of critical capacities such as trust and intimacy, peer groups foster learning about cooperation and leadership.

Throughout middle childhood, the importance of **group norms** is highly evident. Children are sensitive, sometimes exceedingly so, to their peers' standards for behavior, appearance, and attitudes. Rhoda, for instance, is devaluing herself because she recognizes the discrepancy be-tween her appearance and group norms. Not until early adolescence do group norms become more flexible and allow for more individuality, matching the increasing flexibility of cognition.

In most middle childhood peer groups, **dominance hierarchies** establish a social order among group participants. Those hierarchies may predict outcomes when conflict arises (Pettit, Bakshi, Dodge, & Coie, 1990; Savin-Williams, 1979); typically, the more dominant children pre-vail. Furthermore, through reinforcement, modeling, and direct pressure to conform to expecta-tions, children's dominance hierarchies contribute to socialization.

Throughout middle childhood, gains in cognitive abilities promote more complex commu-nication skills and a greater awareness of social norms. These developments, in turn, facilitate more complex peer interaction, which is a vital resource for the development of **social compe-tence**—the ability to engage in sustained, positive, and mutually satisfactory peer interactions.

Cultural values, however, may influence the type and quantity of peer interaction observed among school-age children. Specifically, sociability, cooperativeness, and the value placed on play activities are all culturally shaped phenomena.

Peer acceptance is a powerful predictor of psychological adjustment. One study asked chil-dren to nominate other children who fit particular categories. From the results, the researchers developed five general categories of social acceptance: popular, rejected, controversial, neglected, and average (Coie, Dodge, & Coppotelli, 1982). Common predictors of popular status include physical appearance (Adams & Crane, 1980) and prosocial behaviors in the social setting (Newcomb, Bukowski, & Pattee, 1993). Rejected children like Rhoda are those who are actively disliked by their peers. They are particularly likely to be unhappy and to experience achievement and self-esteem issues. Rejected status is strongly associated with poor school performance, an-tisocial behavior, and delinquency in adolescence (DeRosier, Kupersmidt, & Patterson, 1994; Ollendick, Weist, Borden, & Greene, 1992).

Support for rejected children may include interventions to improve peer relations and psychological adjustment. Most of these interventions are based on social learning theory and involve modeling and reinforcing positive social behavior—for example, initiating interaction and responding to others positively. Several of these programs have indeed helped children develop social competence and gain peer approval (Lochman, Coie, Underwood, & Terry, 1993; Mize & Ladd, 1990).

## Gender Roles

During middle childhood, boys and girls seem to follow different paths in gender role development. Often, boys' identification with "masculine" role attributes increases, while girls' identification with "feminine" role attributes decreases. As adults, females are the more androgynous of the two genders, and this movement toward androgyny appears to begin in middle childhood (Serbin, Powlishta, & Gulko, 1993).

These distinct paths have multiple causes including both social and cognitive forces. Societal acceptance of cross-gender behavior in girls is more widespread than acceptance of such behavior among boys. Most research to date suggests that, for both genders, a traditionally "masculine" identity is associated with a higher sense of overall competence and better academic performance (Boldizar, 1991; Newcomb & Dubas, 1992).

Our understanding of the structure of gender roles is derived from various theoretical perspectives. A behavioral perspective proposes that gender-related behaviors precede self-perception in the development of gender role identity; in other words, girls start imitating feminine behavior before they begin thinking of themselves as distinctly female, and boys go through the same sequence in developing a masculine identity. Cognitive developmental theory, however, assumes that self-perceptions emerge first and then guide children's behavior. Gender schema theory (see Bem, 1993), an information-processing approach to gender, combines behavioral and cognitive developmental theories, suggesting that social pressures and children's cognition work together to perpetuate gender-linked perceptions and behaviors.

In general, as children progress through middle childhood, gender stereotypes gradually become more flexible and children begin to accept that males and females can engage in the same activities and occupations (Carter & Patterson, 1982). In addition, children increasingly rely on unique characteristics, rather than a gender label, in attempting to predict the nature and behavior of a specific individual (Biernat, 1991).

Differences in gender stereotyping also exist. Boys appear to hold more gender stereotypical views throughout childhood than girls (Archer, 1992; Levy, Taylor, & Gelman, 1995). For instance, boys are more likely than girls to label a chore as a "girl's job" or a "boy's job." African American children may also hold less stereotyped views of females than do European American children (Bardwell, Cochran, & Walker, 1986). In addition, children from middle-income backgrounds appear to hold more flexible views of gender than children from lower-income backgrounds (Serbin et al., 1993).

The implications of gender stereotyping for individual gender role adoption are not clear-cut. Even children well aware of gender role expectations may not conform to gender role stereotypes in their actual behavior (Downs & Langlois, 1988; Serbin et al., 1993). For example, girls who enjoy sports may readily refer to themselves as "tomboys." Perhaps children acquire gender role preferences before acquiring knowledge of gender role stereotypes, or perhaps they learn and interpret gender role stereotypes in diverse ways.

## *Friendship and Intimacy*

Throughout middle childhood, children develop their ability to look at things from others' perspectives. In turn, their capacity to develop more complex friendships—based on awareness of others' thoughts, feelings, and needs—emerges (Selman, 1976). Thus, complex and fairly stable friendship networks begin to form for the first time in middle childhood (Hartup, 1983). Although skills such as cooperation and problem solving are learned in the peer group, close friendships facilitate understanding and promote trust and reciprocity. Most socially competent children maintain and nurture both close friendships and effective peer group interaction.

As children move through middle childhood, friendship begins to entail mutual trust and assistance and thus becomes more psychologically rather than behaviorally based (Damon, 1977). For example, Jane and Rhoda's friendship is based on the emotional support they provide for one another as much as, if not more than, their common interests and activities. The concept of friend is transformed from the playmate of early childhood to the confidant of middle childhood. Violations of trust during this period are perceived as serious violations of the friendship bond. As children move out of middle childhood and into adolescence, the role of intimacy and loyalty in friendship becomes even more pronounced. Moreover, children increasingly value mutual understanding and loyalty in the face of conflict among peers (Berndt, 1988).

## *Team Play*

The overall incidence of aggression during peer activities decreases during middle childhood, and friendly rule-based play increases. This transition is due in part to the continuing development of perspective-taking ability. In addition, school-age children are exposed to peers who differ in a variety of ways, including personality, ethnicity, and interests.

Peer communication also benefits from cognitive developments. School-age children are able to take their new understanding of others' needs and desires into account in peer interaction. Thus, their interaction reflects an enhanced ability to understand the role of multiple participants in activities. These developments facilitate the transition to rule-based activities, such as team sports (Rubin, Fein, & Vandenberg, 1983). Malik is a good example of this transition. Although he still gets into occasional fights with peers, he appears to excel at and derive great satisfaction from involvement with team sports.

# Special Challenges in Middle Childhood

American society is changing. Families no longer simply consist of two heterosexual parents, one of whom is employed outside the home. Single-parent and dual-income families are now commonplace. Economic trends are forcing more and more parents into the workforce in order to make ends meet. New legislation requires single mothers who receive public assistance to enter the workforce. Many children can no longer come from school to a home supervised by a stay-at-home parent. The school day often does not coincide with parents' work schedules. Parents are thus forced to find affordable child care, which is rarely available, or leave their children home alone (McWhirter, McWhiter, McWhirter, & McWhirter, 1993). These are just a few of the challenges facing children in middle childhood—along with their parents and schools—as we enter the 21st century.

## Poverty

Foremost among threats to development is poverty, which creates challenges at multiple levels. For a growing number of children, poverty is a persistent experience throughout childhood.

The past two decades, while bringing great progress in preventing poverty among the elderly, have seen a dramatic rise in the poverty rate among young children. That children should be protected from poverty is not disputed; in fact, this societal value dates back to the colonial period (Trattner, 1994). In practice, this belief has resulted in policies and programs targeted at ensuring that the minimal daily needs of children are met. The nature of these policies and programs, however, has shifted over time, as has our success in meeting this goal (Chase-Lansdale & Vinovskis, 1995).

The poverty rate for children in the United States currently exceeds that of all other Western industrialized nations with the exception of Australia (Smeeding & Rainwater, 1995). Moreover, the situation does not appear to be improving: The child poverty rate increased by 39 percent between 1975 and 1994. Today, as noted in Chapter 4, one child in four lives in poverty. The proportion of children in extreme poverty (families with income less than 50 percent of the federal poverty line) doubled during the same period, from 6 to 12 percent. Interestingly, the poverty rate among children grew at a much greater pace in the suburbs (59 percent) than in the cities (34 percent) (National Center for Children in Poverty, 1996/97).

Although in absolute numbers European American children comprise the majority of poor children, children from Hispanic and African American families are consistently overrepresented among all children in poverty. Typically, the percentage of African American or Hispanic children living in poverty is at least twice as high as the percentage of European American children (Children's Defense Fund, 1996; U.S. Bureau of the Census, 1995).

Contrary to stereotypes, most poor children live in working families (National Center for Children in Poverty, 1996/97). Also, research demonstrates small or nonexistent differences between welfare children and poor children whose families do not receive welfare, with respect to both the developmental problems of the children and the quality of their home environments (Zill, Moore, Smith, Stief, & Coiro, 1995). Thus, moving parents off welfare and onto payrolls does not necessarily improve the overall well-being of their school-age children, perhaps because the challenges to development associated with poverty often remain constant.

Risk factors associated with child poverty are numerous, especially when poverty is sustained. Children who grow up in poverty are more likely (as Chapter 4 explains) to be born with low birth weight, to experience serious and chronic health problems, and to receive poorer health care and nutrition than children who grow up in better financial circumstances (Sroufe et al., 1996). In addition, poor families often experience much higher levels of stress than families with adequate incomes, potentially leading to a wide variety of negative outcomes for children, including heightened risk of exposure to **child maltreatment** (abuse and neglect) and exposure to domestic violence between adults in the home (Halpern, 1990; McLoyd, 1990). Children who have spent any part of their infancy or early childhood in poverty are likely to have already encountered several developmental challenges by the time middle childhood begins. Children who enter, progress through, and leave middle childhood in poverty are at much greater risk of negative developmental outcomes than those who briefly enter and then exit poverty while still in middle childhood.

In the United States, low income predicts child development problems more often than in other industrialized countries. U.S. social policies tend to exaggerate rather than minimize the impact of family income on access to human services such as health care and child care (Bronfenbrenner, 1986). For example, in the United States, health care availability and quality are linked to family income.

But what does it actually mean to be poor? Garbarino (1992, 1995), attempting to address the psychosocial implications of poverty for children, focuses on the significance of relative wealth. Being poor is a relative concept, the meaning of which is defined by perceptions of inclusion. In our society, one must be *not* poor in order to be included; thus, poverty results in a sense of exclusion and feelings of inability and inadequacy. Lack of income and certain goods makes poor people feel that they do not possess what is expected among those who belong. This, to Garbarino, is the essence of **relative poverty**. Fundamentally, then, poverty is more a social than an economic phenomenon.

The meaning of poverty for the school-age child is particularly profound. As evidence, Garbarino (1995) points to an innocent question once asked of him by a child: "When you were growing up, were you poor or regular?" (p. 137). As the child struggles with the normal developmental tasks of feeling included and socially competent, poverty is a persistent reminder of exclusion and social incompetence.

## Biculturalism

Juan, who speaks Spanish at home but English at school, represents many school-age children. Current estimates indicate that approximately 6 million American school-age children speak a language other than English at home, a figure that is expected to increase steadily over the next century (U.S. Bureau of the Census, 1995).

A traditional view of bilingualism holds that bilingual, or **English as a second language (ESL),** children often suffer from cognitive and language deficits. However, significant research evidence suggests that bilingualism may have a positive impact on development. Bilingual children often perform better than monolingual children on tests of analytical reasoning, concept formation, and cognitive flexibility (Hakuta, Ferdman, & Diaz, 1987). Moreover, bilingual children may be more likely to acquire capacities and skills that enhance their reading achievement (Campbell & Sais, 1995). Despite such findings, however, bilingual children rarely receive support for their native language and culture in the classroom.

How can social
workers help
children from
nondominant
cultures develop a
healthy identity?

For European American children, ethnicity does not typically lead to comparison with others or exploration of identity (Rotheram-Borus, 1993). But for most children who are members of nondominant groups, ethnicity may be a central part of the quest for identity that begins in middle childhood and continues well into adolescence and young adulthood. Thus, as children like Malik and Juan mature, they may become more aware of the discrimination and inequality to which they are subjected. Issues related to ethnicity—including skin color, language, and culture—may in fact present overwhelming challenges for the school-age child belonging to a nondominant group. At a time when development of a sense of belonging is critical, these issues may set bicultural children apart from members of dominant groups and may increase the prejudice to which they are subjected.

A particular challenge for bicultural children like Juan may be contradictory values, standards, and traditions. His mother and his father are giving him two different messages about who he is. Juan may respond to such cultural contradictions by identifying with the mainstream American culture in which he is immersed and rejecting his Mexican roots or by developing negative attitudes about his subcultural group. Research evidence indicates that rejection of ethnic identity is particularly likely among members of nondominant groups lacking a supportive social movement that stresses ethnic pride (Phinney, 1989). On the other hand, minority children whose experience in the mainstream culture challenges self-esteem and raises barriers to academic success may reject the dominant culture and define themselves in reaction against majority values (Matute-Bianchi, 1986). Other minority children begin to develop their own unique blend of the two cultures. Individuals' reactions, like those of Juan and Malik, will be shaped by their unique experiences and social influences.

Segregation based on ethnicity and social class is common in friendships at all ages, including middle childhood. Like adults, children are more likely to hold negative attitudes toward groups to which they do not belong. However, children, like adults, vary in the extent to which they hold ethnic and social class biases. Research evidence suggests that specific learning experiences are influential in the development of childhood prejudice (Powlishta, Serbin, Doyle, & White, 1994). Verbalized prejudice declines during middle childhood, as children learn to obey social norms against overt prejudice. However, children belonging to nondominant groups continue to face institutional discrimination, such as biased tracking systems, and other significant challenges throughout this period of the life course (Bigler & Liben, 1993).

The particular challenge for bicultural children is blending the values of both dominant and nondominant groups in a manner that promotes their self-esteem. Because this task may be difficult and confusing, children may avoid confronting their ethnic identity (Markstrom-Adams & Adams, 1995). Individuals and organizations within the child's social system can provide support by being sensitive to issues related to ethnic origin and ethnic distinctions. They can also help by celebrating cultural diversity and trying to increase the cultural competence of European American children (Berk, 1997). Such interventions appear to encourage less negative stereotypes of peers belonging to nondominant groups (Rotheram-Borus, 1993). Ensuring that schools respect nondominant cultures and learning styles is thus an important step in facilitating the development of self-identity and other aspects of social and emotional adjustment.

## *Attention Deficits*

In recent years, children who have trouble concentrating on tasks have been among those most frequently referred to outside sources for help (Hinshaw, 1994). These children, who are often first recognized as "problems" in their middle years, may be stigmatized by teachers and peers alike because they are unable to control their behavior in large group settings. They often display high activity levels, inattention, aggression, defiance, poor academic performance, and antisocial behaviors (Hinshaw, 1994). Teachers often refer children displaying these behaviors to physicians, psychologists, and social workers.

How might attention deficits affect psychosocial development?

Children referred to professionals because of suspected **attention deficit disorder (ADD)** or **attention deficit hyperactivity disorder** (**ADHD**) are a heterogenous group (Hinshaw, 1994). Thus, these children must obtain a comprehensive assessment from a professional who specializes in attention deficit disorders. Part of that assessment is a complete history of the disorder from a variety of sources. The specialist will also observe the child over time to detect variations in the child's behavior (Hinshaw, 1994).

Children who are accurately diagnosed as ADD or ADHD may benefit from drug therapy, behavioral therapy, and cognitive behavioral therapy. The drug treatment must be well administered and monitored to avoid complications. Furthermore, it must be coupled with behavioral, or cognitive behavioral, interventions that teach the ADD or ADHD child the skills needed for school success. The key point here is that drug therapy typically leads to desired outcomes only when combined with additional interventions, including behavioral therapy (Dedmon, 1997).

Children who do not receive a comprehensive assessment by a qualified specialist are often misdiagnosed. Drug therapy may be prescribed hastily, with only a halfhearted recommendation for additional therapies. ADD and ADHD have become very popular labels for children who do not conform to school settings. Teachers often suggest to parents that their children have the disorder, parents in turn suggest to their family physician or pediatrician that their child has the disorder, and thus a misdiagnosis is made. One result of this scenario is that children from nondominant groups are disproportionately misdiagnosed with ADD and ADHD, because their behavior often does not conform to classroom standards. Thus, those with social or emotional difficulties may be moved inappropriately to a special education class, where they face an increased risk of academic failure and premature departure from school (Oakes, 1985).

The popularity of the ADD and ADHD diagnoses most likely results from a combination of factors, including teachers' inability to control the classroom environment, too few resources for teachers to draw on in dealing with active children in the classroom, overcrowded classrooms, and discrimination. When resources are scarce and a teacher's time is limited, the easiest solution to the problem child is either drug therapy or transfer to a different class. Neither route may be absolutely necessary to change or control a child's behavior, however. In some cases, individual attention or skill training may achieve the same end without unnecessary trauma to the child.

## *Family Disruption*

The divorce rate in the United States is currently the highest in the world. More than 1 million children experience the divorce of their parents each year, and at any given time approximately one child in four lives in a single-parent household (Meyer & Garasky, 1993). Between two-thirds and three-fourths of divorced parents marry a second time, and thus for many school-age children divorce leads to new family relationships. But the likelihood of divorce is even greater for second marriages, and approximately half of these children experience the end of a parent's second marriage. Divorce thus often leads to a parade of new people and situations, including new housing and income arrangements and new family roles and responsibilities (Hetherington & Jodl, 1994).

What sorts of intervention might help with the psychological aspects of adjustment to divorce?

Divorce, or the loss of one or both parents, is stressful for all children. Great variation exists, however, in how children respond to this stressor. Critical factors in outcomes for children include social supports within the family and surrounding community, the child's characteristics, and the psychological well-being of the parents. In addition, because middle childhood spans a wide age range, school-age children exhibit a wide range of cognitive and emotional responses to divorce. They may blame themselves and suffer from separation anxiety or may demonstrate a mature understanding of the reasons behind the divorce.

Children experiencing family disruption without supports or those who have experienced difficulties preceding the disruption are most likely to experience long-term emotional and behavioral problems. Children placed in foster care or exposed to domestic violence fall into this group. These children are likely to face additional trauma associated with the loss of familiar space, belongings, and social networks (Groves, 1997). Reaction to such trauma should be expected. However, with appropriate support and intervention, many children experiencing family disruption adjust over time (Hetherington & Clingempeel, 1992).

## Physical Disabilities

Children's adjustment to their physical disabilities is highly dependent on the adjustment of those around them. Families may respond in a number of ways to a diagnosis of a disability or serious illness. Ziolko (1993) proposes that parents move through the following stages when they discover that a child is disabled: withdrawal or rejection, denial, fear and frustration, and ideally, adjustment and acceptance. Awareness of and sensitivity to these stages is critical for those assessing the need for intervention. Typically, the parents of disabled children are helped by advocacy and support groups and access to information and resources.

Middle childhood is a critical time for children with either physical disabilities or chronic illness. For such children to acquire a clear sense of self and an ability to care for themselves and their own health needs, they need positive self-regard. The positive development of children with disabilities is facilitated by support at the micro, meso, and macro levels that promotes independence (Green, 1994).

Families of children with disabilities also typically desire independence and self-determination for their children. As Gallagher (1993) points out, family empowerment was an explicit focus of the Education for All Handicapped Children Act (P.L. 94-142) of 1975, which stresses parental participation in the development of an **individual education plan (IEP)** for each child. The IEP charts a course for ensuring that each disabled child achieves as much as possible in the academic realm.

The need to include the family in decision making and planning is also embodied in the **Individuals with Disabilities Education Act** (Part H of P.L. 101-476) of 1990, which replaced the

Education for All Handicapped Children Act. The 1990 act assures all children the right to a free and appropriate public education and supports the placement of children with disabilities into integrated settings. Prior to this act, the education of children with disabilities was left to individual states. As a result, the population labeled disabled and the services provided to them varied greatly among the states. Today, however, through various pieces of legislation and several court decisions, society has stated its clear preference to educate children with disabilities in integrated settings to the maximum extent possible (Gent & Mulhauser, 1993).

Only full inclusion in family, school, and community life can allow children with special challenges to feel valued and to integrate their disabilities with other aspects of their lives (Green, 1994). The critical task for the school-age child with a disability is to confront successfully the reactions of other children, adults, and institutions. The critical task for individuals and institutional structures is to respond appropriately and supportively (Gallagher, 1993). Interventions that promote acceptance and support among children and adults without disabilities are thus necessary.

## Family and Community Violence

Children are increasingly witness or subject to violence not only in their homes but also in their schools and neighborhoods (Guterman & Cameron, 1997). Although child maltreatment and domestic violence have always existed, they have been recognized as social problems only recently. And community violence is slowly becoming recognized as a social problem of equal magnitude, impacting a tremendous number of children and families. Exposure to violence is a particular problem in areas where a lack of economic and social resources already produces significant challenges for children (Groves, 1997).

Witnessing violence deeply affects children, particularly when the perpetrator or victim of violence is a family member. In the United States, approximately 3.3 million children a year witness domestic violence between adults in the home (Children's Defense Fund, 1993). But being a victim of violence is even more devastating. In the United States, the average number of children killed by gunfire increased from 8 a day in 1983 to 14 a day in 1995 (Children's Defense Fund, 1998). In addition, violence committed by children against other children is on the rise (Wilburn & Bates, 1997). Furthermore, 2.9 million child maltreatment cases—including physical abuse, sexual abuse, neglect, and emotional abuse—were reported to authorities in 1993, an increase of 132 percent over the previous decade (Children's Defense Fund, 1996). Research indicates a high, and increasing, incidence of maltreatment among school-age children, specifically among children ages 6 to 11 (Sedlack & Broadhurst, 1996). However, lower rates among other age groups may simply indicate difficulties in detection and reporting. Prior to entering school, children are less observable and maltreatment less detectable by teachers and other professionals. Older children may also be more likely to take steps toward self-protection—for example, running away from home.

A variety of factors contribute to child maltreatment and family violence. Exhibit 5.3 outlines Belsky's (1993) ecological model of maltreatment, which specifies the multiple factors involved in children's victimization. These factors include parental, child, family, community, and cultural characteristics. Typically, the dynamic interplay of such characteristics leads to maltreatment.

**EXHIBIT 5.3**
An Ecological
Model of Child
Maltreatment

| Risk Category | Examples |
|---|---|
| Parental | Psychological disturbance<br>Substance abuse |
| Child | Developmental disability<br>Difficult temperament |
| Family | Low income<br>Limited social support network |
| Community | Social isolation<br>Limited family support services |
| Cultural | Condoned use of physical force<br>History of valuing children as property |

*Source:* Based on Belsky, 1993.

Sternberg et al. (1993) found that children who experience abuse report more unhappiness and troubled behavior than children who only witness abuse. Witnesses, in turn, report more adjustment difficulties than children who have neither been abused nor witnessed domestic violence. Because of the strong association between domestic violence and child maltreatment, however, many children are likely to experience these challenges to healthy development simultaneously (McCloskey, Figueredo, & Koss, 1995).

Child maltreatment broadly affects the development of secure attachments, peer relationships, and cognitive and language skills (Groves, 1997). If Juan has been maltreated, as it appears, the major impact to date appears to be on his cognitive development. Emotionally abused or neglected children often experience lowered self-esteem and elevated anxiety (Sternberg et al., 1993). Also, over time, maltreated children show a variety of learning and adjustment problems, including difficulties with peers, academic failure, depression, substance abuse, and delinquency (Hotaling, Finkelhor, Kirkpatrick, & Strauss, 1988). Severe and chronic maltreatment may lead to more severe consequences, including a variety of psychopathologies (Terr, 1991).

Children who experience trauma, induced by either indirect or direct exposure to violence, may experience **post–traumatic stress disorder**—a set of symptoms that include feelings of fear and helplessness, reliving of the traumatic experience, and attempts to avoid reminders of the traumatic experience (Groves, 1997; Jenkins & Bell, 1997; Kaplan & Sadock, 1998). Researchers have also found changes in the brain chemistry of children exposed to chronic violence (Perry, 1997). Clearly, witnessing or experiencing violence adversely affects children in a number of areas, including the ability to function in school and the ability to establish stable peer relationships (Dyson, 1989). Evidence suggests that perhaps as many as one-half of all children exposed to violence before the age of 10 develop psychiatric problems in adulthood (Davidson & Smith, 1990).

Prolonged exposure to violence has multiple implications for child development. Such children are forced to learn lessons about loss and death, perhaps before they have acquired the cognitive ability to understand. They may therefore come to believe that the world is unpredictable and violent, a belief that threatens children's natural curiosity and desire to explore the social environment. Multiple experiences in which adults are unable to protect them often lead children to conclude that they must take on such responsibility for themselves, a prospect that can easily overwhelm the resources of a school-age child.

Experiencing such helplessness may also lead to feelings of incompetence and hopelessness, to which children who experience chronic violence react in diverse ways. Responses may be passive, including withdrawal symptoms and signs of depression; or they may be active, including the use of aggression as a means of coping with and transforming the overwhelming feelings of vulnerability (Groves, 1997; Guterman & Cameron, 1997).

The emotional availability of a parent or other caretaker who can support the child's need to process traumatic events is critical. However, in situations of crisis stimulated by child maltreatment or domestic violence, families are often unable to support their children psychologically. Even with the best of parental resources, moreover, children developing in violent and chronically dangerous communities continue to experience numerous challenges to development. The child's need for autonomy and independence is directly confronted by the parent's need to protect the child's physical safety. Hours spent indoors to avoid danger do not promote the much-needed peer relationships and sense of accomplishment, purpose, and self-efficacy so critical during this phase of development (Groves, 1997).

# Risk and Resilience in Middle Childhood

School-age children face a variety of risks that undermine their struggles to develop a sense of purpose and self-worth. These risks include poverty, prejudice, and violence (Garbarino, 1995). More generally, risk factors are anything that increases the probability of a problem condition, its progression into a more severe state, or its maintenance (Fraser & Galinsky, 1997). Risk factors are moderated, however, by protective factors, either internal or external, that help children resist risk (Garmezy, 1993, 1994; Werner & Smith, 1992).

To Fraser and Galinsky (1997), resilience—or "survival against the odds"—arises from an interplay of risk and protective factors and manifests as adaptive behavior producing positive outcomes. As Exhibit 5.4 illustrates, a variety of factors influence resilience during middle childhood. Whether a factor manifests as a risk or a protective factor often depends on its interaction with other factors influencing the individual child.

This multidimensional perspective on resilience provides a tool for understanding middle childhood development. This tool also facilitates intervention efforts (discussed in greater detail in Chapter 4). As social workers, we must recognize that resilience is rarely an innate characteristic. Rather, it is a process (Egeland, Carlson, & Sroufe, 1993) that may be facilitated by influences within the child's surrounding environment. A primary goal of the social work profession is to facilitate this process by enhancing the person/environment fit so as to maximize the protective factors and minimize the risk factors.

**EXHIBIT 5.4**

Factors Influencing
Resilience during
Middle Childhood

| Dimension | Factors |
|-----------|---------|
| Individual (child) | Earlier developmental history |
| | Personality |
| | Appearance |
| | Social competence |
| | Learning style |
| | Group membership (dominant/nondominant) |
| Family | Approach to child |
| | Continuity with school |
| | Social, emotional, and financial resources |
| | Group membership (dominant/nondominant) |
| Peer group | Approach to child |
| | Values, norms, and rules |
| School | Continuity with family |
| | Values, norms, and rules |
| | General child/parent/family orientation |
| | Flexibility and responsiveness |
| | Financial and social resources |
| Community | Approach to child and family |
| | Social, emotional, and financial resources |
| | General child/parent/family orientation |
| Socioeconomic system | Values, norms, and rules |
| | Societal orientation (preventive/reactive) |
| | Acceptance of cultural diversity |

## IMPLICATIONS FOR SOCIAL WORK PRACTICE

This discussion of middle childhood suggests several practice principles for social workers:

■  Support family and community attempts to stabilize the environment for children.

- Support parents as the most important emotional resources for their children.

- Recognize and support resilience in children and families. Support the efforts of children and families to cope with adversity.

- Recognize the critical influence of the school environment on growth and development, and encourage attempts by school personnel to be responsive to all children and families.

- Understand the important role of peer groups in psychosocial growth and development; facilitate the development and maintenance of positive peer relationships.

- Understand the ways in which the organization of schools supports the status quo present in the larger society. Support schools in their efforts to alter discrepancies based on race, ethnicity, gender, and class.

- Collaborate with other professionals to develop comprehensive school-based services.

- Facilitate teacher-parent-child communication and school responsiveness to children with special needs.

- Understand the effects of violence on children, and establish a nurturing and nonviolent environment when possible.

- Become familiar with methods of teaching nonviolent conflict resolution skills to children and adults.

- Provide opportunities for moral and spiritual mentoring in the school environment.

- Normalize diversity in children's physical development and ability levels.

- Intervene with "nonclients" to promote understanding and acceptance in various social settings.

## MAIN POINTS

1. In middle childhood, reasoning becomes more logical, an internally based system of morality develops, the child becomes able to understand the perspectives of others, and the child acquires an enhanced sense of mastery.

2. School is the primary context for development in middle childhood. In school, children are evaluated on the basis of how well they perform tasks.

3. Although public schools are intended to equalize opportunities, children who are poor or who are members of racial and ethnic minority groups are often educated in inferior schools.

4. The physical and symbolic organization of schools typically reinforces hierarchal relationships. Students are often divided into groups based on perceived ability or attainment. Minority and poor students are disproportionately found in the special education, non-college-bound, and nonaccelerated groups.

5. Students in middle childhood, with their individual cognitive styles, benefit from diverse educational materials and varied activities. American schools have been criticized for putting in too little time, not asking students to think enough, providing too few substantive courses, and encouraging ineffective teaching methods.

6. Grouping students in small heterogeneous groups has resulted in positive gains for both high- and low-achieving students.

7. Middle childhood is a period with many physical changes, and physical development affects the way a child is treated by peers and teachers.

8. Schools can help children develop positive self-evaluations by providing a variety of activities that allow children with different strengths to succeed.

9. Full-service schools attempt to provide school-based health and social services for schoolchildren and their families.

10. Children who experience vastly different cultures at home and in school are likely to have difficulty accommodating the two worlds.

11. As children progress through middle childhood, peers have an increasingly important impact on social behavior, activities, and dress. Peer acceptance becomes very important for psychological adjustment. Socially competent children begin to develop close friends and fairly stable friendship networks.

12. As children progress through middle childhood, gender stereotypes generally become more flexible, with girls tending to hold more flexible gender role stereotypes than boys.

13. Poverty, biculturalism, attention deficits, family disruption, physical disabilities, and family and community violence pose significant challenges for many children in middle childhood.

14. Risk factors—factors that increase the probability of developmental problems—are moderated by protective factors, both internal and external, that help children resist risk. Whether a factor manifests as a risk or a protective factor often depends on its interaction with other factors influencing the individual child.

## KEY TERMS

attention deficit disorder (ADD)
attention deficit hyperactivity disorder
  (ADHD)

child maltreatment
collaborative team
dominance hierarchy

English as a second language (ESL)
full-service school
group norm
heterogeneous grouping
individual education plan (IEP)
Individuals with Disabilities Education Act
institutional discrimination
mainstreaming
mastery
peer group

post–traumatic stress disorder
prepubescence
prosocial behavior
pubescence
relative poverty
self-competence
social competence
tracking
zone of proximal development

## WORLD WIDE WEB RESOURCES

Education Reforms and Students at Risk
**http://www.ed.gov/pubs/EdReformStudies/EdReforms/**
Site maintained by the Department of Education's National Institute on the Education of At-Risk
Students. Contains a report on education in the United States with sections on diversity, social status, cultural deprivation, socioeconomic disadvantages, prevention, multicultural
education, and much more.

A.D.H.D. Clinic
**http://www.addclinic.com/**
Site written and maintained by Corydon Clark, M.D. Contains information on attention deficit
and hyperactivity disorder, including an introduction and overview, understanding and
coping, medications, questionnaires, family evaluations, and publications.

Child Abuse: Statistics, Research, and Resources
**http://www.jimhopper.com/abstats**
Site written and maintained by Jim Hopper, Ph.D., of HRI Hospital Trauma Center in Brookline,
Massachusetts. Contains information on sexual and physical child abuse, methodology, sections exclusive to boys and girls, the issue of memory, and additional resource links.

Resilience Research
**http://www.ncrel.org/sdrs/cityschl/city1_1b.htm**
Site maintained by the North Central Regional Educational Library. Contains research paper on
resiliency in children, including sections on why some children succeed, protective processes, the Minneapolis approach, resilience indicators and strategies, and a resource guide.

# CHAPTER 6

# Adolescence

*Susan A. McCarter, Virginia Commonwealth University*

### DAVID'S COMING OUT PROCESS

As a social worker at Jefferson High School, you see many facets of adolescent life. Nothing much surprises you—especially not the way some of the kids hem and haw when they're trying to tell you what's really on their mind. Take David Cunha, for instance. When he shows up for his first appointment, you simply ask him to tell you about himself.

"Let's see, I'm 17," he began. "I'm a forward on the varsity soccer team. What else do you want to know? My parents are from Bolivia. My dad, David Sr., teaches history and is the varsity baseball coach here at Jefferson. My mom is a geriatric nurse. I have a younger sister, Patti. Patti Perfect. She goes to the magnet school and is in the ninth grade."

"How are things at home?" you ask him. "Whatever. Patti is perfect, and I'm 'a freak.' They think I'm 'different, arrogant, stubborn.' I don't know what they want me to be. But I don't think that's what I am. That may be because . . . because I'm gay. I haven't come out to my parents. That's all I need!"

This was obviously a difficult confession for David to make to an adult, but with a little encouragement he continues: "There are two other soccer players who are gay, and then we have some friends outside of soccer. Thank God! But basically when the whole team is together or when I'm with other friends, I just act straight. I talk about girls' bodies just like the other guys. I think that is the hardest. Not being able to be yourself. I'm at least glad that I've met other gay guys. It was really hard when I was about 13. I was so confused. I knew that men were supposed to be with women, not other men. What I was feeling was not 'normal,' and I thought I was the only one. I wanted to kill myself. That was a bad time."

David's tone changes. "Let's talk about something good. Let me tell you about Theo. I find Theo very attractive. I hope he likes my soccer build. I wonder if he would like to hang out together—get to know one another? He's a junior, and if we got together the other guys would razz me about seeing a younger guy. But I keep thinking about him. And looking at him during practice. I just need to say something to him. Some guys off the team are going out Thursday night after practice. He hasn't been invited in the past. Maybe if I invite him, he'll come."

### CARL'S STRUGGLE FOR IDENTITY

Whereas David sought you out, Carl Fleischer, another 17-year-old, was sent to see you. He matter-of-factly tells you that he is "an underachiever." He used to get an occasional B in his classes, but now it's mostly Cs with an occasional D.

When you ask Carl what he likes to do in his spare time, he replies, "I like to get high and surf the Net." Further probing elicits one-word answers until you ask Carl about girlfriends. His face contorts as he slaps his ample belly: "I'm not exactly a sex symbol. According to my doctor, I'm a fatso. He says normal boys my age and height weigh at least 50 pounds less than I do. He also tells me to quit smoking and get some exercise. Whatever. My mom says I'm big-boned. She says my dad was the same way. I wouldn't know. I never met the scumbag. He left when my mom was pregnant. But you probably don't want to hear about that."

Carl won't say more on that topic, but you finally get him to talk about his job, delivering pizzas two nights a week and on the weekends. "So if you need pizzas, call me at Antonio's. I always bring pies home for my mom on Tuesday and Friday nights. She works late those nights, and so we usually eat pizza and catch the Tuesday and Friday night lineups on TV. She lets me smoke in the house—cigarettes, not weed. Although I have gotten high in the house a couple times. Anyway, I am not what you would call popular. I am just a fat, slow geek and a pizza guy. But there are some heads who come into Antonio's. I exchange pies for dope. Works out pretty well: they get the munchies, and the pies keep me in with the heads."

## MONICA'S QUEST FOR MASTERY

Monica Golden, one of the peer counselors at Jefferson High, hangs around to chat after a meeting of the peer counselors. Monica is the youngest and tallest daughter in a family of five kids, with one younger brother. Monica's mother is the assistant principal at Grover Middle School, and her father works for the Internal Revenue Service. This year Monica is the vice president of the senior class, the treasurer for the Young Republicans, a starter on the track team, a teacher at Sunday School, and a Jefferson peer counselor.

When you comment on the scope of these activities, Monica replies: "I really do stay busy. I worked at the mall last year, but it was hard to keep my grades up. I'm trying to get into college, so my family and I decided I shouldn't work this year. So I just baby-sit sometimes. A lot of my aunts and uncles have me watch their kids, but they don't pay me. They consider it a family favor. Anyway, I am waiting to hear back from colleges. They should be sending out the letters this week. You know, the fatter the envelope the better. It doesn't take many words to say 'No. We reject you.' And I need to either get into a state school or get a scholarship so that I can use my savings for tuition."

---

**CASE STUDIES**

You talk a little about Monica's options, and she tells you that her first choice is Howard University. "I want to be a pediatrician, you know. I love kids," Monica says. "I tried tons of jobs—that's where I got the savings. And, well, those with kids I enjoyed the most. Like I said, I've worked retail at the mall. I've worked at the supermarket as a cashier. I've worked at the snack bar at the pool. And I've been baby-sitting since I was 12. That's what I like the most."

"I'd love to have kids someday. But I don't even have a boyfriend. I wear glasses. My parents say I don't need contacts; they think I'm being vain. Not that I don't have a boyfriend because I wear glasses. Guys think I'm an over-achiever. They think I'm driven and demanding and incapable of having fun. That's what I've been told. I think I'm just ambitious and extroverted. But really, I just haven't had much time to date in high school. I've been so busy. Well, gotta run."

---

# The Transition from Childhood to Adulthood

Adolescence is the transitional period between childhood and adulthood. The word *adolescence* originates from the Latin verb *adolescere,* which means "to grow into maturity." It is a period of life filled with transitional themes in every dimension of the configuration of person and environment: biological, psychological, social, spiritual. These themes do not occur independently or without affecting one another. For example, David's experience may be complicated because he is gay and because his family relationships are strained, but it is also strengthened by his supportive friendships and his participation in athletics. Carl's transition is marked by several challenges—his weight, his substance use, his relationship with his father, his academic performance—but also by the promise of his developing computer expertise and entrepreneurial skills. Monica's movement through adolescence may be eased by her academic, athletic, and social success, but it also could be taxed by her busy schedule and high expectations for herself.

Many cultures have specific **rites of passage**—ceremonies that demarcate the transition from childhood to adulthood. Often these rites include sexual themes, marriage themes, themes of becoming a man or a woman, themes of added responsibility, or themes of increased insight or understanding. For example, many American Jews celebrate the bar mitzvah for boys and bas mitzvah for girls at the age of 13 to celebrate their transition to adulthood and to mark their assumption of religious responsibility. Mainstream American culture, however, has no such rites. In the United States, the closest thing to a rite of passage may be getting a driver's license, graduating from high school, registering to vote, graduating from college, or getting married. But these

**EXHIBIT 6.1**

Typical Adolescent Development

| Stage of Adolescence | Biological Changes | Psychological Changes | Social Changes |
|---|---|---|---|
| Early (11–14) | Hormonal changes<br><br>Beginning of puberty<br><br>Physical appearance changes<br><br>Possible experimentation with sex and substances | Reactions to physical changes, including early maturation<br><br>Concrete/present-oriented thought<br><br>Body modesty<br><br>Moodiness | Changes in relationships with parents and peers<br><br>Less school structure<br><br>Distancing from culture/tradition<br><br>Seeking sameness |
| Middle (15–17) | Completion of puberty and physical appearance changes<br><br>Possible experimentation with sex and substances | Reactions to physical changes, including late maturation<br><br>Increased autonomy<br><br>Increased abstract thought<br><br>Beginning of identity development<br><br>Preparation for college or career | Heightened social situation decision making<br><br>Consideration of physical attractiveness |
| Late (18–20) | Slowing of physical changes<br><br>Possible experimentation with sex and substances | Formal operational thought<br><br>Continuation of identity development<br><br>Moral reasoning | Very little school/life structure<br><br>Beginning of intimate relationships<br><br>Renewed interest in culture/tradition |

events all occur at different times and thus do not provide a discrete point of transition. Moreover, not all youth participate in these rites of passage.

Even without a cultural rite of passage, all adolescents experience profound biological, psychological, psychosocial, social, and spiritual changes. In advanced industrial societies, these changes have been divided into three phases: early adolescence (ages 11 to 14), middle adolescence (ages 15 to 17), and late adolescence (ages 18 to 20). Exhibit 6.1 summarizes the typical biological, psychological, and social developments in these three phases. Of course, adolescent development varies from person to person and with time, culture, and other aspects of the environment. Yet deviations from the normative patterns of adolescent change may have psychological ramifications because adolescents are so quick to compare their own development to that of their peers.

# Biological Aspects of Adolescence

Those "raging hormones of adolescence" that we hear about are truly influential at this time of life. The hypothalamus, pituitary gland, adrenal glands, and **gonads** (ovaries and testes) begin to interact to stimulate increased hormone production. Although androgens are typically referred to as male hormones and estrogens as female hormones, males and females in fact produce all three major sex hormones: androgens, progestins, and estrogens. However, during **puberty** (the years during which adolescents become capable of reproduction), increased levels of androgens in males stimulate the development and functioning of the male reproductive system; increased levels of progestins and estrogens in females stimulate the development and functioning of the female reproductive system.

Sex hormones affect the development of the gonads, functioning of the gonads (including sperm production and ova maturation), and mating and child-caring behavior. Specifically, testosterone, which is produced in males by the testes, affects the maturation and functioning of the penis, prostate gland, and other male genitals; the secondary sex characteristics; and the sex drive. Estrogen, which is produced in females by the ovaries, affects the maturation and functioning of the ovaries, uterus, and other female genitals; the secondary sex characteristics; and child-caring behaviors.

Generally, puberty is thought to begin with the onset of menstruation in girls and production of sperm in boys. Menstruation is the periodic sloughing off of the lining of the uterus. This lining provides nutrients for the fertilized egg. If the egg is not fertilized, the lining sloughs off and is discharged through the vagina. However, for a female to become capable of reproduction, she must not only menstruate but also ovulate. Ovulation, the release of an egg from an ovary, usually does not begin until several months after **menarche**, the onset of menstruation. For males to reproduce, **spermarche**—the onset of the ability to ejaculate mobile sperm—must occur. Spermarche does not occur until after several ejaculations.

Generally, females begin puberty two years earlier than males. Tanner (1990) suggests that normal pubertal rates (meaning they are experienced by 95 percent of the population) are for girls to begin menstruating between the ages of 9 and 16 and for boys to produce sperm between the ages of 10 and 19. The age at which puberty begins has been declining in this century, although it seems to be plateauing in industrialized countries (Friedman, 1992, p. 346).

**Primary sex characteristics** are those directly related to the reproductive organs and external genitalia. For boys, these include growth of the penis and scrotum. During adolescence, the penis typically doubles or triples in length. Girls' primary sex characteristics are not so visible but include growth of the ovaries, uterus, vagina, clitoris, and labia.

**Secondary sex characteristics** are those not directly related to the reproductive organs and external genitalia. Secondary sex characteristics are enlarged breasts and hips for girls, facial hair and deeper voices for boys, and hair and sweat gland changes for both sexes. Female breast development is distinguished by growth of the mammary glands, nipples, and areola. The tone of the male voice lowers as the larynx enlarges and the vocal cords lengthen. Both boys and girls begin to grow hair around their genitals and then under their arms. This hair begins with a finer texture and lighter color and then becomes curlier, coarser, and darker. During this period, the sweat glands also begin to produce noticeable odors.

Females typically first notice breast growth, then growth of pubic hair, then body growth, especially hips; they then experience menarche, then growth of underarm hair, and finally an increase in production of glandular oil and sweat, possibly with body odor and acne. Males typically follow a similar pattern, first noticing growth of the testes, then growth of pubic hair, body growth, growth of penis, change in voice, growth of facial and underarm hair, and finally an increase in the production of glandular oil and sweat, possibly with body odor and acne.

In addition to changes instigated by raging sex hormones, adolescents experience growth spurts. Bones are augmented by cartilage during adolescence, and the cartilage calcifies later, during the transition to adulthood. Typically, boys develop broader shoulders, straighter hips, and longer forearms and legs; whereas girls typically develop narrower shoulders and broader hips. These skeletal differences are then enhanced by the development of additional upper body musculature for boys and the development of additional fat deposits on thighs, hips, and buttocks for girls. These changes account for differences in male and female weight and strength.

# Psychological Aspects of Adolescence

Psychological development in adolescence is multifaceted. Adolescents have psychological reactions, sometimes dramatic, to the biological, social, and cultural dimensions of their lives. They become capable of and interested in discovering and forming their psychological selves. They may show heightened creativity, as well as interest in humanitarian issues, ethics, religion, and reflection and record keeping, as in a diary (Kaplan, Sadock, & Grebb, 1994, p. 53). Two areas of psychological development are particularly noteworthy: reactions to biological changes and changes in cognition.

## *Psychological Reactions to Biological Changes*

Imagine—or remember—being a sweaty, acne-ridden, gangly teenager whose body is changing every day, and who's concerned with fitting in and being normal. The penis comparisons in the boys' locker room and the discussions of breasts, bras, and periods in the girls' locker room are examples of how adolescents try to cope with biological change.

How might social workers address the biological and psychosocial dimensions of teen sexuality?

Because the onset and experience of puberty vary greatly, adolescents need reassurance regarding their own growth patterns. Some adolescents will be considered early maturers, and some will be considered late maturers. Early maturing boys seem to get more attention than the other boys because they look more like adults (Brooks-Gunn, 1988). Perhaps as a result, early maturing boys seem to be more self-confident, but adult appearance can carry additional adult responsibilities as well. Conversely, late maturing boys tend to get less favorable attention. Because they still look like children, that is how they are often treated; for the most part, they are not given the additional responsibilities that are expected of early maturers. This difference in treatment may negatively affect their self-confidence.

For girls, unlike boys, early maturation often brings awkwardness (Alsaker, 1992; Brooks-Gunn, Petersen, & Eichorn, 1985) and even psychological distress (Ge, Conger, & Elder, 1996; Hayward et al., 1997). Early maturing girls may be taller and heavier than other girls and may find themselves having to wear a bra before their friends who want to wear a bra even pick one out. In addition to the psychological impact, early maturing girls may also feel early sexual pressure. Late maturing girls seem to be the least affected of all boys and girls. They seem to be given more psychological space to develop at their own pace.

Adolescents trying to make psychological accommodations to the dramatic biological changes they are experiencing benefit greatly from the compassion and support of caring adults. Judy Blume's *Are You There, God? It's Me, Margaret* (1970) captures the mixed feelings that some girls experience with their first menstrual period and models useful adult support. The book ends with the following scene (pp. 147–148):

> Then I looked down at my underpants and I couldn't believe it. There was blood on them. Not a lot—but enough. I really hollered, "Mom—hey Mom—come quick!"
>
> When my mother got to the bathroom she said, "What is it? What's the matter?"
>
> "I got it," I told her.
>
> "Got what?"
>
> I started to laugh and cry at the same time. "My period. I've got my period!" My nose started running and I reached for a tissue.
>
> "Are you sure, Margaret?" my mother asked.
>
> "Look—look at this," I said, showing her my underpants.
>
> "My God! You've really got it. My little girl!" Then her eyes filled up and she started sniffling too. "Wait a minute—I've got the equipment in the other room. I was going to put it in your camp trunk, just in case."
>
> "You were?"
>
> . . .
>
> Then I got dressed and looked at myself in the mirror. Would anyone know my secret? Would it show? Would Moose, for instance, know if I went back outside to talk to him? Would my father know right away when he came home for dinner? I had to call Nancy and Gretchen and Janie right away. Poor Janie! She'd be the last of the [group] to get it. And I'd been so sure it would be me! How about that! Now I am growing for sure. Now I am almost a woman!

This fictional representation mirrors what Martin (1996) calls a "normative cultural scenario." A girl is "supposed to begin her period at home, with a supportive, informative mother, with knowledge of what is happening to her, with pads (or occasionally tampons) available" (p. 24). Margaret was indeed prepared, but not everyone has this experience. In any case, the reactions of significant others influence how the adolescent female begins to think and feel about her changing body.

From the male perspective, masturbation is a similarly sensitive topic. A young man interviewed by Martin (1996) had this to say:

How can social workers intervene with adolescents whose parents are less compassionate?

> I pretty much knew everything. I was only worried about getting AIDS through like masturbating or something (laughs), but umm, I actually talked to my dad about that, so I wasn't really worried about anything after sixth grade. [Researcher asks what his dad said when he talked to him.] He said, he sort of laughed. He told me stories about how he used

to do it too, and he said, "No, you can't get AIDS from doing that." And so I was happy, and he was happy, and that sort of opened the door for whatever conversations. (p. 50)

How the topic of masturbation is handled by adolescents and their families and peers may have lasting effects. Like Margaret's experience with menarche, this young man's situation was managed by a compassionate parent. A range of responses are possible, however, and some of them create enduring problems with attitudes toward the body and sex.

## Changes in Cognition

How might cognitive developments change social workers' approach to maturing clients?

During adolescence, most individuals develop cognitive abilities beyond those of childhood (Damon & Hart, 1988; Friedman, 1992), including

- Contemplation of the future
- Comprehension of the nature of human relationships
- Consolidation of specific knowledge into a coherent system
- Ability to envision possible consequences from a hypothetical list of actions (foresight)
- Abstract thought
- Empathy
- Internal control

Many of these abilities are components of Jean Piaget's stage of cognitive development called formal operational thought (see Chapter 4). **Formal operational thought** suggests the capacity to apply hypothetical reasoning to various situations and the ability to use symbols to solve problems. David Cunha, for example, demonstrated formal operational thought when he considered the possibility of getting to know Theo. He considered the reactions from his other friends if he were to get together with Theo; he thought about his thoughts; and he formulated a strategy based on the possibilities and on his thoughts.

# Psychosocial Aspects of Adolescence

Adolescents are fundamentally concerned with the question "Who am I?" This issue of defining a self or an identity could be considered a psychological task of adolescence, but I discuss identity as a psychosocial concept because it is developed in social transactions. **Identity** is a combination of what you're born with and into; who you associate with; how others see you; what you've done; your attitudes, traits, abilities, habits, tendencies, and preferences; and what you look like.

What does the identity we so laboriously construct during adolescence do for us? Adams and Marshall (1996, p. 433) suggest that identity has five common functions:

- To provide a structure for understanding who one is
- To provide meaning and direction through commitments, values, and goals

- To provide a sense of personal control and free will

- To enable one to strive for consistency, coherence, and harmony among values, beliefs, and commitments

- To enable one to recognize one's potential through a sense of future possibilities and alternative choices

Mature adults often incorporate all five functions of identity.

## Theories of Self and Identity

A number of prominent psychologists have put forward theories that address self or identity development in adolescence. Exhibit 6.2 provides an overview of five theorists: Freud, Erikson, Marcia, Piaget, and Kohlberg. All five help to explain how a concept of self or an identity develops, and all five suggest that it cannot develop fully before adolescence. Piaget and Kohlberg suggest that some individuals may not reach these higher levels of identity development at all.

Sigmund Freud thought of human development as a series of five psychosexual stages in the expression of libido (sensual pleasure). The fifth stage, the genital stage, occurs in adolescence, when reproduction and sexual intimacy become possible.

Building on Freud's work, Erik Erikson (1950, 1959b, 1963, 1968) proposed eight stages of psychosocial development, with each stage requiring the mastery of a particular developmental task related to identity. The fifth stage, identity versus role diffusion, is relevant to adolescence. The developmental task is to develop a coherent sense of identity; failure to complete this task successfully leaves the adolescent without a solid sense of identity.

**EXHIBIT 6.2**
Theories of Self
or Identity in
Adolescence

| Theorist | Developmental Stage | Major Task or Processes |
|----------|---------------------|--------------------------|
| Freud | Genital stage | To develop libido capable of reproduction and sexual intimacy |
| Erikson | Identity versus role diffusion | To find one's place in the world through self-certainty versus apathy, role experimentation versus negative identity, and anticipation of achievement versus work paralysis |
| Marcia | Ego identity statuses | To develop one of these identity statuses: identity diffusion, foreclosure, moratorium, or identity achievement |
| Piaget | Formal operational thought | To develop the capacity for abstract problem formulation, hypothesis development, and solution testing |
| Kohlberg | Postconventional morality | To develop moral principles that transcend one's own society: individual ethics, societal rights, and universal principles of right and wrong |

James Marcia (1966, 1980) expounded upon Erikson's notion that adolescents struggle with the issue of identity versus role diffusion. Marcia proposed that adolescents vary in how easily they go about developing personal identity and described four categories of identity development in adolescents:

1. *Identity diffusion.* No exploration of or commitment to roles and values.

2. *Foreclosure.* Commitment made to roles and values without exploration.

3. *Moratorium.* Exploration of roles and values without commitment.

4. *Identity achievement.* Exploration of roles and values followed by commitment.

Jean Piaget proposed four major stages leading to adult thought. He expected the last stage, the stage of formal operations, to occur in adolescence, enabling the adolescent to engage in more abstract thinking about "who I am." Piaget (1972) also thought that adolescents begin to use formal operational skills to think in terms of what is best for society.

Lawrence Kohlberg (1976, 1984) expanded on Piaget's ideas about moral thinking to describe three major levels of moral development:

1. *Preconventional morality.* Moral reasoning based on fear of punishment and hope of reward.

2. *Conventional morality.* Moral reasoning based on adherence to social rules.

3. *Postconventional morality.* Moral reasoning based on moral principles that may transcend social rules.

Kohlberg thought that adolescents become capable of postconventional morality but that many never go beyond conventional morality.

On perhaps a more practical level, Morris Rosenberg, in his book *Conceiving the Self* (1986), provides a very useful model of identity to keep in mind while working with adolescents—or perhaps to share with adolescents who are in the process of identity formation. Rosenberg suggests that identity comprises three major parts: social identity, dispositions, and physical characteristics (p. 9).

**Social identity,** in turn, is made up of several elements, all derived from interaction with other people and social systems:

- **Social statuses**—basic classifications or demographic characteristics, such as sex, age, and socioeconomic status.

- **Membership groups**—groups with which the individual shares an interest, a belief, an origin, or physical or regional continuity. Examples are groups formed on the basis of religion, political party, race, or other interest.

- **Labels**—identifiers that result from social labeling. Rosenberg (1986) suggests that social labeling occurs when descriptors move from verbs to nouns. For example, the woman who drinks too much becomes an alcoholic, and the boy who skips school becomes a delinquent.

- **Derived statuses**—identities based on the individual's role history. Examples are veteran, high school athlete, or Harvard alumnus.

- **Social types**—interests, attitudes, habits, or general characteristics. Some social types common among adolescents are jock, geek, head, playboy, and go-getter.

- **Personal identities**—unique labels attached to individuals. Depending on the forum, personal identity could be your first name, your first and last names, your social security number, your fingerprints, or your DNA.

Rosenberg uses the concept of **dispositions** to discuss self-ascribed aspects of identity. Some examples of dispositions are attitudes (conservatism, liberalism), traits (generosity, bravery), abilities (musical talent, athletic skill), values (efficiency, equality), personality traits (introversion, extroversion), specific habits (making lists, getting up early), tendencies (to arrive late, to exaggerate) and likes or preferences (enjoys romance novels, likes pizza).

Finally, **physical characteristics,** in Rosenberg's model, are simply one's physical traits. Height, weight, body build, facial features, and the like all contribute a great deal to our sense of self.

Exhibit 6.3 uses Rosenberg's model to analyze the social identities of David, Carl, and Monica. Notice that disposition is an element of identity based on how the youth defines him/herself. In contrast, a label is determined by others, and physical characteristics are genetically influenced. David Cunha has an athletic body and thinks of himself as athletic, but his parents—and perhaps others—label him as a freak. He is working to incorporate the fact that he's different into his identity. Carl Fleischer has been labeled as a fatso, an underachiever, and a

**EXHIBIT 6.3**

Examples of Adolescent Identity

| Element of Identity | David | Carl | Monica |
|---|---|---|---|
| *Social Identity* | | | |
| Social statuses | Male, 17, middle-class | Male, 17, working-class | Female, 17, upper-middle-class |
| Membership groups | Bolivian American, gay | European American, heads | African American, Christian, Young Republican |
| Labels | Freak | Fatso, underachiever, smoker | Overachiever |
| Derived statuses | Soccer player | Pizza deliverer | Senior class vice president, baby-sitter, supermarket cashier, track athlete |
| Social types | Jock | Geek, head (affiliate) | Brain, go-getter |
| *Personal Identity* | | | |
| Disposition | Athletic | Underachiever, not popular, fat, slow, likes to get high, likes to surf the Internet | Athletic, ambitious, extroverted, likes children |
| Physical characteristics | Soccer build | Overweight | Tall |

smoker. He seems to have incorporated these negative labels into his identity. Monica Golden has been labeled as an overachiever, but she does not absorb the negative label, reframing it instead as ambitious.

## Identity Formation

How do adolescents construct an identity? We can think of adolescent identity formation as a trip to the salad bar of life. As adolescents move through the salad bar, they first have to decide on a base of iceberg lettuce or maybe romaine or perhaps spinach. Then they exercise more free will: broccoli, carrots, or tomatoes? cheese? croutons? sunflower seeds?

Scholars suggest that identity formation is structured by the sociocultural context (Adams & Marshall, 1996; Baumeister & Muraven, 1996). Thus, the options offered by any given salad bar will vary depending on the restaurant. Think about David, Carl, and Monica. What is the sociocultural context of their trip to the salad bar? What salad ingredients can they choose, given the restaurant they find themselves in?

For those salad options that individuals are able to choose—for those aspects of identity that we shape ourselves—individuals have four ways of trying on and developing a preference for certain identities:

1. **Future orientation**. By adolescence, youth have developed two important cognitive skills. They are able to consider the future, and they are able to construct abstract thoughts. These skills allow them to choose from a list of hypothetical behaviors based on the potential outcomes resulting from those behaviors. David demonstrates future orientation in his contemplation regarding Theo. Adolescents also contemplate potential future selves.

2. **Role experimentation**. According to Erikson (1963), adolescence provides a psychosocial moratorium—a period during which youth have the latitude to experiment with social roles. Thus, adolescents typically sample membership in different cliques, build relationships with various mentors, take various academic electives, and join assorted groups and organizations—all in an attempt to further define themselves. Monica, for example, sampled various potential career paths before deciding on becoming a pediatrician.

3. **Exploration**. Whereas role experimentation is specific to trying new roles, exploration refers to the comfort an adolescent has with trying new things. The more comfortable the individual is with exploration, the easier identity formation will be.

4. **Self-evaluation**. During the quest for identity, adolescents are constantly sizing themselves up against their peers. Erikson (1968) suggested that the development of identity is a process of personal reflection and observation of oneself in relation to others. George Herbert Mead (1934) suggested that individuals create a **generalized other** to represent how others are likely to view and respond to them. The role of the generalized other in adolescents' identity formation is evident when adolescents act on the assumed reactions of their families or peers. For example, what Monica wears to school may be based not on what she thinks would be most comfortable or look the best, but rather on what she thinks her peers expect her to wear. Thus, she does not wear miniskirts to school because "everyone" (generalized other) will think she is loose.

# Social Aspects of Adolescence

The social environment—family, peers, certain institutions, culture, and so on—is a significant element of adolescent life. For one thing, as already noted, identity develops through social transactions. For another, as adolescents become more independent and move into the world, they develop their own relationships with more elements of the social environment.

## *Relationships with Family*

*In what ways is the environmental dimension of family still a factor in adolescents' lives?*

Answering the question "Who am I?" includes a consideration of the question "How am I different from my brothers and sisters, my parents, and other family members?" For many adolescents, this question begins the process of **individuation**—the development of a self or identity that is unique and separate. David seems to have started the process of individuation; he recognizes that he may not want to be what his parents want him to be. He does not yet seem comfortable with this idea, however. Carl is not sure how he is like and different from his absent father. Monica has begun to recognize some ways that she is different from her siblings, and she is involved in her own personal exploration of career options that fit her dispositions. It would appear that she is the furthest along in the individuation process.

Moore (1987) suggests that separation from parents has four components:

1. **Functional independence**—literally being able to function with little assistance or independently from one's parents. An example would be getting ready for school: selecting an appropriate outfit, getting dressed, compiling school supplies, and feeding oneself.

2. **Attitudinal independence**—not merely having a different attitude from parents, but developing one's own set of values and beliefs. An example might be choosing a presidential candidate based not on your parents' choice but on your values and beliefs.

3. **Emotional independence**—not being dependent on parents for approval, intimacy, and emotional support. Emotional independence might mean discovering your own way to overcome emotional turmoil—for example, listening to your favorite CD after a fight with your girlfriend/boyfriend rather than relying on support from your parents.

4. **Conflictual independence**—being able to recognize one's separateness from parents without guilt, resentment, anger, or other negative emotions. Conflictual independence is being comfortable with being different. Thus, instead of ridiculing your dad for wearing those shorts to the picnic, you are able to go to the picnic realizing that you would not wear those shorts but that your father's taste in shorts is not a reflection on you.

The concept of independence is largely influenced by culture. And mainstream American culture places a higher value on independence than do other cultures. As social workers, we need to recognize that the notion that the adolescent should be developing an identity separate from family is not acceptable to all cultural groups. Our assessments of adolescent individuation should be culturally sensitive. Likewise, we must be realistic in our assessments of the functional independence of adolescents with disabilities.

Even when it is consistent with their cultural values, not all parents and adolescents are able to achieve functional independence, attitudinal independence, emotional independence, and conflictual independence. Instead, many maintain a high level of conflict. Conflict is particularly evident in families experiencing additional stressors, such as divorce and economic difficulties (Flanagan, 1990; Smetana, Killen, & Turiel, 1991). Galambos and Almeida (1992) have refuted the notion that parent/adolescent conflict increases uniformly during early adolescence. Their research suggests that, compared with childhood, overall conflict regarding chores, appearance, and politeness decreases; conflict regarding substance use stays the same; and conflict regarding finances increases.

## Relationships with Peers

What signs might indicate that an adolescent is having problems with peer groups?

Most adolescents would rather be anywhere with their peers than anywhere with their parents. In the quest for autonomy and identity, adolescents begin to differentiate themselves from their parents and associate with their peers. Teens are recognizing their differences from their parents and seeking similarity with their peers. Whereas children seek same-sex peer groups, adolescents begin socializing more with opposite-sex peers.

Peer relationships are a fertile testing ground for youth and their emerging identities (Connolly, White, Stevens, & Burstein, 1987). Many adolescents seek out a peer group with compatible members, and inclusion or exclusion from certain groups can affect their identity and overall development. David Cunha's peer groups include the soccer team and a group of gay males from school. Carl Fleischer seems to be gravitating toward the "heads" for his peer group—although this choice appears to be related to a perception of rejection by other groups. Monica Golden enjoys easy acceptance by several peer groups: the peer counselors at high school, the senior class officers, the Young Republicans, and the track team.

Interaction with peers contributes significantly to the development of personal and social competence. Based on their study of 266 ninth-grade students (approximately 14 years old), Jarvinen and Nicholls (1996) suggest that adolescents have six goals in relationships with their peers: intimacy, nurturance, dominance, leadership, popularity, and avoidance. In addition, the researchers discovered six behaviors or circumstances that their adolescent participants believe contribute to success in peer relationships: being sincere, having status, being responsible, pretending to care, entertaining others, and being tough. When social workers interact with adolescents who are having trouble with peer relations, it is helpful to explore with them their goals in peer relationships and their perceptions about what behaviors are valued by their peers.

## Relationships with Institutions

How do two institutions—school and work—differ in the demands they place on adolescents?

As adolescents loosen their ties to parents, they develop more direct relationships with such institutions as school, employment, and leisure activities. To study adolescent relationships with such institutions, Mihaly Csikszentmihalyi and Reed Larson (1984) gave pagers to 75 diverse 9th- through 12th-grade boys and girls. Throughout the day, the researchers periodically beeped their participants. When beeped, the adolescents were to complete a log identifying where they were, what they were doing, and who else was with them.

The researchers found that these adolescents spent 41 percent of their time at home, 32 percent of their time at school, and 27 percent of their time in public. They spent 40 percent of their time in leisure activities such as socializing, playing sports, watching television, and listening to music. They spent 29 percent of their time on school or work activities: 13 percent in class, 12 percent on homework, and 4 percent on jobs. The other 31 percent was spent on maintenance activities, such as eating, personal hygiene, transportation, rest, and errands. More than half of these adolescents' time was spent with peers: 29 percent with friends and 23 percent with classmates. Another 27 percent was spent alone, and 19 percent was spent with family. The remaining 2 percent was spent with others, including bosses, coworkers, and coaches (Csikszentmihalyi & Larson, 1984). As you can see, adolescents spend a substantial portion of their time interacting with, and in the context of, social institutions.

*School.*   From the 32 percent of their time that is spent at school, adolescents are gaining skills and knowledge for their next step in life, either moving into the workforce or continuing their education. In school, they also have the opportunity to evolve socially and emotionally; school is a fertile ground for practicing future orientation, role experimentation, exploration, and self-evaluation.

How might the transition from one level of formal school organization to another create problems?

Middle schools have a very structured format and a very structured environment; high schools are less structured in both format and environment, allowing a gradual transition to greater autonomy. The school experience changes radically, however, at the college level. Many college students are away from home for the first time and are in very unstructured environments. David, Carl, and Monica have had different experiences with structure in their environments to date. David's environment has required him to move flexibly between two cultures. That experience may help to prepare him for the unstructured college environment. Carl has had the least structured home life. It remains to be seen whether that has helped him to develop skills in structuring his own environment, or left him with insufficient models for doing so. Monica is accustomed to juggling multiple commitments and should have little trouble with the competing attractions and demands of college.

School is also an institutional context where cultures intersect, which may create difficulties for students who are not familiar or comfortable with mainstream culture. You may not realize how Eurocentric the American educational model is until you view it through a different cultural lens. We can use a Native American lens as an example. Native Americans have the highest school dropout rate (35.5 percent) of any ethnic group in the nation (Hodgkinson, 1990). Michael Walkingstick Garrett (1995) details the plight of Native American youth in the American classroom in his article "Between Two Worlds: Cultural Discontinuity in the Dropout of Native American Youth." He uses the experiences of the boy Wind-Wolf as an example of the incongruence between Native American culture and the typical education model:

> Wind-Wolf is required by law to attend public school. . . . He speaks softly, does not maintain eye contact with the teacher as a sign of respect, and rarely responds immediately to questions knowing that it is good to reflect on what has been said. He may be looking out the window during class, as if daydreaming, because he has been taught to always be aware of changes in the natural world. These are interpreted by his teacher as either lack of interest or dumbness. (p. 204)

Similar stories exist for many other cultures and many other children. The reality is that scholastic expectations and interpretations vary based on sex, race, ethnicity, disability, and other factors with a cultural aspect.

***Work.***   Like many adolescents, Carl and Monica also play the role of worker in the labor market. Work can provide an opportunity for personal growth, social interaction, and greater financial independence. Work may contribute to personal growth by promoting contribution, responsibility, egalitarianism, self-efficacy, the development of values and preferences for future jobs—answers to questions like "What kind of job would I like to have in the future?" and "What am I good at?" (Mortimer & Finch, 1996, p. 4). Monica tried many jobs before deciding that she loves working with children and wants to become a pediatrician. In addition, employment may also offer the opportunity to develop job skills, time management skills, customer relation skills, money management skills, market knowledge, and other skills of value to future employers.

On the other hand, work may also detract from development, by cutting into time needed for sleep, exercise, maintenance of overall health, school, family relations, and peer relations. Adolescents who work more than 10 hours per week have been found to be at increased risk for poor academic performance; psychological problems, such as depression, anxiety, fatigue, and sleep difficulties; and physical problems, such as headaches, stomachaches, and colds. They are also more likely to use cigarettes, alcohol, or other drugs, regardless of ethnicity, socioeconomic status, or age (Mortimer & Finch, 1996). Although we cannot draw causal conclusions, Carl is a good example of this linkage: He works more than 10 hours a week and also has declining grades and uses tobacco and marijuana. According to Greenberger and Steinberg's (1986) research, employed adolescents demonstrate higher rates of school tardiness and spend less time completing homework.

***Leisure.***   Shaw, Kleiber, and Caldwell (1995) examined the relationship between leisure and identity formation for adolescents and found that the patterns of influence are different for girls and boys. Their research suggests that participation in sports and physical activities has a positive effect on identity development for female adolescents but shows no effect for males. Watching television has a negative effect on identity development for male adolescents but shows no effect for females. And involvement in social activities and other leisure activities was not significantly correlated with identity development for either gender.

Research suggests that girls and boys spend their leisure time differently (Eder & Parker, 1987; Garton & Pratt, 1987). Shaw, Kleiber, and Caldwell (1995) assert that adolescent girls need to be encouraged to undertake activities that stimulate independence and autonomy, because many of the activities they are involved in during their free time feature connectedness and social relationships. Conversely, perhaps males need activities that support connectedness and social relationships.

Leisure activities for rural adolescents are also different from leisure activities for urban youth. Adolescents living in urban areas have greater access to transportation and to recreational and public activities and programs (Garton & Pratt, 1991). Rural youth lack this access and thus rely more heavily on school-related leisure activities (Garton & Pratt, 1991). Access to leisure activities also increases with socioeconomic status (SES).

Finally, whatever an adolescent's gender, region, or SES, research suggests that those who consider their leisure time to be boring are more likely to use substances (Iso-Ahola & Crowley, 1991). They are also more likely to drop out of school (Widmer, Ellis, & Trunnell, 1996).

## Relationships with Culture

What can social workers do to help adolescent immigrants adjust to a new culture?

Adolescents in the United States who are not of European American background face additional challenges as they encounter the many changes of adolescence. Following a five-year longitudinal study of immigrants, Arrendondo (1984) proposed the following three factors as necessary for satisfactory adjustment to a new culture:

■ Willingness and ability to confront the issue of belonging versus estrangement

■ Ability to rely on the values of the native culture

■ Supportive family relationships

Youth from a minority culture must also decide whether to be

■ Traditional—speaking in their native language and practicing traditional beliefs and practices

■ Transitional—speaking both their native language and English and not participating fully in either traditional practices or mainstream culture

■ Bicultural—participating in both native culture and mainstream culture

■ Assimilated—practicing only mainstream culture and values (Garrett, 1995).

For some youth, this decision is not theirs to make; it is imposed on them by family and community.

Many youth will seek to distance themselves from their minority culture in early adolescence in order to emphasize their similarities with peers. These youth may then readopt their native culture in late adolescence, if their self-concept and identity are adequately formed and allow the reconnection. For some youth, their heritage is a source of great pride; for others, it carries shame. These responses certainly affect the self or identity of minority adolescents.

# Spiritual Aspects of Adolescence

In what other ways might adolescents exhibit development of the spiritual dimension of person?

Another potential facet of adolescent development is spirituality or religiosity. As adolescents become capable of advanced thinking and begin to contemplate their existence, identity, and future, many also undertake spiritual exploration. Gallup and Bezilla (1992) found that 76 percent of adolescents between the ages of 13 and 17 believe in a personal God; 29 percent believe they have experienced the presence of God; 74 percent pray at least occasionally; and 48 percent report attendance at religious services in the previous seven days. Yet, spirituality during adolescence has been largely unstudied.

Donahue and Benson (1995) suggest that cross-sectional research on religiousness by age reveals a persistent overall decline in religiousness during adolescence. Some attribute this decline to the period of questioning associated with the cognitive changes in adolescence; others suggest that during this period religiousness is merely evidenced in ways other than those typically studied, such as attendance at worship service (Donahue & Benson, 1995). Research also rather consistently finds that females demonstrate greater religiousness than males across all ages (Batson, Schoenrade, & Ventis, 1993; Donahue & Benson, 1995; Gallup & Bezilla, 1992). Regarding racial differences, Benson, Yeager, Wood, Guerra, and Manno (1986) report that both African American and Hispanic youth ascribe more importance to religion than do their European American counterparts.

Through a review of the literature, Donahue and Benson (1995) studied the effects of religion on the well-being of adolescents (controlling for sociodemographic variables). They found a link between religiousness and "prosocial values and behavior." Religious adolescents are less likely to think of or attempt suicide, to abuse substances, to become prematurely involved in sexual activity, and to become "delinquent." Religiousness is "unrelated to self-esteem," however (p. 145).

# Issues, Challenges, and Problems during Adolescence

The adolescent period is quite complex all on its own, and sexuality, substance use, juvenile delinquency, and other threats to physical and mental health further complicate the picture. Again, not all adolescents face all of these issues, and those who do face some of them follow no strict time line. We do know, however, that adolescents who are considered at risk may be more susceptible than others to these challenges or problems of adolescence. In the introduction to her book, *Adolescents at Risk,* Joy Dryfoos (1990) states:

> Many children are growing up in the United States today without a hope of enjoying the benefits that come with adulthood. They are not learning the skills necessary to participate in the educational system or to make the transition into the labor force. They cannot become responsible parents because they have limited experience in family life and lack the resources to raise their own children. The gap between achievers and nonachievers is expanding. A new class of "untouchables" is emerging in our inner cities, on the social fringes of suburbia, and in some rural areas: young people who are functionally illiterate, disconnected from school, depressed, prone to drug abuse and early criminal activity, and eventually, parents of unplanned and unwanted babies. (p. 3)

## *Sexuality*

Sexual identity is a significant component in the transition to adulthood. For the adolescent, sexual identity encompasses becoming familiar with the physical changes of puberty, recognizing one's sexual orientation, and making decisions about sexual activity; it may also include dealing with pregnancy and childbearing, sexually transmitted disease, and acquaintance rape.

***Masturbation.***   As the pubertal hormones cause changes throughout the body, adolescents spend time becoming familiar with those changes. For many, exploration includes masturbation, the self-stimulation of the genitals for sexual pleasure. Almost 50 percent of boys and 30 percent of girls report masturbating by age 13; boys masturbate earlier and more often than girls (Leitenberg, Detzer, & Srebnik, 1993).

However, masturbation has negative associations for some boys and girls. Martin (1996) suggests that since most girls do not like to touch or look at their genitals, it makes sense that few masturbate. She also found that for boys, any negative or anxious associations with sex at adolescence are usually in regard to masturbation (Martin, 1996, p. 49). Thus, masturbation may have psychological implications for adolescents, depending on the way they feel about masturbation and on how they think significant others feel about it.

***Sexual Orientation.***   During adolescence, many individuals, both homosexual and heterosexual, have homosexual experiences. But not all form a sexual identity based on those experiences. In a study of 38,000 7th through 12th graders, 88 percent classified themselves as heterosexual, 1 percent classified themselves as homosexual or bisexual, and 10 percent classified themselves as uncertain about their sexual orientation (Remafedi, Resnick, Blum, & Harris, 1992).

Still, adolescence is the time when most people develop some awareness of their sexual orientation. In their comprehensive investigation of gay and lesbian sexuality, Saghir and Robins (1973) found that most adult gay men and lesbians reported the onset of homosexual arousal, homosexual erotic imagery, and homosexual romantic attachment during adolescence, before age 15. There are gender differences, however, with gay males tending to begin homosexual activity during early or middle adolescence and lesbians tending to begin homosexual activity closer to age 20 (Bell, Weinberg, & Hammersmith, 1981).

Gay and lesbian youth typically suffer from the awareness that they are different from most of their peers in an aspect of identity that receives a great deal of attention in our culture. Consider David's conflict over his homosexuality. Dennis Anderson (1994) suggests that a "crisis of self-concept occurs because the gay adolescent senses a sudden involuntary joining to a stigmatized group" (p. 15). He goes on to elaborate:

> To some gay and lesbian adolescents the experience of watching boys and girls in school walk hand-in-hand down the hallway, while their own desires must be kept secret, produces feelings of rage and sadness that are difficult to resolve. In addition to having no opportunity to experience social interactions with gay or lesbian peers, there is little likelihood that they will see gay or lesbian adult role models in their day-to-day lives. Low self-esteem, academic inhibition, truancy, substance abuse, social withdrawal, depressed mood, and suicidal ideation are not unusual and may be difficult to differentiate from depressive disorders. (p. 18)

Recall David's feelings of abnormality, isolation, depression, and suicidal thoughts in regard to his sexual orientation. As an adolescent, he is struggling to develop a sense of identity, including sexual identity, but society discourages him from expressing what he finds.

Parents are often not very helpful to their gay and lesbian children:

> Unlike teenagers from other oppressed minority groups, gay teenagers find little or no support or understanding at home for their societal difference. Most often, family members are the most difficult people to reveal sexual orientation to, and are often the last to know. Considering the consequences, this is often a wise choice. Many teenagers who reveal their sexual orientation (or "come out") to their parents face extreme hostility, violence or sudden homelessness. ( O'Connor, 1994, p. 10)

*What other social movements might affect adolescent clients?*

To forestall such damaging responses, the Federation of Parents and Friends of Lesbians and Gays [PFLAG] (1984), a social movement with the goal of promoting a more supportive environment for gay males and lesbians, produced a brochure titled "Read This Before Coming Out to Your Parents." This brochure lists 12 questions to ponder prior to coming out, reproduced in Exhibit 6.4. These are heavy questions for any adolescent, and few nonfamilial supports are available to assist adolescents in resolving their questions related to sexual orientation or easing the process of coming out.

Perhaps we should not be surprised at the elevated risk of suicide among gay and lesbian youth. A task force on youth suicide commissioned by the U. S. Department of Health and Human Services (1993) found that

- Gay male and lesbian youth account for approximately 30 percent of all teen suicides.
- One in three gay male and lesbian youth reports committing at least one self-destructive act.
- Of the gay and lesbian youth who make one suicide attempt, nearly half attempt suicide repeatedly.
- Gay male and lesbian youth compose approximately one-fourth of all homeless youth in the United States.

**EXHIBIT 6.4**

Questions to Ponder Prior to Coming Out

1. Are you sure about your sexual orientation?
2. Are you comfortable with your gay sexuality?
3. Do you have support?
4. Are you knowledgeable about homosexuality?
5. What's the emotional climate at home?
6. Can you be patient?
7. What's your motive for coming out now?
8. Do you have available resources?
9. Are you financially dependent on your parents?
10. What is your general relationship with your parents?
11. What is their moral societal view?
12. Is this your decision?

*Source:* Federation of Parents and Friends of Lesbians and Gays, 1984.

Remafedi, Farrow, & Deisher (1991) also examined suicidal behavior among gay and bisexual youth and found that 30 percent reported at least one suicide attempt. Following these attempts, only 21 percent received medical or psychiatric intervention; 74 percent went without any professional intervention. Many of the youth cited strife regarding their sexual orientation as impetus for the suicide attempt.

*Sexual Decision Making.* The decision to engage or not to engage in sexual activity is yet another decision that most adolescents make. Biological, psychological, social, cultural, spiritual, and moral factors all play a part in the decision. Biologically, changes in hormone production and the reaction to the changes in appearance based on hormones have been cited as possible catalysts for sexual activity (Udry, Billy, Morris, Groff, & Raj, 1985). Psychologically, adolescents are involved in making a wide range of decisions and developing their own identities, and sexuality is just one more decision. Socially, youth are influenced by the attitudes toward sexual activity that they encounter in the environment, at school, among peers, siblings, and family, in their clubs/organizations, in the media, and so on. Furstenberg, Moore, and Peterson (1986) contend that "initiation of sexual behavior is highly associated with what is perceived as normative in one's peer group" (p. 1221). Research suggests that youth who are not performing well in school are more likely to engage in sexual activity than are those who are doing well (Hofferth & Hayes, 1987). Finally, beliefs and behaviors regarding sexuality are also shaped by one's culture, religion/spirituality, and value system.

Data suggest that one in four to five adolescents from Belgium, Canada, Hungary, the United Kingdom, and the United States engage in sexual intercourse by their 16th birthday; by age 18, more than 50 percent of youth from these countries have experienced sexual intercourse (Friedman, 1992, p. 347). According to the Population Division of the United Nations, however, global sexual intercourse data may not be particularly reliable. Reported rates of sexual intercourse among 17-year-olds in sub-Saharan Africa range from 17 percent to 71 percent; in Latin America and the Caribbean, the range is from 6 percent to 65 percent (United Nations, 1989). Meanwhile, across the nations, puberty is occurring earlier and earlier, whereas marriage is occurring later and later (Friedman, 1992). Thus, sexual intercourse outside of marriage is occurring earlier and more commonly worldwide. In the United States, studies of AIDS transmission by the Centers for Disease Control, conducted every two years, indicate that approximately 75 percent of high school students have had sexual intercourse by the 12th grade; less than 50 percent report using latex condoms, and about 20 percent have had more than four sexual partners (Healthtouch, 1997).

In 1995, 73 percent of African American students (median age of first intercourse, 15.0 years) reported having participated in sexual intercourse, compared with 58 percent of Hispanic American students (median age of first intercourse, 16.2 years) and 49 percent of European American students (median age of first intercourse, 16.7 years) (Warren et al., 1998).

Early engagement in sexual intercourse has some negative consequences. Costa, Jessor, Donovan, and Fortenberry (1995) found that the earlier a youth begins engaging in sexual intercourse, the more likely she or he is to become involved in delinquent behavior, problem drinking, and marijuana use. Shrier, Emans, Woods, and DuRant (1996) found that young age, as well as use of substances, is associated with an increased number of sexual partners and nonuse of condoms. Their findings suggest that adolescents who report first sexual intercourse before age 13 are more likely to have nine or more sexual partners by the age of 20 (Shrier et al., 1996).

Rates of sexual activity among teens in the United States are comparable to those in Western Europe, yet the incidence of adolescent pregnancy, childbearing, and sexually transmitted diseases in the United States far exceeds the level of most other industrialized nations. This discrepancy is due to poor contraceptive use among American teenagers (Jones et al., 1985). Almost 50 percent of American teens participate in unprotected sex the first time they engage in sexual relations (Zelnik & Shah, 1983). Only 29 percent of sexually active teens surveyed in one study reported consistent use of condoms (Brown, DiClemente, & Park, 1992). Seventy-three percent of teen girls wait an average of 23 months after first intercourse to visit a family planning clinic, and only 17 percent visit a clinic prior to engaging in sexual intercourse (Mosher & Horn, 1988).

To what extent is teens' attention to safer sex an effect of the environmental dimension of culture?

Why are American adolescents engaging in so much unprotected sex? Many teens blame a double standard: Teens are taught about the benefits of condom use and are expected to practice safer sex, but they find condoms difficult to obtain. They report that they are harassed at local drug stores for buying condoms, and they find the price of condoms prohibitive (McCarter, 1998). Also, whereas few teens mention difficulty in communicating with sexual partners, they often cite reasons such as "He just won't wear one [a condom]," "He told me to trust him," "She was trying to trick me" (McCarter, 1998). Finally, substance use may cloud an adolescent's decision to engage in protected or safer sex (Shrier et al., 1996). (For a discussion of contraceptive methods, please refer to Chapter 3.)

***Pregnancy and Childbearing.*** Approximately 1 million adolescent girls become pregnant each year in the United States (U.S. Department of Health and Human Services, Bureau of Maternal and Child Health, 1995). Thus, approximately 2,800 adolescents become pregnant each day; of those, 400 will miscarry, 1,100 will have an abortion, and 1,300 will give birth (Henshaw, 1993).

As discussed in Chapter 3, adolescent pregnancies carry increased physical risks to mother and infant, including less prenatal care and higher rates of miscarriage, anemia, toxemia, prolonged labor, premature delivery, and low birthweight. In many Asian, eastern Mediterranean, African, and Latin American countries, the physical risks of adolescent pregnancy are mitigated by social and economic support (Friedman, 1992, p. 346). In the United States, however, adolescent mothers are more likely than their counterparts elsewhere to drop out of school, to be unemployed or underemployed, to receive public assistance, and to have subsequent pregnancies and lower educational and financial attainment. Teenage fathers may also experience lower educational and financial attainment (Marsiglio, 1986).

Even pregnant teens who choose to abort are at greater risk than older pregnant women:

> While an overall decline in fertility rates in adults in [Western] societies is largely attributable to contraceptive methods, the unmarried adolescent is more likely to choose induced abortion. Although safe abortion is generally more readily available than in traditional societies, the adolescent with less knowledge, resources, and experience, and often fearing the reaction of service providers, will go late or to the inappropriate sources, thus greatly increasing the danger of septic abortions, illness, future infertility, and death. (Friedman, 1992, p. 346)

The developmental tasks of adolescence are typically accomplished in this culture by going to school, socializing with peers, and exploring various roles. For the teenage mother, these avenues to development may be radically curtailed. The result may be long-lasting disadvantage. Consider Monica's path. She obviously loves children and would like to have her own someday, but she would also like to become a pediatrician. If Monica were to become pregnant unexpectedly, an abortion would challenge her religious values, and a baby would challenge her future goals.

***Sexually Transmitted Diseases.***  Youth have always faced pregnancy as a consequence of their sexual activity, but other consequences now include infertility and death as a result of **sexually transmitted diseases (STDs)**. As noted earlier, many adolescents are engaging in sexual intercourse without protection (Healthtouch, 1997). "Adolescents are particularly prone to engage in behaviors that place them at higher risk of exposure to STDs" (Shrier et al., 1996, p. 377). They are likely to experiment with sex and be persuaded by potential partners about whom they know little. Health and sex education at home and in the schools often does not prepare adolescents for the difficult sexual decisions they must make, and they may be particularly ill informed about STDs (Brooks-Gunn & Furstenberg, 1989). Thus, the prevalence of STDs and their consequences have been increasing among adolescents (Shrier et al., 1996). More than two-thirds of the reported STD cases in the United States are in persons under the age of 25 (State Legislatures, 1996). Three million teenagers—one in every six individuals ages 13 to 19—contract an STD every year in the United States, and one-fifth of U.S. AIDS cases occur in young people between the ages of 13 and 29 (State Legislatures, 1996).

Social workers providing services to adolescents need to be knowledgeable regarding these sexually transmitted diseases:

1. **Chlamydia**. Each year, more people in the United States become infected with the bacterium *Chlamydia trachomatis*, or *T-strain Mycoplasma*, than any other sexually transmitted disease. Approximately 4 million new infections occur each year (National Institutes of Health–National Institute of Allergy and Infectious Diseases [NIH-NIAID],1996). The U.S. annual reported rate of chlamydia cases increased 262 percent (from 48 to 182 cases per 100,000 people) from 1987 to 1995 (NIH-NIAID, 1996). The American Social Health Association (1995) estimates that 29 to 30 percent of sexually active teenage girls have chlamydia. The disease is typically transmitted through sexual contact, but can also be spread nonsexually, through contact with the mucus or feces of an infected person. The symptoms of chlamydia include vaginal itching and discharge in women (most women remain asymptomatic) or a thin, whitish discharge in men (approximately 40 percent remain asymptomatic). These symptoms appear one to three weeks after contact. Chlamydia is most often treated with tetracycline, but if left untreated can result in pelvic inflammatory disease (PID) a leading cause of infertility in women.

2. **Genital warts**. Approximately 1 million Americans a year become infected with the human papilloma virus (HPV), which causes genital warts (NIH-NIAID, 1996). Estimating adolescent rates of HPV infection is difficult, but the American Social Health Association (1995) suggests that approximately 30 percent of sexually active adolescents are infected with the human papilloma virus. Genital warts may be contracted during vaginal or anal intercourse or during childbirth. The warts begin as hard, painless bumps that may appear six weeks to eight months

after transmission and may then become soft and resemble tiny cauliflower florets. They can appear in the vaginal area, on the penis, or around the anus, and they may itch. Genital warts may be hard to see without a colposcope, which magnifies them. Pap tests may reveal precancerous circumstances caused by HPV; more than 80 percent of invasive cervical cancer is associated with HPV. HPV can be treated with acid or podophyllin or with surgical, laser, or freezing treatments. Early treatment may prevent cancer of the cervix, vulva, or penis.

3. **Gonorrhea**. An estimated 800,000 people a year are infected with gonorrhea in the United States (NIH-NIAID, 1996). For 1993, the rate of infection among adolescents ages 15 to 19 was 742.1 per 100,000 population (Centers for Disease Control [CDC], 1994). Gonorrhea is caused by the gonococcus bacteria *Neisseria gonorrhoeae,* which live in mucous membranes such as those found in the mouth, vagina, urethra, and anus. Transmission can occur through oral, anal, or vaginal sexual activity with an infected person. Because gonorrhea can also be transmitted during childbirth, drops of silver nitrate are routinely placed in newborns' eyes immediately following delivery to prevent serious eye infections. Platt, Rice, and McCormack (1983) report that after having intercourse once with an infected person, women have a 50 percent chance and men a 25 percent chance of contracting gonorrhea. Symptoms, which usually appear within 2 to 30 days after contact (average is three to seven days), may include a change in vaginal discharge, painful urination, pelvic discomfort, or abnormal menstruation in women (approximately 80 percent experience mild or no symptoms) and painful urination with foul-smelling, thick, yellow urethral discharge in men (approximately 10 percent experience no symptoms). Gonorrhea is detected by microscopic examination of cultures taken from urethral or vaginal discharges and is treated orally by amoxicillin or ampicillin or intravenously by procaine penicillin. If left untreated, gonorrhea can cause arthritis, heart problems, central nervous system disorders, and pelvic inflammatory disease in women and prostate, testes, and epididymis infections and/or sterility in men.

4. **Syphilis**. Rates of syphilis infection are rising in this country, with more than 130,000 cases reported annually (NIH-NIAID, 1996). This reported rate is almost 60 times greater for African Americans than for European Americans, a disparity not seen in the other STDs. Syphilis is caused by a spirochete bacterium, *Treponema pallidum,* acquired through sexual contact. It can be a four-stage disease. First, infection results in the formation of a chancre or sore on the mouth, cervix, vagina, urethra, rectum, anus, external genitals, or nipples, which appears two weeks to a month after exposure. This first symptom is relatively mild and goes away, often unnoticed. During the second stage, two weeks to two months after the chancre disappears, infected persons may experience body rash, headache, fever, indigestion, sore throat, and painful joints. Syphilis is highly contagious during the first and second stages. During the third stage, syphilis becomes latent, with no external symptoms, but the spirochetes are actively invading the skeletal, cardiovascular, and nervous systems. For individuals who progress to the fourth stage of syphilis, treatment can kill the bacteria, but damage to internal organs may be irreparable at this point. Thus, syphilis should be detected as early as possible and treated with benzathine penicillin G.

5. **Genital herpes**. Approximately 500,000 new cases of genital herpes occur each year, with an estimated 31 million Americans already infected (NIH-NIAID, 1996). The disease is caused by the herpes simplex II virus and is contracted by physical contact with the open herpes sores

of an infected person (the disease is less contagious in the dormant phase). Genital herpes is characterized by small blisters, which appear in women on the labia, the clitoral hood, and the cervix and in men on the glans or foreskin of the penis, three to seven days after infection. The initial outbreak of blisters is typically the most painful and prompts many individuals to seek medical attention. There is no cure for genital herpes, but the medication acyclovir may reduce the pain in herpes outbreaks. Approximately 6 percent of women with genital herpes develop cervical cancer, and more than 80 percent of women with cervical cancer have herpes simplex II antibodies (Trimble, Gay, & Docherty, 1986).

6. **Acquired immunodeficiency syndrome (AIDS).** Nearly one-fifth of all AIDS cases in the United States involve persons 13 to 29 years old (CDC, 1994). HIV/AIDS has been the sixth leading cause of death among 15- to 24-year olds in the United States since 1991 (CDC, 1994). Hispanic and African American youth are overrepresented among persons with AIDS. In addition, the proportion of adolescent girls among those with AIDS has more than doubled, from 14 percent in 1987 to 32 percent by June 1994 (CDC, 1994). AIDS is caused by the human immunodeficiency virus (HIV), which attacks the immune system and reduces the body's ability to combat other diseases. Transmission of the virus can occur through sexual contact, intravenous drug use, blood transfusion, and birth. Symptoms of HIV infection may include swollen lymph nodes, unexplained weight loss, loss of appetite, persistent fevers, night sweats, chronic fatigue, unexplained diarrhea, bloody stools, skin rashes, easy bruising, persistent and severe headaches, and unexplained chronic dry cough, all of which can result from opportunistic infections. As of today, there is no cure for AIDS. There are several experimental treatments for HIV, but none have been tested extensively with children or adolescents.

*What other biological issues might enter into practice with adolescent clients?*

Exhibit 6.5 lists some facts that social workers can use as a starting point for discussing STDs with adolescents. Some social workers who work with adolescents may face issues of infection, but all social workers should discuss prevention. Teaching communication skills to youth will probably benefit them the most, but in addition, they should be educated to

- Recognize the signs and symptoms of STDs
- Refrain from sexual contact if they suspect themselves or a partner of having any of these signs or symptoms and instead get medical attention as soon as possible
- Use a condom correctly during sexual activity
- Have regular checkups that include STD testing

For AIDS information, the U.S. Public Health Service has a confidential toll-free hotline (1-800-342-2437). The American Social Health Association provides an STD hotline at 1-800-227-8922, where callers can obtain STD information without leaving their names.

*Acquaintance Rape.*   **Acquaintance rape** can be defined as forced, manipulated, or coerced sexual contact by someone you know. According to the Illinois Coalition Against Sexual Assault (1990), women between 15 and 24 are the primary victims of acquaintance rape, but junior high school girls are also at great risk.

In the late 1980s, a nationwide study of rape on college campuses found that 25 percent of female students had been victims of rape or attempted rape (Koss, Gidycz, & Wisniewski, 1987).

**EXHIBIT 6.5**

Facts about STDs

1. STDs affect men and women of all backgrounds and economic levels and are most prevalent among teenagers and young adults. Nearly two-thirds of all STDs occur in people younger than 25 years of age.
2. The incidence of STDs is rising.
3. Many STDs initially cause no symptoms, particularly in women. When symptoms develop, they may be confused with those of other diseases not transmitted through sexual contact. However, even when an STD causes no symptoms, a person who is infected may be able to pass the disease on to a sex partner. For this reason, many doctors recommend periodic testing for people who have more than one sex partner.
4. Health problems caused by STDs tend to be more severe and more frequent for women than for men, in part because the frequency of asymptomatic infection means that many women do not seek care until serious problems have developed.
5. When diagnosed and treated early, almost all STDs can be treated effectively.

*Source:* National Institutes of Health–National Institute of Allergy and Infectious Diseases, 1992b.

Muehlenhard and Linton (1987) found that more than three-fourths of the college women they surveyed reported that they had experienced sexual aggression, ranging from pressured kissing to forcible sexual intercourse. "The risk of a woman being sexually assaulted by an acquaintance is four times greater than her risk of being raped by a stranger" (Illinois Coalition Against Sexual Assault, 1990).

Although not a national study, a more recent four-year study of adolescent date rape and sexual assault produced similar findings: 23 percent of the sample experienced unwanted sexual activity by dates or boyfriends, and 15 percent were victims of date rape (Vicary, Klingaman, & Harkness, 1995). This research suggests that predictors of unwanted sexual activity may include early age of menarche, being sexually active, having sexually active same-sex friends, poor peer relationships, and poor emotional status. The researchers conclude that parents, teachers, counselors, the legal system, and communities should be informed of the seriousness of this problem and should adequately address it (Vicary et al., 1995).

Although much research supports the notion that the majority of female victims know their assailants (Mynatt & Algeier, 1990; Russell, 1984), stranger rape is overrepresented in FBI statistics because acquaintance rape is much less likely to be reported. Stranger rape is also more likely to involve the use of a weapon and to result in physical injury to the victim (Mynatt & Algeier, 1990; Russell, 1984).

## Substance Use and Abuse

Throughout this book, you have encountered a multiplicity of factors that contribute to the way individuals behave. Substance use is yet another variable in that mix. For example, Carl's use of tobacco and marijuana has several likely effects on his general behavior. Tobacco may make him feel tense, excitable, or anxious, and these feelings may amplify his concern about his weight, his

**EXHIBIT 6.6**

Percentage of Students Who Have Ever Used Alcohol, Tobacco, or Other Drugs

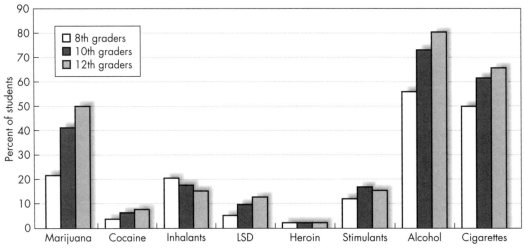

*Source:* National Institutes of Health–National Institute on Drug Abuse, 1998.

grades, and his family relationships. On the other hand, the marijuana may make Carl feel relaxed, and he may use it to counteract or escape from his concerns.

According to the 1997 Monitoring the Future Study (National Institutes of Health–National Institute on Drug Abuse [NIH-NIDA], 1998), 54.3 percent of students in the 1997 high school graduating class had used an illicit drug at least once (up from 40.7 percent in 1992, but still below the peak of 65.6 percent in 1981). Use of any illicit drug by seniors in the past year and in the past month also increased. Between 1992 and 1997, the number of students who had ever used marijuana increased for 10th and 12th graders and leveled off for 8th graders. Inhalants were the most widely abused substances—after alcohol, tobacco, and marijuana—and inhalant use among 8th graders was higher than for 10th or 12th graders in 1997. Daily use of alcohol and cigarettes increased as much as tenfold, particularly among 8th graders (NIH-NIDA, 1998). Exhibit 6.6 summarizes some of the findings about drug use in 1997.

Adolescents typically follow a pattern of substance use (Kandel & Logan, 1984, 1991; O'Malley, Johnston, & Bachman, 1991), beginning with tobacco, coffee, and alcohol. Thus, tobacco is considered a gateway drug to further substance use and abuse. According to the National Cancer Institute (1991), more than half of all smokers begin smoking before they turn 14, and 90 percent begin by the age of 19. Exhibit 6.7 reveals other substance use by high school smokers compared with nonsmokers.

Alcohol use usually begins with beer and wine (Kandel & Logan, 1984, 1991; O'Malley et al., 1991). The Carnegie Council on Adolescent Development (1995) reports that 66 percent of eighth graders who smoked admitted they had tried alcohol, and 28 percent said they had been drunk at least once. According to a national study, 38 percent of high school seniors reportedly abuse alcohol—that is, they had five or more drinks in a row during the preceding two weeks (Johnston, O'Malley, & Bachman, 1988).

**EXHIBIT 6.7**

Substance Use by
High School
Seniors: Smokers
versus Nonsmokers

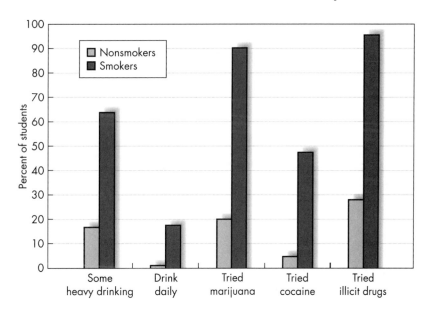

Adolescent substance use has some demographic predictors (Johnston et al., 1988; Oetting & Beauvias, 1987; O'Malley et al., 1991; Windle, 1990). Males are more likely to use substances than are females. Youth planning to attend college have lower rates of alcohol, cigarette, and illicit drug use than do those not planning to go to college. Rates of substance use are higher in metropolitan areas. Marijuana and cigarette use is greatest in the Northeast; cocaine and PCP use is greatest in the West; sedative and tranquilizer use is greatest in the South. Native American high school seniors have the highest usage rates for cigarettes, alcohol, and most illicit drugs, followed by European Americans, Hispanic Americans (except for cocaine use), African Americans (except for marijuana use), and Asian Americans, who have the lowest substance usage rates among high school seniors (Bachman et al., 1991). Kandel and Logan (1984) suggest that adolescence is the primary risk period for initiating substance use; those who have not experimented with licit or illicit drugs by age 21 are unlikely to do so thereafter.

***Decision Making about Substance Use.*** When asked why youth choose to use alcohol, adolescents cite the following reasons: to have a good time with friends, to relieve tension and anxiety, to deal with the opposite sex, to get high, to cheer up, and to alleviate boredom. When asked why youth use cocaine, the additional responses were to get more energy and to get away from problems. Overall drug use at a party is also cited quite often as a reason (O'Malley et al., 1991; Segal & Stewart, 1996). Segal and Stewart (1996) suggest that the following factors are involved in adolescents' choice of drugs: the individual characteristics of the drug, the individual characteristics of the user, the availability of the drug, the current popularity of the drug, and the sociocultural traditions and sanctions regarding the drug.

Adolescents who choose to abuse substances seem to differ from those who do not. In a 12-year longitudinal study, Jessor (1987) found that adolescent problem drinkers differ from other adolescents in their personal qualities, their social environment, and their other patterns of be-havior. Problem drinkers are less likely to hold traditional values about education, religion, or conformity. Problem drinkers perceive large differences between their family's values and their peers' values, are more influenced by their peers, and have peers who are also engaged in prob-lem drinking. Finally, problem drinkers are also more likely to participate in other risk-taking behaviors, such as sexual activity and delinquency (Jessor, 1987).

How do the biological and psychological dimensions interact in cases of substance abuse?

*Consequences of Substance Use and Abuse.*    According to Segal and Stewart (1996), chemical substances pose a profound threat to the health of adolescents, because substance abuse affects metabolism, internal organs, the central nervous system, emotional functioning, and cognitive functioning. Alcohol and opiates can cause severe intoxication, coma, and withdrawal symp-toms. Sedative drugs can depress the nervous and respiratory systems; withdrawal may lead to disturbances in breathing, heart function, and other basic body functions. Intravenous use of cocaine has been linked to adolescent cases of hepatitis, HIV, heart inflammation, loss of brain tissue, and abnormally high fever. Extended use of inhalants can cause irreparable neuropsycho-logical damage (Segal & Stewart, 1996). And finally, substances can weaken the immune system and increase a youth's likelihood of disease or general poor health.

Substance abuse has significant psychosocial implications for adolescents as well:

> [It] compromises their adjustment and school performance, contributes to low achieve-ments, poor academic performance and high school dropout. It disrupts normal psychoso-cial functioning, decreases social support, limits participation in age-appropriate activities, reduces psychological resources and produces anxiety, tension, and low self-esteem. Substance induced psychological reactions interfere with eating and sleeping, modify health related behavior and may be a cause of serious psychiatric disorders. (Segal & Stewart, 1996, p. 202)

As mentioned earlier, substance use can also affect the decision to engage in sexual activity. After substance use, youth are more likely to engage in sexual activity and are less likely to use protection; thus, they are more likely to become pregnant or impregnate and to contract a sexu-ally transmitted disease (Brooks-Gunn & Furstenberg, 1989; Segal & Stewart, 1996; Shrier et al., 1996). In general, adolescents who use tobacco products, alcohol, marijuana, and other sub-stances are more likely to be sexually active and to have more sexual partners (Lowry et al., 1994).

## Juvenile Delinquency

Almost every adolescent violates rules at some time, disobeying parents or teachers, lying, cheating, and perhaps even stealing or vandalizing. Many adolescents smoke cigarettes, drink al-cohol, skip school, or stay out past curfew. For some adolescents, this behavior is a phase, pass-ing as quickly as it appeared. Yet for others, it becomes a pattern. These are the adolescents who are likely to come into contact with the juvenile justice system.

In the United States, persons older than 7 but younger than 18 can be arrested for anything for which an adult can be arrested. (Children under 7 are said not to possess *mens rea*, which means "guilty mind," and thus are not considered capable of criminal intent.) In addition, they can be arrested for what are called **status offenses**, such as running away from home, skipping school, violating curfew, and possessing tobacco or alcohol—behaviors not considered crimes when engaged in by adults. When adolescents are found guilty of committing either a crime (by adult standards) or a status offense, we refer to their behavior as **juvenile delinquency**. Recently, the philosophy of the courts has shifted from reform and rehabilitation of delinquent adolescents to punishment and restitution.

The Office of Juvenile Justice and Delinquency Prevention reports that in 1994, American juvenile courts processed more than a million and a half delinquency cases (Butts, 1996). Between 1985 and 1994, the number of delinquency cases increased 41 percent. More serious cases increased at an even faster rate: Person offenses increased 93 percent; property offenses, 22 percent; drug offenses, 62 percent; and weapons offenses, 156 percent.

Of the delinquency cases reported in 1994, 79 percent involved a male, and 61 percent involved a juvenile under 16 years of age. As has been reported in the popular media, black teens are disproportionately represented among those brought to court. In 1994, the American juvenile population was 80 percent European American and 15 percent African American, but 32 percent of the delinquency cases involved African American juveniles and 64 percent involved European Americans (Butts, 1996). Research suggests that this disparity is based on a complex blend of psychological, racial, socioeconomic, familial, educational, structural, and political factors (McCarter, 1997).

## Threats to Physical and Mental Health

The U.S. Department of Health and Human Resources (1991, 1995) has reported the following statistics:

- Unintentional injury was the leading cause of death of adolescents.

- Homicide was the second leading cause of death for adolescents aged 15 to 19 (this rate is eight times higher for African Americans than for European Americans), and the third leading cause of death for those aged 10 to 14.

- Suicide is the third leading cause of death for adolescents aged 15 to 19, and the fourth leading cause for those aged 10 to 14.

- Approximately 3 million adolescents contract an STD annually, and more than 1 million adolescent girls become pregnant each year (the highest rate of the world's developed countries).

- Among adolescents aged 12 to 17, 15 percent report having used illegal drugs, 41 percent report alcohol use, and 20 percent of teenagers will be smoking by the time they finish high school.

- Of youth aged 10 to 18, 20 percent have no health insurance.

- Between 15 and 30 percent of American adolescents are obese, and the rate has increased over the past 20 years.

- More than half of underweight adolescents report being terrified of becoming overweight.

Thus, threats to adolescent health and well-being include not only pregnancy, sexually transmitted diseases, and substance abuse, which have already been discussed, but also violence, poor nutrition, obesity, eating disorders, and suicide.

How might social workers intervene to reduce violence within communities?

*Violence.*     Although researchers have studied the effects of family violence on youth, they are only beginning to address the effects of community violence on adolescents. A recent study of 935 urban and suburban youth found that "over 45 percent of the students reported witnessing severe forms of violence such as a shooting or stabbing in their communities or schools during the year prior to the study" (O'Keefe, 1997, p. 368). This violence may be a significant predictor of aggressive acting-out behavior for both male and female adolescents (O'Keefe, 1997). Also, urban African American youth exposed to high levels of community violence have been found to experience more distress, such as anxiety and depression, than those with less or no exposure to community violence (Fitzpatrick & Boldizar, 1993).

How might the biological dimension overlap with the social dimension in these cases?

*Nutrition, Obesity, and Eating Disorders.*     The dietary practices of some adolescents put them at risk for overall health problems. These practices include skipping meals, usually breakfast or lunch; snacking, especially on high-calorie, high-fat, low-nutrition snacks; eating fast foods; and dieting. Poor nutrition can affect a youth's growth and development, sleep, weight, cognition, mental health, and overall physical health.

This chapter has emphasized how tenuous self-esteem can be during adolescence, but the challenges are even greater for profoundly overweight or underweight youth. An increasing minority of American adolescents are obese. According to the third National Health and Nutrition Examination Survey, 1988–1994 (NHANES III), approximately 12 percent of adolescents aged 12 to 17 are overweight (Centers for Disease Control and Prevention, 1997)—a significant increase over NHANES II in 1980. American teenagers are overweight as a result of biological tendency, diet, family attitudes and behaviors toward food, and lack of exercise (Maloney & Klykylo, 1983). Overweight adolescents may suffer exclusion from peer groups and discrimination in education, employment, marriage, housing, and health care (DeJong, 1993). Carl Fleischer has already begun to face some of these challenges. He thinks of himself as a "fat, slow geek" and assumes females would not be interested in him because of his weight.

Keel, Fulkerson, and Leon (1997) examined problematic eating attitudes or behaviors in pre- and early adolescent (fifth- and sixth-grade) girls and boys. They found that girls reported more body dissatisfaction, depression, and lower self-esteem than boys and endorsed more of the items on the survey that indicate disordered eating habits or attitudes (p. 213). Girls' body dissatisfaction reflects the incongruence between the societal ideal of thinness and the beginning of normal fat deposits in pubescent girls. The result is often fad diets and unsafe nutrition. These disordered eating attitudes and behaviors are also precursors for anorexia nervosa and bulimia nervosa.

**Anorexia nervosa** means literally "loss of appetite due to nerves," but the disorder is actually characterized by a dysfunctional body image and voluntary starvation in the pursuit of weight loss. According to the DSM-IV (American Psychiatric Association [APA], 1994), the essential features of anorexia nervosa are that "the individual refuses to maintain a minimally normal body weight, is intensely afraid of gaining weight, and exhibits a significant disturbance in the perception of the shape or size of his or her body" (p. 539).

**Bulimia nervosa** is characterized by a cycle of binge eating; feelings of guilt, depression, or self-disgust; and purging (producing vomiting or evacuation of the bowels). The DSM-IV (APA, 1994) suggests that individuals with bulimia nervosa are also excessively influenced by body shape and weight and exhibit binge eating followed by purging at least twice a week for at least three months.

How might status as a minority affect the psychological health of adolescents?

*Depression and Suicide.* Research literature concerning adolescent mental health suggests that approximately 30 percent of adolescents have general emotional difficulties and approximately 5 percent have a major depressive disorder (Kaplan et al., 1994; Kovaks, 1989). Adolescent and adult females are twice as likely as their male counterparts to be diagnosed with a major depressive disorder (APA, 1994, p. 341). Some research also suggests that African American and Mexican American youth may be at increased risk for depression (Roberts, Roberts, & Chen, 1997).

Adolescent depression may be difficult to detect and thus may be underdiagnosed. Many parents and professionals expect adolescence to be a time of ups and downs, moodiness, melodrama, anger, rebellion, and increased sensitivity. There are, however, some reliable outward signs of depression in adolescents: poor academic performance, truancy, social withdrawal, antisocial behavior, changes in eating or sleeping patterns, changes in physical appearance, excessive boredom or activity, low self-esteem, sexual promiscuity, substance use, propensity to run away from home, and excessive family conflict. Additional symptoms of depression not unique to adolescence include pervasive inability to experience pleasure, severe psychomotor retardation, delusions, and a sense of hopelessness (Kaplan et al., 1994, p. 1116).

This chapter has outlined many of the challenges of adolescence, and for many youth these challenges prove overwhelming. I have already discussed the risk of suicide among gay male and lesbian adolescents. Overall, suicide is the third leading cause of death for adolescents in the United States (National Center for Health Statistics, 1993b); it is number two (behind accidents) for European American males aged 15 to 24. The American Academy of Child and Adolescent Psychiatry (1995) provides a list of warning signs for adolescent suicide shown in Exhibit 6.8, and recommends that if one or more of these signs occur, professional help be sought.

**EXHIBIT 6.8**
Suicide Signs in Adolescents

- Change in eating and sleeping habits
- Withdrawal from friends and family, and from regular activities
- Violent actions, rebellious behavior, or running away
- Drug and alcohol use
- Unusual neglect of personal appearance
- Marked personality change
- Persistent boredom, difficulty concentrating, or a decline in the quality of schoolwork
- Frequent complaints about physical symptoms, often related to emotions, such as stomachaches, headaches, and fatigue
- Loss of interest in pleasurable activities
- Intolerance of praise or rewards

*Source:* American Academy of Child and Adolescent Psychiatry, 1995.

## IMPLICATIONS FOR SOCIAL WORK PRACTICE

Adolescence is a vulnerable period. Adolescents' bodies and psyches are changing rapidly in transition from childhood to adulthood. Youth are making some very profound decisions during this life course period. Thus, the implications for social work practice are wide-ranging.

- When working with adolescents, meet clients where they are "at," because that place may change frequently.

- Be familiar with typical adolescent development and with the possible consequences of deviations from developmental time lines.

- Be aware of and respond to the adolescent's level of cognition and comprehension. Assess the individual adolescent's ability to contemplate the future, to comprehend the nature of human relationships, to consolidate specific knowledge into a coherent system, and to envision possible consequences from a hypothetical list of actions.

- Recognize that the adolescent may see you as an authority figure who is not an ally. Develop skills in building rapport with adolescents.

- Assess the positive and negative effects of the school environment on the adolescent, in relation to such issues as early or late maturation, popularity/sociability, culture, and sexual orientation.

- Where appropriate, advocate for change in maladaptive school settings, such as those with Eurocentric models or homophobic environments.

- Provide information, support, or other interventions to assist adolescents in resolving questions of sexual identity and sexual decision making.

- Where appropriate, link youth to existing resources, such as extracurricular activities, education on STDs, prenatal care, and gay and lesbian support groups.

- Provide information, support, or other interventions to assist adolescents in making decisions regarding use of tobacco, alcohol, or other drugs.

- Develop skills to assist adolescents with physical and mental health issues, such as nutritional problems, obesity, eating disorders, depression, and suicide.

- Participate in research, policy, and advocacy on behalf of adolescents.

- Work at the community level to develop and sustain recreational and social programs and places for young people.

## MAIN POINTS

1. Adolescence can be divided into three phases: early (ages 11 to 14), middle (ages 15 to 17), and late (ages 18 to 20). It is characterized by significant physical change, increased hormone production, sexual maturation, increased cognitive functioning, formative identity development, increased independence, and possible experimentation with sex and substances.

2. During adolescence, increased hormone production results in a period called puberty, during which persons become capable of reproduction. Other physical changes during this period include skeletal, musculature, and fat distribution changes as well as development of primary and secondary sex characteristics.

3. Psychological changes during this period include reactions to physical, social, and cultural changes confronting the adolescent, as well as cognitive development. During adolescence, most individuals develop the abilities to contemplate the future, to comprehend the nature of human relationships, to consolidate specific knowledge into a coherent system, and to envision possible consequences from a hypothetical list of actions.

4. The greatest task of adolescence is identity formation—determining who one is. Identity comprises social identity, dispositions, and physical characteristics. Identity may be formed through future orientation, role experimentation, exploration, and self-evaluation.

5. Separation from parents has four elements: functional independence, attitudinal independence, emotional independence, and conflictual independence.

6. Just as adolescents seek to release the tether to their parents, they seek to connect with a group of their peers.

7. Adolescents spend nearly a third of their waking hours at school, where they should receive skills and knowledge for their next step in life. School may be a negative experience, however. For instance, a school that follows a Eurocentric educational model without regard for other cultures may damage the self-esteem of students from minority ethnic groups.

8. Work can provide adolescents an opportunity for personal growth, social interaction, and greater financial independence. However, work can also detract from sleep, exercise, overall health, and school, family, and peer relations.

9. Identity development can be particularly complicated for children and adolescents belonging to ethnic and racial minority groups in the United States.

10. A link has been found between religiousness and prosocial values and behavior in adolescence.

11. Sexual identity formation is a major task for most adolescents. Gay male and lesbian youth may face social risks for both the decision to come out and the decision not to come out.

12. Most adolescents face the decision to engage or not to engage in sexual activity. A possible result, especially in the United States, is early pregnancy. Adolescent pregnancies may carry increased physical risks to mother and infant. Youth who engage in sexual activity also face possible infertility or death as a result of sexually transmitted diseases. Finally, adolescent females are at high risk for sexual assault.

13. Adolescence is the primary risk period for the initiation of substance use. Chemical substances are a threat to the physical, mental, and psychosocial health of adolescents.

14. Anyone older than 7 but younger than 18 can be arrested for any adult crime or for status offenses (such as underage drinking, truancy, and running away from home). The philosophy of the juvenile courts has recently shifted from reform and rehabilitation to punishment and restitution.

15. Among the physical and mental health risks to today's adolescents are violence, poor nutrition, obesity, eating disorders, depression, and suicide.

## KEY TERMS

acquaintance rape
acquired immunodeficiency syndrome
  (AIDS)
anorexia nervosa
attitudinal independence
bulimia nervosa
chlamydia
conflictual independence
derived statuses
dispositions
emotional independence
exploration
formal operational thought
functional independence
future orientation
generalized other
genital herpes

genital warts
gonads
gonorrhea
identity
individuation
juvenile delinquency
labels
membership groups
menarche
personal identities
physical characteristics
primary sex characteristic
puberty
rites of passage
role experimentation
secondary sex characteristic
self-evaluation

sexually transmitted diseases (STDs)
social identity
social statuses
social types

spermarche
status offenses
syphilis

## WORLD WIDE WEB RESOURCES

Puberty in Boys
**http://www.public.health.wa.gov.au/hp2106.htm**
Site maintained by the Health Department of Western Australia. Contains information on the
beginning of puberty, biology, cancer, sexual feelings, friends and relationships, and communication.

Adolescence:  Change and Continuity
**http://www.personal.psu.edu/faculty/n/x/nxdlo/adolesce.htm#top**
Site maintained by Pennsylvania State University. Information on biological, cognitive, and social changes, family changes and influences, peer groups, schools, work and leisure, identity
development, intimacy, sexuality, parenthood, psychosocial problems, delinquency, and
adolescents with disabilities.

Puberty in Girls
**http://www.public.health.wa.gov.au/hp2107.htm**
Site maintained by the Health Department of Western Australia.  Contains information on the female body, periods, discharges, sexual feelings and involvement, friends, relationships, love,
and communication.

DHHS—Youth Info
**http://youth.os.dhhs.gov/**
Site maintained by the Department of Health and Human Services. Contains the latest information on America's adolescents, statistical profiles, reports and publications, information for
parents and teens, and links to additional resources.

# CHAPTER 7

# Adulthood

# CASE STUDIES

## SONJA PUKALSKI, AGE 22

At age 22, Sonja Pukalski is a pretty young woman with brown eyes and long brown hair, but you first notice the fatigue in her face and the droop in her shoulders. Sonja is the third and youngest daughter of a working-class family. Her life was relatively uneventful until she was 12. Her father worked in a factory, and her mother went to work at the neighborhood grocery store once the children were in school. A large extended family, including both sets of grandparents, lived in the neighborhood. Sonja was somewhat shy, but she had a few close friends, and she got on well with her sisters and cousins. She was an average student at school.

When Sonja was 12, her mother was diagnosed with colon cancer. She died one year later. This was a tough time for the family, both emotionally and economically. With the help of extended family and people from the church parish, Sonja's father managed to hold the family together, but Sonja and her sisters were suddenly expected to carry a much heavier load of housework, as well as to supplement the family income. Sonja's father remarried when she was 15, and she and her sisters did not get along well with their stepmother. Sonja began spending at lot of time at the home of her boyfriend, Scott.

When Sonja became pregnant, both families insisted that she and Scott should marry. Sonja dropped out of high school before the baby was born and had a second baby when she was 18. By age 20, Sonja was divorced, and she now receives very little child support from Scott, who is not steadily employed. After the divorce, Sonja and the children received welfare for a while. Now, at age 22, she and the children live with a maternal aunt, who provides child care while Sonja works as a waitress in the evenings. Various members of Sonja's extended family provide occasional child care and financial assistance. Sonja often feels hopeless about her future, but she dreams that she will marry again someday, to someone who will love her and the children and share the financial load with her. She still misses her mother very much.

## ROBERT JOHNSON, AGE 41

Robert Johnson was born into a stable working-class family. His father was a longtime laborer in the steel industry, with an income that allowed the family to maintain a middle-class lifestyle. Robert's mother was a full-time housewife. Robert currently lives about two miles from his parents and keeps in close touch with them and with his two younger sisters and their families. He is proud of and grateful for the type of upbringing he was provided by his hardworking parents.

Robert's father had the good fortune, as many other black male workers did, of getting into the relatively high-paying, unionized steel industry before it began to crumble in the mid-1950s. Drawing on the equity accumulated in the family's modest home, he was able to provide financial assistance for Robert to attend college. Robert was the first member of his family to attend college, and now he has undergraduate and law degrees from a prestigious university.

With a good education, strong earning potential, and a positive self-image, Robert worked steadily toward building the kind of independence that is characteristic of the American middle class. He set his career goals high: to become a partner in his prestigious law firm. Soon after beginning work at the law firm, Robert set about repaying his school loans. At the same time, he began building his own investment program for the future.

After living together for three years, Robert and Cindy Marsh, an interior decorator, felt financially secure enough to get married. Soon after they were married, they bought a house. Once the house was furnished and Robert became a partner in the law firm, Robert and Cindy began to plan to have children. They were excited about this prospect and confident that they would make excellent parents. As the months went by and Cindy did not get pregnant, they became increasingly distressed. They attended a fertility clinic for about a year but found that their relationship was suffering from the constant pressure to become pregnant.

Finally, Robert and Cindy decided to go away for an extended vacation and take time to think and talk about their plan to have children. They talked about their sadness over their inability to get pregnant, their love for each other, and their desire to share their many resources with children. They decided to work with children at their church, and they recently began working toward adoption with you at Family Services, Inc.

### VERONICA PALMORE, AGE 54

Veronica married her high school boyfriend, Simon, when she graduated from college at age 22. Simon was 24 at the time and had been working as a laborer since he graduated from high school. Veronica had dreams of a career in teaching, but she did not know how she could combine that dream with her desire to have a family, because both she and Simon had very traditional expectations about gender roles. Veronica became pregnant during her first year of teaching and quit at age 23 to have a family, planning to return when the children were older.

**CASE STUDIES**

Simon and Veronica's parents were thrilled about the baby, but Veronica did not feel ready to be a mother. She felt overwhelmed and was weepy for much of the first year, saying in retrospect that she was struggling with a stubborn postpartum depression. To make matters worse, Simon was laid off from work for a few months, and it became financially necessary to move in with Veronica's parents.

By the time Veronica was 25, Simon had a better job and they had an apartment of their own. Veronica decided it was time to have another baby, and to her surprise, she really enjoyed the second baby. Both she and Simon developed close relationships with the children.

When the younger child was 2, Veronica decided to try substitute teaching, and she found that she enjoyed being in the classroom more than she had during her earlier teaching experience. A year later, she took a full-time teaching position and hired a sitter for the children. Soon she began to take evening courses toward a master's degree. Simon seemed happy to help with household chores, and family was the center of his life. Work was important to him only because it allowed him to provide for his family. With Veronica and Simon both working, they could afford to buy their own house in a more middle-class neighborhood.

Veronica's starting salary was half that received by men in starting positions, and Veronica felt that she had to prove to her male colleagues that she was dedicated to her work. She was careful never to say that she couldn't stay for a meeting because she had to get home to her children. After a few years as a full-time teacher, Veronica felt more confident and made a commitment to take a particular interest in children who were struggling in school.

When Veronica was 34, her father died suddenly of a heart attack, and her bereft mother lived with Veronica and Simon for two years until she remarried and moved out of town. Veronica was sad to lose the safety net of having a dependable mom and dad close by. About the same time, she and Simon decided that they no longer needed organized religion for their spiritual anchor.

When Veronica was 39, Simon was seriously injured in an accident at work. He was hospitalized for several weeks, followed by a lengthy period in a rehabilitation center. This was a very hard time for the family. Veronica and the children missed Simon very much, and Veronica became concerned about whether she was giving too much responsibility to her adolescent daughters. She was happy for an opportunity to talk to the social worker at the rehabilitation center about the impact Simon's accident was having on the family. During these conversations, Veronica acknowledged that she and Simon were very different, but she also began to have a deep appreciation for the support Simon had offered to her over the years and for his close relationship with the children.

Simon made an excellent recovery from his accident and was able to return to work. A few years later, he was promoted into a better-paying position, the children were doing well in college, and Veronica was earning a reputation as a humane and dedicated teacher. She was assertively challenging school policies and enjoyed mentoring younger teachers. In her late 40s, she turned down an offer to be department head. As she approached 50, she looked forward to another 15 years of teaching, but she began to have occasional worries that she would either burn out or be pushed out.

Today, the question of "what next" is troublesome to Veronica. She was recently asked to join a coalition of county teachers who are developing guidelines for managing diversity in the public schools. She is also busy with family matters: Simon's parents have begun to have major health problems, and Simon and Veronica are actively involved in the lives of their children and grandchildren, who live nearby. Religion is, once again, becoming important to Simon and Veronica.

# The Meaning of Adulthood

You have just read about three people whose lives are in process: Sonja Pukalski, Robert Johnson, and Veronica Palmore. With such different histories and current circumstances, they are likely to have very different futures. Despite the many differences in their life course trajectories, we think of each of them as an adult.

Although much has been written about adult development in the past few decades, definitions of adulthood are rare. In an edited book (Erikson, 1978) written two decades ago for the purpose of clarifying the meaning of adulthood, the following phrases were used, some repeatedly, by the various authors: "grown up," "a fully grown individual," "mature," "responsible," "age of majority."

The limited attempts to define adulthood have been based on biological age, psychological age, or social age. In terms of *biological* age, Katchadourian (1978) proposes that any definition of adulthood must include "completion of growth and reproductive capacity" (p. 54). That definition raises the question of whether Sonja and Scott should have been considered adults when Sonja became pregnant in their mid-teens. Katchadourian acknowledges the difficulty with this biological definition of adulthood, commenting that a comprehensive definition will be based not only on biology but also on psychosocial characteristics and "mind and spirit that lend meaning to life" (p. 54).

> *SANITY*
>
> *NORMALITY*
>
> *RATIONALITY*
>
> *CONTINUITY*
>
> **SOBRIETY**
>
> *RESPONSIBILITY*
>
> **WISDOM**
>
> *CONDUCT AS OPPOSED TO MERE BEHAVIOR*

*Source:* Based on Stegner, 1978, p. 227.

And what of attempts to define *psychological* adulthood? Stegner (1978, p. 227) suggests a list of words, found in Exhibit 7.1, that have been identified with psychological adulthood. This list of qualities, however, reflects the biases of modern Western cultures (Lapidus, 1978; Rudolph & Rudolph, 1978). Some have suggested that any listing of adult psychological qualities serves only as an ideal type; it does not accurately reflect the psychological state of many persons considered adult (for example, Bouwsma, 1978). Indeed, government does reserve the right to declare an age-qualified adult to be incompetent. Stuart Kirk and Herb Kutchins (1992) remind us that judging competence is not an easy matter, however, because secular law must rely on vague, ambiguous, and unreliable psychiatric models for making evaluations of mental status.

How might institutional definitions of adulthood influence social work practice?

*Social* definitions of adulthood focus on family and work roles. David Lipsky and Alexander Abrams (1994) suggest that benchmarks such as financial independence, "a place of my own," marriage, and parenthood have been a part of the informal social definition of adulthood. Social definitions of adulthood are also formalized by secular law, which specifies who is recognized by government as adults. To be an adult in the eyes of secular law, one must have reached the **statutory age of majority**, which is based solely on chronological age. The statutory age of majority has changed over time, varies among states, and sometimes varies within a state for different purposes (Goldstein, 1978). For example, the federal voting age was reduced from 21 to 18 in 1971 by the Twenty-Sixth Amendment to the Constitution, but federal legislation in the 1980s resulted in states' establishing 21 as the drinking age. Exhibit 7.2 demonstrates regional variations in four adult benchmarks. Given the variation, we cannot be surprised that many 18- to 21-year-olds question the rationale for the drinking age.

Obviously, definitions of adulthood are somewhat arbitrary. In this chapter, adulthood will be defined as beginning approximately at age 18 and ending approximately at age 65, almost a half century. Indeed, there is a difference of 31 years between the ages of Sonja Pukalski and Veronica Palmore, who are both adults.

# Theoretical Approaches to Adulthood

Religious, philosophical, and literary texts suggest that humans have long contemplated questions about their personal biographies and the adult life course. In the past quarter century, theorizing about the adult life course in the behavioral sciences has also grown steadily. This

**EXHIBIT 7.2**

Four Adult
Benchmarks for
Selected States

| State | Driver's Age | Marriage Age | Voting Age | Drinking Age |
|---|---|---|---|---|
| California | 16–18 | 18 | 18 | 21 |
| Georgia | 16 | 16 | 18 | 21 |
| Hawaii | 15 | 16 | 18 | 21 |
| Idaho | 17 | 18 | 18 | 21 |
| Mississippi | 16 | 17(M), 15(F) | 18 | 21 |
| Nebraska | 16 | 19 | 18 | 21 |
| Pennsylvania | 17–18 | 18 | 18 | 21 |
| Vermont | 18 | 18 | 18 | 21 |

*Source:* Based on *World almanac and book of facts 1997,* 1996.

chapter will not attempt a thorough discussion of recent theorizing about adulthood but will summarize the central ideas from two theoretical perspectives: stage theories and the process theoretical approach.

## Stage Theories

The idea that people pass through a sequence of stages of development—the basis of **stage theories**—is not a new idea. Mark Tennant and Philip Pogson (1995, p. 69) cite a number of historic stage theories, including Aristotle's three-stage model, Solon's nine seven-year stages, Confucius's six stages, the 14 stages of the Sayings of the Fathers from the Talmud, and Shakespeare's seven stages. The identification of stages of life has been one of the ways that people have tried to bring order and predictability to changing configurations of person and environment across the life course.

Stage theories can be criticized for their rigidity. A critical analysis of stage theories is included in Chapter 2, however, and will not be repeated in this chapter.

*Erikson's Psychosocial Life Span Theory.*    The most influential modern stage theory of adulthood is Erik Erikson's psychosocial life span theory (Erikson, 1950, 1959a, 1980, 1982). (Elements of this theory have been discussed in Chapters 4 though 6.) Erikson describes a sequence of eight psychosocial stages across the life span that result from the interaction between internal instincts and drives and external social and cultural demands. He bases his theory on the **epigenetic principle,** which holds that development occurs in clearly defined, sequential stages and that each stage must be satisfactorily completed for healthy development to continue.

A major focus of Erikson's theory is the development of *identity,* a concept that he never explicitly defines but that appears to include a sense of self that distinguishes "who I am" from other people and that is enduring over time. Identity develops as the person encounters physiological changes and the changing demands of society, demands that produce a **psychosocial crisis**—a struggle or turning point that defines the particular stage. A well-resolved psychosocial crisis leads to strength; a poorly resolved psychosocial crisis sets the stage for psychopathology.

The first five stages in Erikson's model build on Freud's psychosexual stages and are postulated to occur in childhood and adolescence. The last three stages are adult stages, generally referred to as the stages of young adulthood, middle adulthood, and later adulthood. Young adulthood and middle adulthood are the subject of this chapter; later adulthood is discussed in Chapter 8.

According to Erikson, the psychosocial struggle in *young adulthood* is intimacy versus isolation. **Intimacy** is "the ability to fuse your identity with somebody else's without fear that you're going to lose something yourself" (Erikson, in H. Bee, 1996, p. 57). When young adults are not ready for the demands of intimacy, their relationships remain shallow, and they experience isolation and loneliness. Robert Johnson and Veronica Palmore were successful in negotiating the demands of intimacy, but Sonja Pukalski confronted those demands before she was ready for them. As a social worker, you will find that people often need help to resolve issues of intimacy.

The psychosocial struggle in *middle adulthood* is generativity versus stagnation. **Generativity** is the ability to transcend personal interests to provide care and concern for generations to come; it "encompasses procreativity, productivity, and creativity" (Erikson, 1982, p. 67). Failure to find a way to contribute to future generations, or to make a contribution to the general well-being, results in self-absorption and a sense of stagnation. Robert Johnson and Veronica Palmore are both finding a variety of ways to experience generativity, but as a social worker you will most likely encounter people who struggle with a sense of stagnation in middle adulthood.

*Levinson's Theory of Seasons of Adulthood.*  Although Erikson's psychosocial theory has had the most influence on stage theories of adulthood, Daniel Levinson's theory of **seasons of adulthood** is one of the best known and most often quoted stage theories (Levinson, 1978, 1980, 1986, 1990, 1996). Levinson conceptualizes the life course as a sequence of **eras** (see Exhibit 7.3), each with its own biopsychosocial character (Levinson, 1996), with major changes from one era to the next and smaller changes within eras. The eras are partially overlapping, with **cross-era transitions**, in which characteristics of both the old era and the new are evident, lasting about five years. Adult life is, therefore, composed of alternating periods of relative stability and periods of transition. Every era begins and ends at a clearly defined average age, with a range of approximately two years above and below this average.

Levinson postulates that the eras and the cross-transition periods are universal, found in all human lives, but they accommodate innumerable "variations related to gender, class, race, culture, historical epoch, specific circumstances, and genetics" (1996, p. 5). Just consider the variations at age 40 among the people whose stories you read at the beginning of the chapter: Robert Johnson was trying to become a parent, Veronica Palmore was preparing to launch her first child, and Sonja Pukalski may be a grandmother.

A key concept of Levinson's theory is **life structure**, by which he means "the underlying pattern or design of a person's life at a given time" (1996, p. 22). Relationships are the primary components of a life structure. Levinson uses the concept **central components** to designate the relationships that have the greatest significance to a life structure. He suggests that usually no more than two central components exist in a life structure, but the structure may also involve **peripheral components** and **unfulfilled components.** In most cases, family and occupation are the central components in the life structure, but people vary widely in how much weight they assign

**EXHIBIT 7.3**

Levinson's Seasons
of Adulthood

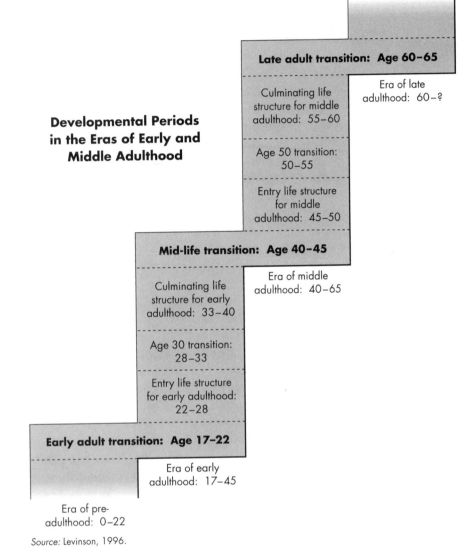

**Developmental Periods
in the Eras of Early and
Middle Adulthood**

**Late adult transition: Age 60–65**

Era of late
adulthood: 60–?

Culminating life
structure for middle
adulthood: 55–60

Age 50 transition:
50–55

Entry life structure
for middle
adulthood: 45–50

**Mid-life transition: Age 40–45**

Era of middle
adulthood: 40–65

Culminating life
structure for early
adulthood: 33–40

Age 30 transition:
28–33

Entry life structure
for early adulthood:
22–28

**Early adult transition: Age 17–22**

Era of early
adulthood: 17–45

Era of pre-
adulthood: 0–22

*Source:* Levinson, 1996.

to each. These variations are quite evident in the life course trajectories of Robert Johnson, Cindy Marsh, and Veronica and Simon Palmore. During transition periods, the pattern of central, peripheral, and unfulfilled components are reexamined and often reworked. The desire for children is an unfulfilled component for Robert and Cindy in their midlife transition; work and family have taken on different meanings for Veronica and Simon across several transitions.

You can see in Exhibit 7.3 that Levinson recognizes three eras of adulthood: early adulthood, middle adulthood, and late adulthood. He focuses most of his work on the first two eras, however, and that is the only part of his work reported in this chapter. According to Levinson's theory, each era of adulthood begins with a cross-era transition that terminates one era and begins the next. This transition is followed by an **entry life structure** for the era, then a mid-era transition in which the entry life structure is reassessed, and finally a **culminating life structure** for the era.

According to Levinson, early adulthood, from about 17 to 45, is the adult era of greatest vigor but also of "greatest contradiction and stress" (1996, p. 19). The 20s and 30s are peak years biologically. Psychosocially, early adulthood offers only limited life experience for making crucial decisions about domestic partnerships, family, work, and lifestyle. Heavy financial obligations are likely to be incurred, but earning power is still comparatively low. Both the rewards and costs of this era are enormous. Although they managed these contradictions and competing demands in different ways, Sonja Pukalski, Robert Johnson, and Veronica Palmore would probably agree that they experienced both strong rewards and strong costs in early adulthood.

The era of middle adulthood, from about 40 to 65, is a time of reduced biological capacities but also a period when many people are energized by satisfying intimate relationships and gratifying contributions at work and in the community. This certainly seems to be the case for Robert Johnson and Veronica Palmore. For others, however, middle adulthood is a time of progressive decline, self-absorption, and emptiness.

*Sheehy's New Passages.*   Gail Sheehy (1976, 1995) was strongly influenced by both Erikson and Levinson and shares Levinson's interest in developing a stage theory focused specifically on adulthood. In her recent work (Sheehy, 1995), however, she challenges the idea that the timing and content of the stages of adulthood are universal, and she pays particular attention to the influence of culture and historical time. Sheehy uses the concept of **passages** in the same way that Erikson uses "psychosocial crises" and Levinson uses "transitions": to refer to predictable crises or turning points between stages of adulthood.

Sheehy's first book on the adult life stages, *Passages,* appeared in 1976. Almost 20 years later, she began *New Passages* by suggesting that adult stages have been "fundamentally altered" since the publication of *Passages* by monumental changes in social institutions. She suggests that people are now moving from childhood to adolescence earlier but moving from adolescence to adulthood later, resulting in a prolonged adolescence. Age norms for marker events in adulthood such as marriage, are also shifting upward and becoming highly flexible, with a diversity of pathways through adulthood. People are also living longer.

Sheehy (1995, p. 8) maps out what she calls "three adult lives" or periods of adulthood: Provisional Adulthood (age 18–30), First Adulthood (age 30–45), and Second Adulthood (age 45–85+). She divides Second Adulthood into two stages: Age of Mastery (45–65) and Age of Integrity (65–85+).

How can social workers accommodate the cultural influences on clients from different cohorts?

Sheehy superimposes a cohort analysis onto her stage analysis of adulthood (see the discussion of cohort in Chapter 1), proposing that experience with these different stages is highly influenced by the historical time in which one is born. She delineates five cohort groups, which she also refers to as **generations**, born between 1914 and 1980. The shared cultural influences and historical events of each cohort group proposed by Sheehy are summarized in Exhibit 7.4. Like other cohort analysts, Sheehy emphasizes that "the playing field is quite different for each generation when its young members start the journey into adulthood" (1995, p. 24) and that these differences will affect the journey through each stage of adulthood. Also, like other life course

**EXHIBIT 7.4**

Cohort Groups Identified by Gail Sheehy

| Cohort (Birth Years) | Shared Cultural Influences and Historical Events |
|---|---|
| 1. World War II Generation (1914–1929) | Motto: "I want to fly." Young through Depression and World War II. 6.4 percent of women and 14 percent of men completed college. Men married in mid-20s. Strict gender roles. |
| 2. Silent Generation (1930–1945) | As children, taught to prepare for thermonuclear war. Born before television. Products of the repressive 1950s. Earliest marrying and baby-making generation in American history. Second smallest generation in 20th century. Plentiful career opportunities in young adulthood. Surge of women entered college after age 40. Produced leaders of modern civil rights and feminist movements. Never a U.S. president from this cohort. |
| 3. Vietnam Generation (1946–1955) | Motto: "I want to be different." Children during child-centered, prosperous era. Believed they could do anything. Expected everything will always get better. First TV generation. Highly individualistic, irreconcilably divided. Young women could assert independent identities. Postponed marriage, fewer children. More college graduates, both women and men. Active in social movements, social consciousness. |
| 4. Me Generation (1956–1965) | Prosperity taken for granted. Sense of entitlement. Expected to "have it all." More women than men in graduate schools. Largest population bulge in U.S. today. Avoiding commitments. Culturally alienated from parents. Women became working mothers. Faced a tightened economy in their 30s. |
| 5. Endangered Generation (1966–1980) | Motto: "Whatever." Disillusioned by parental divorce. Living at home longer. Drugs, guns. Widening gap between poor and elites. Adolescent suicide, AIDS, teen pregnancy. Watergate, Iranian hostages, Challenger blowing up. Delaying or forgoing marriage. Competition for jobs, jobs without benefits. More racial and ethnic diversity, accepting of multiculturalism. High educational achievement. |

*Source:* Based on Sheehy, 1995.

scholars (Farley, 1996; Schulenberg, Bachman, Johnston, & O'Malley, 1995), she suggests that events experienced in late adolescence and young adulthood have the most influence on enduring attitudes.

Consider the signs of Sheehy's cohort effects in the life course trajectories of Sonja Pukalski, Robert Johnson, and Veronica Palmore. Veronica Palmore, a member of the Silent Generation, was married at 22 and had her first baby at 23. Cohabitation prior to marriage would have been unthinkable to her and Simon. She moved in and out of the workforce with ease because career opportunities were plentiful when she was a young woman. Veronica and Simon started their marriage with traditional gender role expectations, but reworked them over time. Veronica continued to experience tension about gender roles at work, however.

Robert Johnson is on the cusp between the Vietnam Generation and the Me Generation. His childhood seems to have been influenced by the prosperity of the time, and his strong self-esteem and achievement motivation probably reflect not only this prosperity but also a child-centered family life. Unlike Veronica and Simon, however, Robert and Cindy began their relationship without strong gender role biases (which also may be influenced by race), chose cohabitation over marriage in their late 20s, and postponed marriage until they were financially secure. They will experience the stages of parenthood at later ages than Veronica and Simon.

Sonja Pukalski is a member of the Endangered Generation. She was a teen mother and is now a divorced single mother. At age 22, however, she appears to be in an adolescent holding pattern, highly dependent on older relatives and awaiting a day when she will remarry and have a place of her own. Her journey through adulthood could follow many possible pathways, but her status as a single mother without a high school education makes her and her children vulnerable to the growing economic disparities in U.S. society.

## Process Theoretical Approaches

Many theorists prefer not to think of adult behavior in terms of discrete stages that are experienced universally. Instead, they see adulthood as a continuous transaction among various biological, psychological, and sociocultural processes. These scholars are interested in the diversity of pathways through adulthood and the diversity of coping strategies used in the journey. I refer to their formulations as **process theoretical approaches** because they are interested in the processes by which adults cope with the unique configuration of life experiences they face and because their ideas are not as well developed as the stage theories.

***Riegel's Dialectical Approach to Human Development.***    Klaus Riegel (1976, 1979) explicitly criticized stage theories of adulthood, calling instead for a dialectical understanding of human development. He proposed that adult development is characterized by conflicting forces and "consists of continuing changes along several dimensions of progressions at the same time" (1979, p. 13). This perspective is very consistent with the changing person/environment configurations discussed in this book.

Riegel was particularly critical of the stage theorists' emphasis on completion of developmental tasks, arguing that developmental tasks are never completed. New questions and new doubts always arise as both person and society evolve. For example, as they confront new events, Veronica and Simone Palmore continue to develop their capacity for intimacy within the context of their relationship. Riegel identified at least four dimensions along which human development moves: the inner-biological dimension, the individual-psychological dimension, the cultural-sociological dimension, and the outer-physical dimension.

***Baltes's Life Span Perspective.***    Unlike Riegel, Paul Baltes (1987) does not reject the idea that shared stages of adult development might exist, but he and his colleagues argue that developmental processes may begin at any point in the life course and are not necessarily linear. They identify three major influences on human behavior across the adult life course:

- *Normative age–graded influences*—influences based both in biology and in socially constructed age norms.

- *Normative history–graded influences*—influences shared by a cohort group.
- *Nonnormative influences*—unexpected life events, such as the premature death of Sonja Pukalski's mother, Robert Johnson and Cindy Marsh's infertility, or Simon Palmore's serious accident.

This perspective, like other process theoretical approaches, assumes that change occurs throughout the life course and recognizes both general influences on human behavior and unique configurations of person and environment.

*What signs might indicate that the psychological dimension is a source of an adult's problems?*

***Pearlin's Theory of Psychological Distress.***    Leonard Pearlin has been interested in the sources of distress in adulthood and in the ways that adults cope with distress (Pearlin, 1980, 1982a, 1982b; Pearlin & Skaff, 1996). He begins with the premise that "because people are at the same age or life cycle phase, it cannot be assumed that they have either traveled the same route to reach their present locations or that they are headed in the same future directions" (1982a, p. 64). Pearlin delineates three types of sources of distress:

- *Chronic or durable strains*—the everyday strains that are built into life, such as role conflicts of work and family and time and resource management problems.
- *Scheduled or predictable change or events*—such as birth of child, empty nest, and retirement.
- *Unexpected, unscheduled changes*—such as job loss, serious illness or accident, or changes wrought by a natural disaster.

How a person copes with any of these types of distress depends on individual factors (gender, race or ethnicity, social or economic class), her or his coping skills, the person's social support network, and the nature and timing of the sources of distress.

Like other process theorists, Pearlin does not negate the contribution of stagelike life course markers to adult behavior. After all, he identifies scheduled or predictable change or events as one of the three types of distress. His research suggests, however, that these scheduled changes have much less effect on perceived well-being than do unexpected or unscheduled events. Indeed, the death of Sonja's mother, Robert and Cindy's infertility, and Simon's accident have been very influential events in the life course trajectories of Sonja Pukalski, Robert Johnson, and Veronica Palmore. Pearlin and a colleague (Pearlin & Skaff, 1996) have recently proposed the marriage of a life course perspective with stress theory to encourage researchers to examine the shifting nature of stressors and resources over the life course. This approach seems to have promise for assisting social workers to look at risk factors and protective factors in adulthood.

# Love and Work: Major Themes in Adulthood

*How are love and work related to the spiritual dimension of person?*

As a social worker getting acquainted with Sonja Pukalski, Robert Johnson, and Veronica Palmore, you would undoubtedly take note of the ways in which they are involved in family and work roles. Indeed, from Sigmund Freud to Daniel Levinson, theorists have identified love and work as the two central phenomena of adulthood. Freud (in Erikson, 1950) suggests that the capacity to love and to work is the measure of adult maturity, and Levinson (1996) suggests that family and work are the central components of the life structure for most adults. In an attempt to define the adult phenomena of love and work, Smelser (1980) proposes that in the adult years people reach "their maximum of mutually gratifying attachments to other individuals" as well as "whatever heights of purposeful, organized mastery of the world they are capable of reaching" (pp. 4–5).

Love and work are valued differently across cultures and times, and their interrelationship is organized in various ways as well. In agrarian societies, love and work are fused, and families work together. In contrast, since the Industrial Revolution, the European American tradition has been to make a sharp split in the social organization of love and work and a sharp division in our thinking about them. Major social institutions were constructed to specialize in either love (family) or work (labor market). A belief system—often referred to as the "separate spheres" philosophy—was also developed that assigned the world of emotions, including love, to women and the world of work to men. The central mission of the feminist social movement has been to oppose this social organization of love and work.

Despite our tendency to relegate love and work to separate spheres, the behavioral science literature often reminds us that the two phenomena overlap "almost to the point of fusion" (Smelser, 1980, p. 5). Many people love to work and have close relationships with work colleagues, and it has become common to hear people talk about "working at love." Both spheres, love and work, involve interpersonal relationships, which are central to personal identity. Our behavior in matters of love and family are inseparable, intertwined with, our behavior in matters of work.

The behavioral science literature also remarks on the interdependence of our love and work lives (for example, Farley, 1996; Lipsky & Abrams, 1994; Smelser, 1980). For example, choosing a professional work life often means postponing romantic partnership and childbearing. This was the case for Robert Johnson. Family relationships are influenced by workplace policies, such as family leave and child and elder care programs.

Behavioral scientists have used a variety of theoretical and empirical tools to help us in thinking about the effects of love and work on adult behavior and well-being, and they have produced a very large body of literature that crosses academic disciplines. However, with a predominant focus on people who are white and middle-class, the literature is not always helpful in understanding the diversity of individuals' experiences. The one aspect of diversity that has received attention is gender differences, because the gender-based "separate spheres" philosophy has had a pervasive influence on the lives of men and women. But before talking more specifically about current variations in love and work, I should review briefly the general trends in these arenas.

In the realm of love, young adults are delaying formation of domestic partnerships (Farley, 1996; Poston & Dan, 1996). They are living at home with their parents, and receiving financial assistance from their parents, until a later age (Bahr, Dechaux, & Stiehr, 1994; Farley, 1996). They are also delaying childbearing and having fewer children (Caldwell, Stiehr, Modell, & Del Campo, 1994; Farley, 1996; Poston & Dan, 1996). Cohabitation has become more common, but cohabitation is also being delayed (Farley, 1996). Thus, there is a trend toward greater diversity of household types. Adults of all ages are spending more time living alone or with nonrelatives over their life course than earlier cohorts (Farley, 1996). At the same time, the proportion of children living in two-parent homes has declined, with an increase in both mother-only and father-only families (Bahr et al., 1994; Farley, 1996). High divorce rates, as well as rising rates of childbearing by never-married mothers, contribute to this picture. Fertility is declining among two-parent families and increasing among single-parent families (Bahr et al., 1994; Farley, 1996; Poston & Dan, 1996).

As for work, five recent trends in the labor force are likely to continue into the 21st century (Farley, 1996; Noll & Langlois, 1994; Reskin & Padavic, 1994):

- Economic restructuring, with decreased employment in manufacturing and increased employment in services

- Downsizing of organizations, resulting in mass layoffs

- Upgrading of some jobs and deskilling of others

- Increased proportion of contingent workers, which includes temporary and part-time workers and independent contractors

- Increased diversity of the workforce, with a larger presence of women and ethnic minorities

These trends are resulting in less job security and greater economic inequality.


# Variations in Love

When the word *love* appears in the behavioral science literature, it is often not defined, and no consistent definition is used among scholars who do provide definitions. *Love* is used as a synonym for a variety of other concepts, including attachment, intimacy, affiliation, bonding, and social support. Some scholars have insisted that there are important distinctions among these concepts, however. For the sake of clarity about a topic that seems inherently fuzzy, I begin by defining these concepts as they are being used in this chapter.

**Attachment relationships** are a special kind of relationship—a "dyadic relationship in which proximity to a special and preferred other is sought or maintained to achieve a sense of security" (West & Sheldon-Keller, 1994, p. 19). In short, attachment relationships are the ones most important to our sense of security. For children and adolescents, these are typically relationships with parents (Bowlby, 1969). Colin (1996) suggests that "most marriages, many lasting sexual relationships, and many sibling relationships" (p. 294) can be considered attachment relationships. In the European American tradition, attachment relationships for adults are often thought of as romantic partnerships that offer reciprocal security. Although attachment theory recognizes that we may have several attachment relationships in our lives, it suggests that we form a hierarchy of attachment relationships, with one relationship more central than others to our sense of security (Colin, 1996). Chapter 4 explains that this emphasis on a primary attachment relationship may obscure or distort the attachment relationships between infants and adults of racial and ethnic minority groups. It may also obscure the attachments between adults in extended family networks of these groups.

Our interactions in adult attachment relationships are thought to be highly influenced by the **working model** for attachment relationships that is developed out of our earliest experiences with caregivers and revised in subsequent experiences with other attachment relationships (for example, see West & Sheldon-Keller, 1994). As social workers, we often help clients—particularly those who have a pattern of problems in relationships—to analyze and revise their working models. According to attachment theory, loss of an attachment figure leads to grief, whether or not the attachment relationship provided a secure base. We might wonder if Sonja Pukalski is grieving the loss of her husband to divorce as well as the loss of her mother to cancer.

Intimacy, like love, is not consistently defined and is used with different shades of meaning in the theoretical, research, and professional literature. You have already seen one definition, the one provided by Erikson. In a more nuanced approach, Karen Prager (1995) suggests thinking of intimacy as comprising two basic concepts:

■ **Intimate interaction,** "in which partners share personal, private material; feel positively about each other and themselves; and perceive a mutual understanding between them" (Prager, 1995, p. 22). Intimate interactions involve both intimate behaviors and perceptions of intimacy. Intimate behaviors may be either verbal or nonverbal (Prager, 1995; Reis & Shaver, 1988), as Exhibit 7.5 indicates. Perceptions of intimacy involve feelings of warmth, affection, involvement, and acceptance.

■ **Intimate relationship**—a relationship with a history of multiple and regular intimate interactions, as well as affection and cohesion. Some, but not all, intimate relationships are attachment relationships; only unique intimate relationships that are used to seek security are also considered attachment relationships.

Although definitional inconsistencies confound interpretation of the research, intimate interactions and relationships seem to serve as a buffer against stress and to provide health benefits (for a review of this research, see Prager, 1995). The literature on intimacy usually assumes that the dyad is the unit of intimate interactions, but intimate interactions may involve units larger than dyads. Family discussions, for instance, may be intimate even though they involve three or more people. Small groups, particularly mutual aid and self-help groups, may also be intimate.

Love can also be defined more broadly as affiliation, bonding, and social support. In these broader terms, love is experienced at the group, community, and organizational level. **Affiliation** is typically used to refer to a sense of belonging, of unity with other people. Bonding is used here to mean **social bonding,** or the experience of mutual commitment to some common good. *Social support* includes any interactions or relationships that support and nurture the well-being of individuals. It may be emotional support, which requires intimate interactions, or instrumental

*What might be some signs in adult clients of deficient community and small group support?*

**EXHIBIT 7.5**

Examples of Intimate Behaviors

| Noverbal Intimate Behaviors | Verbal Intimate Behaviors |
| --- | --- |
| Meaningful glances | Self-disclosure |
| Affectionate touches | Statements of acceptance |
| Shared emotional expressions, such as tears and laughter | |
| Shared sexuality | |

*Source:* Based on Prager, 1995.

support, which provides tangible aid and does not require intimate interactions. Social workers often help link clients to sources of social support.

A transactional perspective reminds us to think broadly about how human adults work at love, to include the larger-scale involvements of affiliation, bonding, and social support as well as the more intimate dyadic interactions. After extensive interview research, Weiss (1973) divided relationships into attachment relationships and community relationships. He reported that both types are beneficial resources in times of stress and that loneliness occurs if either type is missing. Thus, the following discussion includes six types of relationships that may take on great importance in adulthood, including both attachment and community relationships: romantic relationships, relationships with parents, relationships with children, other family relationships, relationships with friends, and community/organizational relationships.

## Romantic Relationships

Over time and across cultures, families have formed in a variety of ways. In Western advanced industrial societies, following the Christian tradition, monogamous marriage based on a romantic partnership has been the legally, socially, and psychologically acceptable form (Prager, 1995; Valsiner, 1989a). There is a cultural expectation that a long-term commitment to a romantic relationship, formalized in marriage, will occur sometime in young adulthood. The spousal relationship is generally assumed to be the primary adult attachment relationship, providing a secure base for employment, child rearing, and community involvement, and is assumed to provide for most of an adult's intimacy needs (O'Connor, 1992).

In 1989, 95 percent of U.S. adults had been married at some point in their lives (U.S. Bureau of Census, 1989), but some experts believe that the current trend toward delayed marriage will mean that higher proportions of men and women will never marry. Current Census Bureau projections suggest that about 90 percent of white women and 75 percent of black women will eventually marry (Farley, 1996). The lower rate of marriage among black women is related to the growing disadvantage of black men in the labor market, their overrepresentation as victims of homicide, and their increasing rates of incarceration (Tucker & Mitchell-Kernan, 1995). These rates of ever-married adults give an inflated view of the proportion of adults who are currently married, however. Because of high rates of divorce and increasing trends toward cohabitation, living alone, and living with nonrelatives, 44 percent of whites, 68 percent of blacks, and 53 percent of Hispanics were not living with a spouse in 1997 (U.S. Bureau of Census, 1998). In 1993, cohabiting couples accounted for 6.2 percent of couples living together (Farley, 1996). Gay and lesbian couples are counted as cohabiting, regardless of the nature of the commitment, because current law does not allow them to form a legal marriage.

Research suggests that the first year of heterosexual marriage is a time of strong romantic feelings, affectionate expression, and frequent sexual activity (Huston, McHale, & Crouter, 1986). A similar pattern has been found among newly cohabiting couples as well, including gay male and lesbian couples (Kurdek, 1994). Heterosexual cohabiters and gay male couples have been found to have the most frequent sexual activity in the early stage of the relationship (Blumstein & Schwartz, 1983). However, the divorce rate is exceptionally high after the first year among married couples (Prager, 1995).

Married couples who stay together after the first year show a steady decline in intimate interaction and marital satisfaction. The same pattern exists but is not as strong among cohabiting couples (Kurdek, 1991). Among married couples, this trend toward devitalization occurs in childless couples as well as couples with children, but the findings are conflicting about whether childless couples experience less decline in intimacy and satisfaction than couples with children (Adelmann, Chadwick, & Baerger, 1996; Huston et al., 1986; Prager, 1995). Although intimate interactions decrease over several years before beginning to increase again, couples seem to make steady progress in minimizing their negative interactions. One study found negative marital interactions to decline steadily over the course of marriage. On the other hand, positive marital interactions show a U-shaped curve, starting high, declining steadily until middle adulthood, and then beginning to increase again (Adelmann et al., 1996). It appears that this pattern is the case with Veronica and Simon Palmore.

Although Sonja Pukalski is divorced, she hopes to remarry someday. In the contemporary era in the United States, divorce and remarriage have become common occurrences. An estimated one-half of marriages begun in the 1970s will end in divorce at some time (Farley, 1996). Cross-national data indicate that the divorce rate in the United States is currently two to three times the divorce rate in other advanced industrial nations (Bahr et al., 1994). The remarriage rate is also high, but declined steadily in the 1970s and 1980s and was cut in half between 1960 and 1990 (Farley, 1996). These trends tear at the previously stated cultural assumption that romantic relationships among monogamous marital partners are the primary adult attachment relationships. That is probably not the case for many adults. For remarried couples with children, family relationships may resemble those in polygamous marriages (marriages with more than one spouse) more than they resemble relationships in the traditional monogamous marriage. As social workers, we often help remarried families develop more realistic models for family relationships.

Research has identified variations in the experience of romantic relationships based on race, ethnicity, social class, gender, and sexual orientation. For instance, although blacks have the same patterns of marital quality as whites over the life course, they have been consistently found to have lower levels of marital quality than whites (Adelmann et al., 1996; Creighton-Zollar & Williams, 1992; Oggins, Veroff, & Leber, 1993; Woody, 1996). These differences do not disappear when number of children or income is controlled. However, marital satisfaction has been found to decline with increasing financial strain (Adelmann et al., 1996). What is not clear is whether there are cultural biases in the instruments used to measure marital satisfaction.

What sorts of cultural differences in marriage practices might U.S. social workers encounter?

In a qualitative study of partner interdependence over the life course, comparing Japanese and American marriages, one research team found that the marital relationship is experienced in culturally specific ways (Ingersoll-Dayton, Campbell, Kurokawa, & Saito, 1996). American couples emphasized the "partnership" aspect of their relationship and valued role sharing. In middle adulthood, they were looking for more separateness in their marriage. By contrast, Japanese couples had entered arranged marriages and lived in extended families, often with the husband's family, at the time of marriage. In these arrangements, the husband's relationship with extended family members was as central as his relationship with his wife. In addition, clearly defined gender roles meant that husbands and wives lived in very different spheres. Intimacy for these couples did not begin until their parents were dead. So in middle adulthood, Japanese couples were looking for intimacy, not separateness.

Given the history of separate spheres based on gender, it is not surprising that women and men have been found to have different experiences in romantic relationships. Engel and Saracino (1986) found that in both heterosexual and homosexual romantic relationships, men value sexual intimacy more than verbal intimacy and women value verbal intimacy more than sexual intimacy. This gender difference may help explain the lower levels of sexual activity found among long-term lesbian couples (Blumstein & Schwartz, 1983). Women have also been found less likely than men to withdraw from conflict in the romantic relationship (Christensen & Heavy, 1990; Christensen & Shenk, 1991; Gottman, 1994). Distressed wives often ask for more intimacy; distressed husbands ask for less conflict (Kobak & Hazan, 1991). Men also say that sharing activities and interests is as important a pathway to intimacy as self-disclosure, which is favored by women. Note in Exhibit 7.5, however, that the research on intimacy does not count sharing activities and interests as intimate behavior. Keep in mind, when reading about gender differences in intimacy, that the researchers may not be sensitive to all male and female differences.

Two measures of contemporary tensions in romantic relationships are the divorce rate and the rate of interpersonal violence between domestic partners. The high rate of divorce in the United States has already been discussed. Research indicates that both men and women have high levels of distress for months, and sometimes years, following a divorce (Hetherington, Cox, & Cox, 1977; Wallerstein & Kelly, 1977). As for violence, its true incidence in romantic relationships is not known, because many instances are probably not reported. But available data indicate that women are the victims in more than 90 percent of these violent incidents (Bachman, 1994). One recent survey found that more than half (56%) of respondents know someone who has been involved in violent interactions between romantic partners (Liz Claiborne Inc.'s Women's Work program, cited in Family Violence Preservation Fund, 1997). The U.S. Surgeon General declared domestic violence to be a "public health crisis" in 1992 (The Family Place, 1996).

## Relationships with Parents

How might social workers intervene to reduce inter-generational conflicts within a family?

Relationships with parents appear to be an important part of the stories of Sonja Pukalski, Robert Johnson, and Veronica Palmore. Contrary to public perception, Americans repeatedly demonstrate a strong sense of intergenerational solidarity. Bengtson and Harootyan (1994) and their colleagues have advanced our understanding of adult relationships with parents by analyzing six interdependent dimensions of these relationships: physical proximity, contact, emotional closeness, shared opinions, helping behavior, and sense of responsibility. Here are some findings on several of these dimensions:

1. *Physical proximity.* It is unusual for adults to live under the same roof as their parents, with the exception of 18- to 24-year olds, for whom it has become a common occurrence. Labor market requirements for higher levels of education, delayed marriage, and the rising cost of housing all contribute to a trend of delayed exit from the parental home. Census data show that by 1993, 53 percent of young adults ages 18–24 lived with their parents (Farley, 1996).

Lawton, Silverstein, and Bengtson (1994) found that 59 percent of this age group live with their mothers and 46 percent with their fathers. If the father is divorced, the young adult is far less likely to live with him (18%), and even less likely if he remarries (10%).

2. *Contact.* Although most adults do not live with their parents, Lawton et al. (1994) found high rates of contact between adults and their parents. More respondents have weekly contact with mothers (69%) than with fathers (56%). Adults are less likely to have contact with fathers who are divorced and remarried and with mothers who are remarried (Lawton et al., 1994).

3. *Emotional closeness.* The majority of adult respondents in the Lawton et al. study reported feeling very close to their parents, with 72 percent feeling very close to mothers and 55 percent feeling very close to fathers. Parental divorce does not have a significant effect on closeness with mothers, but it is associated with a significant decrease in closeness with fathers. Blacks were more likely than other groups to feel close to their mothers, but they were no more likely to feel close to their fathers.

4. *Helping behavior.* Earlier studies had found high levels of mutual aid between middle-age adults and their late-adult parents, with 70 percent of adult children and parents reporting such exchanges (Bahr et al., 1994). But focusing on noneconomic assistance and including young adult respondents, Lawton et al. (1994) found a more modest rate of helping behavior, approximately 30–35 percent. Interestingly, both adult children and their parents perceived that they gave more assistance than they received. Sons and daughters provided the same amount of noneconomic aid to mothers, but sons were more likely than daughters to provide aid to fathers. Adult children with paid employment are more likely than those without paid employment to provide assistance to both mothers and fathers. Parents over 65 are more likely than younger parents to receive aid from their adult children. Thus, middle-aged adults may provide more assistance than they receive in their relationships with both their young-adult children and their late-adult parents. Currently, Veronica and Simon Palmore are in this "squeezed middle."

When all dimensions of intergenerational solidarity are considered together, mother/daughter pairs have the closest relationships, followed by mother/son pairs, with father/daughter relationships the most distant (Bahr et al., 1994; Lawton et al., 1994).

It also appears that mothers continue to be the kin keepers—the glue that holds families together—and that divorce weakens fathers' ties with adult children. Although our culture emphasizes the marital relationship, Bahr et al. (1994, p. 116) suggest that the parent/child relationship is the "single most important kinship tie in Western industrial societies," particularly because marital relationships are becoming less stable. Bahr et al. also report that, given the declining birthrates, we now have more parent/adult child pairs than parent/minor child pairs.

In spite of this evidence of strong solidarity between adults and their parents, elder abuse is an increasing concern. The true incidence of abuse of older adults by their adult children is not known, but in 1994, approximately 820,000 older adults were estimated to be victims of some type of domestic abuse (National Center on Elder Abuse, 1997). The National Center on Elder Abuse (NCEA) identifies six types of elder abuse: physical abuse, sexual abuse, emotional abuse, financial/material exploitation, neglect, and abandonment. More than half the reports of elder abuse involve neglect (NCEA, 1997).

## Relationships with Children

In previous chapters, you have read about the influence of parent/child relationships on child and adolescent behavior. Consistent with the transactional approach of this book, I assume that parent/child relationships are bidirectional, with influence flowing both ways, and that relationships with children influence the behaviors of parents as well as children.

How do inadequacies in social institutions affect parent/child relationships?

In a comprehensive review of the effects of minor children on parents, Anne-Marie Ambert (1992) suggests that parent/minor child relationships are influenced by characteristics of the child, by characteristics of the parent, and by the ways a society is organized to meet the needs of parents and children. Ambert suggests some societal traits that will produce more positive outcomes for both children and parents: adequate, affordable, and accessible housing, child-care alternatives, schools, health and mental health resources, and recreational facilities; work opportunities that do not put parents at a disadvantage; safe neighborhoods; positive peer group cultures for children and adolescents; positive mass media; and societal regard for the contributions of parents. Currently, our social institutions are falling short in many of these areas, making them fruitful areas for social work planning and advocacy.

*The Costs and Benefits of Parenting.*    Research about the influence of parenting on adult behavior is in its infancy and is fraught with underdeveloped conceptualizations and methodological weaknesses. Social scientists commonly use a rational choice, social exchange perspective to analyze trends in childbearing and childrearing (Ambert, 1992; Bahr et al., 1994; Farley, 1996). The result is the sort of cost/benefit analysis shown in Exhibit 7.6. Although the evidence to date suggests that parenting has both benefits and costs, such analyses also typically suggest

**EXHIBIT 7.6**

Benefits and Costs of Parenting Found in Research

| Benefits of Parenting | Costs of Parenting |
|---|---|
| ■ Generativity | ■ Less time in intimate interactions with adults |
| ■ More anticipation of the future | ■ More marital discord |
| ■ More complex thinking | ■ Increased financial costs |
| ■ Improved perspective-taking | ■ Disruptions in mother's career |
| ■ Self-awareness and maturity in identity | ■ Increased role strain |
| ■ Improved emotional regulation | ■ Loss of freedom |
| ■ Expanded interactional repertoire | ■ Feelings of fatigue and confinement when caring for infants |
| ■ More sense of responsibility | ■ Increased sex typing in gender roles |
| ■ Increased clarity about religious and moral beliefs | |
| ■ More playfulness | |
| ■ Companionship, nurturance, and physical affection | |
| ■ More community involvement | |

*Source:* Based on Ambert, 1992.

that parenting has more costs than benefits in societies like ours with a market-based economy and a high value on individualism. Such societies may need to develop incentives to parent in order to ensure an adequate labor pool for the future. Some child welfare researchers also suggest that the current cost/benefit equation helps to explain why so many parents become child abusers (Gelles, 1983). I will start, however, with a discussion of the benefits of parenting and move to a discussion of the costs.

Eriksonian theorists often consider parenthood as necessary, but not sufficient, for adult achievement of generativity. John Snarey (1993), for example, proposes that the experience of involved parenting promotes generativity at the wider community and societal levels, and his research does show an association between parental generativity and broader-based generativity. However, Erikson did not consider parenting a necessary condition for generativity. Adults who are not parents may find different pathways to generativity, as Robert Johnson and his wife seem to be doing while waiting to adopt.

The research suggests that low levels of involvement, with little priority given to the parental role, do not produce the benefits that come with more active involvement (Palkovitz, 1996; Snarey, 1993). Researchers frequently use Lamb's (1986) three-pronged definition of parental involvement: accessibility, interaction, and responsibility.

In a rational choice, social exchange approach, these benefits are weighed against the costs of parenting. Whereas the benefits appear to be primarily cognitive and emotional, most of the costs appear to be in three primary areas: finances, personal freedom, and time. In agrarian societies, children are financial benefits, but they become financial costs in industrialized, urbanized societies. The research currently indicates that the costs in personal freedom and time are experienced more by mothers than by fathers, because mothers continue to be the primary caregivers in most families (Ambert, 1992).

***Motherhood and Fatherhood.***   Because of the historical societal assignment of child care to mothers, mothering has been studied in a plethora of ways over time. All too often, the research has emphasized the things that mothers do to harm their children or the negative aspects of motherhood. The study of fathering is relatively new, however, and is currently thriving.

The contemporary literature on both mothering and fathering is hopelessly tangled with gender politics, which have become highly contentious. A preponderance of research (Googins, 1991; Snarey, 1993) does show that maternal involvement in paid labor has outpaced paternal involvement in child and home care. Authors in the feminist tradition, both men and women, thus call for a "new fatherhood," where fathers do their share on the home front (Coltrane, 1995; Hanson & Bozett, 1985). In response, some of the proliferating fatherhood literature complains about the emphasis on the failings of fathers, suggests that the financial caring that fathers do is not appreciated, and calls for a return to separate spheres, where women do not impinge on men's opportunities in the labor market (Mackey, 1996).

Ralph LaRossa's (1997) historical analysis of the social and political history of fatherhood suggests that the involved style of the "new fatherhood" is not totally new and provides evidence of an ongoing struggle throughout the 20th century to rework the gender-based division of labor that accompanied industrialization. He also provides evidence that a variety of fathering styles have coexisted at any given historical time.

More evidence of multiple fathering styles has been provided by Snarey's (1993) four-decade, longitudinal intergenerational study of father/child relationships in a sample of 240 lower- and working-class families. The sample was not ethnically diverse, but it does have the benefit of being based on the reports of fathers and children, whereas most research on fathering activities is based on reports of mothers. Snarey found that 35 percent of the fathers in his study were "not very active," 41 percent were "substantially involved," and 24 percent were "highly involved." Fathers' involvement was higher during childhood than during either adolescence or infancy. The most common father/child interaction provided socioemotional support, followed by support of physical/athletic development and support of intellectual/academic development. Fathers provided equal levels of child care to sons and daughters. It is important to note that Snarey included play and shared activities as involvement in child care, but most researchers do not. His findings suggest that both fathers and children often consider these activities to be intimate interactions.

***Parenthood and Divorce.*** Researchers consistently find one large and growing group of parents to have low rates of financial support for and contact with their children: fathers who do not reside with their children because they are separated or divorced from the mother or because they never married her (Braver, Wolchik, Sandler, Fogas, & Zventina, 1991; Bray & Berger, 1990, 1993; Furstenberg, Nord, Peterson, & Zill, 1983; Seltzer, 1991). A large majority of children (85% to 90%) reside primarily with the mother after divorce (Glick, 1988). One study found that black nonresidential fathers are more likely than other nonresidential fathers to have contact with their children and to participate in child-rearing decisions, but they are no more likely than others to provide financial support (Seltzer, 1991). Nonresidential fathers have reported a number of reasons for discontinuing contact and financial support (Braver, Wolchik, Sandler, & Sheets, 1993):

- Awkward or painful visitation
- Conflict with the mother
- Visitation blocked by the mother
- Competing interpersonal relationships
- Economic hardship
- Physical distance
- Perceived abuse of child support by the mother
- Belief that visitation is not in the best interest of the child

By assuming the role of mediator, social workers can often help families resolve some of these impediments to the continuity of relationships between divorced fathers and their children.

Approximately 85 percent of divorced men and 75 percent of divorced women remarry (London, 1991), often further complicating the parent/child relationship. Del Carmen and Virgo (1993) report that remarriage is more common among European American whites than among racial and ethnic minority groups because of the strong bias toward the nuclear family model among European Americans. This bias is not shared, at least not to the same degree, by some racial and ethnic minority groups, for whom strong multigenerational family networks exist, often transcending household boundaries (Hatchett & Jackson, 1993; Lin & Liu, 1993; Sudarkasa, 1993). Nevertheless, research indicates that economic support and contact by the nonresidential parent often decrease once either parent remarries (Peterson & Nord, 1990). The role of the stepparent or stepparents must also be negotiated. Bray and Berger (1993) suggest that many divorced and remarried families struggle with parental role definitions because they are trying to adapt to family role prescriptions that are based on a nuclear family structure.

## Other Family Relationships

In the United States, marital relationships and parent/child relationships are considered the primary family relationships, and these relationships have been the subject of the preponderance of research on family relationships. One notable exception is the line of research that studies extended kinship systems (Hatchett & Jackson, 1993; Paz, 1993). The grandparent/grandchild relationship has received the next greatest amount of research attention, followed by a growing body of research on sibling relationships. In the Lawton et al. (1994) study, 44 percent of adult grandchildren said that they felt "very close" to grandparents. Major findings in the limited research on sibling relationships indicate that adult siblings provide more emotional support than financial support. Sibling contact in adulthood is much less frequent than parent/child contact, and sibling pairs consisting of at least one sister are closer than those involving brothers only (Gold, 1989).

## Relationships with Friends

*What might be the effect on adult clients of changing friendship patterns over the life course?*

When one group of researchers asked respondents to list types of love, the most frequent response was friendship (Fehr & Russell, 1991). There is considerable evidence that friendships are important relationships in adulthood (Fehr, 1996). Relationships with friends also appear to undergo changes across the adult life course. In adolescence, friends replace family members as the most important intimate relationships, and even young adults have high levels of contact and intimate interactions with friends. Close friends serve as primary confidants, even when young adults are in a romantic relationship (Prager, 1995). Although the number of friends doesn't change with marriage and parenthood, time spent with friends declines significantly after marriage and shows another significant decline after parenthood (Carbery, 1993). Friendship in middle adulthood has not been studied much, but the number of continuing friends appears to decline (Nardi, 1992), as does frequency of contact with friends (Dickens & Perlman, 1981) and the number of new friends (Lowenthal, Thurnher, & Chiriboga, 1977). Levels of intimacy with friends, however, does not decline (Dickens & Perlman, 1981).

The two most frequently cited places for forming friendships are workplace and neighborhood (Fischer & Phillips, 1982). Friendships at work take on greater importance to people who are highly committed to their work (Rawlins, 1992), and having friends at work has been found to be associated with job satisfaction (Winstead, Derlega, & Montgomery, 1995). Friendships are also more likely to develop in cooperative rather than competitive workplaces (Rawlins,

1992). In choosing friends, one researcher found that gay men and lesbians are more willing than heterosexuals to include previous sexual partners among their friends (Nardi & Sherrod, 1994).

Much research has focused on gender differences in friendships, and several controversies have developed. A preponderance of research suggests that women's friendships are characterized by talk and men's friendships by activities, but that finding has been challenged in recent research (Walker, 1994). Gender differences in the level of intimacy in friendships are also a matter of controversy (Fehr, 1996), but both women and men report that their most intimate relationships are with women (Buhrke & Fuqua, 1987). Little attention has been paid to cultural variations in gender differences in friendship relationships (Berman, Murphy-Berman, & Pachauri, 1988).

## Community/Organizational Relationships

Adults experience affiliation, social bonding, and social support in a variety of community/organizational relationships, but the focus here will be on three types of community-based activities: formal volunteering, informal assistance, and self-help groups. Adults in the United States spend considerable time in these activities.

*How might such community relationships help the volunteers as well as the recipients of services?*

One study found that 54 percent of U.S. adults are involved in formal volunteering with organizations such as religious organizations, schools, civic groups, and charities (Harootyan & Vorek, 1994). The same study found that informal assistance to others is even more prevalent, involving 89 percent of adults, although this number drops to 70 percent when only informal help to nonrelated members of the community is considered (Harootyan & Vorek, 1994). As social workers, we need to recognize these forms of informal helping as important resources for helping clients resolve problems of living.

Robert Wuthnow (1994) suggests that the small group movement is "beginning to alter American society" (p. 3). Wuthnow found that 40 percent of adults in the United States belong to a "small group that meets regularly and provides caring and support for its members" (p. 4). He also found that these groups provide a forum for important relationships and intimate interactions and that nearly two-thirds of these groups have some connection to religious organizations.

# Variations in Work

In earlier eras, people did not think of work as something distinct from the rest of life. Life *was* work. Most people consumed what they produced and received no pay for their work. But with the development of capitalism and industrialization, work came to be seen as a paid activity. Thus, **domestic work,**—"the work people do around their homes for themselves and members of their household" (Reskin & Padavic, 1994, p. 2)—was no longer considered work.

Today, involvement in paid work is a central component of the adult life structure (Levinson, 1978, 1996), a central dimension of personal identity, and the central yardstick of social value (Clair, Karp, & Yoels, 1993). Work is a major social role of adult life.

**EXHIBIT 7.7**

Three Eras of
American Work
Values

| Era | Time Period | Work Values |
|-----|-------------|-------------|
| Work as Salvation | 1620s to 1730s | Work as an expression of devotion to family, community, and society. |
| Work as Alienation and Opportunity | 1730s to 1930s | Work as a way to "get ahead." |
| Work as Self-Fulfillment | 1930s to present | Work as an opportunity to grow and learn. |

*Source:* Based on Bernstein, 1997.

## The Meaning of Work

Paul Bernstein (1997) has traced the evolution of the meaning of work in Western culture over the past five centuries and has identified three eras in American history with very different work values, as shown in Exhibit 7.7. In the first era, work values were derived from the religious beliefs brought to America by the Puritan settlers, for whom work was a "sign of eternal reward" (p. 15). In this view, work was an expression of devotion to family, community, and society. Industrialization and a market economy then brought a major shift in the work ethic, leading to a new era in which work was viewed in terms of both alienation and opportunity. The emphasis on religious obligation was replaced with a work ethic that focused on work as the way to "get ahead," to achieve personal success. A shortage of labor and an abundance of land made the new colonies a "land of opportunity" for many. For others, however, slave labor on the plantations or long hours in dirty and dangerous factories produced alienation, not opportunity. The growing alienation of workers helped to usher in a new era with greater attention to the needs of workers, an era in which work was equated with self-fulfillment. This era began when owners and managers tried to win the cooperation of workers, but the 1960s brought a new twist on the work ethic, emphasizing work as an opportunity to grow and learn.

Bernstein's analysis may be an accurate portrayal of the dominant cultural work values in different eras. In the current era, however, I propose that subcultural variations in work values are woven together in complex ways. Veronica and Simon Palmore are good examples of this mix. For Veronica, work seems to represent commitment to community and society, as well as an opportunity to grow and learn. For Simon, work seems to represent primarily commitment to family and, perhaps secondarily, an opportunity to get ahead.

Bernstein (1997) suggests that, although work values have shifted over time, four themes have been present consistently throughout the three eras: search for job security, belief in opportunity, commitment to hard work, and the work and welfare debate. Bernstein proposes that market economies will always have booms and busts, and thus job security will never be certain. Belief in opportunity must therefore be tempered by the uncertainties of the market. In the contemporary era, the commitment to hard work is also being challenged, by questions about the rationality of employee loyalty to organizations that provide no job security.

The work and welfare debate has always been highly contentious, and it has been particularly so of late. The different positions in the current debate reflect the work values of all three historical eras identified by Bernstein. They also reflect different beliefs about how much job security can be assumed, how open the opportunities are for some groups, and the rationality of commitment to hard work. In addition, the current debate is also fueled by controversies about whether domestic work should be counted as work.

## Social Work and Work

*Today, what types of social movements are relevant to social workers' concerns?*

Sheila Akabas (1993) suggests that "the close connection between work and well-being has been clear to social workers from the outset of the profession" (p. xviii). Both she and Lawrence Root (1993) cite the strong role played by workers in the settlement house movement to respond to problems of employment and unemployment that resulted from urban, capitalist industrialism. Their activities were broad-based, including English-language classes for immigrant workers, day care, community-based economic development, and advocacy for standards of occupational health and safety.

Bertha Reynolds (1951/1975) provided a rationale for work-based social work, which has come to be known as **occupational social work**, with her premise that social work activities should occur in the "natural life space" of clients. Since the 1970s, social workers have been active participants in the development of **employee assistance programs (EAPs),** which have the goal of assisting workers with a variety of personal, emotional, and behavioral problems that interfere with their work performance (Kurzman, 1993). Unlike the early settlement house interventions, which focused on reforms in the workplace, these programs focus on service to individual workers.

Recent literature on occupational social work identifies three key issues related to work and adult behavior: conflict between work and family life, the impact of work on health and mental health, and marginalization in the labor market.

*What sorts of programs might help adult clients balance work and family life?*

***The Conflict between Work and Family Life.***    Balancing work and family relationships is a primary concern of adults who are employed full-time (Snarey, 1993; Voydanoff, 1993). A generation ago, the typical two-adult family spent approximately 40 hours per week in paid work. Today, the typical two-adult family spends approximately 80 hours per week in work outside the home. However, the workplace is still organized in much the same way that it was when men did paid work with the support of a wife doing the domestic work at home. The rapid influx of women into the labor market has outpaced changes in cultural, economic, and political systems. Consequently, families have borne most of the weight of the changing configuration of work and family life. In the United States, both government and employers have been slower than in some other advanced industrial nations to assist families to balance work and family (Googins, 1991; Reskin & Padavic, 1994). This reluctance is largely ideological; a higher value is placed on individualism in the United States than in European countries, where it is generally assumed that societies have a responsibility and a stake in family well-being.

Managing time has become a major challenge for both men and women, but a disproportionate share of the burden of coping with the competing demands of work and family falls to women. Time management is especially problematic for three types of domestic work:

1. *Housework.* Cooking, cleaning, home repair, and shopping are time-consuming activities. Families with high incomes can afford to pay to have some of this housework done for them, but such assistance is not feasible for most low- and middle-income families. Currently, few employers sponsor programs that assist with housework. In general, families must negotiate how to manage housework internally. Housework is a common source of marital conflict in families where husbands and wives have different expectations about the fair division of household chores (Googins, 1991; Reskin & Padavic, 1994).

2. *Child Care.* Obtaining adequate child care is the major source of stress among employed mothers, but both mothers and fathers report worrying about their children while at work (Googins, 1991). Demand exceeds supply for both formal and informal child-care services (Reskin & Padavic, 1994). As noted in Chapter 5, even when children reach school age, the school hours of children generally do not match the work hours of parents. Care of sick children and children on school vacations also presents a challenge. Many large companies provide some kind of assistance with child care, but the majority of workers are employed by small companies where such assistance is not available (Reskin & Padavic, 1994). Care for preschoolers in Europe is considered a responsibility of government regardless of the work status of parents, but the U.S. government is much more reluctant to "interfere" in family life.

3. *Elder Care.* Given the current birthrates, most families will spend more years caring for elderly relatives than caring for children. Although most elderly relatives care for themselves, the rapidly growing population of persons over 85 increases the likelihood that families will need to provide elder care at some point (Googins, 1991). The preponderance of elder care is provided by families, the bulk of it by women (Googins, 1991). As Veronica and Simon Palmore are discovering, the need to provide elder care generally arises in emergency situations and cannot be planned in advance. As with child care, the demand for resources to assist families exceeds the supply, and few employers provide meaningful assistance with elder care (Reskin & Padavic, 1994). I am reminded of an experience that my husband and I had—one that I suspect is shared by many families. When we found our job performance suffering because of the considerable time we were spending transporting my mother-in-law to medical appointments, my husband contacted the employee assistance program at his place of employment to inquire about resources for transportation. He was told, "We don't have information about transportation resources, but we do provide counseling if you are having problems caring for your mother." My husband responded, "We may need that counseling someday if we can't get assistance with the transportation."

***The Impact of Work on Physical and Mental Health.***   Much has been written about the negative impact of work-related stress on the physical and mental health of adults (Beehr, 1995; Sauter & Murphy, 1995). The most frequently cited physical illness thought to be related to job stressors is cardiovascular disease (Beehr & Newman, 1978; Cooper & Marshall, 1976; Ironson,

1992). The most frequently cited psychiatric illnesses are anxiety and depression (Jackson & Schuler, 1985; Jex & Beehr, 1991). Smoking behavior has also been found to be related to job stressors (Beehr & Newman, 1978).

The increasing interdependence of home and work stressors complicates the interpretation of research findings. Researchers have identified two very different processes involved in transactions between home and work (Bronfenbrenner & Crouter, 1982). One is **spillover:** Positive and negative emotions, attitudes, and behaviors related to one setting can influence the other setting. Family stressors can spill over to the work setting, and some researchers have found a positive spillover from work to the family lives of women. The other process is **compensation,** whereby adults achieve better overall life satisfaction and health because satisfactions in one domain balance out dissatisfactions in the other domain.

Another important research topic in this area is **job burnout**, a process in which a previously committed worker disengages from his or her work in response to stress and strain experienced in the job. Researchers studying job stressors and adult health have found that job situations providing low control, excessive uncertainty, and low social support have deleterious effects (Beehr, 1995; Golembiewski, 1994).

Four aspects of work's effects on health have recently begun to receive more research attention:

1. How to restore trust and certainty in workplaces in the midst of rampant corporate downsizing and mergers (Jaffe, Scott, & Tobe, 1994).    •

2. How to measure the impact of hostile environments on minority workers (Fisher, Semko, & Wade, 1995).

3. The impact of the threat of violence on worker health, given recent findings that violence is the third leading cause of death to workers (National Institute for Occupational Safety and Health, 1993), occurring most commonly among service workers (Fong, 1995).

4. How workers can manage the stress involved in doing **emotional work**—the "management of feeling to create a publicly observable facial and bodily display" (Adelmann, 1995; Hochschild, 1983, p. 7). Such emotional work is prominent in the growing service sector and is a feature of most social work positions.

How might social workers try to influence these changes in social institutions and social structure?

*Marginalization in the Labor Market.*    Employment is the principal source of income for individuals and families in the United States, and economic security is based on access to employment opportunities. Thus, patterns of poverty and inequality originate in the labor market. Marginalization in the labor market leads to economic insecurity, which has serious negative effects on most other aspects of life, including family relationships, community relationships, housing alternatives, and physical and mental health (Root, 1993).

In the United States, we are in the midst of a transformation of the labor market that is having a monumental impact on patterns of poverty and inequality (Reich, 1992). The trend toward greater inequality in the United States, with a widening gap between rich and poor, is related to the growing divergence in how much money people receive from their employment, which in turn is related to level of education (Chirot, 1994; Reich, 1992). In 1960, the typical CEO earned about 12 times what the line worker earned; by 1988, the CEO's earnings were about 70 times the earnings of line workers. Between 1980 and 1990, the gap in wages between a typical high school graduate and a typical college graduate doubled (Reich, 1992).

In the previous industrial phase, poverty was due to unemployment. In the current era, unemployment plays a smaller role; the major issue is the growing proportion of low-wage and no-benefit jobs.

Marginalization in the labor market in adulthood is the result of "cumulative disadvantage" over the life course (O'Rand, 1996). Some groups are more likely than others to accumulate disadvantage for competition in the labor market. Black men with a high school education or less have been particularly disadvantaged in the current phase of industrialization, largely because of the declining numbers of routine production jobs (Reich, 1992; Reskin & Padavic, 1994).

In addition, West (1991, p. xi) suggests, "Americans with disabilities are the largest, poorest, least employed, and least educated minority in America." Beginning in 1990, when the employment provisions of the Americans with Disabilities Act (ADA) were put into effect, persons with disabilities were ensured the opportunity to participate in the world of work. Much remains to be done to open educational and work opportunities to persons with disabilities, however (Akabas & Gates, 1993). A 1994 Harris poll found that 79 percent of working-age people with disabilities who were not working would like to work (Stoddard, Jans, Ripple, & Kraus, 1998).

# Challenges to Physical and Mental Health in Adulthood

*How might problems in the biological person affect a client's psychosocial well-being?*

Young adults are the healthiest age group in the United States, and the typical middle-aged adult is quite healthy. But physical health problems are more common, and show up earlier, among adults with less education and low income, and among members of racial and ethnic minority groups. Many, but not all, of the racial and ethnic differences disappear when income is controlled (Keil, Sutherland, Knapp, & Tyroler, 1992). These differences in health status are probably related to differences in access to health care, differences in health practices, and special strains related to discrimination and economic insecurity (Bee, 1996).

The leading causes of death in the United States today are coronary heart disease and cancer. Coronary heart disease (CHD) is a disease caused by the narrowing of the coronary arteries. It is possible to have heart disease without symptoms, but the common symptoms are shortness of breath, chest pain, fatigue, fainting, and palpitations (Texas Heart Institute, 1996). Heart attack, or myocardial infarction, occurs when there is complete blockage of a coronary artery. The risk factors for CHD include older age, smoking, lack of exercise, diet high in fat, overweight, and high blood pressure.

Cancer is an "unregulated growth of previously normal cells" (Fintel & McDermott, 1993, p. 15), produced when mistakes are made in the normal process of cell division. Cancer cells differ from normal cells in two ways: they proliferate wildly, and they become virtually immortal. Common risk factors include viruses; radiation; exposure to chemicals; lifestyle issues, such as smoking, heavy alcohol consumption, and a high-fat, low-fiber diet; stress; a weak immune system; and genetic factors (Fintel & McDermott, 1993).

**EXHIBIT 7.8**
Seven Major
Adaptive Tasks
in Coping with
Serious Illness

- Dealing with the physiological consequences of the illness.
- Dealing with treatment.
- Developing and maintaining relationships with health care providers.
- Maintaining emotional equilibrium.
- Maintaining a sense of a competent self.
- Maintaining relationships with family and friends.
- Preparing for future contingencies.

*Source:* Based on Aldwin, 1994.

New treatments for both CHD and cancer have improved the life chances for people with these serious illnesses, but survivors face the challenge of living with chronic diseases. Aldwin (1994) has identified seven major adaptive tasks in coping with serious illness, listed in Exhibit 7.8.

**How might environmental dimensions be related to the biological and psychological dimensions?**

Our understanding of mental health in adulthood has been altered greatly in recent years by efforts in biological research and increasing attention to the intricacies of biopsychosocial transactions. Following are three of the most common mental health problems in adulthood:

1. **Anxiety disorders** are diagnosed when the normal anxious state is exceeded in either intensity or duration. In threatening situations, we have all experienced the vague sense of apprehension known as anxiety, often accompanied by unpleasant physical symptoms, such as headache, sweating, dizziness, stomach discomfort, and tightness in the chest. When the symptoms become severe and interfere with social functioning, personal relationships, or work, an anxiety disorder may be diagnosed. Several types of anxiety disorders have been identified, including panic disorder, phobias, obsessive-compulsive disorder, and post–traumatic stress disorder (Kaplan, Sadock, & Grebb, 1994).

2. **Mood disorders** are disturbances in mood, either depressed or elevated. Depressed mood is characterized by loss of energy and interest in life, difficulty concentrating, loss of appetite, feelings of guilt and sadness, and thoughts of death. Elevated mood is characterized by heightened self-esteem, grandiose ideas, decreased sleep, and flight of ideas. Two major mood disorders have been identified: major depressive disorder (depression) and bipolar disorder (which must include at least one episode of elevated mood).

3. **Substance-related disorders** are diagnosed when use of a substance, or substances, is interfering with role performance in some area of a person's life. **Substance abuse** is a pattern of substance use that begins to interfere with the person's life. **Addiction** is a chronic, relapsing disorder involving progressive loss of control over use of the substance (Kaplan et al., 1994). Substance-related disorders are sometimes considered to be the number one health problem in the United States. More than 15 percent of the U.S. adult population is estimated to have serious substance abuse problems; for two-thirds of them, the primary substance of abuse is alcohol. The current trend is toward polydrug abuse, or the abuse of more

than one substance by the same person. Substance use can affect both mood and behavior, and we are just beginning to understand the biological, brain-based connections between substance-related disorders and other psychiatric disorders (Kaplan et al., 1994).

With an awareness of these disorders, you will be better equipped to practice social work with an adult clientele.

## IMPLICATIONS FOR SOCIAL WORK PRACTICE

This discussion has several implications for social work practice with adults:

- Be familiar with the unique pathways your clients have traveled to reach adulthood. Assess the history and current circumstances of clients' love and work roles in the context of rapid changes in the family and economic institutions.

- Recognize that the configuration of love and work roles in adulthood has many variations. Be aware of individual variations as well as variations related to gender, social class, race, ethnicity, sexual orientation, disability, historical era, religion and spirituality, biology, and special life events.

- Recognize the interrelatedness of love and work roles in clients' lives.

- Engage clients in mutual assessment of their working models of attachment relationships.

- Engage clients in mutual assessment of their involvement in a variety of relationships, including romantic relationships, relationships with parents, relationships with children, other family relationships, relationships with friends, and community/organizational relationships.

- When appropriate, coach clients in the use of intimate interactions.

- Assist divorced and remarried families to develop a realistic model of family life for their circumstances.

- Be aware of the potential of small groups for intimate interactions and social support.

- Engage clients in mutual assessment of work-related stressors.

- Collaborate with other social workers and other disciplines to advocate for governmental and corporate solutions to work and family life conflicts.

- Contribute to the public dialogue on the widening gap between rich and poor.

- Collaborate with social workers and members of other disciplines to continue to open educational and work opportunities to persons with disabilities.

- Where appropriate, support the efforts of clients to adapt to living with chronic diseases.

## MAIN POINTS

1. The limited attempts in the literature to define adulthood are based on biological age, psychological age, and social age. In this chapter, the period of adulthood is considered to span the ages from approximately 18 to approximately 65.

2. The two major theoretical perspectives on adulthood are stage theories and process theoretical approaches.

3. Stage theorists suggest that people pass through a sequence of adult stages. Erik Erikson describes two stages of adulthood, each with its psychosocial crisis: the crisis of intimacy versus isolation in young adulthood, and the crisis of generativity versus stagnation in middle adulthood. Daniel Levinson sees the adult life course as alternating periods of relative stability and transition, with young adulthood and middle adulthood as two universal, age-based periods. Gail Sheehy identifies three stages of adulthood—Provisional Adulthood, First Adulthood, and Second Adulthood—but she sees these stages as highly influenced by culture and historical time.

4. Process theoretical approaches see adult behavior as a continuous transaction of biological, psychological, and sociocultural processes that do not occur in universal, discrete stages. Riegel's dialectical approach sees the adult life course as progressing through continuing changes in the following dimensions: the inner-biological, the individual-psychological, the cultural-sociological, and the outer physical. Baltes's life span perspective identifies three major influences on adult behavior: normative age-graded influences, normative history-graded influences, and nonnormative influences. Pearlin's theory of psychological distress identifies three sources of distress: chronic or durable strains; scheduled or predictable change or events; and unexpected, unscheduled changes.

5. Love and work have been identified as the two central, and related, phenomena of adulthood. Monumental changes have occurred since 1960 in how individuals experience love and work.

6. Love may be experienced as attachment, intimacy, affiliation, bonding, and social support.

7. Six types of relationships may take on great importance in adulthood: romantic relationships, relationships with parents, relationships with children, other family relationships, relationships with friends, and community/organizational relationships.

8. Social workers have historically recognized close relationships between work and adult well-being.

9. Currently, three important issues are related to work and adult behavior: work and family conflict, the impact of work on physical and mental health, and marginalization in the labor market.

10. Some of the most common health and mental health problems in adulthood are coronary heart disease, cancer, anxiety disorders, mood disorders, and substance-related disorders.

## KEY TERMS

addiction

affiliation

anxiety disorder

attachment relationship

central components

compensation

cross-era transitions

culminating life structure

domestic work

emotional work

employee assistance programs (EAPs)

entry life structure

epigenetic principle

eras

generation

generativity

intimacy

intimate interaction

intimate relationship

job burnout

life structure

mood disorder

occupational social work

passages

peripheral components

process theoretical approach

psychosocial crisis

seasons of adulthood

social bonding

spillover

stage theories

statutory age of majority

substance abuse

substance-related disorders

unfulfilled components

working model

## WORLD WIDE WEB RESOURCES

Job Stress Help

**http://www.jobstresshelp.com/**

Site maintained by a group of professional, licensed social workers and other mental health professionals. Contains facts about job stress, frequently asked questions (FAQ), online consultation and information, and links to additional information.

Midlife Moments
**http://www.bestyears.com/**
Site written and maintained by Mike Bellah, Ph.D. Contains articles on midlife issues, including career changes and midlife crisis, question-and-answer page, online chat, and links to additional information.

The Couples Place
**http://www.couples-place.com/**
Site written and maintained by David Sanford, Ph.D., MSW. Provides support for marriage and other "couple" relationships. Contains a relationship library, forums, and links to resources on men, women, relationships, and marriage.

Web of Addictions
**http://www.well.com/user/woa/**
Site written and maintained by Andrew Honer, Ph.D., and Dick Dillon. Contains fact sheets arranged by drug, contact information for a variety of substance abuse groups, in-depth information on special topics, and links to additional resources.

# CHAPTER 8

# Late Adulthood

*Matthias J. Naleppa, Virginia Commonwealth University*

### THE SMITHS IN EARLY RETIREMENT

The Smiths are a couple in their early retirement years who have come to you for couples counseling. Lois Smith is 66 and Gene Smith is 68 years of age. They have lived in the same quiet suburban neighborhood since they married 20 years ago. When they met, Gene was a widower, and Lois had been divorced for three years. They have no children from this marriage, but three children from Lois's first marriage. The Smiths are grandparents to the three children of their married daughter, who lives four hours away. Their two sons are both single and also live in a different city. The Smiths visit their children frequently, but family and holiday gatherings usually take place at the Smiths' house.

The Smiths live in a comfortable home, but their neighborhood has changed over the years. When they bought the house, many other families were in the same life stage, raising adolescent children and seeing them move out as young adults. Many of the neighbors from that time have since moved, and the neighborhood has undergone a change to young families with children. Although the Smiths feel connected to the community, they do not have much interaction with the people in their immediate neighborhood. Only one other neighbor, a woman in her mid-80s, is in the same age group. This neighbor has difficulty walking and no longer drives a car. The Smiths help her with chores around the house and often take her shopping.

Until her divorce, Lois had focused primarily on raising her children. After the divorce at age 43, she needed to enter the job market. Without formal education beyond high school, she had difficulty finding employment. She worked in a number of low-paying short-term jobs before finding a permanent position as a secretary at a small local company. She has only a small retirement benefit from her 12 years on that job. Gene had worked as bookkeeper and later assistant manager with a local hardware store for more than 30 years. Although their combined retirement benefits enable them to lead a comfortable retirement, Gene continues to work at the hardware store on a part-time basis.

The transition into retirement has not been easy for the Smiths. Both Gene and Lois retired last year, which required them to adjust all at once to a decrease in income. Much more difficult, however, has been the loss of status and feeling of void that they are experiencing. Both were accustomed to the structure that was provided by work. Gene gladly assists in his former company on a part-time basis, but he worries that his employer will think he's getting too old. Lois has no plans to reenter the workforce. She would like her daughter to live closer so she could spend more time with the grandchildren. Although the infrequency of the visits with the grandchildren has placed some strain on Lois's relationship with her daughter, especially in the period following her retirement, Lois has now begun to enjoy the trips to visit with her daughter as a welcome change in her daily routine. But those visits are relatively infrequent, and Lois often wishes she had more to do.

## THE MOROS' INCREASING NEEDS FOR CARE

Frank Moro is an 82-year-old married man who lives with his 80-year-old wife, Camille, in their own home. Both Frank and Camille are second-generation Italian Americans. Frank had a stroke one year ago that resulted in a right-side paralysis. He has several other limiting medical conditions, including arthritis, hypertension, and a partial loss of vision. He perceives his health to be fair, even though his level of functioning in activities of daily living is very low. He needs assistance in using the toilet, rising from a chair, getting in and out of bed, moving around, and personal care. Frank has a wheelchair that he rarely uses. He shows a slight cognitive decline on a standardized measurement tool. Camille is the primary caregiver, assisting her husband in his personal care, helping him in and out of bed, and assisting him with toileting. The two sons who live in the area also provide assistance, especially with home repairs and financial arrangements.

Frank was referred by his physical therapist to the case management program for which you work as a case manager. Since his stroke, he is not able to ambulate independently. His wife and sons have reported being overwhelmed by round-the-clock caregiving.

During your first home visit, you identified several needs: Frank needed assistance with his personal care and mobility, and he did not use his wheelchair. Furthermore, Camille needed some respite. After exploring Frank's personal care needs, you told the Moros about the services available to them. Then the three of you agreed to undertake a couple of tasks: You would contact a home health aide to set up a meeting, and the Moros would discuss their needs and make arrangements with the home health aide. These tasks were completed quickly, and the aide began providing services within a week.

The second target problem related to Frank's physical mobility and Camille's need for respite. After some discussion, it was decided that Frank would benefit from medical adult day care, which could assist in maintaining his mobility. Day care would also provide respite for Camille. Implementing this plan took a little longer, however, because the Moros had to visit an adult day-care center, apply, and arrange for transportation before Frank could begin to attend.

A third area of need, identified by Camille, related to Frank's unwillingness to use the wheelchair. In his culture, he said, men do not advertise physical limitations and dependence on others. His self-esteem as well as cultural factors seemed to be hindering efforts to increase his mobility. With a great deal of persuasion, you helped Frank see the benefits of using a wheelchair, and he finally agreed to try it out for a few days. Although he began very reluctantly, after several weeks Frank got used to the wheelchair. He uses it on a daily basis now, and concedes that it has significantly enhanced his independence.

### THE INSTITUTIONALIZATION OF ROSE GOLDBERG

Rose had lived on her own since her husband died 12 years ago. Her two brothers also died several years ago. Now, at age 89, she is the last family member of her generation who is still alive. Rose's only daughter, Marion, who is 60, lives and works close to Rose's home. Marion would come almost every day for a brief visit on her way home from work, and Rose often spent the weekends at her daughter's house. Although Rose was occasionally confused and got lost twice within the last year, she still made a daily trip to the little neighborhood market to go shopping.

Several months ago, however, Rose was coming back from the market when she fell and broke her hip. She was taken to the hospital for emergency surgery. The healing of the fracture proceeded fairly slowly, and she ran into several medical complications. While she was in the hospital, Rose became more and more confused, at times not remembering where she was. When it came time to discharge her, it was not feasible for her to return home on her own because her memory and her cognitive abilities were rapidly declining.

As the social worker assigned to Rose's case, you were involved in the discharge planning. You met with Rose and Marion to discuss the options. Unfortunately, Marion was not able to take her mother into her home. There was no extra room, and Marion could not afford to stop working full-time to provide the care that Rose needs. In-home health care services did not seem a viable option, either, because Rose needs constant supervision and assistance. Thus, the very difficult decision was made to pursue a nursing home placement.

Rose participated in planning the move into the nursing home, but was very quiet and withdrawn. She knew that it was not feasible to move in with her daughter. Nevertheless, she expressed anger and hurt. No one in her family had lived in a nursing home before, and it was not the way she had planned to spend her last years. She reluctantly accepted the fact that she did not have any other alternative.

**CASE STUDIES**

Fortunately, you found a nursing home with an immediate opening, and Rose was moved from the hospital within a few days. But Rose's first days in the nursing home were even more difficult than she thought they would be. She had to share a room with a woman experiencing dementia, who repeated the same phrases over and over again. During the day, Rose did not want to spend any time in her new room. So, in addition to being upset about losing her independence and the hope of returning home, Rose felt trapped in an unfamiliar environment without a place to retreat. During these first days, Rose felt very lonely and had a hard time finding companionship among the nursing home residents. You encouraged Rose to establish some new routines to take the place of her old ones. Now, her weekly visits to the hairdresser and participation in a social activity group provide a welcome change of pace. Rose's daughter continues to visit daily, and they spend time together on the weekends. They continue to be close and are planning to spend a week together at the beach next summer.

# Demographics of the Older Population

How might the psychological concept of self affect social work practice with older persons?

Every client in these stories could be considered old. The term *old* can have many meanings. In discussing life course trajectories, we commonly use the terms *older population* or *elderly persons* to refer to those over 65 years of age. But an Olympic gymnast is "old" at age 25, while a President of the United States is "young" at age 50, and a 70-year-old may not consider herself "old" at all.

*Late adulthood* is perhaps a more precise term than *old,* but it still encompasses a very wide range of ages. Late adulthood ranges from age 65 to more than 100, a span of almost 50 years. Only "adulthood" includes a similar age range. With a life expectancy in the United States of 79 years for women and 72 years for men, many people today reach the life stage of late adulthood (Hobbs & Damon, 1997). Just a century ago, it was not so common to reach even 65 years of age. The first population census of the United States, conducted in 1870, estimated about 3 percent of the population to be over 65 years of age. Today, more than 12 percent of the U.S. population is in this age group, and a person reaching this age can expect to live another 17 years (Hobbs & Damon, 1997). The U.S. Census Bureau estimates that in the next 50 years the elderly population will double to 80 million, representing approximately 20 percent of the estimated total population.

An interesting side effect of the growing elderly population is a shifting **dependency ratio**—a demographic indicator that expresses the degree of demand placed on society by the young and the aged combined (Morgan & Kunkel, 1996). The U.S. dependency ratio has changed gradually over the past century, as the percentage of children in the population has decreased and

**EXHIBIT 8.1**

Dependency Ratio:
Percentage of
Children and Elderly
in the U.S.
Population, 1900,
1980, and 2030

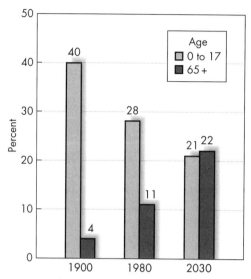

*Source:* Moody, 1998, p. 220.

the percentage of dependent older adults has increased. Currently, the dependency ratio is stable, because the increase in elderly dependents is being offset by a decrease in dependents under 18 (Soldo & Agree, 1988). This demographic shift toward aged dependents suggests, as Exhibit 8.1 shows, that by the year 2030 more Americans will be over 65 than under 18 (Moody, 1998).

Because today it empasses such a broad age range, the older population is often categorized into subgroups: the **young-old** (age 65 to 74), the **middle-old** (age 75 to 84), and the **oldest-old** (over 85). The Smiths exemplify the young-old, the Moros the middle-old, and Rose Goldberg the oldest-old members of our society. The oldest-old, the fastest-growing subgroup, already constitute 10 percent of the elderly population and 1 percent of the general population (Hobbs & Damon, 1997).

Among the older population, women outnumber men across all racial and ethnic groups. Approximately 59 percent of the elderly population are women, 41 percent men (Hobbs & Damon, 1997). The difference is even bigger for the oldest-old, where the ratio is 5 women for every 2 men.

One of the biggest differences in life circumstances for elderly women and men is the difference in their martial status. While 75 percent of the elderly men not living in an institutional setting were married in 1993, only 41 percent of the elderly women were married (Hobbs & Damon, 1997). About 48 percent of the elderly women were widowed, compared to 14 percent of the elderly men. Moreover, the current cohort entering the older population is seeing an increase in divorced or separated elderly.

Not surprisingly, given these statistics, elderly women are more likely than elderly men to live alone. Approximately 80 percent of the noninstitutionalized elderly living alone are female. You may recall that Rose Goldberg lived alone for 12 years prior to her institutionalization.

Fewer elderly persons are institutionalized than we generally assume, but the risk for entering a nursing home increases significantly with age. Only 1 percent of the young-old, but almost a quarter of the oldest-old live in a nursing home (Hobbs & Damon, 1997). Rose Goldberg was almost 90 before she entered a nursing home. It remains to be seen whether Gene, Lois, Frank, or Camille will spend some time before death in a nursing home.

The elderly population is becoming increasingly diverse in race and ethnic background. Currently about 10 percent of older adults are nonwhite. This number is projected to increase to approximately 20 percent in the next 50 years. The Hispanic elderly population is expected to increase from 4 percent currently to 16 percent of the elderly population by the year 2050 (Hobbs & Damon, 1997).

*How are such differences in social status likely to affect the experience of aging?*

The economic status of elderly individuals varies significantly with gender, race, and ethnicity. According to U.S. Census data (Hobbs & Damon, 1997), the median income for an elderly person in 1992 was $14,548 for men and $8,189 for women. Elderly men have a significantly lower poverty rate than elderly women (9 percent versus 16 percent). The poverty rates also differ for racial groups, with black elderly persons having the highest poverty rate (33 percent), followed by Hispanics (22 percent), and whites (11 percent). However, the poverty rate is currently declining for all racial and ethnic groups of older adults. Within the elderly population, the poverty rate is lower for the young-old (11 percent) than for those over 75 (16 percent). The current trend is toward an elderly population of increasingly higher economic status (Hobbs & Damon, 1997).

The geographic distribution of the elderly population is not uniform across the country. U.S. Census Bureau data reveal that the states with the largest populations—California, Florida, New York, Pennsylvania, Texas, Ohio—are also the states with the most elderly persons (Hobbs & Damon, 1997). While Florida (19 percent) and Pennsylvania (16 percent) lead the country in terms of highest percentage of elderly residents, many states with high proportions of elderly inhabitants are located in the midwestern farm belt.

Residential mobility has a significant impact on the distribution of the elderly population. The migration of older persons to Florida after retirement contributes to its high percentage of elderly residents. On the other hand, high percentages of elderly residents in states such as Nebraska and North Dakota are the result of outward migration by younger people. The areas with the greatest increase in older persons are the western states and the coastal Southeast (Hobbs & Damon, 1997).

*How might social workers help older clients cope with such changes in community?*

Residential mobility can also lead to changing age structures within neighborhoods and thus impact the elderly person's life. For example, the Smiths used to be a "typical" family in their neighborhood. Now, as one of two households with elderly occupants, they are the exception.

# Theoretical Perspectives on Social Gerontology

How we as social workers see and interpret aging will inspire our interventions with an older adult. **Social gerontology**—the social science that studies human aging—offers several theoretical perspectives that can explain the process of growing old. Eight predominant theories of social gerontology are introduced here. An overview of the primary concepts of each theory is presented in Exhibit 8.2.

**EXHIBIT 8.2**
Theoretical
Perspectives on
Social Gerontology

| Theory | Primary Concept |
|---|---|
| Disengagement theory | Elderly persons gradually disengage from society. |
| Activity theory | Level of life satisfaction is related to level of activity. |
| Continuity theory | Elderly persons continue to adapt and continue their interaction patterns. |
| Social construction theory | Self-concepts arise through interaction with the environment. |
| Feminist theory | Gender is an important organizing factor in the aging experience. |
| Social exchange theory | Resource exchanges in interpersonal interactions change with age. |
| Life course perspective | Aging is a dynamic, lifelong process characterized by many transitions. |
| Age stratification perspective | Society is stratified by age, which determines people's roles and rights. |

*Disengagement Theory.*    Initially proposed by Cumming and Henry (1961), **disengagement theory** suggests that as elderly individuals grow older, they gradually decrease their social interactions and ties and become increasingly self-preoccupied. Considering Frank Moro, for example, you might interpret his initial lack of initiative to increase his mobility by using the wheelchair as a sign of his disengagement from others. In addition, society disengages itself from older adults. While disengagement is seen as a normative and functional process of transferring power within society, the theory does not explain, for example, the fact that a growing number of older persons like Gene and Lois Smith continue to assume active roles in society. Disengagement theory has received much criticism and little research support (Neugarten, Havighurst, & Tobin, 1968).

*Activity Theory.*    **Activity theory** states that higher levels of activity and involvement are directly related to higher levels of life satisfaction in elderly people (Havighurst, 1968). If they can, individuals stay active and involved, and carry on as many activities of middle adulthood as possible. Activity theory has received some criticism for not addressing what occurs when individuals like Frank Moro and Rose Goldberg cannot maintain their level of activity. It also does not address the choice made by many older individuals to adopt a more relaxed lifestyle.

*Continuity Theory.*    **Continuity theory** was developed in response to critiques of the disengagement and activity theories. According to continuity theory, individuals adapt to changes by using the same coping styles they have used throughout the life course, and new roles substitute for roles lost because of age (Neugarten et al., 1968). Individual personality differences are seen as a major influence in adaptation to old age. Those individuals who were active earlier stay active in later life, while those who adopted a more passive lifestyle continue to do so in old age. For example, older adults typically retain the same stance concerning religion and sex as they always did; those who were interested and active earlier in life usually remain so, as circumstances permit. Continuity theory might help you counsel someone like Lois Smith. Just as she adapted actively to her divorce by reentering the job market later in life, she might actively seek new roles in retirement. She might find great satisfaction in volunteering in her church and in being a grandmother.

*Social Construction Theory.*　The social construction of aging has its historical background in symbolic interactionism, phenomenology, and ethnomethodology. This theory aims to understand and explain the influence of social definitions, social interactions, and social structures on the individual elderly person. The individual's self-conceptions about aging arise through interaction with the social environment (Dannefer & Perlmutter, 1990). You may recall Mrs. Clark from Chapter 2, who had developed a definition of aging that included "helpless" old woman.

*Feminist Theory.*　Proponents of **feminist theories** of aging suggest that gender is a key factor in understanding a person's aging experience. They contend that because gender is an organizing principle in our society, we can only understand aging by taking gender into account (Arber & Ginn, 1995). Think, for example, about Camille Moro's experience as a caregiver to her husband and about Rose Goldberg's experience as a single older woman. How might their personal situations differ if they were men?

*Social Exchange Theory.*　First proposed by Homans (1961) and Blau (1964), social exchange theory is built on the notion that an exchange of resources takes place in all interpersonal interactions. Individuals will only engage in an exchange if they perceive a favorable cost/benefit ratio or if they see no better alternatives (Hendricks, 1987). As individuals become older, however, the resources they are able to bring to the exchange begin to shift. Exchange theory bases its explanation of the realignment of roles, values, and contributions of older adults on this assumption. For example, many older persons get involved in volunteer activities; this seemingly altruistic activity may also be seen as fulfilling an emotional need that provides a personal gain. Older individuals who withdraw from social activities may perceive their personal resources as diminished to the point where they have little left to bring to an exchange, thus leading to their increasing seclusion from social interactions. You might want to explore how Frank and Camille Moro are dealing with the shift in resources within their relationship.

*Life Course Perspective.*　From the life course perspective, aging is a dynamic, lifelong process. Individuals go through many transitions in the course of their life span. The era they live in, the cohort they belong to, and personal and environmental factors influence these transitions.

*Age Stratification Perspective.*　The framework of **age stratification** proposed by Riley (1971) and Foner (1995) falls into the tradition of the life course perspective. The age stratification perspective suggests that, similar to the way society is structured by socioeconomic class, it is also stratified by age. Roles and rights of individuals are assigned based on their membership in an age group or cohort. Individuals proceed through their life course as part of that cohort. Their experience of aging differs because cohorts differ in size, composition, and experience with an ever-changing society.

# The Concepts of Time and Age in Late Adulthood

As suggested in Chapter 1, time and the related concept of age are important considerations in discussing human behavior. Three aspects of time are relevant in dealing with elderly persons: chronological, biological, and psychological.

*Chronological Time.*   Physical time—measured in seconds, minutes, days, and so on—is the most widely used concept of time. An individual's **chronological age** is measured by the units of chronological time—typically, years—that have elapsed since birth. Thus, Lois Smith is 66 years of age, Gene Smith is 68, Frank Moro is 82, Camille Moro is 80, and Rose Goldberg is 89. We celebrate our chronological age every year on our birthday. The definition of late adulthood as the phase of life beginning at age 65 is based on chronological time. Measuring age in terms of chronological time is a very useful approach, but it should not be the sole measure of a person's place in the life course. Schroots and Birren (1990) point out that the first 20 years of a person's life are not equal to the next 20 years in terms of human development.

*Biological Time.*   Individuals of the same chronological age exhibit significant biological variations. Biological age is the individual's age in relation to his or her potential life span (Schroots & Birren, 1990). Let us assume, for example, that the 66-year-old Lois Smith functions biologically and physically like a typical 55-year-old woman. If the average life expectancy for women is 79 years, she has a life expectancy of 90 years. Biological time, as you can see, adds a dimension to our understanding of the person beyond chronological time. Because biological age is complex to measure, however, its usefulness to social work may be limited.

Another biological concept with some relevance to social work is **biological rhythms**— events that occur on a regular basis and are in synchronization with cycles in the environment. A well-known example is the rhythm of the oceans. In the same way, our body goes through many different biological rhythms, including the wake/sleep cycle and the cycle of cellular renewal. As the body ages, some of these cycles are disrupted, thus limiting the adaptive capacity of a person's body.

*Psychological Time.*   Some of a person's adaptive capacities, such as memory and learning, are related to age. Schroots and Birren (1990) suggest that one way of measuring **psychological time** is by the time needed to complete a psychological event. For example, memorizing a new task may take longer for an older adult.

Related to psychological time is social age, which refers to age-appropriate behavior. Social age is determined by the norms of the society in which an individual lives. What constitutes age-appropriate behavior also changes over time. For example, not so long ago it may have seemed peculiar for an elderly individual to visit a fitness center. Today, even some nursing homes have a workout room.

# The Effects of Aging on Functional Capacity

How are such biological changes linked to the psychological and environmental dimensions?

Every day, our bodies are changing. In a sense, then, our bodies are constantly aging. As social workers, however, we need not be concerned with the body's aging until it begins to affect the person's ability to function in her or his world, which typically begins to occur in old age.

Several physiological theories of aging try to explain how and why our bodies age. The four theories described here are popular, but none has received uniform support in the scientific community:

- **Wear and tear theory.** As we age, our body simply wears out. This theory suggests that each species has a maximum life span, determined by its genes.

- **Cross-linkage theory.** This theory, also termed *collagen theory,* is based on the fact that collagen changes as we age. Collagen, the connective tissue of the body, stiffens with age. The wrinkling of skin is a visible result of this process. Other effects are the slower healing of wounds, decreased elasticity of muscle tissue and blood vessels, and changes in the eyes and other organs (Hooyman & Kiyak, 1988).

- **Autoimmune theory.** The aging body loses some of its ability to recognize foreign bacteria, viruses, and other invaders. The body also starts to attack some of its own healthy cells by producing antibodies against itself, thus possibly producing autoimmune diseases.

- **Cellular aging theory.** Cells cannot replicate themselves indefinitely. A slowing down in the replication of cells occurs as we become older. Hayflick (1987) has proven that human cells can only divide a limited number of times, approximately 50 times. On this basis, the upper limit of the human life span would be 110 to 120 years.

However the complex process of physiological aging is described, it has an impact on the functional capacity of both the body and the mind.

## *Health and Longevity*

In the 220 years since the United States was founded, a person's life expectancy has more than doubled, from 35 years in 1776 to 75 years (Hobbs & Damon, 1997). The Moros and Rose Goldberg have all reached the 80-year benchmark, and Rose may well live to be 90. Factors that influence a person's life expectancy include gender (women live longer), heredity, lifestyle, personality characteristics, and health.

**Mortality**—the rate at which death occurs within a population—has declined significantly since 1970. Declining mortality is a consequence of a reduction in acute health conditions, namely a significant decrease in stroke and heart disease (Manton & Soldo, 1985).

Together, cancer, stroke, and heart disease account for about 70 percent of all deaths among older adults (Hobbs & Damon, 1997).

As mortality has decreased, **morbidity**—the incidence of disease—has increased (Wolfe, 1993). In other words, the proportion of the population suffering from age-related chronic conditions has increased in tandem with the population of elderly persons. Health conditions correlated to old age include arthritis, osteoporosis, diabetes, senile dementia, and impairments in the performance of activities of daily living (Wolfe, 1993). Almost 80 percent of today's elderly adults endure at least one chronic condition (Soldo & Agree, 1988), and many have several limiting conditions. For example, Frank Moro has several chronic conditions that limit him: right-side paralysis, arthritis, hypertension, and a partial loss of vision.

For many people, illness and death can be postponed through lifestyle changes. In recent years, the importance of preventing illness by promoting good health has received considerable attention. Hess (1991) summarizes the goals of health promotion for older adults as preventing or delaying the onset of chronic disease and disability; reducing the severity of chronic diseases; and maintaining mental health, physical health, and physical functioning as long as possible. Ways to promote health in old age include improving dietary habits, increasing activity levels and physical exercise, stopping smoking, and getting regular health screenings (blood sampling, blood pressure measurement, mammography, glaucoma screening).

## Age-Related Changes in Physiology

The nervous system is made up of the central nervous system, which includes the brain and the spinal cord; the peripheral nervous system, which comprises the nerves that connect the central nervous system with other body parts; and the autonomic nervous system, which controls cardiovascular, gastrointestinal, genitourinary, and respiratory systems. Neurons and synapses are the transmitters of information throughout the nervous system. Since neurons are not replaced by the body after birth, the number of neurons decreases throughout the life span (Santrock, 1995). The result is a slow decrease of brain mass after age 30. Because we are born with many more neurons and synapses than we need to function, problems usually do not arise (Spence, 1989). However, a neurological injury or disease may result in more permanent and serious consequences for an older person.

Our cardiovascular system changes in several ways as we become older. The cardiac output—the amount of blood pumped per minute—decreases throughout adult life, and the pulse slows with age (Spence, 1989). The arteries become less elastic and harden, which can result in arteriosclerosis. Fatty lipids accumulate in the walls of the blood vessels and make them narrower, which can cause atherosclerosis. As a result of these changes, less oxygen is available for muscular activities (Spence, 1989).

The respiratory system, too, changes with age. Beginning at about 20 years of age, a person's lung capacity decreases throughout the lifespan (Spence, 1989). The typical decrease from age 20 to age 80 is about 40 percent for a healthy person.

The most important age-related change in our skeletal system occurs after age 30, when the destruction of bones begins to outpace the reformation of bones. The gradual decrease in bone mass and bone density can cause osteoporosis (Spence, 1989). As the cartilage between the joints wears thin, arthritis, a chronic inflammation of the joints, begins to develop. Although many individuals suffer from some form of arthritis in their 40s, the symptoms are often not painful until late adulthood. Some of these changes can be ameliorated by diet and exercise and by avoiding smoking and alcohol. Another change in our skeletal system is that we get shorter with age. An older adult normally loses 2–4 cm of height per decade (Spence, 1989).

With increasing age, the muscular system declines in strength and endurance. As a consequence, an elderly person may become fatigued more easily. In addition, muscle contractions begin to slow down, which contributes to deteriorating reflexes and incontinence, which become more prevalent with age. However, the muscular system of older individuals can be successfully strengthened through weight training and changes in diet and lifestyle (Chopra, 1993).

*How could the physical environment be adapted to accommodate age-related changes in the senses?*

Changes in the neurological, muscular, and skeletal systems have an impact on the sensory system and the sense of balance, which contributes to the increase in accidental falls and bone fractures in late adulthood. Vision decreases with age, and older persons need more light to reach the retina in order to see. The eye's adaptation to the dark slows with age, as does visual acuity, the ability to detect details (Fozard, 1990). Age-related decreases in hearing are caused by degenerative changes in the spiral organ of the ear and the associated nerve cells. Many older adults have a reduced ability to hear high-pitch sounds (Fozard, 1990). Since taste receptors are constantly replaced, age-related changes in taste are minimal (Bornstein, 1992). Differences may reflect individual factors, such as exposure to environmental conditions like smoking, rather than general processes of aging. The smell receptors in the nose can decrease with age and become less sensitive.

The **integumentary system** includes the skin, hair, and nails. The skin comprises an outer layer (epidermis) and an inner layer (dermis). With age, the epidermis becomes thinner and pigment cells grow and cluster, creating age spots on the skin (Thomas, 1992). The sweat and oil-secreting glands decrease, leaving the skin dryer and more vulnerable to injury (Spence, 1989). Much of the fat stored in the hypodermis, the tissue beneath the skin, is lost in age, causing wrinkles. The skin of an older person often feels cool because the blood flow to the skin is reduced (Spence, 1989).

## Intellectual Changes, Learning, and Memory

*How can social workers encourage older adults to exercise their cognitive abilities?*

Answering the question about how our intellectual capabilities change in late adulthood is a complex and difficult task. One often-cited study on age-related intellectual changes found that **fluid intelligence** (the capacity for abstract reasoning) declines with age, but **crystallized intelligence** (based on accumulated learning) increases (Horn, 1982). This theory has received much criticism, however, because it was based on a cross-sectional comparison of two different age groups. Researchers who followed a single cohort over time found no general decline of intellectual abilities in late adulthood (Schaie, 1984). Rather, they found considerable individual variation.

Learning and memory are closely related; we must first learn before we can retain and recall. When we process information, it moves through several stages of memory (Kaplan & Sadock, 1998; Thomas, 1992):

1. **Sensory memory.** New information is initially recorded in sensory memory. Unless the person deliberately pays attention to the information, it is lost within less than a second. There seems to be little age-related change in this type of memory.

2. **Primary memory.** If the information is retained in sensory memory, it is passed on to the primary memory, also called *recent* or *short-term memory.* Primary memory has only limited capacity; it is used to organize and temporarily hold information. **Working memory** refers to the process of actively reorganizing and manipulating information that is still in primary memory. While there are some age-related declines in working memory, there seems to be little age-related decline in primary memory.

3. **Secondary memory.** Information is permanently stored in secondary memory. This is the memory we use daily when we remember an event or memorize facts for an exam. The ability to recall seems to decline with age, but recognition capabilities stay consistent.

4. **Tertiary memory.** Information is stored for extended periods in tertiary memory, also called remote memory. This type of memory experiences little age-related changes.

Another way to distinguish memory is between intentional and incidental memory (Sinnott, 1986). **Intentional memory** relates to events that you plan to remember. **Incidental memory** relates to facts you have learned without the intention to retain and recall. Research by Sinnott (1986) suggests that while incidental memory declines with old age, intentional memory does not.

## Mental Health and Mental Disorders

Most older adults living in the community are in good mental health (Young & Olson, 1991). Although older individuals are more predisposed than other people to certain mental disorders, these disorders are not a part of the normal aging process. However, many of the more common mental disorders associated with older age are diagnosed and treated in elderly persons much as they would be in earlier adulthood (Hooyman & Kiyak, 1988).

*Anxiety.*    Anxiety in older adults is similar to that in the younger population. Diagnosis and treatment, however, are often more complex and difficult, because anxiety in older adults often does not follow any direct stimulus. Rather, anxiety is frequently an indication of an underlying mental or physical disorder (Tueth, 1993). Situational stressors that may trigger anxiety in older adults include financial concerns, physical stressors, and loss and loneliness. Symptoms of anxiety include tension, worry, apprehension, and physiological symptoms such as dizziness, gastrointestinal distress, palpitations, urinary disturbance, sweating, and tremors.

*Depression.*    The most common mental health problem in older adults is depression, and major depression is the leading cause of suicide in late adulthood (Blazer, 1995). Many depressive episodes in older adults are associated with problems in coping with difficult life events, such as death of a loved person or physical illness. Symptoms of depression include sadness and depressed mood, loss of interest, weight loss, insomnia, and fatigue. To be diagnosed, the depressive episode has to persist for at least two weeks.

*Delirium.*    One of the two most prevalent cognitive disorders in the elderly population (Kaplan, Sadock, & Grebb, 1994), **delirium** is characterized by an impairment of consciousness. The syndrome has a sudden onset—a few hours or days—follows a brief and fluctuating course that includes an impairment of consciousness, and has the potential for improvement when the causes are treated. Prevalent causative factors include not only central nervous system disturbances, but also outside factors such as renal or hepatic failure (Kaplan et al., 1994). The prevalence of delirium is high among hospitalized elderly persons, with approximately 30–40 percent of hospital patients over age 65 experiencing an episode (Kaplan et al., 1994). Toxicity from prescribed medications is a very common cause of delirium.

*Dementia.*    The other most prevalent cognitive disorder among older adults is **dementia**. It has a slower onset than delirium and is not characterized by an impairment of consciousness. Rather, dementia is characterized by multiple impairments of the person's cognitive functioning caused by damage in the brain tissue. Dementia is not part of the brain's normal aging process, but its prevalence increases with age. Approximately 5 percent of persons over 65, and 20 percent of those over 80, show signs of severe dementia (Kaplan et al., 1994).

There are two types of dementia, reversible and irreversible. Reversible dementia is caused by factors such as drug and alcohol use, nutritional deficits, a brain tumor, or severe depression, and the cognitive decline is reversible if identified and treated early enough (Kaplan et al., 1994). Irreversible dementia is not curable. The two most prevalent types of irreversible dementia are senile dementia of the Alzheimer's type (SDAT) and vascular dementia (multi-infarct dementia), which together account for approximately 75 percent of all cases. SDAT alone accounts for almost two-thirds of all dementia cases (Moody, 1998). Other causes of dementia include Parkinson's disease, Huntington's disease, Pick's disease, Creutzfeldt-Jakob disease, and HIV. Having a family member with dementia is emotionally trying for all involved. In the advanced stages, the person may repeat the same words over and over again, may have problems using appropriate words, and may not recognize a spouse or other family members. At the same time, the person may still be able to recall and vividly describe events that happened many years ago.

Is abuse of legal and illegal drugs by older adults likely to meet with such reactions in years to come?

*Substance Abuse.*    Alcohol is the drug of choice among today's older adults. The prevalence of alcoholism in the older population is estimated to be between 10 and 18 percent. It is the second most frequent reason (after depression) for admitting older adults to an inpatient psychiatric facility (Moss, Mortens & Brennan, 1993). The general consumption of alcohol is lower for older adults than for younger adults, but many heavy drinkers do not reach old age, and alcohol abuse is often more hidden among older adults. Although the consequences of alcoholism are the same for older adults as for younger persons, the attitudes held by family members and society are often very different. Notions such as "He's too old to change," "If I were old I would drink too," or "Don't take away her last pleasure" often prevent efforts to intervene. Contrary to these common attitudes, however, many older persons respond as well to treatment as younger adults do.

# Role Transitions and Life Events of Late Adulthood

Transitions are at the center of the life course perspective, and people experience many transitions, some of them very abrupt, in late adulthood. Retirement, death of a spouse or partner, institutionalization, and one's own death are among the most stressful events in human existence, and they are clustered in late adulthood. Several other events are more benign but may still enter into the social worker's analysis of the changing configuration of person and environment represented by each case.

## *Families in Later Life*

As you saw with the Smiths, the Moros, and Rose Goldberg, families continue to play an important role in the life of an older person. With increased longevity, however, the post-empty-nest and postretirement period lengthens. Thus, the significance of the marital or partner relationship increases in late adulthood. As older individuals are released from their responsibilities as parents and members of the workforce, they are able to spend more time together. Some studies have suggested a U-shaped curve of marital satisfaction, with the highest levels during the first period of the marital relationship and in late adulthood, and lower levels during the childbearing years (Bengtson, Rosenthal, & Burton, 1990). Moreover, overall satisfaction with the quality of life seems to be higher for married elderly individuals than for the widowed or never married. For married couples, the spouse is the most important source of emotional, social, and personal support in times of illness and need of care

How might social workers help never-married elderly persons obtain the support they need?

The never married constitute a very small group of the current elderly population. It will further decrease for some time as the cohort of babyboomers, with its unusually high rate of marriage, enters late adulthood (Bengtson et al., 1990). However, the proportion of elderly singles and never married will probably increase toward the middle of the next century, because the cohort that follows the baby boomers has had an increase in the number of individuals remaining single.

Singlehood due to divorce in late adulthood is increasing, however, as divorce is becoming more socially accepted in all population groups. As in all stages of life, divorce in later life may entail financial problems, especially for older women, and it may be especially difficult to recuperate financially in postretirement. Divorce also results in a change of kinship ties and social networks, which are important sources of support in later life. The incidence of remarriage after divorce or widowhood is significantly higher for older men than for older women. The fact that there are more elderly women than men contributes to this trend.

Sibling relationships play a special role in the life of older adults. Siblings share childhood experiences and are often the personal tie with the longest duration. Siblings are typically not the primary source of personal care, but they often play a role in providing emotional support. Sibling relationships often change over the life course, with closer ties in preadulthood and later life and less involvement in early and middle adulthood.

One group of elderly that has often been neglected in the discussion of late adulthood are elderly gay men and lesbians. Estimates of the proportion of gay men and lesbians among eld-

What social institutions serving older adults are structured to discriminate against elderly gay men and lesbians?

erly persons are similar to those for younger age groups (Teitelman, 1995). Being faced not only with ageist but also with homophobic attitudes, elderly gay men and lesbians may be confronted by a double jeopardy. Eligibility requirements for many services to elderly adults continue to be based on a norm of heterosexuality. Although growing in number, services catering directly to older gay or lesbian persons are still few and far between in many parts of the country. But the most problematic aspect of being an elderly homosexual may be the lack of societal sanction to grieve openly when the partner dies (Teitelman, 1995).

The "myth of the golden age" suggests that in the past older people were respected, lived in a multigenerational family, were well taken care of, and had valued emotional and economic roles. This heartwarming picture is a myth, however; because people died earlier, multigenerational families were less prevalent than they are in our era of increased longevity (Nydegger, 1983). Furthermore, even in the past, elderly individuals valued independent living, and respect in the community was linked to their wealth or prestige.

In fact, multigenerational families have become more common in recent years, resulting in more interactions and exchanges across generations. Contrary to common belief, **intergenerational exchanges** between adult children and elderly parents are not one-directional. Children often take care of their elderly parents, but healthy elderly persons also provide significant assistance to their adult children. Research on elderly parents living with their adult children suggests that for the young-old, more assistance flows from the elderly parents to the adult children than the other way around (Speare & Avery, 1993). In another study (Ward, Logan, & Spitze, 1992), older parents living with their adult children reported doing more than three-quarters of the housework. Patterns of coresidence between parents and adult children vary by race. Non-Hispanic white elderly are the least likely to coreside with their children; Asian elderly are the most likely to live with their children (Speare & Avery, 1993).

## Grandparenthood

Grandparenthood is a normative part of the family lifecycle. More than 94 percent of the older persons who have children will become grandparents (Hooyman & Kiyak, 1988). The timing of grandparenthood influences the way it is experienced and the roles and responsibilities that a grandparent will take on. Many first-time grandparents are middle-aged adults in their early 50s. Yet others do not become grandparents until they are 70 or 80 years old. Because individuals are enjoying longer lives, more and more assume the role of grandparent, and they assume it for more years. Many spend the same number of years being a grandparent as being a parent of a child under the age of 18. It should also be mentioned that an increasing number of older Americans are assuming full responsibility for parenting their grandchildren, as their children have problems with drugs, HIV infection, or crime. Being a grandparent is a welcome and gratifying role for most individuals, but it may increase in significance and meaning for an older person. The Smiths, for example, both enjoy being grandparents, and Lois Smith especially gains pleasure and satisfaction from her role as grandmother to her daughter's children.

In their classic study of middle-class grandparents, Neugarten and Weinstein (1964) identified several styles of grandparenting:

**EXHIBIT 8.3**

Meaning of
Grandparenthood

| Dimension | Description |
|---|---|
| Centrality | Grandparenthood is a central part of the individual's life and meaning. |
| Valued elder | Grandparenthood is characterized by the traditional concepts of the respected and wise elder. |
| Immortality through clan | Grandparenthood is a way of achieving immortality through procreation. |
| Reinvolvement with personal past | The individual's life review is assisted by being a grandparent. |
| Indulgence | An attitude of lenience and indulgence is expressed toward the grandchild. |

*Source:* Adapted from Kivnick, 1983.

- *Formal grandparents* fulfill the proper and prescribed roles. They are interested in the grandchild, but do not take on any parenting responsibilities.

- *Fun seekers* are the playful grandparents who have very informal interactions with the grandchildren and like spending leisure time with them.

- *Distant figures* have a relationship with their grandchildren characterized by little closeness and infrequent interactions, limited mostly to special holidays and family events.

- *Surrogate parents* are grandparents, often grandmothers, who assume the parent role for the grandchild, spending more time taking care of and raising the child than the actual parents do.

- *Mentors.* Often grandfathers serve as the reservoir of family wisdom and teach special skills to the grandchildren.

How can social workers promote growth of the spiritual person in old age?

Regardless of the grandparenting style, the meaning of grandparenthood has five dimensions that are shared by grandparents in varying degrees (Kivnick, 1983). These five dimensions of meaning—centrality, valued elder, immortality through clan, reinvolvement with the personal past, and indulgence—are summarized in Exhibit 8.3.

## Work and Retirement

Some older individuals continue to work for many years after they reach age 65 and are eligible to retire from the workforce (Morgan & Kunkel, 1996). Individuals who continue to work fall into two groups: those who could afford to retire but choose to continue working, and those who continue to work because of a financial need. Elderly of the first group usually receive great satisfaction in sharing their knowledge and expertise and gain a feeling of purpose from being productive. Members of the second group continue to work out of necessity. Since economic status in old age is influenced by past employment patterns and the resultant retirement benefits, this

**EXHIBIT 8.4**

Seven Phases
of Retirement
Adjustment

| Stage | Primary Tasks |
|---|---|
| Remote stage | Only few thoughts spent on upcoming retirement. |
| Near stage | More thoughts about retirement; evaluation of benefits. |
| Honeymoon stage | Period of elation; adjustment to recent retirement. |
| Disenchantment stage | Sense of loss experienced in varying degrees. |
| Reorientation stage | Reevaluation of lifestyle and routine. |
| Stability stage | Feeling well-adapted; few thoughts about retirement. |
| Termination stage | Declining health; facing the end of retirement and of life. |

*Source:* Adapted from Atchley, 1976.

second group consists of individuals who had lower-paying employment throughout their life. This group also includes elderly divorced or widowed women who depended on their husband's retirement income and are now faced with poverty or near poverty. Gene Smith falls into the first category, because he continued working even though he and his wife had sufficient combined benefits to retire. However, Lois Smith's own benefits would not have enabled her to lead a financially comfortable retirement if she were not married, and she would probably face some financial hardship if she were to become a widow. Although some older persons continue to work, it is more common for a person over 65 to be in retirement than to be an active member of the workforce.

When we think about retirement, we often picture individuals cleaning up their desks to stop working completely and sit in a rocking chair on the front porch. Yet there are many ways of retiring from the workforce. Some individuals do cease work completely, but others continue with part-time or part-year employment. Others may retire for a period and then reenter the labor market, as Gene Smith did when his former employer offered him a part-time position. Retirement is a socially accepted way to end an active role in the workforce. Most persons retire because of advancing age, mandatory retirement policies, health problems, or simply the wish to relax and lead the life of a retiree.

*What aspects of a formal work organization might a retired person miss?*

Retirement brings with it a shift in roles, social interactions, and financial resources. These changes typically occur in seven stages of adjustment (Atchley, 1976), summarized in Exhibit 8.4:

1. *Remote stage.* Before actual retirement, most individuals spend little time thinking about it. They may do some financial planning, but the actual event of retiring still seems far away.

2. *Near stage.* As retirement comes closer, individuals begin thinking about what it will be like not to work. Many start looking into their retirement benefits and pensions.

3. *Honeymoon stage.* In the period immediately following the retirement event, individuals often experience a feeling of elation accompanied by a sense of loss.

4. *Disenchantment stage.* Many feel a continuing sense of loss that lasts from a few months to several years. Not everything works out as they had planned for retirement. For some elderly, this disenchantment may cause depression. Those whose life centered around work

often have a harder time adjusting than those who were more actively involved in activities outside of work.

5. *Reorientation stage.* Most people progress to the next stage, which involves reevaluation of the lifestyle and the routine adopted in retirement. Some, like Gene Smith, may decide at this point to return to work. Others may decide that the choices they made are satisfying.

6. *Stability stage.* During this phase, the individual feels well-adapted and does not spend much time thinking about retirement. Adjustment to retirement seems to be easiest for those who are healthy and active, are better educated, have a higher retirement income, and participate in an active social network (Palmore, Burchett, Fillenbaum, George, & Wallman, 1985).

7. *Termination stage.* The end of retirement nears when a person becomes dependent on others for care and assistance because of frailty and declining health and begins to face death.

Every person goes through these phases of retirement at a different pace, and different individuals experience different phases with more or less intensity. Also, not everyone proceeds through the phases in order. Some individuals end their first retirement by returning to the workforce. Others are faced with death before going through all stages of adjustment to retirement.

## Caregiving and Care Receiving

Women are the primary source of caregiving in old age (Soldo & Agree, 1988). Daughters are more likely than sons to take care of elderly parents. Moreover, elderly men tend to be married and thus are more likely to have a wife available as caregiver (T. Brubaker, 1990).

How can small groups ease the burden for weary caregivers?

Caregiving can be a 24-hours, around-the-clock task and often leaves caregivers overwhelmed and exhausted. Camille Moro is a good example of the burden that can be experienced by an elderly spouse. Programs that can assist caregivers like Camille in reducing their exceptional levels of stress have received much attention. Many programs combine educational components—for example, information about and training in adaptive coping skills—with ongoing support through the opportunity to share personal feelings and experiences. Respite programs for caregivers are also available. In-home respite programs provide assistance through a home health aide or a visiting nurse. Community-based respite is often provided through adult day care and similar programs.

When caregiving becomes too overwhelming, a nursing home placement may be pursued. Yet, caregiving often continues after a family member enters a nursing home. Although caregivers are relieved from direct care, they continue to be involved in the emotional and social aspects of care in the nursing home.

Stress and burden are not experienced only by the caregiver. The care recipient also often experiences significant strain. Requiring care is a double loss: The person has lost the capability to perform the tasks for which he or she needs assistance and has lost independence. Having to rely on others for activities that a person has carried out independently throughout adult life can be the source of tremendous emotional and psychological stress. Some individuals respond by emotional withdrawal; others become agitated and start blaming others for their situation. According to Brubaker, Gorman, and Hiestand (1990), the levels of stress that an elderly care recipient may experience depend on "(1) personal and situational characteristics of the elderly recipient; (2) characteristics of the caregiver; (3) social support provided to caregiver and recipient; (4) aspects of the relationship between family caregiver and recipient; and (5) characteristics of caregiving" (p. 268).

Think of Frank Moro. His stress was amplified by culturally defined norms promoting individuality and pride. Helping Frank overcome his uneasiness about receiving assistance and support was a matter of asking him to verbalize his worries, listening to him express his feelings, and looking together at ways that he could overcome his uneasiness in small steps. Getting him to accept a wheelchair also reduced his stress by increasing his independence. Such assistive technology can often greatly reduce the care recipient's reliance on help and thus decrease her or his stress.

## Institutionalization

Another myth of aging is that older individuals are being abandoned and neglected by their families and being pushed into nursing homes to get them out of the way. Despite the myth, most children and spouses do not use nursing homes as a dumping ground for their elderly relatives. They turn to nursing homes only after they have exhausted all other alternatives. Nor is institutionalization a single, sudden event. It is a process that starts with the need to make a decision, continues through the placement itself, and ends in the adjustment to the placement (Naleppa, 1996).

Researchers have taken a close look at the factors that predict a person's entry into a nursing home. Among the most important are the condition and needs of the elderly individual. Functional and behavioral deficits, declining health, previous institutionalization, and advanced age all contribute to the decision to enter a nursing home. Family characteristics that are good predictors of institutionalization include the need for 24-hour caregiving, caregiver feelings of distress, caregiver health and mental status, and caregiving environment (Naleppa, 1996). Marital status is a strong predictor of institutionalization for elderly men. Unmarried and never married men have the highest risk of entering a nursing home (Dolinsky & Rosenwaike, 1988; Hanley, Alecxih, Wiener, & Kennell, 1990). Individuals without a spouse who live alone in the community are at a higher risk of entering a nursing home than those living with spouses, family members, or friends (Montgomery & Kosloski, 1994).

The placement decision itself is emotionally stressful for all involved and can be viewed as a family crisis. Yet it can be considered a normative part of the family life cycle. Gonyea (1987) has identified four stages in the process of making a placement decision: "the recognition of the potential for institutionalization; discussion of the institutionalization option; implementation of actions steps toward institutionalization; and placement of the relative in the institutional setting" (p. 63). Because many nursing home placements are arranged from the hospital for an elderly individual who entered the hospital expecting to return home, many people may not have time to progress well through these stages. For those who unexpectedly enter a nursing home from the hospital, it may be advisable to arrange a brief visit home to say farewell to their familiar environment. While society has developed rituals for many occasions, unfortunately no rituals exist for this difficult life transition.

What features in the physical environment might help nursing home residents feel more in control?

Entering a nursing home means losing control and adjusting to a new environment. How well a person adjusts depends on many factors. If the elderly individual sees entering the nursing home in a favorable light and feels in control, adjustment may proceed well. In the case of Rose Goldberg's entry into the nursing home, her adjustment to the new surroundings could have been facilitated by decorating the room with familiar things such as pictures or wallhangings. Frequent visits by relatives and friends also help in adaptation to the new living arrangement. For example, her daughter's visits helped Rose adjust to the new situation. Despite the commonly held belief that families do not visit their relatives, continued family involvement seems to be the norm. About two-thirds of nursing home residents receive one or more visitors a week, and only a very small group is never visited (Bitzan & Kruzich, 1990).

## *Widowhood*

The death of a spouse is one of the most stressful events in a person's life. In most cases, it is the loss of someone with whom the individual has shared a major part of life. Moreover, the marital relationship is one of the most important relationships for a person in later life. Since they have a longer life expectancy, more women than men face this life event.

Losing a spouse signifies the end of one phase in a person's life course and the beginning of a new phase called widowhood. It requires the individual to readjust to a new social role and a new way of relating to others. It also confronts the person with his or her own mortality. There seems to be some evidence that the loss of a spouse is associated with subsequent illness and earlier mortality (Minkler, 1985). The family is the most important source of emotional, social, and financial support during this time.

There is strong ethnographic evidence that people of all cultures have strong, painful reactions to the death of attachment figures (Counts & Counts, 1991). Sadness, loneliness, disbelief, and anxiety are only a few of the feelings a person may experience in times of bereavement. Several models of the grief process have been presented in recent years (Averill, 1968; Bowlby, 1961; Lindemann, 1944; Parkes, 1987; Raphael, 1983; Volkan & Zintl, 1993). Therese Rando (1984, 1993) proposes the following three phases of grief and mourning:

1. *Avoidance phase.* Immediately following the loss, a person feels denial and disbelief. For several days, emotional numbness alternates with weeping. During this time, many short-term, death-related tasks have to be completed, such as making funeral arrangements and reviewing financial arrangements.

2. *Confrontation phase.* During the next phase, the survivor experiences a painful longing for the lost person. Many memories of the deceased come up. This period of increased sadness and restlessness usually lasts several weeks but can last one or two years or longer.

3. *Accommodation phase.* Individuals readjust and begin to move adaptively into new roles and responsibilities, without forgetting the old.

The rituals associated with death vary in historical and cross-cultural context (Counts & Counts, 1991). In some cultures, the dead are buried; in other cultures, the dead are burned and the ashes are spread. In some places and times, a surviving wife might have burned together with her husband. In the United States, death rituals can be as different as a traditional New Orleans funeral with street music and mourners dressed in white or a somber and serene funeral with mourners dressed in black. Some cultures prescribe more emotional expressions than others. Some cultures build ritual for expression of anger, and some do not. Counts and Counts (1991) identify the following commonalities in death rituals across cultures:

- Social support provided to grievers
- Ritual and ceremony used to give meaning to death
- Visual confrontation of the dead body
- A procession

*How could social workers help surviving caregivers rebuild links with a community?*

Adjustment to widowhood is facilitated by a person's own inner strength, family support, a strong network of friends and neighbors, and membership in a church or an active community. It may be especially difficult if the surviving spouse provided intensive caregiving for a prolonged period. In this case, the partner's death may be a relief from the burdensome caregiving task, but it may also mean the loss of a role and sense of purpose. In addition, during the period of intensive caregiving, the person may have had to give up many social interactions and thus have a shrunken social support network. Those who saw the world through the eyes of a spouse have to learn to see everything from a new perspective.

## The Search for Personal Meaning

*Why does life review promote growth in the spiritual dimension of person?*

As adults become older, they spend more time reviewing their life achievements and searching for personal meaning. In gerontology, the concept of life review was introduced by Robert Butler (1963). He theorized that this self-reflective review of one's life is not a sign of losing short-term memory, as had been assumed. Rather, **life review,** a developmental task of late adulthood, is a process of evaluating and making sense of one's life. It includes a reinterpretation of past experiences and unresolved conflicts.

The life review can lead to diverse outcomes, including depression, acceptance, or satisfaction (Butler, 1987). If the life review is successful, it leads the individual to personal wisdom and inner peace. But the reassessment of one's life may also lead to despair and depression. This idea that the process of life review may lead to either acceptance or depression is similar to the eighth stage of Erikson's theory of adult development: Through the life review, the individual tries to work through the conflict between ego integrity (accepting oneself and seeing one's life as meaningful) and despair (rejecting oneself and one's life).

The ways in which individuals review their lives differ considerably. Some undertake a very conscious effort of assessing and reevaluating their achievements; for others, the effort may be subtle and not very conscious. Regardless of how they pursue it, life review is believed to be a common activity for older adults that occurs across cultures and time.

The concept of **reminiscence** is closely related to life review. Most older persons have a remarkable ability to recall past events. They reminisce about the past and tell their stories to anyone who is willing to listen, but they also reminisce when they are on their own. This reminiscing can serve several functions (Sherman, 1991):

- Reminiscing may be an enjoyable activity that can lift the spirits of the listener and of the person telling the story.

- Some forms of reminiscing are directed at enhancing a person's image of self, as when individuals focus on their accomplishments.

- Reminiscing may help the person cope with current or future problems, letting her or him retreat to the safe place of a comfortable memory or recall ways of coping with past stressors.

- Reminiscing can assist in the life review, as a way to achieve ego integrity.

Sherman suggests that reminiscing combines past, present, and future orientations. It includes the past, which is when the reviewed events occurred. However, the construction of personal meaning is an activity that is also oriented to the present and the future, providing purpose and meaning to life.

## The Dying Process

Current mainstream American culture could be described as in "death denial." Talking about death and dying continues to be taboo, although thinking about death becomes more dominant in late adulthood.

Many factors influence the ways in which a person adjusts to death and dying, including the person's religion and philosophy of life, culture, personality, and other individual traits. It is also affected by the conditions of dying. A person with a long terminal illness has more time to accept death than someone with a very short time to face death.

In her classic book *On Death and Dying*, Elisabeth Kübler-Ross (1969) identified five phases a dying individual goes through:

1. *Denial.* The person denies that death will occur: "This is not true. It can't be me." This denial is succeeded by temporary isolation from social interactions.

2. *Anger.* The individual asks "Why me?" The person projects his or her resentment and envy onto others and often starts to display anger toward caregivers, family members, and friends.

3. *Bargaining.* The individual starts bargaining in an attempt to postpone death: "Yes, me, but I will do . . . in exchange for a few more months."

4. *Depression.* A sense of loss follows. Individuals grieve about their own end of life and about the ones that will be left behind. A frequent reaction is withdrawal from close and loved persons: "I just want to be left alone."

5. *Acceptance.* The person accepts that the end is near and the struggle is over: "It's O.K. My life has been. . . ."

Most individuals experience these five reactions if they have the time. However, they often shift back and forth between phases and do not experience them in a linear way. Kübler-Ross (1969) suggests that, on some level, hope of survival persists through all phases of dying.

# Resources for Meeting the Needs of Elderly Persons

The persons in the stories at the beginning of the chapter needed several kinds of assistance. Lois and Gene Smith, for example, needed some counseling to help them settle comfortably into retirement together. Gene went back to work to fill some of his leisure hours, but Lois needed some suggestions about the volunteer opportunities that could give meaning to her life. The Moros' needs were quite different. Frank is confronted with several chronic conditions for which he needs assistance. Much of this assistance has been provided by his wife. Camille, in turn, needs some respite services to prevent her from being overwhelmed by the demands of giving care. Rose Goldberg, with restricted mobility and some cognitive decline, requires a level of assistance most practically provided in a nursing home.

The types of support and assistance that elderly persons receive can be categorized as either formal or informal resources. Formal resources are those provided by formal service providers. They typically have eligibility requirements that a person has to meet in order to qualify. Some formal resources are free, but others are provided on a fee-for-service basis, meaning that anyone who is able to pay can request the service.

## Informal Resources

Informal resources are those provided through families, friends, neighbors, and churches. Elderly persons receive a considerable amount of support through these informal support networks.

The family is the most important provider of informal resources for many older individuals. It is estimated that 80 to 90 percent of the care provided to elderly persons living in the community is provided by family members (Manton & Liu, 1984). Usually family members can provide better emotional and social support than other providers of services. Family members know the person better and are more available for around-the-clock support. Different family members tend to provide different types of assistance. Daughters tend to provide most of the caregiving and are more involved in housekeeping and household chores. Sons are more likely to provide assistance with household repairs and financial matters.

However, the family should not be considered a uniformly available resource. Not all family networks are functional and able to provide needed support. As Rose Goldberg's story illustrates, even when family members are involved in the elderly person's life, other competing demands may prevent them from supplying all the needed caregiving and assistance. The increased presence of women in the labor market places them in a particularly difficult position—trying to balance the demands of raising children, taking care of their parents, and being part of the workforce. Furthermore, the size of the family network available to support elderly persons is decreasing as a consequence of the decreasing average number of children in a family (T. Brubaker, 1990).

A second source of informal resources is friends and neighbors, who often provide a significant amount of care and assistance. While they may be less inclined than family members would be to provide personal care, friends and neighbors like Gene and Lois Smith in our first story often offer other forms of assistance, such as running errands or performing household chores. Sometimes a system of informal exchanges evolves—for example, an elderly woman invites her elderly neighbor over for meals, while he mows her lawn and drives her to medical appointments.

Finally, informal resources are also provided by church and community groups. Church-related resources include social and emotional support through group activities and community events. It is this form of support that an active retired person like Lois Smith finds most helpful. In addition, some churches are involved in providing more formal resources, such as transportation or meal services.

## Formal Resources

How might the formal nature of these organizations affect the aging person?

The second source of support is the formal service delivery system, which offers a wide range of services. Four different **Social Security trust funds** are the backbone of formal resources to older Americans:

1. **Old-Age and Survivors Insurance (OASI).** The retirement and survivors' component of the U.S. Social Security system is a federally administered program that covers almost all workers. To qualify, a person must have worked at least 10 years in employment covered by the program. The benefit is based on the individual's earnings and is subject to a maximum benefit amount. Through cost-of-living adjustments, the amount is adjusted annually for inflation. Many older individuals are able to supplement this benefit with private pension benefits.

2. **Hospital Insurance Trust Fund (Medicare Part A).** This fund covers a major part of the cost of hospitalization, as well as a significant part of the costs of skilled nursing facility care, approved home health care, and under certain conditions, hospice care. Depending on the type of service needed, beneficiaries pay a one-time co-payment or a percentage of the actual costs. Most beneficiaries do not need to pay a monthly premium (Kingson & Berkowitz, 1993).

3. **Supplementary Medical Insurance (Medicare Part B).** This fund covers medical costs such as physicians' services, inpatient and outpatient surgery, and ambulance services, as well as laboratory services, medically necessary home health care, and outpatient hospital treatment. Beneficiaries pay a small monthly premium (Kingson & Berkowitz, 1993). Some services require a co-payment or a deductible.

4. **Disability insurance.** This component provides benefits for workers younger than 62 with a severe long-term disability. There is a five-month waiting period, but the benefits continue as long as the disability exists.

In addition, **Supplementary Social Security Income (SSI)** is a financial need–based program that provides cash benefits to low-income, aged, blind, and disabled persons. It is not part of the Social Security trust funds but is a federal welfare program.

Other formal services are available regionally. Here is an overview of some of the most important ones:

- *Adult day care.* Some elderly individuals have conditions that prevent them from staying at home while their caregiver is at work, or the caregiver may benefit from respite. Two forms of adult day care exist for such situations. The **social adult day care** model provides meals, medication, and socialization, but no personal care. The **medical adult day care** model is for individuals who need medical care, nursing services, physical or occupational therapy, and more intensive personal care.

- *Senior centers.* Community forums for social activities, educational programs, and resource information are available even in small communities.

- *Home health care services.* Several types of home health care are available, varying greatly in level of assistance and cost. They range from homemakers who assist with household chores, cleaning, and errands to registered nurses who provide skilled nursing service, use medical equipment, and provide IV therapy.

- *Hospice programs.* The purpose of a **hospice** program is to provide care to the terminally ill. Through inpatient or outpatient hospice, patients typically receive treatment by a team of doctors, nurses, social workers, and care staff.

- *Senior housing.* An elderly person may require a change in his or her living arrangement for a number of reasons, and several alternative living arrangements are available. Senior apartments and **retirement communities** are for persons who can live independently. They typically offer meals and housekeeping services, but no direct care. Many offer transportation, community rooms, and senior programs. **Adult homes** are for seniors in need of more assistance. They usually have rooms, rather than apartments, and provide meals, medication management, and supervision. **Health-related senior facilities** are for those in need of nursing care and intensive assistance with activities of daily living. Rooms are private or semiprivate, and residents share living and dining rooms. Medications, meals, personal care, and some therapeutic services are provided. The **skilled nursing facility** provides the highest level of care, including nursing and personal care and an array of therapeutic services. Several noninstitutional alternatives to the nursing home exist, including **adult foster care** programs that operate in a similar way to foster care programs for children and adolescents.

- *Nutrition programs.* Deficits in nutrition can affect a person's health and the aging process. Nutritional services are provided through a number of programs, the best known being Meals on Wheels (Wacker, Roberto, & Piper, 1997).

- *Transportation services.* Public and private providers offer transportation for elderly persons with mobility problems.

- *Power of attorney.* Some elderly persons have difficulty managing their legal and financial affairs. A **power of attorney (POA)** is a legal arrangement by which a person appoints another individual to manage his/her financial and legal affairs. The person given the POA should be a person the client knows and trusts. Standard POA forms are available at stationery stores, but the POA can be tailored to the individual's situation. It then needs to be notarized, a service provided by attorneys and some banks. A POA can be limited (for a limited time period), general (no restrictions), or durable (begins after the client reaches a specified level of disability) (Wacker et al., 1997).

With so many types of services available, the social worker's most daunting task is often assessing the elderly person's needs. It may also be a challenge, however, to find quality services that are affordable. Thus, advocacy on behalf of older adults remains a concern of the social work profession.

## IMPLICATIONS FOR SOCIAL WORK PRACTICE

Several practice principles for social work with older adults can be recommended:

- Develop a general understanding of the complex influences that emotional, physical, biological, psychological, spiritual, and social factors have on the functioning of persons in late adulthood.
- When working with an older adult, take into account the person's life history.
- Develop self-awareness of your views on aging and how different theoretical perspectives may influence your practice.
- Do a thorough and multidimensional assessment when working with older adults. Do not solely look at an individual's chronological age, but consider biological, psychological, and social age.
- Be conscious that age-related social roles change over time and that they vary for different cohorts.
- Identify areas in which you can assist an elderly client in preventing future problems, such as health-related difficulties.
- Develop an understanding of and skills to assess the difference between the physical, biological, psychological, and socioemotional changes that are part of normal aging and those that are indicative of a problematic process. Develop an understanding of how such factors may impact on the intervention process.
- Develop an understanding of the different types of families in later life. Because older adults continue to be part of their families, it may be beneficial to work with the entire family system.
- Develop an understanding of the different roles and styles of grandparenting and how they may influence an older adult's behavior.
- Develop an understanding of the retirement process and how individuals adjust differently to this new life stage.

- Carefully assess an elderly person's caregiving network. Be conscious of the difficulties that the caregiving situation poses for both the caregiver and the care recipient. Be conscious of the potential for caregiver burnout, and familiarize yourself with local caregiver support options.

- Develop an understanding of the process of institutionalizing an older adult. Be careful not to label it as an act of abandonment. Rather, be aware that institutionalization is stressful for all involved and is typically done only as a last resort. Develop an understanding of the process of adaptation to nursing home placement, and skills to assist an older adult and his or her family with that adaptation.

- Develop an understanding of the grieving process, and skills to assist in the process.

- Develop an understanding of the process of reacting to a terminal illness, and skills to assist in the process.

- When assessing the need for service, be conscious of the availability of formal and informal support systems. Develop an understanding and knowledge of the formal service delivery system.

- Avoid treating an older person as if he or she were incapable of making decisions simply because he or she may not be able to carry out the decision. Rather, involve the person to the maximum extent possible in any decisions relating to his or her personal life and care, even if he or she is not able to carry out the related actions.

## MAIN POINTS

1. Because the older population is a very heterogeneous group, we distinguish among the young-old (65–74 years), the middle-old (75–84 years), and the oldest-old (85 and above). The oldest-old are the fastest growing segment of the U.S. population.

2. U.S. average life expectancy has continuously increased and is currently at 79 years for women and 72 years for men. A decrease in deaths by heart disease and stroke has contributed to a decreased mortality rate.

3. Older women outnumber older men by approximately 2 to 1. Older men are more likely to be married than older women.

4. Theories of social gerontology provide us with a perspective on aging. The most commonly discussed theories are disengagement theory, activity theory, continuity theory, social construction of aging, feminist theories of aging, social exchange

theory, life course theory, and age stratification. Biological theories of aging explain the aging of our physical systems. The most common theories include wear and tear theory, cross-linkage theory, autoimmune theory, and cellular aging theory.

5. Several physiological changes typically occur in late adulthood. An older person may recover more slowly from neurological injury because of changes in the nervous system. Cardiac output decreases, and the pulse becomes slower. The capacity of the lungs decreases throughout adulthood. Changes in the skeletal system include a decrease in bone mass and bone density. The abilities to hear, see, and smell also decrease. Changes occur differently in every person.

6. Information is processed through several stages of memory. Sensory memory stores new information for less than a second. If it is retained, it moves on to the primary or short-term memory. Secondary memory permanently stores information, and tertiary memory is the long-term repository. While some phases of the memory processing are affected by age, others are not.

7. The most prevalent mental health problems among older adults include anxiety, depression, and dementia. Assessment and diagnosis of these mental disorders may be especially complex with the older adult population.

8. Families play an important role in late adulthood. Older adults live in increasingly diverse family forms, including as marital couples, never married or divorced singles, remarried couples, or in gay and lesbian relationships. As a result of increased longevity, multigenerational families are more common than ever. Intergenerational exchanges are not unidirectional, but benefit all generations.

9. Some individuals continue to work in late adulthood even after they are eligible to retire, either out of financial necessity or by choice. Some work full-time; others change to part-time or part-year positions. However, most persons enter retirement and adjust to this phase of life through a series of stages: remote, near, honeymoon, disenchantment, reorientation, stability, and termination.

10. Women tend to be the primary caregivers for disabled elderly persons. Caregiving can be emotionally and physically exhausting. Respite and support programs can assist overburdened caregivers.

11. Receiving care also places a significant strain on the recipient. Having to rely on others for assistance signifies a loss of independence that can be highly stressful.

12. Institutionalization is a process that encompasses the decision to pursue a placement, the actual placement and transition into the nursing home, and the postplacement adjustment to the new living situation. Despite common belief, most placements are only made as a last resort when there are no feasible alternatives.

13. Losing a spouse is one of the most stressful and consequential life events. Individuals typically go through several phases of grief and bereavement, which include

shock, despair, and recovery. Widowhood is a new life phase that requires an adjustment to new social roles.

14. Late adulthood is a time when persons search for personal meaning. Life review and reminiscence are directed at reinterpreting past experiences and unresolved conflicts in an effort to achieve ego integrity.

15. Rituals related to death and dying vary across time and culture. Kübler-Ross suggests that individuals move through several phases in the process of accepting the end of their life: denial, anger, bargaining, depression, and acceptance.

16. Informal resources include spouses, other family members, neighbors, friends, and community and church groups. They provide a significant amount of care.

17. The major formal resources for older adults that are provided on a national level are Old-Age and Survivors Insurance (OASI), the Hospital Insurance Trust Fund (Medicare Part A), Supplementary Medical Insurance (Medicare Part B), disability insurance, and Supplementary Social Security Income (SSI). Other resources, such as alternative living programs, nutritional programs, transportation, hospice, and adult day care, vary regionally.

## KEY TERMS

activity theory
adult foster care
adult home
age stratification
autoimmune theory
biological rhythm
cellular aging theory
chronological age
continuity theory
cross-linkage theory
crystallized intelligence
delirium
dementia
dependency ratio
disability insurance
disengagement theory
feminist theory
fluid intelligence
health-related senior facility

hospice
Hospital Insurance Trust Fund
    (Medicare Part A)
incidental memory
integumentary system
intentional memory
intergenerational exchanges
life review
medical adult day care
middle-old
morbidity
mortality
Old-Age and Survivors Insurance (OASI)
oldest-old
power of attorney (POA)
primary memory
psychological time
reminiscence
retirement community

secondary memory

sensory memory

skilled nursing facility

social adult day care

social gerontology

Social Security trust funds

Supplementary Medical Insurance
   (Medicare Part B)

Supplementary Social Security Income (SSI)

tertiary memory

wear and tear theory

working memory

young-old

## WORLD WIDE WEB RESOURCES

Aging in a Social Context

**http://www.gl.umbc.edu/~vdotte1/index.html**

Site maintained by the University of Maryland–Baltimore County. Contains on-line articles and
   journals, research aids, and links to additional information, including government sites on
   aging.

Social Gerontology & the Aging Revolution

**http://www.trinity.edu/~mkearl/geron.html**

Site maintained by Trinity University. Contains many resources including theoretical and methodological issues, biology of aging, psychology of aging, social psychology of aging, old age
   across culture and time, politics of aging, aging and the economy, aging and religion, and
   much more.

AgePage.Com

**http://www.agepage.com/articles.htm**

Contains information on issues of aging, the elderly, seniors, and their caregivers. Topics include
   arthritis, crime and the elderly, incontinence, medical care, nursing homes, medications,
   sexuality, and links to other resources.

GeroWeb

**http://www.iog.wayne.edu/GeroWebd/GeroWeb.html**

Site maintained by Wayne State University's Institute of Gerontology. Contains many links to articles and resources on gerontology, from Alzheimer's to retirement.

# Hacer es Poder: *A Community Prevention Project with a Life Course Framework*

*Elizabeth D. Hutchison, Virginia Commonwealth University*
*Marian A. Aguilar, University of Texas at Austin*

Ernesto Arce is a prevention specialist for the state department of mental health. For the past two years, he has directed *Hacer es Poder* (Action Is Power), a prevention project in a community where he lived as a child—a community that is predominantly Mexican American but has a growing population of other Latino groups. Located in the central city of a major urban center in the Southwest, this community has been identified as an area of concentrated poverty. The housing stock is deteriorating, and rates of unemployment and early school leaving are high. Some residents are new immigrants; some are the children of immigrants; some have ancestors whose presence in the region predated the Anglo-American settlers; and some have moved back and forth across the border with changing labor conditions in both the United States and Mexico. Some are U.S. citizens, and some are undocumented. Some speak English, some speak Spanish, and many are bilingual. Most are Catholic, but some are Protestant; some weave Christian beliefs with healing rituals.

Having grown up in the community, Ernesto is well aware of its problems. Since Ernesto was a child, he has heard a lot about problems in the community. In his work at the state department of mental health, he is familiar with data that indicate a variety of community troubles: high rates of unemployment, teen pregnancy, early school leaving, substance abuse, depression and anxiety, serious health problems, and family and community violence. Ernesto is also familiar with many strengths in the community: the natural support systems made up of extended family, *compradzo* (church sponsors or godparents), and the *barrios* (tightly knit neighborhoods); the religious institutions; the merchants who run the cultural *hierberia* shops (that sell herbs) and grocery shops; and the social and recreational clubs. He knows that the community has been able to absorb and support new immigrants and to survive prejudice and discrimination from the outside world.

In the early days of *Hacer es Poder*, Ernesto and project staff wanted to identify community assets and community problems—from the perspective of community members. They talked to a lot of community people, including community leaders (from teens to older adults), religious leaders, traditional healers, merchants, members of the social and recreational clubs, self-help groups, advocacy groups, parent groups in the schools, youth groups, and so on. They also talked to staff in the schools, social service agencies, the medical clinic, and the legal clinic, and to leaders in civic organizations that have provided resources to the community.

These conversations identified an assortment of community assets—many of them already familiar to Ernesto, but some new ones as well—including

- strong family and neighborhood support systems, including mutual support between older adults and grandchildren
- deep religious faith of many community members and their involvement in church activities such as religious education, fund-raisers, social activities, and social services
- committed merchants who provide many kinds of aid to community members
- an active Catholic Services agency, St. Vincent de Paul, that provides a soup kitchen, a clothing closet, a legal clinic, and adult education programs
- interested and committed organizations from outside the community, such as the Junior League, a suburban church, and the university medical school
- community festivals that help to develop cultural pride
- community activists who have formed safety patrol groups

The conversations also identified the community problems most troublesome to community members:

- financial hardship
- child and maternal health problems
- parenting difficulties
- early school leaving
- family conflict about acculturation issues
- caregiver burden
- substance abuse
- youth gangs creating unsafe schools, playgrounds, and neighborhoods
- physical and mental health problems among community elders

An Advisory Council was formed to help the *Hacer es Poder* staff develop programs that use community assets to address community problems. The council is made up of people who represent the community, rather than those who come from the outside to offer services—community leaders from teens to older adults. They recommended a life course perspective as the best framework for improving community life and strengthening families (see Mrazek & Haggerty, 1994). This framework was used to analyze the risk factors and protective factors for each age group in the community, and the following targets were identified for intervention specific to each age-graded period:

- *Conception, pregnancy, and birth.* Provide better information for community women of childbearing age about the hazards of tobacco, alcohol, and other drugs, diabetes, and HIV during pregnancy. Secure early, regular, and comprehensive prenatal care for pregnant women.

- *Infancy and early childhood.* Provide more widespread immunization. Strengthen parenting skills. Develop more child-care options. Develop programs to improve nutrition.

- *Middle childhood.* Strengthen relationships between home and school. Provide earlier intervention for children with behavioral problems or at risk for school failure. Prevent the use of alcohol and other drugs.

- *Adolescence.* Improve school retention rates. Reduce the use of alcohol and other drugs. Prevent HIV, teen pregnancy, and gang involvement. Strengthen cultural pride.

- *Adulthood.* Reduce stress related to unemployment, work conditions, immigrant status, caregiver burden, and chronic illness.

- *Late adulthood.* Reduce depressive symptoms and social isolation among elder widows. Enhance mutual aid with younger generations.

Still in an early stage, *Hacer es Poder* counts the following activities among its accomplishments:

1. The department of mental health and the public health department have provided brochures—written in both Spanish and English—on the hazards of tobacco, alcohol, and other drugs, diabetes, and HIV during pregnancy. These brochures are now prominently displayed in the *hierberia* shops, grocery shops, music stores, and beauty shops. Local merchants—who received some training about these hazards—often engage customers in conversations about the content of the brochures.

2. Catholic Services is collaborating with the public health department and the medical school to ensure that more pregnant women in the community—regardless of citizenship status—receive prenatal care. They are working to ensure that language interpretation will be available when needed. In addition, the public health department has provided brochures on physiological and emotional changes during pregnancy and on fetal development—in both Spanish and English—to community merchants. These brochures are prominently displayed, and merchants draw them to the attention of pregnant customers, asking if they have received prenatal care.

3. The medical clinic—located in the community and run by the medical school—has stepped up its efforts to vaccinate infants and young children. They are collaborating with community merchants, religious leaders, and social clubs to get the word out about the immunization program.

4. Catholic Services, Head Start, and the Junior League are working together to seek funding to expand parent education in the community. They hope to provide weekend workshops for mothers and fathers. They also hope to begin a mother-to-mother program

that pairs experienced mothers (trained in parenting skills) with new mothers and provides home visitation and telephone reassurance.

5. A subcommittee of the *Hacer es Poder* Advisory Council is exploring several options for addressing the shortage of child-care providers in the community. With project staff, they are investigating funding possibilities for a child development center.

6. The Advisory Council has worked with primary and secondary schools in the community—public and private—to develop collaborative teams of administrators, teachers, other school personnel, parents, and students to resolve school problems and to promote academic success. This process has not always been smooth, but there have been important breakthroughs in relationships between parents and school personnel, particularly with regard to the "hot" topic of honoring the bicultural and bilingual nature of the students' lives. Parents have begun to feel a greater sense of "ownership" of the schools. Teachers have learned how much the parents value education. An elementary school collaborative team has sought help from the department of mental health to develop special programs for aggressive and peer-rejected children and children at risk of school failure. The collaborative team at the high school has focused on the inability of many parents to help their children with schoolwork. They have begun to think about ways to support parents in their efforts to support their children's educational achievement. They have also used community heroes as role models of school achievement.

7. With consultation from the department of mental health and the Advisory Council, school social workers and the Girls and Boys Clubs are developing a peer education program to prevent substance abuse. They are also exploring alternatives for jobs for adolescents, neighborhood safety, and recreation sites.

8. The *Hacer es Poder* Advisory Council has worked with the legal clinic, churches, and merchants to publicize materials developed by national immigrants' rights groups and to assist in legalizing status whenever possible. *Hacer es Poder* staff have made efforts to educate teachers, social workers, and medical providers about the special stresses of undocumented immigrants—to help them understand the fear behind the evasive and resistant behaviors they sometimes encounter.

9. Catholic Services and *Hacer es Poder* staff, with consultation from the Advisory Council, have developed separate curricula for teens and for parents to help them understand the family conflict and emotional problems that develop when teens and parents have different approaches to handling their bicultural existence. Cultural pride is emphasized in the teen curriculum. These curricula are being used by school social workers, the Girls and Boys Clubs, and the churches.

10. The medical clinic is developing a support group for family caregivers of chronically ill and disabled community members and another support group for community members with disabilities. They are seeking funds for assistive technology for community members with disabilities.

11. Catholic Services has developed two widow support groups in the community. One of these groups has begun to plan a program to pair older adults and youth for mentoring and mutual aid. They are also providing Meals on Wheels and transportation to health facilities

## Something to Think About

Ernesto Arce knew that this community had many troubles. His social work education has helped him to think about the relationships among these troubles. Ernesto also knew that this community had many assets. His social work education has taught him how to assess and enhance those assets. The following questions will help you think about how you might use what you have been learning to minimize risks and strengthen protective factors for people of every age:

- How did Ernesto and his staff go about assessing the assets and problems of this community? What information did they use? Whom did they involve in the assessment process? How did they make sure their assessment was grounded in the culture and tradition of the community?

- *Hacer es Poder* is targeting interventions at all age periods of the life course. Why do you think this approach is important to them? If prevention is their goal, why not confine the focus to prenatal and early childhood issues? How important do you think it is for the Advisory Council to include people of different ages?

- The assessment indicated that financial hardship is a major community problem. Given the pervasive risks of poverty for all age groups, how does action bring power to this community? Do you see any risk factors being reduced? Protective factors strengthened?

- What have you learned about the life course that could help you be a competent member of the *Hacer es Poder* staff? How might you use what you have learned about conception, pregnancy, and birth? What you have learned about early childhood? Middle childhood? Adolescence? Adulthood? Late adulthood?

- In what ways does this project build on family and neighborhood support systems? What other ways could it use?

# WORKS CITED

Abel, E. L., & Sokol, R. J. (1987). Incidence of fetal alcohol syndrome and economic impact of FAS-related anomalies. *Drug and Alcohol Dependence, 19,* 51–70.

Aberman, S., & Kirchoff, K. T. (1985). Infant-feeding practices: Mother's decision-making. *Journal of Obstetric, Gynecologic, and Neonatal Nursing, 14,* 394–398.

Achata, C. (1993). Immunization of Mexican migrant farm workers' children, on site at a day care center in a rural Tennessee County: Three successful summers. *Journal of Health and Social Policy, 4*(4), 89–101.

Adams, G. R., & Crane, P. (1980). An assessment of parents' and teachers' expectations of preschool children's social preference for attractive or unattractive children and adults. *Child Development, 51,* 224–231.

Adams, G. R., & Marshall, S. K. (1996). A developmental social psychology of identity: Understanding the person-in-context. *Journal of Adolescence, 19,* 429–442.

Adams, J., & Jacobsen, P. (1964). Effects of wage inequities on work quality. *Journal of Abnormal and Social Psychology, 69,* 19–25.

Adelmann, P. (1995). Emotional labor as a potential source of job stress. In S. Sauter & L. Murphy (Eds.), *Organizational risk factors for job stress* (pp. 371–381). Washington, DC: American Psychological Association.

Adelmann, P., Chadwick, K., & Baerger, D. (1996). Marital quality of black and white adults over the life course. *Journal of Social and Personal Relationships, 13,* 361–384.

Adler, L. (1993). Introduction and overview. *Journal of Education Policy, 8*(5–6), 1–16.

Ainsworth, M., Blehar, M., Waters, E., & Wall, S. (1978). *Patterns of attachment: A psychological study of the strange situation.* Hillsdale, NJ: Erlbaum.

Akabas, S. (1993). Introduction. In P. Kurzman & S. Akabas (Eds.), *Work and well-being: The occupational social work advantage* (pp. xvii–xxiv). Washington, DC: NASW Press.

Akabas, S., & Gates, L. (1993). Managing disability in the workplace: A role of social workers. In P. Kurzman & S. Akabas (Eds.), *Work and well-being: The occupational social work advantage* (pp. 239–255). Washington, DC: NASW Press.

Aldwin, C. (1994). *Stress, coping, and development.* New York: Guilford.

Allen-Meares, P. (1995). School failure and special populations. In P. Allen-Meares (Ed.), *Social work with children and adolescents* (pp. 143–164). White Plains, NY: Longman.

Allen-Meares, P., & Lane, B. A. (1987). Grounding social work practice in theory: Ecosystems. *Social Casework: The Journal of Contemporary Social Work, 68,* 517–521.

Allen-Meares, P., Washington, R. O., & Walsh, B. (1996). *Social work services in schools* (2nd ed.). Englewood Cliffs, NJ: Prentice Hall.

Alsaker, F. D. (1992). Pubertal timing, overweight, and psychological adjustment. *Journal of Early Adolescence, 12,* 396–419.

Altman, I., & Rogoff, B. (1987). World views in psychology: Trait, interactional, organismic, and transactional perspectives. In D. Stokols & I. Altman (Eds.), *Handbook of environmental psychology, Vol. 1* (pp. 7–40). New York: Wiley.

Ambert, A. (1992). *Effect of children on parents.* New York: Haworth.

American Academy of Child and Adolescent Psychiatry. (1995). *Facts for families: Fact no. 10. Teen suicide.*

American Psychiatric Association. (1994). *Diagnostic and statistical manual of mental disorders (DSM-IV)* (4th ed.). Washington, DC: Author.

American Social Health Association. (1995). *STD fact sheet.* Research Triangle Park, NC: Author.

Ameta, E. S., & Sherrard, P. A. (1995). Inquiring into children's social worlds: A choice of lenses. In B. A. Ryan, G. R. Adams, T. P. Gullotta, R. P. Weissberg, & R. L. Hampton (Eds.), *The family-school connection: Theory, research, and practice* (pp. 29–74). Thousand Oaks, CA: Sage.

Anderson, D. A. (1994). Lesbian and gay adolescents: Social and developmental considerations. *The High School Journal, 77* (1–2), 13–19.

Anderson, R., & Carter, I. (1974). *Human behavior in the social environment: A social systems approach.* Chicago: Aldine.

Andrews, L. B. (1994). *Assessing genetic risks: Implications for health and social policy.* Washington, DC: National Academy Press.

Arber, S., & Ginn, J. (1995). *Connecting gender and aging: A sociological approach.* Philadelphia: Open University Press.

Archer, J. (1992). Childhood gender roles: Social content and organization. In H. McGurk (Ed.), *Childhood social development* (pp. 31–62). Hillsdale, NJ: Erlbuam.

Arrendondo, P. M. (1984). Identity themes for immigrant young adults. *Adolescence, 19,* 977–993.

Ashford, J., LeCroy, C., & Lortie, K. (1997). *Human behavior and the social environment: A multidimensional perspective.* Pacific Grove, CA: Brooks/Cole.

Atchley, R. C. (1976). *The sociology of retirement.* Cambridge, MA: Schenkman.

Averill, J. R. (1968). Grief: Its nature and significance. *Psychological Bulletin, 70,* 721–748.

Bachman, J. G., Wallace, J. M., Jr., O'Malley, P. M., Johnston, L. D., Kurth, C. L., & Neighbors, H. W. (1991). Racial/ethnic differences in smoking, drinking, and illicit drug use among American high school seniors, 1976–1989. *American Journal of Public Health, 81,* 372–378.

Bachman, R. (1994). *Violence against women: A national crime victimization survey report.* Washington, DC: U.S. Department of Justice, Bureau of Justice Statistics.

Bahr, H., Dechaux, J., & Stiehr, K. (1994). The changing bonds of kinship: Parents and adult children. In S. Langlois (Ed.), *Convergence or divergence? Comparing recent social trends in industrial societies* (pp. 115–171). Buffalo, NY: McGill-Queen's University Press.

Bailey-Dempsey, C. A. (1993). *A test of a task-centered case management approach to resolve school failure.* Unpublished doctoral dissertation, State University of New York at Albany.

Baillargeon, R. (1987). Object permanence in 3 1/2 and 4 1/2 month old infants. *Developmental Psychology, 23,* 655–664.

Bain, M. D., Gau, D., & Reed, G. B. (1995). An introduction to antenatal and neonatal medicine, the fetal period and perinatal ethics. In G. B. Reed, A. E. Claireaux, & F. Cockburn (Eds.), *Diseases of the fetus and newborn* (2nd ed.) (pp. 3–23). London: Chapman & Hall.

Bakan, R., Birmingham, C. L., & Goldner, E. M. (1991). Chronicity in anorexia nervosa: Pregnancy and birth complications as risk factors. *International Journal of Eating Disorders, 10,* 631–645.

Baker, A. (1990). The psychological impact of the Intifada on Palestinian children in the occupied West Bank and Gaza: An exploratory study. *American Journal of Orthopsychiatry, 60,* 496–505.

Baltes, P. (1987). Theoretical propositions of life-span developmental psychology: On the dynamics between growth and decline. *Developmental Psychology, 23,* 611–626.

Bandura, A. (1977). Self-efficacy: Toward a unifying theory of behavioral change. *Psychological Review, 84,* 191–215.

Bandura, A. (1986). *Social foundations of thought and action: A social cognitive theory.* Englewood Cliffs, NJ: Prentice-Hall.

Baranowski, T. (1983). Social support, social influence, ethnicity, and the breastfeeding decision. *Social Science Medicine, 17,* 1599–1611.

Bardwell, J. R., Cochran, S. W., & Walker, S. (1986). Relationship of parental education, race, and gender to sex role stereotyping in five year old kindergartners. *Sex Roles, 15,* 275–281.

Barr, R. D., & Parrett, W. H. (1995). *Hope at last for at-risk youth.* Boston: Allyn & Bacon.

Bartz, K., & Levine, E. (1978). Childrearing by black parents: A description and comparison to Anglo and Chicano parents. *Journal of Marriage and the Family, 40,* 709–719.

Batson, C. D., Schoenrade, P., & Ventis, W. L. (1993). *Religion and the individual: A social-psychological perspective.* New York: Oxford University Press.

Baumeister, R. F., & Muraven, M. (1996). Identity as adaptation to social, cultural, and historical context. *Journal of Adolescence, 19,* 405–416.

Baumrind, D. (1971). Current patterns of parental authority. *Developmental Psychology Monographs, 41*(1, pt. 2).

Becker, G. (1981). *A treatise on the family.* Cambridge, MA: Harvard University Press.

Beckman, D., & Brent, R. (1994). Effects of prescribed and self-administered drugs during the second and third trimesters. In G. Avery, M. Fletcher, & M. MacDonald (Eds.), *Neonatology: Athophysiology and management of the newborn* (4th ed.) (pp. 197–206). Philadelphia: Lippincott.

Beckwith, L. (1984). Parent interaction with their preterm infants and later mental development. *Early Child Development and Care, 16*(1–2), 27–40.

Becvar, D., & Becvar, R. (1996). *Family therapy: A systemic integration* (3rd ed.). Boston: Allyn & Bacon.

Bee, H. (1996). *The journey of adulthood* (3rd ed.). New York: Macmillan.

Beehr, T. (1995). *Psychological stress in the workplace.* New York: Routledge.

Beehr, T., & Newman, J. (1978). Job stress, employee health, and organizational effectiveness: A facet analysis, model, and literature review. *Personnel Psychology, 31,* 665–699.

Bell, A. P., Weinberg, M. S., & Hammersmith, S. D. (1981). *Sexual preference: Its development in men and women.* Bloomington: Indiana University Press.

Belsky, J. (1987). Infant day care and socioemotional development: The United States. *Journal of Child Psychology and Psychiatry, 29,* 397–406.

Belsky, J. (1993). Etiology of child maltreatment: A developmental ecological analysis. *Psychological Bulletin, 114,* 414–434.

Belsky, J., & Braungart, J. M. (1991). Are insecure-avoidant infants with extensive day care experience less stressed by and more independent in the strange situation? *Child Development, 62,* 567–571.

Bem, S. L. (1993). *The lenses of gender: Transforming the debate on sexual inequality.* New Haven, CT: Yale University Press.

Bengtson, V., & Harootyan, R. (1994). *Intergenerational linkages: Hidden connections in American society.* New York: Springer.

Bengtson, V., Rosenthal, C., & Burton, L. (1990). Families and aging: Diversity and heterogeneity. In R. H. Binstock & L. K. George (Eds.), *Handbook of aging and the social sciences* (3rd ed.) (pp. 405–426). San Diego: Academic Press.

Benson, P. L., Yeager, R. J., Wood, P. K., Guerra, M. J., & Manno, B. V. (1986). *Catholic high schools: Their impact on low-income students.* Washington, DC: National Catholic Educational Association.

Berenson, A. B., San Miguel, V. V., & Wilkinson, G. S. (1992). Prevalence of physical and sexual assault in pregnant adolescents. *Journal of Adolescent Health, 13,* 466–469.

Berk, L. (1997). *Child development* (4th ed.). Boston: Allyn & Bacon.

Berlin, S. (1983). Cognitive-behavioral approaches. In A. Rosenblatt & Diana Waldfogel (Eds.), *Handbook of clinical social work* (pp. 1095–1119). San Francisco: Jossey-Bass.

Berman, J., Murphy-Berman, V., & Pachauri, A. (1988). Sex differences in friendship patterns in India and in the United States. *Basic and Applied Social Psychology, 9,* 61–71.

Berndt, T. J. (1988). Friendships in childhood and adolescence. In W. Damon (Ed.), *Child development today and tomorrow* (pp. 332–348). San Francisco: Jossey-Bass.

Bernstein, P. (1997). *American work values: Their origin and development.* Albany: State University of New York Press.

Berryman, J. C., & Wendridge, K. (1991). Having a baby after 40: A preliminary investigation of women's experience of pregnancy. *Journal of Reproduction and Infant Psychology, 9,* 3–18.

Berryman, J. C., & Wendridge, K. (1996). Pregnancy after 35 and attachment to the fetus. *Journal of Reproduction and Infant Psychology, 14,* 133–143.

Berzoff, J. (1989). From separation to connection: Shifts in understanding women's development. *Affilia, 4,* 45–58.

Biernat, M. (1991). Gender stereotypes and the relationship between masculinity and feminity: A developmental analysis. *Journal of Personality and Social Psychology, 61,* 351–365.

Bigler, R. S., & Liben, L. S. (1993). A cognitive-developmental approach to racial stereotyping and reconstructive memory in Euro-American children. *Child Development, 64,* 1507–1518.

Bishop, K. (1993). Psychosocial aspects of genetic disorders: Implications for practice. *Families in Society, 74,* 207–212.

Bitzan, J. E., & Kruzich, J. M. (1990). Interpersonal relationships of nursing home residents. *The Gerontologist, 30,* 385–390.

Blau, P. M. (1964). *Exchange and power in social life.* New York: Wiley.

Blazer, D. G. (1995). Depression. In G. L. Maddox (Ed.), *The encyclopedia of aging: A comprehensive resource in gerontology and geriatrics* (2nd ed.) (pp. 265–266). New York: Springer.

Blood, R., & Wolfe, D. (1960). *Husbands and wives: The dynamics of married living.* New York: Free Press.

Bloom, M. (1984). *Configurations of human behavior: Life span development in social environments.* New York: Macmillan.

Bloom, M. (1990). *Introduction to the drama of social work.* Itasca, IL: Peacock.

Blume, J. (1970). *Are you there, God? It's me, Margaret.* New York: Dell.

Blumstein, P., & Schwartz, P. (1983). *American couples: Money, work, sex.* New York: Morrow.

Boldizar, J. P. (1991). Assessing sex typing and androgyny in children: The children's sex role inventory. *Developmental Psychology, 27,* 505–515.

Bonne, O. B., Rubinoff, B., & Berry, E. M. (1996). Delayed detection of pregnancy in patients with anorexia nervosa: Two case reports. *International Journal of Eating Disorders, 20,* 423–425.

Bornstein, M. H. (1992). Perception across the life span. In M. H. Bornstein & M. E. Lamb (Eds.), *Developmental psychology: An advanced textbook* (3rd ed.) (pp. 155–210). Hillsdale, NJ: Erlbaum.

Bouwsma, W. (1978). Christian adulthood. In E. H. Erikson (Ed.), *Adulthood* (pp. 81–96). New York: Norton & Norton.

Bowlby, J. (1961). Processes of mourning. *The International Journal of Psychoanalysis, 42,* 317–340.

Bowlby, J. (1969). *Attachment and loss.* New York: Basic Books.

Bowles, S., & Gintis, H. (1976). *Schooling in capitalist America: Educational reform and the contradictions of economic life.* New York: Basic Books.

Brantlinger, E. (1992). Professional's attitudes toward the sterilization of people with disabilities. *Journal of the Association for Severe Handicaps, 17*(1), 4–18.

Braungart, J., Plomin, R., DeFries, J. C., & Fulker, D. (1992). Genetic influences on tester-rated infant temperament as assessed by Bayley's Infant Behavior Record: Nonadoptive and adoptive siblings and twins. *Developmental Psychology, 28,* 40–47.

Braver, S., Wolchik, S., Sandler, I., Fogas, B., & Zventina, D. (1991). Frequency of visitation by divorced fathers: Differences in reports by fathers and mothers. *American Journal of Orthopsychiatry, 61,* 448–454.

Braver, S., Wolchik, S., Sandler, I., & Sheets, V. (1993). A social exchange model of nonresidential parent involvement. In C. Depner & J. Bray (Eds.), *Nonresidential parenting: New vistas in family living* (pp. 87–108). Newbury Park, CA: Sage.

Bray, J., & Berger, S. (1990). Nonresidential parent and grandparent relationships in stepfamilies. *Family Relations, 39,* 414–419.

Bray, J., & Berger, S. (1993). Nonresidential parent-child relationships following divorce and remarriage: A longitudinal perspective. In C. Depner & J. Bray (Eds.), *Nonresidential parenting: New vistas in family living* (pp. 156–181). Newbury Park, CA: Sage.

Brazelton, T. B. (1983). *Infants and mothers: Differences in development.* New York: Delta/Seymour Lawrence.

Bredekamp, S. (Ed.). (1992). *Developmentally appropriate practice in early childhood programs serving children from birth through age 8.* Washington, DC: National Association for the Education of Young Children.

Bricker-Jenkins, M., Hooyman, N. R., & Gottlieb, N. (Eds.). (1991). *Feminist social work practice in clinical settings.* Newbury Park, CA: Sage.

Brinch, M., Isager, T., & Tolstrup, K. (1988). Anorexia nervosa and motherhood: Reproduction pattern and mothering behavior of 50 women. *Acta Psychiatrica Scandinavica, 77,* 611–617.

Bronfenbrenner, U. (1986). Ecology of the family as a context for human development research perspectives. *Developmental Psychology, 22,* 723–742.

Bronfenbrenner, U. (1989). Ecological systems theory. *Annals of Child Development, 6,* 187–249.

Bronfenbrenner, U., & Crouter, A. (1982). Work and family through time and space. In S. Kamerman & C. Hayes (Eds.), *Families that work: Children in a changing world* (pp. 39–83). Washington, DC: National Academy Press.

Brooks-Gunn, J. (1988). Antecedents and consequences of variations in girls' maturational timing. *Journal of Adolescent Health, 9,* 365–373.

Brooks-Gunn, J., & Furstenberg, F. (1989). Adolescent sexual behavior. *American Psychologist, 44,* 249–257.

Brooks-Gunn, J., Petersen, A. C., & Eichorn, D. (1985). The study of maturational timing effects in adolescence. *Journal of Youth and Adolescence, 14,* 149–161.

Brown, J., Eichenberger, S., Portes, P., & Christensen, D. (1991). Family functioning and children's divorce adjustment. *Journal of Divorce and Remarriage, 17*(1/2), 81–97.

Brown, L. K., DiClemente, R. J., & Park, T. (1992). Predictors of condom use in sexually active adolescents. *Journal of Adolescent Health, 13,* 651–657.

Brubaker, E., Gorman, M. A., & Hiestand, M. (1990). Stress perceived by elderly recipients of family care. In T. H. Brubaker (Ed.), *Family relationships in later life* (2nd ed.) (pp. 267–281). Newbury Park: Sage.

Brubaker, T. H. (1990). An overview of family relationships in later life. In T. H. Brubaker (Ed.), *Family relationships in later life* (2nd ed.) (pp. 13–26). Newbury Park: Sage.

Buhrke, R., & Fuqua, D. (1987). Sex differences in same- and cross-sex supportive relationships. *Sex Roles, 17,* 339–352.

Bullis, R. K., & Harrigan, M. (1992). Religious denominational policies on sexuality. *Families in Society, 73,* 304–312.

Burgess, R., & Nielsen, J. (1974). An experimental analysis of some structural determinants of equitable and inequitable exchange relationships. *American Sociological Review, 39,* 427–443.

Burrell, G., & Morgan, G. (1979). *Sociological paradigms and organizational analysis.* London: Heinemann.

Burt, R. (1983). *Corporate profits and cooperation: Networks of market constraints and directorate ties in the American economy.* New York: Academic Press.

Bustan, N. M. (1994). Maternal attitudes toward pregnancy and the risk of neonatal death. *American Journal of Public Health, 84,* 411–414.

Butler, R. N. (1963). The life review: An interpretation of reminiscence in the aged. *Psychiatry, 26,* 65–70.

Butler, R. N. (1987). Life review. In G. L. Maddox (Ed.), *The encyclopedia of aging: A comprehensive resource in gerontology and geriatrics* (2nd ed.) (pp. 397–398). New York: Springer.

Butts, J. A. (1996). *Delinquency cases in juvenile courts, 1994* (Fact Sheet # 47). Washington DC: Office of Juvenile Justice and Delinquency Prevention.

Caldwell, G., Stiehr, K., Modell, J., & Del Campo, S. (1994). Differing levels of low fertility. In S. Langlois (Ed.), *Convergence or divergence? Comparing recent social trends in industrial societies* (pp. 43–87). Buffalo, NY: McGill-Queen's University Press.

Campbell, R., & Sais, E. (1995). Accelerated metalinguistic (phonological) awareness in bilingual children. *British Journal of Developmental Psychology, 13,* 61–68.

Canino, I., & Spurlock, J. (1994). *Culturally diverse children and adolescents.* New York: Guilford Press.

Carbery, J. (1993). *The changing significance of friendship across three young adult phases.* Unpublished doctoral dissertation, University of Texas at Dallas.

Carey, T. A. (1994). "Spare the rod and spoil the child." Is this a sensible justification for the use of punishment in child rearing? *Child Abuse and Neglect, 18,* 1005–1010.

Carnegie Council on Adolescent Development. (1995). *Turning points: Preparing American youth for the 21st century.* Washington, DC: Author.

Carter, B., & McGoldrick, B. (Eds.). (1989). *The changing family life cycle: A framework for family therapy* (2nd ed.). New York: Allyn & Bacon.

Carter, B., & McGoldrick, M. (Eds.). (1988a). *The changing family life cycle* (2nd ed.). New York: Gardner.

Carter, B., & McGoldrick, M. (1988b). Overview: The changing family life cycle: A framework for family therapy. In B. Carter & M. McGoldrick (Eds.), *The changing family life cycle: A framework for family therapy* (2nd ed.) (pp. 3–28). New York: Gardner.

Carter, D. B., & Patterson, C. J. (1982). Sex roles as social conventions: The development of children's conceptions of sex-role stereotypes. *Developmental Psychology, 18,* 812–824.

Carter, H., & Glick, P. (1976). *Marriage and divorce: A social and economic study.* Cambridge, MA: Harvard University Press.

Cavanaugh, J. (1993). *Adult development and aging* (2nd ed.). Pacific Grove, CA: Brooks/Cole.

Centers for Disease Control and Prevention. (1994). *STD surveillance, 1993.* Atlanta: Author.

Centers for Disease Control and Prevention. (1997, March 7). Analysis of the third National Health and Nutrition Examination Survey, 1988–1994 (NHAMES III). *Morbidity and Mortality Weekly Report, 46*(9), 11–32.

Chadiha, L., & Danziger, S. (1995). The significance of fathers for inner-city African-American mothers. *Child and Adolescent Social Work Journal, 12*(2), 83–100.

Chadwick, R., Levitt, M., & Shickle, D. (1997). *The right to know and the right not to know.* Brookfield, VT: Avebury.

Chase-Lansdale, P. L., & Vinovskis, M. A. (1995). Whose responsibility? An historical analysis of the changing roles of mothers, fathers, and society. In P. L. Chase-Lansdale & J. Brooks-Gunn (Eds.), *Escape from poverty: What makes a difference for children?* (pp. 11–37). New York: Cambridge University Press.

Chasnoff, I. J., Landress, H. J., & Barrett, M. E. (1990). The prevalence of illicit-drug and alcohol use during pregnancy and discrepancies in mandatory reporting in Pinellas County, Florida. *New England Journal of Medicine, 322,* 1202–1206.

Chen, Y., Yu, S., & Li, W. (1988). Artificial feeding and hospitalization in the first 18 months of life. *Pediatrics, 81,* 58–62.

Chestang, L. (1972). *Character development in a hostile environment* (Occasional Paper No. 3). University of Chicago, School of Social Service Administration.

Children's Defense Fund. (1993). *The state of America's children, 1993.* Washington, DC: Author.

Children's Defense Fund. (1996). *The state of America's children, 1996.* Washington, DC: Author.

Children's Defense Fund. (1998). *Annual report: The state of America's children.* Washington, DC: Author.

Chirot, D. (1994). *How societies change.* Thousand Oaks, CA: Pine Forge.

Chomsky, N. (1968). *Language and mind.* New York: Harcourt Brace Javanovich.

Chopra, D. (1993). *Ageless body, timeless mind: The quantum alternative to growing old.* New York: Harmony.

Christensen, A., & Heavy, C. (1990). Gender and social structure in the demand-withdraw pattern of marital conflict. *Journal of Personality and Social Psychology, 59,* 73–81.

Christensen, A., & Shenk, J. (1991). Communication, conflict, and psychological distance in nondistressed, clinic, and divorcing couples. *Journal of Consulting and Clinical Psychology, 59,* 458–463.

Chudacoff, H. (1989). *How old are you?* Princeton, NJ: Princeton University Press.

Cingolani, J. (1984). Social conflict perspective on work with involuntary clients. *Social Work, 29,* 442–446.

Clair, J., Karp, D., & Yoels, W. (1993). *Experiencing the life cycle: A social psychology of aging* (2nd ed.). Springfield, IL: Charles C. Thomas.

Clarke-Stewart, K. A. (1988). The effects of infant day care reconsidered, reconsidered: Risks for parents, children, and researchers. *Early Childhood Research Quarterly, 3*(3), 293–318.

Clarke-Stewart, K. A. (1989). Infant day care: Maligned or malignant? *American Psychologist, 17,* 454–462.

Coates, M. M. (Ed.). (1993). Policy statements. In LaLeche League International, *The lactation consultant's topical review and bibliography of the literature on breastfeeding.* Franklin Park, IL: LaLeche League International.

Cohen, P. (1968). *Modern social theory.* New York: Basic Books.

Coie, J. D., Dodge, K. A., & Coppotelli, H. (1982). Dimensions and types of social status: A cross age perspective. *Developmental Psychology, 18,* 557–570.

Cole, S. S., & Cole, T. M. (1993). Sexuality, disability, and reproductive issues through the lifespan. In F. P. Haseltine, S. S. Cole, & D. B. Gray (Eds.), *Reproductive issues for persons with physical disabilities* (pp. 3–21). Baltimore: Brookes.

Coleman, J. (1990). *Foundations of social theory.* Cambridge, MA: Belknap Press of Harvard University Press.

Colin, V. (1996). *Human attachment.* Philadelphia: Temple University Press.

Collins, A., Freeman, E. W., Boxer, A. S., & Tureck, R. (1992). Perceptions of infertility in females as compared to males entering in vitro fertilization treatment. *Fertility and Sterilization, 57,* 350–356.

Collins, A., & Pancoast, D. (1976). *Natural helping networks.* Washington, DC: National Association of Social Workers.

Collins, R. (1981). On the micro-foundations of macro-sociology. *American Journal of Sociology, 86,* 984–1014.

Collins, R. (1988). *Theoretical sociology.* San Diego: Harcourt Brace Jovanovich.

Collins, R. (1990). Conflict theory and the advance of macro-historical sociology. In G. Ritzer (Ed.), *Frontiers of social theory: The new syntheses* (pp. 68–87). New York: Columbia University Press.

Collins, R. (1994). *Four sociological traditions.* New York: Oxford University Press.

Colon, F. (1980). The family life cycle of the multiproblem poor family. In E. Carter & M. McGoldrick (Eds.), *Family life cycle* (pp. 343–381). New York: Gardner.

Coltrane, S. (1995). The future of fatherhood: Social, demographic, and economic influences on men's family involvements. In W. Marsiglio (Ed.), *Fatherhood: Contemporary theory, research, and social policy* (pp. 255–274). Thousand Oaks, CA: Sage.

Comer, J. P. (1980). *School power: Implications of an intervention project.* New York: Free Press.

Comer, J. P. (1994). Home, school, and academic learning. In K. I. Goodland & P. Keating (Eds.), *Access to knowledge: The continuing agenda for our nation's schools.* New York: The College Board.

Connie, T. A. (1988). *Aids and adaptations for disabled parents: An illustrated manual for service providers and parents with physical or sensory disabilities* (2nd ed.). Vancouver: University of British Columbia, School of Rehabilitation Medicine.

Connolly, J., White, D., Stevens, R., & Burstein, S. (1987). Adolescent self-reports of social activity: Assessment of stability and relations to social adjustment. *Journal of Adolescence, 10,* 83–95.

Constable, R. (1996). General perspectives on theory and practice. In R. Constable, J. P. Flynn, & S. McDonald (Eds.), *School social work: Practice and research perspectives* (3rd ed.) (pp. 3–16). Chicago: Lyceum Books.

Constable, R., & Walberg, H. (1996). School social work: Facilitating home-school partnerships in the 1990s. In R. Constable, J. P. Flynn, & S. McDonald (Eds.), *School social work: Practice and research perspectives* (3rd ed.) (pp. 182–196). Chicago: Lyceum Books.

Cook, E. A., Jelen, T. G., & Wilcox, C. (1992). *Between two absolutes: Public opinion and the politics of abortion.* Boulder, CO: Westview Press.

Cook, K. (Ed.). (1987). *Social exchange theory.* Newbury Park, CA: Sage.

Cook, K., O'Brien, J., & Kollock, P. (1990). Exchange theory: A blueprint for structure and process. In G. Ritzer (Ed.), *Frontiers of social theory: The new syntheses* (pp. 158–181). New York: Columbia University Press.

Cooper, C., & Marshall, J. (1976). Occupational sources of stress: A review of the literature relating to coronary heart disease and mental ill health. *Journal of Occupational Psychology, 49,* 11–28.

Corbin, J. M. (1987). Women's perceptions and management of pregnancy complicated by chronic illness. *Health Care Women International, 8*(5–6), 317–337.

Coser, L. (1956). *The functions of conflict.* New York: Free Press.

Coser, L. (1975). Presidential address: Two methods in search of a substance. *American Sociological Review, 40,* 691–700.

Costa, F. M., Jessor, R., Donovan, J. E., & Fortenberry, J. D. (1995). Early initiation of sexual intercourse: The influence of psychosocial unconventionality. *Journal of Research on Adolescents, 5,* 93-121.

Counts, D. R., & Counts, D. A. (1991). *Coping with the final tragedy: Cultural variation in dying and grieving.* Amityville, NY: Baywood.

Creighton-Zollar, A., & Williams, S. (1992). The relative educational attainment and occupational prestige of black spouses and life satisfaction. *Western Journal of Black Studies, 16,* 57–63.

Cronenwett, L. R., & Reinhardt, R. (1987). Social support and breastfeeding: A review. *Birth, 14,* 199–203.

Csikszentmihalyi, M., & Larson, R. (1984). *Being adolescent: Conflict and growth in the teenage years.* New York: Basic Books.

Cumming, E., & Henry, W. (1961). *Growing old.* New York: Basic Books.

Damon, W. (1977). *The social world of the child.* San Francisco: Jossey-Bass.

Damon, W., & Hart, D. (1988). *Self understanding in childhood and adolescence.* Cambridge: Cambridge University Press.

Dannefer, D., & Perlmutter, M. (1990). Development as a multidimensional process: Individuals and social constituents. *Human Development, 33,* 108–137.

Danziger, S. K., & Danziger, S. (1993). Child poverty and public policy: Toward a comprehensive antipoverty agenda. *Daedalus, 122,* 57–84.

David, H. P. (1996). Induced abortion: Psychosocial aspects. In J. J. Sciarra (Ed.), *Gynecology and obstetrics* (Vol. 6, pp. 1–8). Philadelphia: Lippincott-Raven.

Davidson, J., & Smith, R. (1990). Traumatic experiences in psychiatric outpatients. *Journal of Traumatic Stress Studies, 3,* 459–475.

Davis, L. (1986). Role theory. In F. Turner (Ed.), *Social work treatment: Interlocking theoretical approaches* (3rd ed.) (pp. 541–563). New York: Free Press.

Dedmon, S. R. (1997). Attention deficiency and hyperactivity. In M. Fraser (Ed.), *Risk and resilience in childhood: An ecological perspective* (pp. 73–94). Washington DC: NASW Press.

DeJong, W. (1993). Obesity as a characterological stigma: The issue of responsibility and judgments of task performance. *Psychological Reports, 73,* 963–970.

del Carmen, R., & Virgo, G. (1993). Marital disruption and nonresidential parenting: A multicultural perspective. In C. Depner & J. Bray (Eds.), *Nonresidential parenting: New vistas in family living* (pp. 13–36). Newbury Park, CA: Sage.

DeRosier, M. E., Kupersmidt, J. B., & Patterson, C. J. (1994). Children's academic and behavioral adjustment as a function of the chronicity and proximity of peer rejection. *Child Development, 65,* 1799–1813.

deVries, M., & Sameroff, A. (1984). Culture and temperament: Influences on infant temperament in three East African societies. *American Journal of Orthopsychiatry, 54,* 83–96.

Dewey, J., & Bentley, A. F. (1949). *Knowing and the known.* Boston: Beacon.

Dhooper, S., & Schneider, P. (1995). Evaluation of a school-based child abuse prevention program. *Research on Social Work Practice, 5*(1), 36–46.

Dickason, E. J., Schult, M., & Silverman, B. L. (1990). *Maternal-infant nursing care.* St. Louis: Mosby.

Dickason, E. J., Silverman, B. L., & Kaplan, J. A. (1998). *Maternal-infant nursing care* (3rd Ed.). St. Louis: Mosby.

Dickens, W., & Perlman, D. (1981). Friendship over the life cycle. In S. Duck & R. Gilmour (Eds.), *Personal relationships: Vol. 2. Developing personal relationships* (pp. 91–122). London: Academic Press.

Dick-Read, G. (1944). *Childbirth without fear: Principles and practices of natural childbirth.* New York: Harper & Row.

Dodge, D. T. (1995). The importance of curriculum on achieving quality child care programs. *Child Welfare, 74,* 1171–1188.

Dolinsky, A. L., & Rosenwaike, I. (1988). The role of demographic factors in the institutionalization of the elderly. *Research on Aging, 10,* 235–257.

Donahue, M. J., & Benson, P. L. (1995). Religion and the well-being of adolescents. *Journal of Social Issues, 51*(2), 145–161.

Downs, A. C., & Langlois, J. H. (1988). Sex typing: Construct and measurement issues. *Sex Roles, 18*(1–2), 87–100.

Drisko, J. (1992). Intimidation and projective identification in group therapy of physically abused early adolescent boys. *Journal of Child and Adolescent Group Therapy, 2*(1), 17–30.

Dryfoos, J. G. (1990). *Adolescents at risk.* New York: Oxford University Press.

Dryfoos, J. G. (1994). *Full-service schools: A revolution in health and social services for children, youth, and families.* San Francisco: Jossey-Bass.

Dubrow, N., & Garbarino, J. (1989). Living in the war zone: Mothers and young children in a public housing development. *Child Welfare, 68,* 3–20.

Duncan, G. J. (1991). The economic environment of childhood. In A. C. Huston (Ed.), *Children and poverty* (pp. 23–50). New York: Cambridge University Press.

Dunn, J., Brown, J., Slomkowski, C., Tesla, C., & Youngblade, L. (1991). Young children's understanding of other people's feelings and beliefs: Individual differences and their antecedents. *Child Development, 62,* 1352–1366.

DuPlessis, H. M., Bell, R., & Richards, T. (1997). Adolescent pregnancy: Understanding the impact of age and race on outcomes. *Journal of Adolescent Health, 20*(3), 187–197.

Dupper, D. R., & Poertner, J. (1997). Public schools and the revitalization of impoverished communities: School-linked, family resource centers. *Social Work, 42,* 415–422.

Duvall, E. (1962). *Family development.* New York: Lippincott.

Dyson, J. (1989). Family violence and its effects on academic underachievement and behavior problems in school. *Journal of the National Medical Association, 82,* 17-22.

East, P. L. (1996). The younger sisters of childbearing adolescents: Their attitudes, expectations, and behaviors. *Child Development, 67,* 267–282.

East, P. L., & Shi, C. R. (1997). Pregnant and parenting adolescents and their younger sisters: The influence of relationship qualities and younger sister outcomes. *Journal of Developmental and Behavioral Pediatrics, 18*(2), 84–90.

Eder, D., & Parker, S. (1987). The cultural production and reproduction of gender: The effect of extracurricular activities on peer-group culture. *Sociology of Education, 60,* 200–213.

Edwards, C. (1992). Normal development in the preschool years. In E. V. Nuttall, I. Romero, & J. Kalesnik (Eds.), *Assessing and screening preschoolers* (pp. 9–22). Boston: Allyn & Bacon.

Egeland, B., Carlson, E., & Sroufe, L. A. (1993). Resilience as process. *Development and Psychopathology, 5,* 517–528.

Ekeh, P. (1974). *Social exchange theory: The two traditions.* Cambridge, MA: Harvard University Press.

Elder, G. (1992). Life course. In E. Borgatta & M. Borgatta (Eds.), *Encyclopedia of sociology* (pp. 1120–1130). New York: Macmillan.

Elder, G. (1994). Time, human agency, and social change: Perspectives on the life course. *Social Psychology Quarterly, 57*(1), 4–15.

Ellman, B., & Taggart, M. (1993). Changing gender norms. In F. Walsh (Ed.), *Normal family processes* (2nd ed.) (pp. 377–404). New York: Guilford.

Emerson, R. (1972a). Exchange theory: Part I. A psychological basis for social exchange. In J. Berger, M. Zelditch, Jr., & B. Anderson (Eds.), *Sociological theories in progress* (Vol. 2, pp. 38–57). Boston: Houghton Mifflin.

Emerson, R. (1972b). Exchange theory: Part II. Exchange relations and networks. In J. Berger, M. Zelditch, Jr., & B. Anderson (Eds.), *Sociological theories in progress* (Vol. 2, pp. 58–87). Boston: Houghton Mifflin.

Engel, G. (1977). The need for a new medical model: A challenge for biomedicine. *Science, 196,* 129–136.

Engel, J., & Saracino, M. (1986). Love preferences and ideals: A comparison of homosexual, bisexual, and heterosexual groups. *Contemporary Family Therapy, 8,* 241–250.

Engels, F. (1970). *The origins of the family, private property and the state.* New York: International Publishers. (Original work published 1884)

Epstein, J. L., & Lee, S. (1995). National patterns of school and family connections in the middle grades. In B. A. Ryan, G. R. Adams, T. P. Gullotta, R. P. Weissberg, & R. L. Hampton (Eds.), *The family-school connection: Theory, research, and practice* (pp. 108–154). Thousand Oaks, CA: Sage.

Epstein, N., Bishop, D., Ruan, C., Miller, I., & Keitner, G. (1993). The McMaster model: View of healthy functioning. In F. Walsh (Ed.), *Normal family processes* (pp. 138–160). New York: Guilford Press.

Erikson, E. H. (1950). *Childhood and society.* New York: Norton.

Erikson, E. H. (1959a). *Identity and life cycle.* New York: Norton. (Reissued 1980)

Erikson, E. H. (1959b). The problem of ego identity. *Psychological Issues, 1,* 101–164.

Erikson, E. H. (1963). *Childhood and society* (2nd ed.). New York: Norton.

Erikson, E. H. (1968). *Identity: Youth and crisis.* New York: Norton.

Erikson, E. H. (Ed.) (1978). *Adulthood.* New York: Norton.

Erikson. E. H. (1980). Themes of adulthood in the Freud-Jung correspondence. In N. J. Smelser & E. H. Erikson (Eds.), *Themes of work and love in adulthood* (pp. 43–76). Cambridge, MA: Harvard University Press.

Erikson, E. H. (1982). *The life cycle completed.* New York: Norton.

Erikson, R. (1993). Abortion trauma: Application of a conflict model. *Pre- and Peri-natal Psychology Journal, 8* (1), 33–42.

Fahy, T. (1991). Fasting disorders in pregnancy. *Psychological Medicine, 21,* 577–580.

Falicov, C., & Karrer, B. (1980). Cultural variations in the family life cycle: The Mexican American family. In E. Carter & M. McGoldrick (Eds.), *Family life cycle* (pp. 383–425). New York: Gardner.

The Family Place. (1996). Domestic violence statistics [On-line]. Available: http://www.smu.edu/-mlair/family_place/stats.html

Family Violence Preservation Fund. (1997, July 24). News Flash: Work to end domestic violence [On-line]. Available: http://www.fvpf.org/fund/materials/speakup/7-24-97.htm#Differing

Farley, R. (1996). *The new American reality: Who we are, how we got here, and where we are going.* New York: Russell Sage Foundation.

Federation of Parents and Friends of Lesbians and Gays [PFLAG]. (1984). *Read this before coming out to your parents.* Washington, DC: Sauerman.

Fehr, B. (1996). *Friendship processes.* Thousand Oaks, CA: Sage.

Fehr, B., & Russell, J. (1991). The concept of love viewed from a prototype perspective. *Journal of Personality and Social Psychology, 60,* 425–438.

Figueira-McDonough, J. (1990). Abortion: Ambiguous criteria and confusing policies. *Affilia, 5*(4), 27–54.

Finn, J. D. (1989). Withdrawing from school. *Review of Educational Research, 59,* 117–142.

Fintel, W., & McDermott, G. (1993). *Living with cancer.* Dallas: Word.

Fischer, C., & Phillips, S. (1982). Who is alone? Social characteristics of people with small networks. In L. A. Peplau & D. Perlman (Eds.), *Loneliness: A sourcebook of current theory, research and therapy* (pp. 21–39). New York: Wiley Interscience.

Fisher, G., Semko, E., & Wade, F. (1995). Defining and measuring hostile environment: Development of the hostile environment inventory. In S. Sauter & L. Murphy (Eds.), *Organizational risk factors for job stress* (pp. 81–91). Washington, DC: American Psychological Association.

Fitzpatrick, K. M., & Boldizar, J. P. (1993). The prevalence and consequences of exposure to violence among African American youth. *Journal of the American Academy of Child and Adolescent Psychiatry, 56,* 22–34.

Flanagan, C. A. (1990). Change in family work status: Effects on parent-adolescent decision making. *Child Development, 61,* 163–177.

Fletcher, A. B. (1994). Nutrition. In G. B. Avery, M. A. Fletcher, & M. G. MacDonald (Eds.). *Neonatology: Pathophysiology and management of the newborn* (4th ed.) (pp. 330–350). Philadelphia: Lippincott.

Foner, A. (1995). Social stratification. In G. L. Maddox (Ed.), *The encyclopedia of aging: A comprehensive resource in gerontology and geriatrics* (2nd ed.) (pp. 887–890). New York: Springer.

Fong, J. (1995). Patient assaults on psychologists: An unrecognized occupational hazard. In S. Sauter & L. Murphy (Eds.), *Organizational risk factors for job stress* (pp. 273–281). Washington, DC: American Psychological Association.

Fontana, A. (1984). Introduction: Existential sociology and the self. In J. Kotarba & A. Fontana (Eds.), *The existential self in society* (pp. 3–17). Chicago: University of Chicago Press.

Ford, D. J., & Lerner, R. M. (1992). *Developmental systems theory: An integrative approach.* Newbury Park, CA: Sage.

Forrest, G. (1993). Preterm labour and delivery: Psychological sequelae. *Bailliere's Clinical Obstetrics and Gynaecology, 7,* 653–669.

Fost, N. (1981). Counseling families who have a child with severe congenital anomaly. *Pediatrics, 67,* 321–323.

Foucault, M. (1969). *The archaeology of knowledge and the discourse on language.* New York: Harper Colophon.

Fox, C., & Miller, H. (1995). *Postmodern public administration: Toward discourse.* Thousand Oaks, CA.: Sage.

Fozard, J. L. (1990). Vision and hearing in aging. In J. E. Birren & K. W. Schaie (Eds.), *Handbook of the psychology of aging* (3rd ed.) (pp. 150–170). San Diego: Academic Press.

Fracasso, M., Busch-Rossnagel, N., & Fisher, C. (1994). The relationship of maternal behavior and acculturation to the quality of attachment in Hispanic infants living in New York City. *Hispanic Journal of Behavioral Sciences, 16,* 143–154.

Frank, R., Strobino, D., Salkever, D., & Jackson, C. (1992). Updated estimates of the impact of prenatal care on birth weight outcomes by race. *The Journal of Human Resources, 27,* 629–642.

Frankel, A. (1991). Social work and day care: A role looking for a profession. *Child and Adolescent Social Work Journal, 8*(1), 53–67.

Franklin, C. (1995). Expanding the vision of the social contructionist debates: Creating relevance for practitioners. *Families in Society: 76,* 395–407.

Fraser, M. W., & Galinsky, M. J. (1997). Toward a resilience-based model of practice. In M. W. Fraser (Ed.), *Risk and resilience in childhood: An ecological perspective* (pp. 265–275). Washington, DC: NASW Press.

Frederick, I. B., & Auerbach, K. G. (1985). Maternal-infant separation and breastfeeding: The return to work or school. *Journal of Reproductive Medicine, 30,* 523–526.

Freeman, E., & Dyer, L. (1993). High risk children and adolescents: Family and community environments. *Families in Society, 74,* 422–431.

Freeman, L., Shaffer, D., & Smith, H. (1996). Neglected victims of homicide: The needs of young siblings of murder victims. *American Journal of Orthopsychiatry, 66,* 337–345.

Freud, S. (1953). Three essays on the theory of sexuality. In J. Strachey (Ed. and Trans.), *The standard edition of the complete works of Sigmund Freud* (Vol. 7, pp. 135–245). London: Hogarth Press. (Original work published 1905)

Freud, S. (1973). *An outline of psychoanalysis.* London: Hogarth Press. (Original work published 1938)

Frey, A. (1989). Treating children of violent families: A sibling group approach. *Social Work With Groups, 12*(1), 95–107.

Friedman, H. L. (1992). Changing patterns of adolescent sexual behavior: Consequences for health and development. *Journal of Adolescent Health, 13,* 345–350.

Fromm, E. (1941). *Escape from freedom.* New York: Avon.

Fromm, E., & Maccoby, M. (1970). *Social character in a Mexican village.* Englewood Cliffs, NJ: Prentice-Hall.

Fulmer, R. (1988). Lower-income and professional families: A comparison of structure and life cycle process. In E. Carter & M. McGoldrick (Eds.), *The changing family life cycle* (2nd ed.) (pp. 545–578). New York: Gardner.

Furstenberg, F. (1994). Good dads–bad dads: Two faces of fatherhood. In A. S. Skolnick & J. H. Skolnick (Eds.), *Family in transition* (8th ed.) (pp 348–368). New York: Harper Collins.

Furstenberg, F. F., Moore, K. A., & Peterson, J. L. (1986). Sex education and sexual experience among adolescents. *American Journal of Public Health, 75,* 1221–1222.

Furstenberg, F., Jr., Nord, C., Peterson, J., & Zill, N. (1983). The life course of children of divorce: Marital disruption and parental contact. *American Sociological Review, 48,* 656–668.

Galambos, N. L., & Almeida, D. M. (1992). Does parent-adolescent conflict increase in early adolescence? *Journal of Marriage and the Family, 54,* 737–747.

Gallagher, J. J. (1993). The future of professional/family relations in families with children with disabilities. In J. L. Paul & R. J. Simeonsson (Eds.), *Children with special needs: Family, culture, and society* (2nd ed.) (pp. 295–310). Fort Worth, TX: Harcourt Brace Jovanovich.

Gallup, G. H., Jr., & Bezilla, R. (1992). *The religious life of young Americans.* Princeton, NJ: Gallup Institute.

Gambrill, E. (1987). Behavioral approach. In Anne Minahan (Ed.), *Encyclopedia of social work* (18th ed.) (Vol. 1, pp. 184–194). Silver Spring, MD: National Association of Social Workers.

Gambrill, E. (1990). *Critical thinking in clinical practice: Improving the accuracy of judgments and decisions about clients.* San Francisco: Jossey-Bass.

Gandelman, R. (1992). *Psychobiology of behavioral development.* New York: Oxford University Press.

Garbarino, J. (1976). A preliminary study of some ecological correlates of child abuse: The impact of socioeconomic stress on mothers. *Child Development, 47,* 178–185.

Garbarino, J. (1977). The human ecology of child maltreatment: A conceptual model for research. *Journal of Marriage and the Family, 39,* 721–735.

Garbarino, J. (1992). The meaning of poverty to children. *American Behavioral Scientist, 35,* 220–237.

Garbarino, J. (1995). *Raising children in a socially toxic environment.* San Francisco: Jossey-Bass.

Garbarino, J., & Sherman, D. (1980). High-risk neighborhoods and high-risk families: The human ecology of child maltreatment. *Child Development, 51,* 188–198.

Garmezy, N. (1993). Children in poverty: Resilience despite risk. *Psychiatry, 56,* 127–136.

Garmezy, N. (1994). Reflections and commentary on risk, resilience, and development. In R. J. Haggerty, L. R. Sherrod, N. Garmezy, & M. Rutter (Eds.), *Stress, risk, and resilience in children and adolescents: Processes, mechanisms, and interventions* (pp. 1–18). New York: Cambridge University Press.

Garrett, M. W. (1995). Between two worlds: Cultural discontinuity in the dropout of Native American youth. *The School Counselor, 10,* 199–208.

Garton, A. F., & Pratt, C. (1987). Participation and interest in leisure activities by adolescent schoolchildren. *Journal of Adolescence, 10,* 341–351.

Garton, A. F., & Pratt, C. (1991). Leisure activities of adolescent school students: Predictors of participation and interest. *Journal of Adolescence, 14,* 305–321.

Gartrell, N., Hamilton, J., Banks, A., Mosbacher, D., Reed, N., Sparks, C., & Bishop, H. (1996). The national lesbian family study: 1. Interviews with prospective mothers. *American Journal of Orthopsychiatry, 66,* 272–281.

Garver, K. L. (1995). Genetic counseling. In G. B. Reed, A. E. Claireaux, & F. Cockburn (Eds.), *Diseases of the fetus and newborn* (2nd ed.) (pp. 1007–1012). London: Chapman & Hall.

Ge, X., Conger, R. D., & Elder, G. H., Jr. (1996). Coming of age too early: Pubertal influences on girls' vulnerability to psychological distress. *Child Development, 67,* 3386–3401.

Gelles, F. J. (1992). Poverty and violence toward children. *American Behavioral Scientist, 35,* 258–274.

Gelles, R. (1983). An exchange, social control theory. In D. Finkelhor, R. Gelles, G. Hotaling, & M. Straus (Eds.), *The dark side of families* (pp. 289–292). Beverly Hills, CA: Sage.

Gelles, R. (1989). Child abuse and violence in single-parent families: Parent absence and economic deprivation. *American Journal of Orthopsychiatry, 59,* 492–501.

Gelles, R., & Hargreaves, E. (1981). Maternal employment and violence toward children *Journal of Family Issues, 2,* 509–530.

Gent, P. J., & Mulhauser, M. B. (1993). Public integration of students with handicaps: Where it's been, where it's going, and how it's getting there. In M. Nagler (Ed.), *Perspectives on disability* (2nd ed.) (pp. 397–409). Palo Alto, CA: Health Markets Research.

George, L. (1993). Sociological perspectives on life transitions. *Annual Review of Sociology, 19,* 353–373.

Germain, C. (1973). An ecological perspective in casework practice. *Social Casework: The Journal of Contemporary Social Work, 54,* 323–330.

Germain, C. (1994). Human behavior and the social environment. In R. Reamer (Ed.), *The foundations of social work knowledge* (pp. 88–121). New York: Columbia University Press.

Germain, C., & Gitterman, A. (1980). *The life model of social work practice.* New York: Columbia University Press.

Gilligan, C. (1982). *In a different voice: Psychological theory and women's development.* Cambridge, MA: Harvard University Press.

Glass, P. (1994). The vulnerable neonate and the neonatal intensive care environment. In G. B. Avery, M. A. Fletcher, & M. MacDonald (Eds.), *Neonatology: Pathophysiology and the management of the newborn* (4th ed.) (pp. 77–94). Philadelphia: Lippincott.

Glick, P. (1988). The role of divorce in the changing family structure: Trends and variations. In S. A. Wolchik & P. Karoly (Eds.), *Children of divorce: Empirical perspectives on adjustment* (pp. 3–34). New York: Gardner Press.

Gold, D. (1989). Generational solidarity: Conceptual antecedents and consequences. *American Behavioral Scientist, 33,* 19–32.

Goldstein, E. (1984). *Ego psychology and social work practice.* New York: Free Press.

Goldstein, E. (1986). Ego psychology. In F. Turner (Ed.), *Social work treatment* (3rd ed.) (pp. 375–406). New York: Free Press.

Goldstein, J. (1978). On being adult and being an adult in secular law. In E. H. Erikson (Ed.), *Adulthood* (pp. 249–267). New York: Norton & Norton.

Golembiewski, R. (1994). Is organizational membership bad for your health? Phases of burnout as covariants of mental and physical well-being. In A. Farazmand (Ed.), *Modern organizations: Administrative theory in contemporary society* (pp. 211–227). Westport, CT: Praeger.

Gonyea, J. G. (1987). The family and dependency: Factors associated with institutional decision-making. *Journal of Gerontological Social Work, 10,* 61–77.

Googins, B. (1991). *Work/family conflicts: Private lives—public responses.* New York: Auburn House.

Gottman, J. (1994). *What predicts divorce?* Hillsdale, NJ: Erlbaum.

Gouldner, A. (1970). *The coming crisis of western sociology.* New York: Basic Books.

Green, M. (1994). *Bright futures: Guidelines for health supervision of infants, children, and adolescents.* Arlington, VA: National Center for Education in Maternal and Child Health.

Greenberger, E., & Steinberg, L. D. (1986). *When teenagers work: The psychological and social costs of adolescent employment.* New York: Basic Books.

Griffith, S. (1996). *Amending attachment theory: Ambiguities among maternal care, day care peer group experience, general security and altruistic prosocial proclivities in 3, 4 & 5 year old children.* Unpublished doctoral dissertation, Adelphi University, New York.

Grossman, L. K., Fitzsimmons, S. M., Larsen-Alexander, J. B., Sachs, L., & Harter, C. (1990). The infant feeding decision in low and upper income women. *Clinical Pediatrics, 29*(1), 30–37.

Groves, B. M. (1997). Growing up in a violent world: The impact of family and community violence on young children and their families. *Topics in Early Childhood Special Education, 17*(1), 74–102.

Grusznski, R., Brink, J., & Edleson, J. (1988). Support and education groups for children of battered women. *Child Welfare, 67,* 431–444.

Guterman, N. B., & Cameron, M. (1997). Assessing the impact of community violence on children and youths. *Social Work, 42,* 495–505.

Habermas, J. (1984). *The theory of communicative action: Vol. 1. Reason and the rationalization of society.* Boston: Beacon Press.

Habermas, J. (1987). *The theory of communicative action: Vol. 2. Lifeworld and the system: A critique of functionalist reason.* Boston: Beacon Press.

Hack, M., Breslau, N., & Aram, D. (1992). The effects of very low birthweight and social risk on neurocognitive abilities at school age. *Journal of Developmental and Behavioral Pediatrics, 13,* 412–420.

Hack, M., Taylor, G., Klein, N., & Eiben, R. (1994). Outcome of <750 gram birthweight children at school age. *New England Journal of Medicine, 331,* 753–759.

Hakuta, K., Ferdman, B. M., & Diaz, R. M. (1987). Bilingualism and cognitive development: Three perspectives. In S. Rosenberg (Ed.)., *Advances in applied psycholinguistics: Vol. 2. Reading, writing, and language learning* (pp 284–319). New York: Cambridge University Press.

Halpern, R. (1990). Poverty and early childhood parenting: Toward a framework for intervention. *American Journal of Orthopsychiatry, 6,* 6–18.

Halpern, R. (1992). Challenges in evaluating community-based health and social intervention: The case of prenatal care outreach. *Journal of Social Service Research, 16*(3/4), 117–131.

Halpern, R. (1993). Neighborhood based initiative to address poverty: Lessons from experience. *Journal of Sociology and Social Welfare, 20*(4), 111–135.

Hanley, R. J., Alecxih, L. M., Wiener, J. M., & Kennell, D. L. (1990). Predicting elderly nursing home admissions: Results from the 1982–1984 National Long-Term Care Survey. *Research on Aging, 12,* 199–227.

Hannerz, U. (1992). *Cultural complexity: Studies in the social organization of meaning.* New York: Columbia University Press.

Hanson, S., & Bozett, F. (Eds.). (1985). *Dimensions of fatherhood.* Beverly Hills, CA: Sage.

Hareven, T. (1982). American families in transition: Historical perspectives on change. In F. Walsh (Ed.), *Normal family processes* (pp. 446–466). New York: Guilford.

Harkness, S. (1990). A cultural model for the acquisition of language: Implications for the innateness debate. *Developmental Psychobiology, 23,* 727–739.

Harootyan, R., & Vorek, R. (1994). Volunteering, helping, and gift giving in families and communities. In V. Bengtson & R. Harootyan, *Intergenerational linkages: Hidden connections in American society* (pp. 77–111). New York: Springer.

Hart, J. (1970). The development of client-centered therapy. In J. T. Hart & T. M. Tomlinson (Eds.), *New directions in client-centered therapy.* Boston: Houghton Mifflin.

Harter, S. (1988). Developmental processes in the construction of self. In T. D. Yawkey & J. E. Johnson (Eds.), *Integrative processes and socialization: Early to middle childhood* (pp. 45–78). Hillsdale, NJ: Erlbaum.

Hartman, A. (1970). To think about the unthinkable. *Social Casework: The Journal of Contemporary Social Work, 51,* 467–474.

Hartman, A. (1978). Diagrammatic assessment of family relationships. *Social Casework, 59,* 465–476.

Hartman, A. (1995). Diagrammatic assessment of family relationships. *Families in Society, 76,* 111–122.

Hartup, W. W. (1983). Peer relations. In E. M. Hetherington (Ed.), *Handbook of child psychology: Vol. 4. Socialization, personality, and social development* (4th ed.) (pp. 103–196). New York: Wiley.

Harvey, S. M., Carr, C., & Bernheime, S. (1989). Lesbian mothers' health care experiences. *Journal of Nurse-Midwives, 34*(3), 115–119.

Hatchett, S., & Jackson, J. (1993). African American extended kin systems: As assessment. In H. McAdoo (Ed.), *Family ethnicity: Strength in diversity* (pp. 90–108). Newbury Park, CA: Sage.

Hatecher, R. A., Trussel, J., Stewart, F., Stewart, G. K., Kowal, D., Guest, F., Cates, W., & Policar, M. S. (1994). *Contraception technology* (16th ed.). New York: Irvington.

Havighurst, R. J. (1968). Personality and patterns of aging. *The Gerontologist, 8,* 20–23.

Hayflick, L. (1987). The cell biology and theoretical basis of aging. In L. Carstensen & B. A. Edelstein (Eds.), *Handbook of clinical gerontology.* New York: Pergamon.

Hayward, C., Killen, J. D., Wilson, D. M., Hammer, L. D., Litt, I. F., Kraemer, H. C., Haydel, F., Varady, A., & Taylor, C. B. (1997). Psychiatric risk associated with early puberty in adolescent girls. *Journal of the American Academy of Child and Adolescent Psychiatry, 36,* 255–263.

Healthtouch. (1997). [On-line] Available: http://www.healthtouch.com

Healy, J. (1995). Nurturing the growing brain. *NAMTA Journal, 20*(1), 44–66.

Hearn, G. (1958). *Theory building in social work.* Toronto: University of Toronto Press.

Hearn, G. (1969). *The general systems approach: Contributions toward an holistic conception of social work.* New York: Council on Social Work Education.

Hearn, J., & Parkin, W. (1993). Organizations, multiple oppressions and postmodernism. In J. Hassard & M. Parker (Eds.), *Postmodernism and organizations* (pp. 148–162). Newbury Park, CA: Sage.

Helburn, S. W., & Howes, C. (1996). Child care cost and quality. *Future of Children, 6*(2), 62–82.

Hemenway, D., Solnick, S., & Carter, J. (1994). Child-rearing violence. *Child Abuse and Neglect, 18,* 1011–1020.

Hendricks, J. (1987). Exchange theory in aging. In G. L. Maddox (Ed.), *The encyclopedia of aging* (pp. 238–239). New York: Springer.

Henshaw, S. K. (1993). Teenage abortion, birth and pregnancy statistics by state, 1988. *Family Planning Perspectives, 25*(3), 122–127.

Hess, J. P. (1991). Health promotion and risk reduction for later life. In R. F. Young & E. A. Olson (Eds.), *Health, illness, and disability in later life: Practice issues and interventions* (pp. 25–44). Newbury Park, CA: Sage.

Hetherington, E. M., & Clingempeel, W. G. (1992). Coping with marital transitions: A family systems perspective. *Monographs of the Society for Research in Child Development, 57* (2–3, Serial No. 227).

Hetherington, E., Cox, M., & Cox, R. (1977). The aftermath of divorce. In J. H. Stevens, Jr., & M. Matthews (Eds.), *Mother-child, father-child relationships* (pp. 149–176). Washington, DC: NAEYC.

Hetherington, E. M., & Jodl, K. M. (1994). Stepfamilies as settings for child development. In A. Booth & J. Dunn (Eds), *Stepfamilies: Who benefits? Who does not?* (pp. 55–79). Hillsdale, NJ: Erlbaum.

Hill, R. B. (1972). *The strengths of black families.* New York: National Urban League.

Hines, P. (1988). The family life cycle of poor black families. In E. Carter & M. McGoldrick (Eds.), *The changing family life cycle* (pp. 513–544). New York: Gardner.

Hinshaw, S. P. (1994). *Attention deficits and hyperactivity in children.* Thousand Oaks, CA: Sage.

Ho, M. K. (1992). *Minority children and adolescents in therapy.* Newbury Park, CA: Sage.

Hobbs, F., & Damon, B. (1997). *Sixty-five plus in the United States: Statistical brief.* U.S. Census Bureau: www.census.gov/socdemo/www/agebrief (4/25/97).

Hochschild, A. (1983). *The managed heart: Commercialization of human feeling.* Berkeley: University of California Press.

Hodgkinson, H. L. (1990). *The demographics of American Indians: One percent of the people; fifty percent of the diversity.* Washington, DC: Institute for Educational Leadership.

Hofferth, S. L., & Hayes, C. D. (Eds.). (1987). *Risking the future: Adolescent sexuality, pregnancy, and childbearing: 2. Working papers and statistical reports.* Washington, DC: National Academy Press.

Hogoel, L., Van-Raalte, R., Kalekin-Fishman, D., & Shlfroni, G. (1995). Psychosocial and medical factors in pregnancy outcome: A case study of Israeli women. *Social Science and Medicine, 40,* 567–571.

Holmes, M. M., Resnick, H. S., Kilpatrick, D. G., & Best, C. L. (1996). Rape-related pregnancy: Estimates and descriptive characteristics from a national sample of women. *American Journal of Obstetrics and Gynecology, 175,* 320–324.

Homans, G. (1958). Social behavior as exchange. *American Journal of Sociology, 63,* 597–606.

Homans, G. C. (1961). *Social behavior: Its elementary forms.* New York: Harcourt Brace Jovanovich.

Hooyman, N. R., & Kiyak, H. A. (1988). *Social gerontology: A multidisciplinary perspective.* Boston: Allyn & Bacon.

Hopper, R., & Naremore, R. (1978). *Children's speech: A practical introduction to communication development.* New York: Harper & Row.

Horn, J. L. (1982). The theory of fluid and crystallized intelligence in relation to concepts of cognitive psychology and aging in adulthood. In F. I. M. Craik & S. Trehub (Eds.), *Aging and cognitive processes* (237–278). New York: Plenum.

Horney, K. (1939). *New ways in psychoanalysis.* New York: Norton.

Horney, K. (1967). *Feminine psychology.* New York: Norton.

Hotaling, G. T., Finkelhor, D., Kirkpatrick, J. T., & Strauss, M. A. (Eds.). (1988). *Family abuse and its consequences: New directions in research.* Newbury Park, CA: Sage.

Howie, P. W., Forsyth, J. S., Ogston, S. A., Clark, A., & Florey, C. D. (1990). Protective effect of breastfeeding against infection. *British Medical Journal, 300,* 11–16.

Hughes, H. (1988). Psychological and behavioral correlates of family violence in child witnesses and victims. *American Journal of Orthopsychiatry, 58,* 77–90.

Huston, T., McHale, S., & Crouter, A. (1986). When the honeymoon's over: Changes in the marriage relationship over the first year. In R. Gilmore & S. Duck (Eds.), *The emerging field of personal relationships* (pp. 53–90). New York: Academic Press.

Illinois Coalition Against Sexual Assault. (1990). *Date rape.* Springfield, IL: Author.

Imre, R. (1984). The nature of knowledge in social work. *Social Work, 29,* 41–45.

Ingersoll-Dayton, B., Campbell, R., Kurokawa, U., & Saito, M. (1996). Separateness and togetherness: Interdependence over the life course in Japanese and American marriages. *Journal of Social and Personal Relationships, 13,* 385–398.

Ironson, G. (1992). Work, job stress, and health. In S. Zedeck (Ed.), *Work, families, and organizations* (pp. 33–69). San Francisco: Jossey-Bass.

Iso-Ahola, S. E., & Crowley, E. D. (1991). Adolescent substance abuse and leisure boredom. *Journal of Leisure Research, 23,* 260–271.

Jackson, J. (1993). Multiple caregiving among African Americans and infant attachment: The need for an emic approach. *Human Development, 36,* 87–102.

Jackson, S., & Schuler, R. (1985). A meta-analysis and conceptual critique of research on role ambiguity and role conflict in work settings. *Organizational Behavior and Human Decision Processes, 36,* 16–78.

Jaffe, D., Scott, C., & Tobe, G. (1994). *Rekindling commitment.* San Francisco: Jossey-Bass.

Jarvinen, D. W., & Nicholls, J. G. (1996) Adolescents' social goals, beliefs about the causes of social success, and satisfaction in peer relations. *Developmental Psychology, 32,* 435–442.

Jenkins, E., & Bell, C. (1997). Exposure and response to community violence among children and adolescents. In J. Osofosky (Ed.), *Children in a violent society* (pp. 9–31). New York: Guilford.

Jessor, R. (1987). Problem-behavior theory, psychosocial development, and adolescent problem drinking. *British Journal of Addiction, 82,* 331–342.

Jex, S., & Beehr, T. (1991). Emerging theoretical and methodological issues in the study of work-related stress. In G. Ferris & K. Rowland (Eds.), *Research in personnel and human resources management* (Vol. 9, pp. 311-364). Greenwich, CT: JAI Press.

Johnson, H. D., Atkins, S. P., Battle, S. F., Hernandez-Arata, L., Hesselbrock, M., Libassi, M. F., & Parish, M. S. (1990). Strengthening the "bio" in the biopsychosocial paradigm. *Journal of Social Work Education, 26,* 109–123.

Johnston, L. D., O'Malley, P. M., & Bachman, J. G. (1988). *Monitoring the future.* Ann Arbor: Univerity of Michigan, Institute for Social Research.

Jones, E., Forrest, J. D., Goldman, N., Henshaw, S., Lincoln, R., Rosoff, J., Westoff, C., & Wulf, D. (1985). Teenage pregnancy in developed countries: Determinants and policy implications. *Family Planning Perspectives, 17*(2), 53–63.

Jordan, J. (1992). The relational self: A new perspective for understanding women's development. *Contemporary Psychotherapy Review, 7,* 56–71.

Kahneman, E., & Tversky, A. (1982). The psychology of preferences. *Scientific American, 246,* 160–173.

Kahneman, D., & Tversky, A. (1984). Choices, values, and frames. *American Psychologist, 39,* 341–350.

Kail, R. V., & Cavanaugh, J. C. (1996). *Human development.* Pacific Grove, CA: Brooks/Cole.

Kandel, D. B., & Logan, J. A. (1984). Patterns of drug use from adolescence to young adulthood: Periods of risk for initiation, stabilization and decline in use. *American Journal of Public Health, 74,* 660–666.

Kandel, D. B., & Logan, J. A. (1991). Cocaine use in a national sample of U.S. youth: Ethnic patterns, progression and predictors. *NIDA Monographs, 110,* 151–188.

Kaplan, H., & Sadock, B. (1998). *Synopsis of psychiatry* (8th ed.). Baltimore: Williams & Wilkins.

Kaplan, H., Sadock, B., & Grebb, J. (1994). *Synopsis of psychiatry* (7th ed.). Baltimore: Williams & Wilkins.

Katchadourian, H. (1978). Medical perspectives on adulthood. In E. H. Erikson (Ed.), *Adulthood* (pp. 33–60). New York: Norton.

Kaufman, K. J., & Hall, L. A. (1989). Influences of the social network on choice and duration of breast-feeding in mothers of preterm infants. *Research in Nursing and Health, 12,* 149–159.

Keating, P. (1994). Striving for sex equity in schools. In K. I. Goodland & P. Keating (Eds.), *Access to knowledge: The continuing agenda for our nation's schools* (pp. 91–106). New York: The College Board.

Keel, P. K., Fulkerson, J. A., & Leon, G. R. (1997). Disordered eating precursors in pre- and early adolescent girls and boys. *Journal of Youth and Adolescence, 26,* 203–216.

Keil, J., Sutherland, S., Knapp, R., & Tyroler, H. (1992). Does equal socioeconomic status in black and white men mean equal risk of mortality? *American Journal of Public Health, 82,* 1133–1136.

Kellaghan, T., Sloane, K., Alvarez, B., & Bloom, B. S. (1993). *The home environment and school learning: Promoting parental involvement in the education of children.* San Francisco: Jossey-Bass.

Kelley, H., & Thibaut, J. (1978). *Interpersonal relations: A theory of interdependence.* New York: Wiley.

Kenney, J. W., Reinholtz, C., & Angelini, P. J. (1997). Ethnic differences in childhood and adolescent sexual abuse and teenage pregnancy. *Journal of Adolescent Health, 21*(1), 3–10.

Kertzer, D. (1989). Age structuring in comparative and historical perspective. In D. Kertzer & K. W. Schaie (Eds.), *Age structuring in comparative perspective* (pp. 3–20). Hillsdale, NJ: Lawrence Erlbaum Associates.

Keye, W. R. (1995). Psychological issues of infertility. In J. J. Sciarra (Ed.), *Gynecology and obstetrics* (Vol. 5, pp. 1–14). Philadelphia: Lippincott-Raven.

Kimmel, D. (1990). *Adulthood and aging* (3rd ed.). New York: Wiley.

Kingson, E. R., & Berkowitz, E. D. (1993). *Social Security and Medicare: A policy primer.* Westport, CT: Auburn House.

Kinkade, K. (1973). *A Walden Two experiment: The first five years of Twin Oaks Community.* New York: Morrow.

Kirby, L., & Fraser, M. (1997). Risk and resilience in childhood. In M. Fraser (Ed.), *Risk and resilience in childhood* (pp. 10–33). Washington, DC: NASW Press.

Kirk, S., & Kutchins, H. (1992). *The selling of DSM: The rhetoric of science in psychiatry.* New York: Aldine de Gruyter.

Kivnick, H. (1983). Dimensions of grandparenthood meaning: Deductive conceptualization and empirical derivation. *Journal of Personality and Social Psychology, 44,* 1056–1068.

Klaus, M. H., & Kennel, J. H. (1982). *Parent-infant bonding.* St. Louis: Mosby.

Kleinman, J., Fingerhut, L. A., & Prager, K. (1991). Differences in infant mortality by race, nativity status, and other maternal characteristics. *American Journal of Diseases of Children, 145,* 194–199.

Kleinman, J., & Madans, J. H. (1985). The effects of maternal smoking, physical stature, and educational attainment on the incidence of low birth weight. *American Journal of Epidemiology, 121,* 832–855.

Klerman, L. (1991). The health of poor children. In A. C. Huston (Ed.), *Children and poverty* (pp. 136–157). New York: Cambridge University Press.

Kobak, R., & Hazan, C. (1991). Attachment in marriage: The effects of security and accuracy of working models. *Journal of Personality and Social Psychology, 60,* 861–869.

Koeske, G., & Koeske, R. (1992). Parenting locus of control: Measurement, construct validation, and a proposed conceptual model. *Social Work Research and Abstracts, 28*(3), 37–45.

Kohlberg, L. (1969). Stage and sequence: The cognitive developmental approach to socialization. In D. A. Goslin (Ed.), *Handbook of socialization theory and research* (pp. 347–480). Chicago: Rand McNally.

Kohlberg, L. (1976). Moral stages and moralization: The cognitive-developmental approach. In T. Lickona (Ed.), *Moral development and behavior: Theory, research, and social issues* (pp. 31–53). New York: Holt.

Kohlberg, L. (1984). *Essays on moral development: Vol. 2. The psychology of moral development.* San Francisco: Harper & Row.

Koss, M. P., Gidycz, C. A., & Wisniewski, N. (1987). The scope of rape: Incidence and prevalence of sexual aggression and victimization in a national sample of higher education students. *Journal of Consulting and Clinical Psychology, 55,* 162–170.

Kovaks, M. (1989). Affective disorders in children and adolescents. *American Journal of Psychology, 44,* 209–212.

Kozol, J. (1991). *Savage inequalities: Children in America's schools.* New York: HarperPerennial.

Kramer, M. S., Coates, A. L., Michoud, M., & Hamilton, E. F. (1994). Maternal nutrition and idiopathic preterm labor. *Pediatric Research, 35*(4), 277A.

Kramer, M. S., McLean, F. H., Eason, E. L., & Usher, R. H. (1992). Maternal nutrition and spontaneous preterm birth. *American Journal of Epidemiology, 136,* 574–583.

Kravetz, D. (1982). An overview of content on women for the social work curriculum. *Journal of Education for Social Work, 18*(2), 42–49.

Krill, D. (1986). Existential social work. In F. Turner (Ed.), *Social work treatment: Interlocking theoretical approaches* (pp. 181–217). New York: Free Press.

Kropf, N., & Greene, R. (1994). Erikson's eight stages of development: Different lenses. In R. Greene (Ed.), *Human behavior theory: A diversity framework* (pp. 75–114). New York: Aldine de Gruyter.

Kübler-Ross, E. (1969). *On death and dying.* New York: Macmillan.

Kurdek, L. (1991). Correlates of relationship satisfaction in cohabiting gay and lesbian couples: Integration of contextual, investment, and problem-solving models. *Journal of Personality and Social Psychology, 61,* 910–922.

Kurdek, L. (1994). The nature and correlates of relationship quality in gay, lesbian, and heterosexual cohabiting couples: A test of the individual difference, interdependence, and discrepancy models. In B. Greene & G. M. Herek (Eds.), *Lesbian and gay psychology* (pp. 133–155). Thousand Oaks, CA: Sage.

Kurtz, L. (1995). The relationship between parental coping strategies and children's adaptive processes in divorced and intact families. *Journal of Divorce and Remarriage, 24*(3/4), 89–110.

Kurtz, P. D. (1988). Social work services to parents: Essential to pupils at risk. *Urban Education, 22,* 444–457.

Kurtz, P. D., & Barth, R. P. (1989). Parent involvement: Cornerstone of school social work practice. *Social Work, 34,* 407–413.

Kurzman, P. (1993). Employee assistance programs: Toward a comprehensive service model. In P. Kurzman & S. Akabas (Eds.), *Work and well-being: The occupational social work advantage* (pp. 26–45). Washington, DC: NASW Press.

Laing, R. D. (1967). *The politics of experience.* New York: Ballantine.

Laing, R. D. (1969). *The politics of the family.* New York: Pantheon.

Laird, J. (1994). Changing women's narratives: Taking back the discourse. In L. Davis (Ed.), *Building on women's strengths: A social work agenda for the twenty-first century* (pp. 179–210). New York: Haworth Press.

Lamaze, F. (1958). *Painless childbirth: Psychoprophylactic method* (L. R. Celestin, Trans.). London: Burke.

Lamb, M. (1986). The changing roles of fathers. In M. Lamb (Ed.), *The father's role: Applied perspectives* (pp. 3–27). New York: Wiley.

Lapidus, I. (1978). Adulthood in Islam: Religious maturity in the Islamic tradition. In E. H. Erikson (Ed.), *Adulthood* (pp. 97–112). New York: Norton & Norton.

LaRossa, R. (1997). *The modernization of fatherhood: A social and political history.* Chicago: University of Chicago Press.

Larson, E. J. (1995). The effects of maternal substance abuse on the placenta and fetus. In G. B. Reed, A. E. Claireaux, & F. Cockburn (Eds.), *Diseases of the fetus and newborn* (2nd ed.) (pp. 353–361). London : Chapman & Hall.

Lawrence, B. (1996). Organizational age norms: Why is it so hard to know one when you see one? *The Gerontologist, 36*(2), 209–220.

Lawton, L., Silverstein, M., & Bengtson, V. (1994). Solidarity between generations in families. In V. Bengtson & R. Harootyan, *Intergenerational linkages: Hidden connections in American society* (pp. 19–42). New York: Springer.

Leitenberg, H., Detzer, M. J., & Srebnik, D. (1993). Gender differences in masturbation and the relationship of masturbation experience in preadolescence and/or early adolescence and sexual behavior and sexual adjustment in young adulthood. *Archives of Sexual Behavior, 22,* 299–313.

Levi, M., Cook, K., O'Brien, J., & Faye, H. (1990). The limits of rationality. In K. Cook & M. Levi (Eds.), *The limits of rationality* (pp. 1–16). Chicago: University of Chicago Press.

Levinson, D. (1978). *The seasons of a man's life.* New York: Knopf.

Levinson, D. (1980). Toward a conception of the adult life course. In N. J. Smelser & E. H. Erikson (Eds.), *Themes of work and love in adulthood* (pp. 265–290). Cambridge, MA: Harvard University Press.

Levinson, D. (1986). A conception of adult development. *American Psychologist, 41,* 3–13.

Levinson, D. (1990). A theory of life structure development in adulthood. In C. N. Alexander & E. J. Langer (Eds.), *Higher stages of human development* (pp. 35–54). New York: Oxford University Press.

Levinson, D. (1996). *The seasons of a woman's life.* New York: Knopf.

Levy, G. D., Taylor, M. G., & Gelman, S. A. (1995). Traditional and evaluative aspects of flexibility in gender roles, social conventions, moral rules and physical laws. *Child Development , 66,* 515–531.

Lewis, T. (1994). A comparative analysis of the effects of social skills training and teacher directed contingencies on social behavior of preschool children with disabilities. *Journal of Behavioral Education, 4,* 267–281.

Light, J., Irvine, K., & Kjerulf, L. (1996). Estimating genetic and environmental effects of alcohol use and dependence from a national survey: A "quasi adoption" study. *Journal of Studies on Alcohol, 57,* 507–520.

Lin, C., & Liu, W. (1993). Intergenerational relationships among Chinese immigrant families from Taiwan. In H. McAdoo (Ed.), *Family ethnicity: Strength in diversity* (pp. 271–286). Newbury Park, CA: Sage.

Lincoln, Y., & Guba, E. (1985). *Naturalistic inquiry.* Beverly Hills, CA: Sage.

Lindemann, E. (1944). Symptomatology and management of acute grief. *American Journal of Psychiatry, 101,* 141–148.

Lipsky, D., & Abrams, A. (1994). *Late bloomers.* New York: Times Books.

Lochman, J. E., Coie, J.D., Underwood, M. K., & Terry, R. (1993). Effectiveness of a social relationship intervention program for aggressive and nonaggressive, rejected children. *Journal of Consulting and Clinical Psychology, 61,* 1053–1058.

Logan, S. L., Freeman, E. M., & McRoy, R. G. (Eds.). (1990). *Social work practice with black families: A culturally specific perspective.* New York: Longman.

London, K. (1991). Cohabitation, marriage, marital dissolution, and remarriage: United States, 1988. *Advance data from vital and health statistics* (No. 194). Hyattsville, MD: National Center for Health Statistics.

Longres, J. (1995). *Human behavior in the social environment* (2nd ed.). Itasca, IL: Peacock.

Lowenthal, M., Thurnher, M., & Chiriboga, D. (1977). *Four stages of life.* San Francisco: Jossey-Bass.

Lowry, R., Holtzman, D., Truman, B. I., Kann, L., Collins, J. L., & Kolbe, L. J. (1994). Substance use and HIV-related sexual behaviors among U.S. high school students: Are they related? *American Journal of Public Health, 84,* 1116–1120.

Luepnitz, D. (1988). *The family interpreted: Feminist theory and clinical practice.* New York: Basic Books.

Maccoby, E. (1980). *Social development: Psychological growth and the parent-child relationship.* San Diego: Harcourt Brace Jovanovich.

Mackey, W. (1996). *The American father: Biocultural and developmental aspects.* New York: Plenum.

MacLennan, B. (1994). Groups for poorly socialized children in the elementary school. *Journal of Child and Adolescent Group Therapy, 4,* 243–250.

Magwaza, A., Kilian, B., Peterson, I., & Pillay, Y. (1993). The effects of chronic violence on preschool children living in South African townships. *Child Abuse and Neglect, 17,* 795–803.

Maier, S., Watkins, L., & Fleshner, M. (1994). Psychoneuroimmunology: The interface between behavior, brain, and immunity. *American Psychologist, 49,* 1004–1017.

Main, M., & Hesse, E. (1990). Parents' unresolved traumatic experiences are related to infant disorganized attachment status: Is frightened and/or frightening parental behavior the linking mechanism? In M. Greenberg, D. Cicchetti, & E. M. Cumming (Eds.), *Attachment in the preschool years: Theory, research and intervention* (pp. 161–182). Chicago: University of Chicago Press.

Maloney, M. J., & Klykylo, W. M. (1983). An overview of anorexia nervosa, bulimia and obesity in children and adolescents. *Journal of the American Academy of Child Psychiatry, 22,* 99–107.

Mann, M. (1986). *The sources of social power* (Vol. 1). New York: Cambridge University Press.

Manton, K. G., & Liu, K. (1984). *The future growth of the long-term care population: Projections based on the 1977 national nursing home survey and the 1981 long-term care survey.* Washington, DC: Health Care Financing Administration.

Manton, K. G., & Soldo, B. J. (1985). Dynamics of health changes in the oldest old: New perspectives and evidence. *The Millbank Quarterly, 63,* 206–285.

March, J., & Simon, H. (1958). *Organizations.* New York: Wiley.

Marcia, J. E. (1966). Development and validation of ego-identity status. *Journal of Personality and Social Psychology, 3,* 551–558.

Marcia, J. E. (1980). Identity in adolescence. In J. Adelson (Ed.), *Handbook of adolescent psychology* (pp. 159–187). New York: Wiley.

Marcia, J. E. (1993). The ego identity status approach to ego identity. In J. E. Marcia, A. S. Waterman, D. R. Mattesson, S. L. Arcjer, & J. L. Orlofsky (Eds.), *Ego identity: A handbook for psychosocial research.* New York: Springer-Verlag.

Markstrom-Adams, C., & Adams, G. R. (1995). Gender, ethnic group, and grade differences in psychosocial functioning during middle adolescence. *Journal of Youth and Adolescence, 24,* 397–417.

Marsiglio, W. (1986). Teenage fatherhood: High school accreditation and educational attainment. In A. B. Elster & M. E. Lamb (Eds.), *Adolescent Fatherhood.* Hillside, NJ: Erlbaum.

Martin, K. A. (1996). *Puberty, sexuality, and the self: Boys and girls at adolescence.* New York: Routledge.

Martin, P. Y., & O'Connor, G. G. (1989). *The social environment: Open systems applications.* New York: Longman.

Marx, K. (1967). *Capital: A critique of political economy* (Vol. 1) (S. Moore & E. Aveling, Trans.). New York: International Publishers. (Original work published 1887)

Maslow, A. (1962). *Toward a psychology of being.* New York: Van Nostrand.

Matute-Bianchi, M. E. (1986). Ethnic identities and patterns of school success and failure among Mexican-descent and Japanese-American students in a California school: An ethnographic analysis. *American Journal of Education, 95,* 233–255.

McCarter, S. (1997). *Understanding the overrepresentation of minorities in Virginia's juvenile justice system.* Unpublished doctoral dissertation, Virginia Commonwealth University, Richmond.

McCarter, S. (1998). Interviews with adolescents regarding health topics. Work in progress, Virginia Commonwealth University, School of Social Work.

McCarthy, J., & Zald, M. (1977). Resource mobilization in social movements: A partial theory. *American Journal of Sociology, 82,* 1212–1239.

McCarton, C. (1986). The long term impact of a low birth weight infant on the family. *Zero to Three, 267* (16), 6–10.

McCloskey, L. A., Figueredo, A. J., & Koss, M. P. (1995). The effects of systemic family violence on children's mental health. *Child Development, 66,* 1239–1261.

McCormick, M. C., Brooks-Gunn, J., Workman-Daniels, K., Turner, J., & Peckman, J. (1993). The health and developmental status of very low-birth-weight children at school age. *Journal of the American Medical Association, 267,* 2204–2208.

McDermott, S., Cokert, A. L., & McKeown, R. E. (1993). Low birthweight and risk of mild mental retardation by ages 5 and 9 to 11. *Paediatric and Perinatal Epidemiology, 7*(2), 195–204.

McGoldrick, M. (1988). Women and the family life cycle. In E. Carter & M. McGoldrick (Eds.), *The changing family life cycle* (pp. 31–68). New York: Gardner.

McGregor, D. (1960). *The human side of enterprise.* New York: McGraw-Hill.

McLoyd, V. (1990). The impact of economic hardship on black families and children: Psychological distress, parenting, and socioemotional development. *Child Development, 61,* 311–346.

McLoyd, V., & Wilson, L. (1991). The strain of living poor: Parenting, social support and child mental health. In A. C. Huston (Ed.), *Children and poverty* (pp. 105–136). New York: Cambridge University Press.

McWhirter, D., & Mattison, A. (1984). *The male couple: How relationships develop.* Englewood Cliffs, NJ: Prentice-Hall.

McWhirter, J. J., McWhirter, B. T., McWhirter, A. M., & McWhirter, E. H. (1993). *At-risk youth: A comprehensive response.* Pacific Grove, CA: Brooks/Cole.

Mead, G. H. (1934). *Mind, self and society.* Chicago: University of Chicago Press.

Meyer, C. (1976). *Social work practice* (2nd ed.). New York: Free Press.

Meyer, C. (Ed.). (1983). *Clinical social work in an eco-systems perspective.* New York: Columbia University Press.

Meyer, C. (1993). *Assessment in social work practice.* New York: Columbia University Press.

Meyer, D. R., & Garasky, S. (1993). Custodial fathers: Myths, realities, and child support policy. *Journal of Marriage and the Family, 55,* 73–89.

Middleton, P. (1989). Socialism, feminism and men. *Radical Philosophy, 53,* 8–19.

Mikulincer, M. (1994). *Human learned helplessness: A coping perspective.* New York: Plenum.

Milunsky, A. (1987). *How to have the healthiest baby you can.* New York: Simon & Schuster.

Minkler, M. (1985). Social support and health in the elderly. In S. Cohen & S. L. Syme (Eds.), *Social support and health* (pp. 199–216). Orlando: Academic Press.

Mize, J., & Ladd, G. W. (1990). A cognitive-social learning approach to social skill training with low status preschool children. *Development Psychology, 26,* 388–397.

Moen, P. (1995). Introduction. In P. Moen, G. Elder, Jr., & K. Luscher (Eds.), *Examining lives in context: Perspectives on the ecology of human development* (pp. 1–11). Washington, DC: American Psychological Association.

Molfese, V., Holcomb, L., & Helwig, S. (1994). Biomedical and social-environmental influences on cognitive and verbal abilities in children 1 to 3 years of age. *International Journal of Behavioral Development, 17,* 271–287.

Monte, C. (1995). *Beneath the mask: An introduction to theories of personality* (5th ed.). Fort Worth, TX: Harcourt Brace Jovanovich.

Montgomery, R. J. V., & Kosloski, K. (1994). A longitudinal analysis of nursing home placement for dependent elders cared for by spouses vs. adult children. *Journal of Gerontology: Social Science, 49,* S62--S74.

Moody, H. R. (1998). *Aging: Concepts and controversies.* (2nd ed.). Thousand Oaks, CA: Pine Forge.

Moore, D. (1987). Parent-adolescent separation: The construction of adulthood by late adolescents. *Developmental Psychology, 23,* 298–307.

Moore, K. L., & Persaud, T. V. N. (1993). *Before we are born* (4th ed.). Philadelphia: Saunders.

Morgan, L., & Kunkel, S. (1996). *Aging: The social context.* Thousand Oaks, CA: Pine Forge.

Mortimer, J. T., & Finch, M. D. (1996). *Adolescents, work, and family: An intergenerational developmental analysis.* Thousand Oaks, CA: Sage.

Mosher, W. D., & Horn, M. C. (1988). First family planning visits by young women. *Family Planning Perspective, 20*(1), 33–40.

Moss, N. E. (1987). Effects of father-daughter contact on use of pregnancy services by Mexican, Mexican-American, and Anglo adolescents. *Journal of Adolescent Health Care, 8,* 419–425.

Moss, R. H., Mortens, M. A., & Brennan, P. L. (1993). Patterns of diagnosis and treatment among late-middle-aged and older substance abuse patients. *Journal of Studies in Alcohol, 54,* 479–487.

Moyer, K. (1974). Discipline. In *You and your child: A primer for parents* (pp. 40–61). Chicago: Nelson Hall

Moyers, B. (1993). *Healing and the mind.* New York: Doubleday.

Mrazek, P., & Haggerty, R. (Eds.). (1994). *Reducing risks for mental disorder.* Washington, DC: National Academy Press.

Muehlenhard, C. L., & Linton, M. (1987). Date rape and sexual aggression in dating situations: Incidence and risk factors. *Journal of Consulting Psychology, 34,* 186–196.

Mynatt, C. R., & Algeier, E. R. (1990). Risk factors, self-attributions and adjustment problems among victims of sexual coercion. *Journal of Applied Social Psychology, 20,* 130–153.

Naleppa, M. J. (1996). Families and the institutionalized elderly: A review. *Journal of Gerontological Social Work, 27,* 87–111.

Nardi, P. (1992). "Seamless souls": An introduction to men's friendships. In P. Nardi (Ed.), *Men's friendship* (pp. 1–14). Newbury Park, CA: Sage.

Nardi, P., & Sherrod, D. (1994). Friendship in the lives of gay men and lesbians. *Journal of Social and Personal Relationships, 11,* 185–200.

National Cancer Institute. (1991). *Cancer statistics review* (NCI, NIH Pub. No. 91-2789). Bethesda, MD: U.S. Government Printing Office.

National Center for Child Abuse and Neglect. (1995). *Child maltreatment 1995: Reports of the states to the National Child Abuse Neglect Data Systems.* http:www/calib.com/nccanch/services/stats.htm#NIS-3

National Center for Children in Poverty. (1996/97). One in four: America's youngest poor. *News and Issues, 6*(2), 1–2. New York: Author.

National Center for Clinical Infant Programs. (1992). How community violence affects children, parents, and practitioners. *Public Welfare, 50*(4), 25–35.

National Center for Health Services Research. (1988, October). *HIV-related illnesses: Topics for health services research.* Washington, DC: Author.

National Center for Health Statistics. (1990). Advance report of final mortality statistics, 1988. *Monthly Vital Statistics Report, 39*(7) (DHHS Publication No. PHS 90-1120). Hyattsville, MD: Public Health Service.

National Center for Health Statistics. (1993a, September 9). Advance report of final natality statistics, 1991. *Monthly Vital Statistics Report, 42*(3), Suppl. Hyattsville, MD: Public Health Service. http://www.cdc.gov/nchwww/products/pubs/pubd/mvsr/supp/44-43/mvs44_3s.htm

National Center for Health Statistics. (1993b). *Vital statistics of the United States, 1989: Vol 2. Mortality, Part A.* Washington, DC: Public Health Service.

National Center for Health Statistics. (1997, June 10). 1995 birth statistics released. In MVSR Vol. 45, No. 11(S). *Report of final natality statistics, 1995.* Public Health Service. http://www.cdc.gov/nchwww/releases/97facts/97sheets/95natrel.htm

National Center on Elder Abuse. (1997). Statistics. In *Elder abuse in domestic settings* [On-line]. Available: http://interinc.com/NCEA/Statistics/pl.html

National Commission to Prevent Infant Mortality. (1992). One-stop shopping for infants and pregnant women. *Public Welfare, 50*(1), 26–34.

National Institute for Occupational Safety and Health. (1993). *Alert: Request for assistance in preventing homicide in the workplace* (Pub. No. 93-109). Cincinnati: Author.

National Institutes of Health–National Institute of Allergy and Infectious Diseases. (1996, August). Bethesda, MD: U.S. Department of Health and Human Services, Public Health Service.

National Institutes of Health–National Institute on Drug Abuse. (1998). *Monitoring the future study.* Bethesda, MD: U.S. Department of Health and Human Services, Public Health Service.

National Research Council (1990). *Who cares for America's children?* Washington, DC: Author.

Neugarten, B. (1979). Time, age, and the life cycle. *American Journal of Psychiatry, 136,* 887–894.

Neugarten, B. L., Havighurst, R. J., & Tobin, S. S. (1968). Personality and patterns of aging. In B. L. Neugarten (Ed.), *Middle age and aging.* Chicago: University of Chicago Press.

Neugarten, B. L., & Weinstein, K. K. (1964). The changing American grandparent. *Journal of Marriage and the Family, 26,* 199–204.

Newcomb, A. F., Bukowski, W. M., & Pattee, L. (1993). Children's peer relations: A meta-analytic review of popular, rejected, neglected, controversial, and average sociometric status. *Psychological Bulletin, 113,* 99–128.

Newcomb, N., & Dubas, J. S. (1992). A longitudinal study of predictors of spatial ability in adolescent females. *Child Development, 63,* 37–46.

Noll, H., & Langlois, S. (1994). Employment and labour-market change: Toward two models of growth. In S. Langlois (Ed.), *Convergence or divergence? Comparing recent social trends in industrial societies* (pp. 89–113). Buffalo, NY: McGill-Queen's University Press.

Nosek, M. (1995). Findings on reproductive health and access to health care. *National study of women with physical disabilities.* Baylor College of Medicine, Department of Physical Medicine and Rehabilitation, Houston.

Novak, J. C., & Broom, B. (1995). *Maternal and child health nursing.* St. Louis: Mosby.

Nydegger, C. N. (1983). Family ties of the aged in cross-cultural perspective. *The Gerontologist, 23,* 26–32.

O'Connor, P. (1992). *Friendships between women: A critical review.* New York: Guilford.

O'Conor, A. (1994). Who gets called queer in school? Lesbian, gay and bisexual teenagers, homophobia and high school. *The High School Journal, 77* (1–2), 7–12.

O'Keefe, M. (1994). Adjustment of children from maritally violent homes. *Families in Society, 75,* 403–415.

O'Keefe, M. (1997). Adolescents' exposure to community and school violence: Prevalence and behavioral correlates. *Journal of Adolescent Health, 20,* 368–376.

O'Malley, P. L., Johnston, L., & Bachman, J. (1991). Quantitative and qualitative changes in cocaine use among American high school seniors, college students, and young adults. *NIDA Monographs, 110,* 19–43.

O'Rand, A. (1996). The precious and the precocious: Understanding cumulative disadvantage and cumulative advantage over the life course. *The Gerontologist, 36,* 230–238.

Oakes, J. (1985). *Keeping track of tracking: How schools structure inequality.* New Haven, CT: Yale University Press.

Oakes, J., & Lipton, M. (1990). *Making the best of schools: A handbook for parents, teachers, and policymakers.* New Haven, CT: Yale University Press.

Oakes, J., & Lipton, M. (1992). Detracking schools: Early lessons from the field. *Phi Delta Kappan, 73,* 448–454.

Oakley, A., Hickey, D., Rojan, L., & Rigby, A. S. (1996). Social support in pregnancy: Does it have long-term effects? *Journal of Reproductive and Infant Psychology, 14*(1), 7–22.

Oberklaid, F., Sanson, A., Pedlow, R., & Prior, M. (1993). Predicting preschool behavior problems from temperament and other variables in infancy. *Pediatrics, 91,* 113–120.

Oetting, E. R., & Beauvias, F. (1987). Common elements in youth drug involvement, peer clusters and other psychosocial factors. *Journal of Drug Issues, 17*(23), 133–151.

Ogbu, J. U. (1994). Overcoming racial barriers to equal access. In K. I. Goodland & P. Keating (Eds.), *Access to knowledge: The continuing agenda for our nation's schools* (pp. 59–90). New York: The College Board.

Oggins, J., Veroff, J., & Leber, D. (1993). Perceptions of marital interaction among black and white newlyweds. *Journal of Personality and Social Psychology, 65,* 494–511.

Ollendick, T. H., Weist, M. D., Borden, M. C., & Greene, R. W. (1992). Sociometric status and academic, behavioral, and psychological adjustment: A five year longitudinal study. *Journal of Consulting and Clinical Psychology, 60,* 80–87.

Online Mendelian Inheritance in Man (OMIM ™). (1998). Center for Medical Genetics, Johns Hopkins University (Baltimore, MD) and National Center for Biotechnology Information, National Library of Medicine (Bethesda, MD). http://www.ncbi.nlm.nkh.gov/omim/

Opitz, J. M. (1996). Origins of birth defects. In J. J. Sciarra (Ed.), *Gynecology and obstetrics* (rev. ed.) ( pp. 23–30). Philadelphia: Lippincott-Raven.

Osofsky, J. D., Hann, D., & Peebles, C. (1993). Adolescent parenthood: Risks and opportunities for mothers and infants. In C. Zeanah, Jr. (Ed.), *Handbook of infant mental health* (pp. 106–119). New York : Guilford Press.

Osofsky, J. D., Osofsky, H. J., & Diamond, M. O. (1988). The transition to parenthood: Special tasks and risk factors for adolescent mothers. In G. Y. Michaels & W. A. Goldberg (Eds.), *The transition to parenthood* (pp. 209–234). Cambridge: Cambridge University Press.

Palkovitz, R. (1996). Parenting as a generator of adult development: Conceptual issues and implications. *Journal of Social and Personal Relationships, 13,* 571–592.

Palmore, E. B., Burchett, B. M., Fillenbaum, C. G., George, L. K., & Wallman, L. M. (1985). *Retirement: Causes and consequences.* New York: Springer.

Panksepp, J. (1986). The psychobiology of prosocial behaviors: Separation distress, play, and altruism. In C. Zahn-Waxler, E. M. Cummings, & R. Iannotti (Eds.), *Altruism and aggression: Biological and social origin* (pp. 465–492). Cambridge: Cambridge University Press.

Parette, H. (1995, November). *Culturally sensitive family-focused assistive technology assessment strategies.* Paper presented at the DEC Early Childhood Conference on Children with Special Needs, Orlando, FL.

Parkes, C. M. (1987). *Bereavement: Studies of grief in adult life* (2nd ed.). Madison, CT: International Universities Press.

Parten, M. (1932). Social participation among preschool children. *Journal of Abnormal and Social Psychology, 27,* 243–269.

Paz, J. (1993). Support of Hispanic elderly. In H. McAdoo (Ed.), *Family ethnicity: Strength in diversity* (pp. 177–183). Newbury Park, CA: Sage.

Pearlin, L. (1980). Life strains and psychological distress among adults. In N. J. Smelser & E. H. Erikson (Eds.), *Themes of work and love in adulthood* (pp. 174–192). Cambridge, MA: Harvard University Press.

Pearlin, L. (1982a). Discontinuties in the study of aging. In T. K. Hareven & K. J. Adams (Eds.), *Aging and life course transitions: An interdisciplinary perspective* (pp. 55–74). New York: Guilford.

Pearlin, L. (1982b). The social contexts of stress. In L. Goldberger & S. Breznitz (Eds.), *Handbook of stress: Theoretical and clinical aspects* (pp. 367–379). New York: Free Press.

Pearlin, L., & Skaff, M. (1996). Stress and the life course: A paradigmatic alliance. *Gerontologist, 36,* 239–247.

Peck, P. (1997). Study shows puberty hits girls at a young age. *Family Practice News, 27*(16), 61.

Pennekamp, M. (1995). Response to violence. *Social Work in Education, 17,* 199–200.

Perloff, J., & Buckner, J. (1996). Fathers of children on welfare: Their impact on child well being. *American Journal of Orthopsychiatry, 66,* 557–571.

Perry, B. (1997). Incubated in terror: Neurodevelopmental factors in the "cycle of violence." In J. Osofsky (Ed.), *Children in a violent society* (pp. 124–149). New York: Guilford.

Peterson, J., & Nord, C. (1990). The regular receipt of child support: A multistep process. *Journal of Marriage and the Family, 52,* 539–551.

Peterson, M. B., Greisen, G., & Kovacs, R. (1994). Outcome of <750 gm birthweight children at school age. *New England Journal of Medicine, 331,* 753–759.

Pettit, G. S., Bakshi, A., Dodge, K. A., & Coie, J. D. (1990). The emergence of social dominance in young boy's play groups: Developmental differences and behavioral correlates. *Developmental Psychology, 26,* 1017–1025.

Phinney, J. S. (1989). Stages of ethnic identity development in minority group adolescents. *Journal of Early Adolescence, 9,* 34–49.

Piaget, J. (1952). *The origins of intelligence in children.* New York: International Universities Press. (Original work published 1936)

Piaget, J. (1965). *The moral judgment of the child.* New York: Free Press. (Original work published 1932)

Piaget, J. (1972). Intellectual evolution from adolescence to adulthood. *Human Development, 15,* 1–12.

Pincus, A., & Minahan, A. (1973). *Social work practice: Model and method.* Itasca, IL: Peacock.

Pirke, K. M., Dogs, M., Fichter, M. M., & Tuschil, R. J. (1988). Gonadotrophin, oestradiol, and progesterone during the menstrual cycle in bulimia nervosa. *Clinical Endocrinology Metabolism, 60,* 1174–1179.

Platt, R., Rice, P., & McCormack, W. (1983). Risk of acquiring gonorrhea and prevalence of abnormal adnexal findings among women recently exposed to gonorrhea. *Journal of the American Medical Association, 250,* 3205–3209.

Poehlmann, J., & Fiese, B. (1994). The effects of divorce, maternal employment, and maternal social support on toddlers' home environments. *Journal of Divorce and Remarriage, 22*(1/2), 121–135.

Pomeroy, C., & Mitchell, J. E. (1989). Medical complications and management of eating disorders. *Psychiatric Annals, 19*(9), 488–493.

Poston, D., Jr., & Dan, H. (1996). Fertility trends in the United States. In D. Peck & J. Hollingsworth (Eds.), *Demographic and structural change: The effects of the 1980s on American society* (pp. 85–100). Westport, CT: Greenwood Press.

Powlishta, K. K., Serbin, L. A., Doyle, A., & White, D. R. (1994). Gender, ethnic, and body type biases: The generality of prejudice in childhood. *Developmental Psychology, 30,* 526–536.

Prager, K. (1995). *The psychology of intimacy.* New York: Guilford.

Pridham, K., & Chang, A. (1992). Transition to being the mother of a new infant in the first 3 months: Maternal problem solving and self-appraisals. *Journal of Advanced Nursing, 17,* 204.

Rabkin, J., Balassone, M., & Bell, M. (1995). The role of social workers in providing comprehensive health care to pregnant women. *Social Work in Health Care, 20*(3), 83–97.

Rando, T. (1984). Grief, dying, and death. Champaign, IL: Research Press.

Rando, T. (1993). *Treatment of complicated mourning.* Champaign, IL: Research Press.

Raphael, B. (1983). *The anatomy of bereavement.* New York: Basic Books.

Rauch, J. (1988). Social work and the genetics revolution: Genetic services. *Social Work, 9/10,* 389–395.

Rawlins, W. (1992). *Friendship matters.* Hawthorne, NY: Aldine de Gruyter.

Reed, G. B. (1996). Introduction to genetic screening and prenatal diagnoses. In J. J. Sciarra (Ed.), *Gynecology and obstetrics* (rev. ed.) (pp. 999–1003). Philadelphia: Lippincott-Raven.

Reich, R. (1992). *The work of nations: Preparing ourselves for 21st-century capitalism.* New York: Vintage.

Reid, W. (1985). *Family problem solving.* New York: Columbia University Press.

Reid, W., & Smith, A. (1989). *Research in social work* (2nd ed.). New York: Columbia University Press.

Reis, H., & Shaver, P. (1988). Intimacy as interpersonal process. In S. Duck (Ed.), *Handbook of personal relationships: Theory, relationships, and interventions* (pp. 367–389). Chichester, UK: Wiley.

Remafedi, G., Farrow, J. A., & Deisher, R. W. (1991). Risk factors for attempted suicide in gay and bisexual youth. *Pediatrics, 87,* 869–875.

Remafedi, G., Resnick, M., Blum, R., & Harris, L. (1992). Demography of sexual orientation in adolescents. *Pediatrics, 89,* 714–721.

Reskin, B., & Padavic, I. (1994). *Women and men at work.* Thousand Oaks, CA: Pine Forge.

Reynolds, B. (1975). *Social work and social living.* Washington, DC: NASW. (Original work published 1951)

Richmond, M. (1901). Charitable cooperation. In *Proceedings of the National Conference of Charities and Corrections.* Boston: Elles.

Richmond, M. (1917). *Social diagnosis.* New York: Russell Sage.

Riedmann, G. (1996a). Education for childbirth. In J. J. Sciarra (Ed.), *Gynecology and obstetrics.* (2nd ed.) (Vol. 2, pp. 1–9). Philadelphia: Lipincott-Raven.

Riedmann, G. (1996b). Preparation for parenthood. In J. J. Sciarra (Ed.), *Gynecology and obstetrics.* (2nd ed.) (Vol. 2, pp. 1–8). Philadelphia: Lippincott-Raven.

Riegel, K. (1976). The dialectics of human development. *American Psychologist, 31,* 689–699.

Riegel, K. (1979). *Foundations of dialectic psychology.* New York: Academic Press.

Riley, M. W. (1971). Social gerontology and the age stratification of society. *The Gerontologist, 11,* 79–87.

Riley, M. W. (1994). Aging and society: Past, present, and future. *The Gerontologist, 34,* 436–446.

Riordan, J. (1993a). The cultural context of breastfeeding. In J. Riordan & K. Auerbach (Eds.), *Breastfeeding and human lactation* (pp. 167–178). Boston: Jones & Bartlett.

Riordan, J. (1993b). Viruses in human milk. In J. Riordan & K. Auerbach (Eds.), *Breastfeeding and human lactation* (pp. 167–178). Boston: Jones & Bartlett.

Ritzer, G. (1992). *Contemporary sociological theory* (3rd ed.). New York: McGraw-Hill.

Roberts, E., Burchinal, M., & Bailey, D. (1994). Communication among preschoolers with and without disabilities in same-age and mixed-age classes. *American Journal on Mental Retardation, 99,* 231–249.

Roberts, R. E., Roberts, C. R., & Chen, Y. R. (1997). Ethnocultural differences in prevalence of adolescent depression. *American Journal of Community Psychology, 25*(1), 95–111.

The Robert Wood Foundation. (1991). *Challenges in health care: Perspective.* Princeton, NJ: RWJ Foundation.

Rock, P. (1996). Eugenics and euthanasia: A cause for concern for disabled people, particularly disabled women. *Disability & Society, 11*(1), 121–127.

Rodwell, M. (1987). Naturalistic inquiry: An alternative model for social work assessment. *Social Service Review, 61,* 231–246.

Rogers, C. (1951). *Client-centered therapy.* Boston: Houghton Mifflin.

Rogers, R. (1989). Ethnic and birth-weight differences in cause-specific infant mortality. *Demography, 26,* 335–341.

Root, L. (1993). Unemployment and underemployment: A policy and program-development perspective. In P. Kurzman & S. Akabas (Eds.), *Work and well-being: The occupational social work advantage* (332–349). Washington, DC: NASW Press.

Rosenberg, M. (1986). *Conceiving the self.* Malabar, FL: Robert E. Krieger.

Rosenfeld, J. A., & Everett, K. D. (1996). Factors related to planned and unplanned pregnancies. *Journal of Family Practice, 43*(2), 161–166.

Ross, L. J. (1992). African-American women and abortion: A neglected history. *Journal of Health Care for the Poor and Underserved, 3,* 274–284.

Ross, S. (1996). Risk of physical abuse to children of spouse abusing parents. *Child Abuse and Neglect, 20,* 589–598.

Rotheram-Borus, M. J. (1993). Biculturalism among adolescents. In M. Bernal & G. Knight (Eds.), *Ethnic identity* (pp. 81–102). Albany, NY: SUNY Press.

Roueche, J. E., & Baker, G. A., III. (1986). *Profiling excellence in America's schools.* Arlington, VA: American Association of School Administrators.

Rubin, A., & Babbie, E. (1993). *Research methods for social work* (2nd ed.). New York: Columbia University Press.

Rubin, K. (1982). Nonsocial play in preschoolers: Necessarily evil? *Child Development, 53,* 651–657.

Rubin, K. H., Fein, G. G., & Vandenberg, B. (1983). Play. In E. M. Hetherington (Ed.). *Handbook of child psychology: Vol. 4. Socialization, personality, and social development* (4th ed.) (pp. 693–744). New York: Wiley.

Rubin, R. (1995). *Maternal identity and the maternal experience: Childbirth educator.* New York: Springer.

Rudolph, S., & Rudolph, L. (1978). Rajput adulthood: Reflections on the Amar Singh Diary. In E. H. Erikson (Ed.), *Adulthood* (pp. 149–171). New York: Norton & Norton.

Russell, D. E. H. (1984). *Sexual exploitation: Rape, child sexual abuse, and workplace harassment.* Beverly Hills, CA: Sage.

Ryan, B. A., & Adams, G. R. (1995). The family-school relationships model. In B. A. Ryan, G. R. Adams, T. P. Gullotta, R. P. Weissberg, & R. L. Hampton (Eds.), *The family-school connection: Theory, research, and practice* (pp. 3–28). Thousand Oaks, CA: Sage.

Sadker, M., Sadker, D., Fox, L., & Salata, M. (1994). Gender inequity in the classroom. In J. I. Goodlad & P. Keating (Eds.), *Access to knowledge: The continuing agenda for our nation's schools* (rev. ed.) (pp. 321–328). New York: College Entrance Examination Board.

Saghir, M. T., & Robins, E. (1973). *Male and female homosexuality: A comprehensive examination.* Baltimore: Williams & Wilkins.

Saleeby, D. (1992). Biology's challenge to social work: Embodying the person-in-environment perspective. *Social Work, 37,* 112–118.

Saleeby, D. (1994). Culture, theory, and narrative: The intersection of meanings in practice. *Social Work, 39*(4), 351–359.

Santrock, J. W. (1995). *Life-span development* (5th ed.). Madison, WI: Brown & Benchmark.

Sauter, S., & Murphy, L. (Eds.). (1995). *Organizational risk factors for job stress.* Washington, DC: American Psychological Association.

Savin-Williams, R. C. (1979). Dominance hierarchies in groups of early adolescents. *Child Development, 50,* 923–935.

Sawin, K. S. (1998). Health care concerns for women with physical disability and chronic illness. In E. Q. Youngkin & M. S. Davis (Eds.), *Women's health: A primary care clinical guide* (2nd ed.) (pp. 905–941). Stamford, CT: Appleton & Lange.

Schachere, K. (1990). Attachment between working mothers and their infants: The influence of family processes. *American Journal of Orthopsychiatry, 60,* 19–34.

Schaie, K. W. (1984). The Seattle Longitudinal Study: A 21-year exploration of psychometric intelligence in adulthood. In K. W. Schaie (Ed.), *Longitudinal studies of adult psychological development* (pp. 64–135). New York: Guilford Press.

Schild, S., & Black, R. (1984). *Social work and genetics: A guide for practice.* New York: Haworth.

Schmitz, C., & Hilton, A. (1996). Combining mental health treatment with education for preschool children with severe emotional and behavioral problems. *Social Work in Education, 18,* 237–249.

Schriver, J. (1995). *Human behavior and the social environment: Shifting paradigms in essential knowledge for social work practice.* Boston: Allyn & Bacon.

Schroots, J. J. F., & Birren, J. E. (1990). Concepts of time and aging in science. In J. E. Birren & K. W. Schaie, *Handbook of the psychology of aging* (3rd ed.) (pp. 45–64). San Diego: Academic Press.

Schulenberg, J., Bachman, J., Johnston, L., & O'Malley, P. (1995). American adolescents' views on family and work: Historical trends from 1976–1992. In P. Noack, M. Hofer, & J. Youniss (Eds.), *Psychological responses to social change: Human development in changing environments.* New York: Walter de Gruyter.

Schutt, R. (1996). *Investigating the social world: The process and practice of research.* Thousand Oaks, CA: Pine Forge.

Schutz, A. (1967). *The phenomenology of the social world.* (G. Walsh & F. Lehnert, Trans.) Evanston, IL: Northwestern University Press. (Original work published 1932)

Schwartz, M. (1973). Sexism in the social work curriculum. *Journal of Social Work Education, 9*(3), 65–70.

Sedlack, A. J., & Broadhurst, D. D. (1996). *Third national incidence study of child abuse and neglect: Final report.* Washington, DC: U.S. Department of Health and Human Services.

Segal, B. M., & Stewart, J. C. (1996). Substance use and abuse in adolescence: An overview. *Child Psychiatry and Human Development, 26*(4), 193–210.

Seligman, M. (1992). *Helplessness: On depression, development, and death.* New York: Freeman.

Selman, R. L. (1976). Social-cognitive understanding: A guide to educational and clinical practice. In T. Lickona (Ed.), *Moral development and behavior: Theory, research, and social issues* (pp. 219–316). New York: Holt, Rinehart, & Winston.

Seltzer, J. (1991). Relationships between fathers and children who live apart: The father's role after separation. *Journal of Marriage and the Family, 53,* 79–101.

Serbin, L. A., Powlishta, K. K., & Gulko, J. (1993). The development of sex typing in middle childhood. *Monographs of the Society for Research in Child Development, 58*(2, Serial No. 232).

Settersten, R., Jr., & Hagestad, G. (1996). What's the latest? Cultural age deadlines for family transitions. *The Gerontologist, 36,* 178–188.

Shaw, S., Kleiber, D., & Caldwell, L. (1995). Leisure and identity formation in male and female adolescents: A preliminary examination. *Journal of Leisure Research, 27,* 245–263.

Sheehy, G. (1976). *Passages.* New York: Dutton.

Sheehy, G. (1995). *New passages.* New York: Random House.

Shepard, M. (1992). Child visiting and domestic abuse. *Child Welfare, 71,* 357–367.

Shepard, T. H. (1995). Human teratology. In G. B. Reed, A. E. Claireaux, & F. Cockburn (Eds.), *Diseases of the fetus and newborn* (2nd ed.) (pp. 83–93). London: Chapman & Hall.

Sherman, E. (1991). *Reminiscence and the self in old age.* New York: Springer.

Sherman, E., & Reid, W. (1994). *Qualitative research in social work.* New York: Columbia University Press.

Shrier, L. A., Emans, S. J., Woods, E. R., & DuRant, R. H. (1996). The association of sexual risk behaviors and problem drug behaviors in high school students. *Journal of Adolescent Health, 20,* 377–383.

Silvern, L., & Kaersvang, L. (1989). The traumatized children of violent marriages. *Child Welfare, 68,* 421–436.

Sinnott, J. D. (1986). Prospective/intentional and incidental everyday memory: Effects of age and passage of time. *Psychology and Aging, 1,* 110–116.

Siporin, M. (1975). *Introduction to social work practice.* New York: Macmillan.

Skinner, B. F. (1957). *Verbal behavior.* Englewood Cliffs, NJ: Prentice-Hall.

Skocpol, T. (1979). *States and social revolutions.* New York: Cambridge University Press.

Skolnick, A., & Skolnick, J. (1996). *The family in transition* (9th ed.). Reading, MA: Addison-Wesley.

Slater, S. (1995). *The lesbian family life cycle.* New York: Free Press.

Slee, R. (1995). Inclusive education: From policy to school implementation. In C. Clark, A. Dyson, & A. Millward (Eds.), *Towards inclusive schools?* New York: Teachers College Press.

Smeeding, T., & Rainwater, L. (1995). Cross-national trends in income, poverty, and dependence: The evidence for young adults in the eighties. In K. McFate (Ed.), *Poverty, inequality, and the future of social policy.* New York: Russell Sage Foundation.

Smelser, N. J. (1980). Issues in the study of work and love in adulthood. In N. J. Smelser & E. H. Erikson (Eds.), *Themes of work and love in adulthood* (pp. 1–26). Cambridge, MA: Harvard University Press.

Smetana, J. G., Killen, M., & Turiel, E. (1991). Children's reasoning about interpersonal and moral conflicts. *Child Development, 62,* 629–644.

Smith, J., O'Connor, I., & Berthelsen, D. (1996). The effects of witnessing domestic violence on young children's psycho-social adjustment. *Australian Social Work, 49*(4), 3–10.

Smith, J. D., & Polloway, E. A. (1993). Institutionalization, involuntary sterilization, and mental retardation: Profiles from the history of the practice. *Mental Retardation, 314,* 208–214.

Snarey, J. (1993). *How fathers care for the next generation: A four-decade study.* Cambridge, MA: Harvard University Press.

Soldo, B. J., & Agree, E. M. (1988). America's elderly. *Population Bulletin, 43*, 1–51.

Speare, A. Jr., & Avery, R. (1993). Who helps whom in older parent–child families? *Journal of Gerontology, 48*, S64–S73.

Specht, H. (1986). Social support, social networks, social exchange, and social work practice. *Social Service Review, 60*, 218–240.

Speckland, A. (1993). Complicated mourning: Dynamics of impacted post abortion grief. *Pre- and Peri-natal Psychology Journal, 8*(1), 5–32.

Spence, A. P. (1989). *Biology of aging.* Englewood Cliffs, NJ: Prentice Hall.

Sroufe, L. A., Cooper, R. G., & DeHart, G. B. (1996). *Child development: Its nature and course* (3rd ed.). New York: McGraw-Hill.

Stacey, J. (1996). *In the name of the family: Rethinking family values in the postmodern age.* Boston: Beacon.

*State Legislatures.* (1996). Sexually transmitted diseases and adolescents. *State Legislatures, 22*(4), 7.

Stegner, W. (1978). The writer and the concept of adulthood. In E. H. Erikson (Ed.), *Adulthood* (pp. 227–236). New York: Norton & Norton.

Stein, H., & Cloward, R. (1958). *Social perspectives on behavior: A reader in social science for social work and related professions.* New York: Free Press.

Stepp-Gilbert, E. (1988). Sensory integration: A reason for infant enrichment. *Issues in Comprehensive Pediatric Nursing, 11*, 319–331.

Sternberg, K. J., Lamb, M. E., Greenbaum, C., Cicchetti, D., Dawut, S., Cortes, R. M., Krispin, O., & Lorey, F. (1993). Effects of domestic violence on children's behavior problems and depression. *Developmental Psychology, 29*, 44–52.

Stock, R. (1990). Ectopic pregnancy: A look at changing concepts and problems. *Clinical Obstetrics and Gynecology, 33*, 448–453.

Stoddard, S., Jans, L., Ripple, J., & Kraus, L. (1998). *Chartbook on work and disability in the United States, 1998* (An InfoUse Report). Washington, DC: U.S. National Institute on Disability and Rehabilitation Research.

Streeter, C., & Gillespie, D. (1992). Social network analysis. *Journal of Social Service Research, 16*, 201–221.

Stuart, R. (1989). Social learning theory: A vanishing or expanding presence? *Psychology: A Journal of Human Behavior, 26*, 35–50.

Sudarkasa, N. (1993). Female-headed African American households: Some neglected dimensions. In H. McAdoo (Ed.), *Family ethnicity: Strength in diversity* (pp. 81–89). Newbury Park, CA: Sage.

Sue, D. W., & Sue, D. (1990). *Counseling the culturally different: Theory and practice* (2nd ed.). New York: Wiley.

Suh, E., & Abel, E. (1990). The impact of violence on the children of the abused. *Journal of Independent Social Work, 4*(4), 27–43.

Swap, S. M. (1993). *Developing home-school partnerships: From concepts to practice.* New York: Teachers College Press.

Takahashi, E. A., & Turnbull, J. E. (1994). New findings in psychiatric genetics: Implications for social work practice. *Social Work in Health Care, 20*(2), 1–21.

Tanner, J. M. (1990). *Fetus into man: Physical growth from conception to maturity.* Cambridge, MA: Harvard University Press.

Teitelman, J. L. (1995). Homosexuality. In G. L. Maddox (Ed.), *The encyclopedia of aging: A comprehensive resource in gerontology and geriatrics* (2nd ed.) (p. 270). New York: Springer.

Tennant, M., & Pogson, P. (1995). *Learning and change in the adult years.* San Francisco: Jossey-Bass.

Teplin, S. W., Burchinal, M., Johnson-Martin, N., Humphry, R. A., & Kraybill, E. N. (1991). Neurodevelopmental, health, and growth status at age 6 years of children with birth weights less than 1000 grams. *Journal of Pediatrics, 118*, 751–760.

Terr, L. C. (1991). Childhood traumas: An outline and overview. *American Journal of Psychiatry, 148*, 10–20.

Texas Heart Institute. (1996). *Heart owner's handbook.* New York: Wiley.

Thapa, S., Short, R. V., & Potts, M. (1988). Breastfeeding, birthspacing, and their effects on child survival. *Nature, 335*, 679–682.

Thibaut, J., & Kelley, H. (1959). *The social psychology of groups.* New York: Wiley.

Thomas, A., & Chess, S. (1986). The New York longitudinal study: From infancy to early adult life. In R. Plomin & J. Dunn (Eds.), *The study of temperament: Changes, continuities, and challenges* (pp. 39–52). Hillside, NJ: Erlbaum.

Thomas, A., Chess, S., & Birch, H.G. (1968). *Temperament and behavior disorders in children.* New York: New York University Press.

Thomas, A., Chess, S., & Birch, H.G. (1970). The origin of personality. *Scientific American, 223*, 102–109.

Thomas, J. L. (1992). *Adulthood and aging.* Needham Heights, MA: Allyn & Bacon.

Thyer, B. (1991). Behavioral social work: It is not what you think. *Arete, 16*, 1–9.

Thyer, B. (1994). Social learning theory: Empirical applications to culturally diverse practice. In R. Greene (Ed.), *Human behavior theory: A diversity framework* (pp. 133–146). New York: Aldine de Gruyter.

Tracy, E., & Whittaker, J. (1990). The social network map: Assessing social support in clinical practice. *Families in Society, 71*, 461–470.

Trattner, W. I. (1994). *From poor law to welfare state: A history of social welfare in America* (5th ed.). New York: Free Press.

Trimble, J., Gay, H., & Docherty, J. (1986). Characterization of the tumor-associated 38-kd protein of herpes simples virus Type II. *The Journal of Reproductive Medicine, 31*(5), 399–409.

Tucker, M., & Mitchell-Kernan, B. (1995). *The decline in marriage among African-Americans.* New York: Russell Sage Foundation.

Tueth, M. J. (1993). Anxiety in the older patient: Differential diagnosis and treatment. *Geriatrics, 48,* 51–54.

Tutty, L., & Wagar, J. (1994). The evolution of a group for young children who have witnessed family violence. *Social Work With Groups, 17*(1/2), 89–104.

Udry, J. R. (1993). The politics of sex research. *The Journal of Sex Research, 30*(2), 103–110.

Udry, J. R., Billy, J. O. G., Morris, N. M., Groff, T. R., & Raj, M. H. (1985). Serum androgenic hormones motive sexual behavior in boys. *Fertility and Sterility, 43*(1), 90–94.

United Nations. (1989). *Adolescent reproductive behavior: Evidence from developing countries* (Vol. 2). New York: United Nations.

U.S. Bureau of Census. (1989). *Statistical abstract of the United States: 1990* (110th ed.). Washington DC: U.S. Government Printing Office.

U.S. Bureau of the Census. (1995). *Statistical abstract of the United States* (115th ed.). Washington, DC: U.S. Government Printing Office.

U.S. Bureau of Census. (1998). *Marital status of persons 15 years and over by age, sex, race, Hispanic origin, and region: March 1997. Marital status and living arrangements.* [On-line Current Population Reports (Series P-20)]. U.S. Bureau of Census, World Wide Web Site, www. census.gov/prod/3/98pubs/P20-506u.pdf

U.S. Department of Health and Human Services, Public Health Service. (1991). *Healthy people 2000.* Washington, DC: U.S. Government Printing Office.

U.S. Department of Health and Human Services. (1993). Gay male and lesbian youth suicide. *Report of the Secretary's Task Force on Youth Suicide* (Vol. 93, 110–142). Washington, DC: U.S. Government Printing Office.

U.S. Department of Health and Human Services, Health Resources and Services. Administration, Maternal and Child Health Bureau. (1995). *Adolescent health fact sheet.* Washington DC: U.S. Government Printing Office.

U.S. Department of Labor. (1988). Labor force participation among mothers of young children. *News.* Washington, DC: Author.

Valsiner, J. (1989a). *Human development and culture: The social nature of personality and its study.* Lexington, MA: Lexington Books.

Valsiner, J. (1989b). Social development in infancy and toddlerhood. In *Human development and culture: The social nature of personality and its study* (pp. 163–253). Lexington, MA: Lexington Books.

Vekemans, M. (1996). Cytogentics. In J. J. Sciarra (Ed.), *Gynecology and obstetrics* (rev. ed.) (pp. 57–66). Philadelphia: Lippincott-Raven.

Veltkamp, L., & Miller, T., (1994). *Clinical handbook of child abuse and neglect.* Madison, CT: International Universities Press.

Vicary, J. R., Klingaman, L. R., & Harkness, W. L. (1995). Risk factors associated with date rape and sexual assault of adolescents. *Journal of Adolescence, 18,* 289–307.

Viggiani, P. A. (1996). *Social worker—teacher collaboration.* Unpublished doctoral dissertation, State University of New York at Albany.

Volkan, V., & Zintl, E. (1993). *Life after loss.* New York: Scribner's.

Voydanoff, P. (1993). Work and family relationships. In T. Brubaker (Ed.), *Family relations: Challenges for the future* (pp. 98–111). Newbury Park, CA: Sage.

Vygotsky, L. (1986). *Thought and language.* Cambridge, MA: MIT Press.

Wachs, T. (1992). *The nature of nurture.* Newbury Park: Sage.

Wacker, R. R., Roberto, K. A., & Piper, L. E. (1997). *Community resources for older adults: Programs and services in an era of change.* Thousand Oaks, CA: Pine Forge.

Walker, K. (1994). Men, women, and friendship: What they say, what they do. *Gender & Society, 8,* 246-265.

Walker, L. O. (1992). *Parent-infant nursing science: Paradigms, phenomena, methods.* Philadelphia: Davis.

Wallace, R., & Wolf, A. (1995). *Contemporary sociological theory: Continuing the classical tradition* (4th ed.). Englewood Cliffs, NJ: Prentice-Hall.

Wallerstein, I. (1974–1989). *The modern world system* (Vols. 1–3). New York: Academic Press.

Wallerstein, J. S. (1983). Children of divorce: The psychological task of the child. *American Journal of Orthopsychiatry, 53,* 230–243.

Wallerstein, J. S., & Blakeslee, S. (1989). *Second chances: Men, women and children a decade after divorce.* New York: Ticknor & Fields.

Wallerstein, J. S., & Corbin, S. (1991). The child and the vicissitudes of divorce. In M. Lewis (Ed.), *Child and adolescent psychiatry: A comprehensive textbook* (pp. 1108–1118). Baltimore: Williams & Wilkins.

Wallerstein, J. S., Corbin, S., & Lewis, J. (1988). Children of divorce: A ten year study. In E. Hetherington & J. Arasteh (Eds.), *Impact of divorce, single-parenting and step-parenting on children* (pp. 198–214). Hillsdale, NJ: Erlbaum.

Wallerstein, J., & Kelly, J. (1977). Divorce counseling: A community service for families in the midst of divorce. *American Journal of Orthopsychiatry, 47*, 4–22.

Wallerstein, J. S., & Kelly, J. (1980). *Surviving the breakup.* New York: Basic Books.

Ward, R. R., Logan, J., & Spitze, G. (1992). The influence of parent and child needs on coresidence in middle and later life. *Journal of Marriage and the Family, 54*, 209–221.

Ware, L. (1995). The aftermath of the articulate debate: The invention of inclusive education. In C. Clark, A. Dyson, & A. Millward (Eds.), *Towards inclusive schools?* (pp. 127–146). New York: Teachers College Press.

Warren, C. W., Santelli, J. S., Everett, S. A., Kann, L., Collins, J. L., Cassell, C., Morris, L., & Kolbe, L. J. (1998). Sexual behavior among U.S. high school students, 1990–1995. *Family Planning Perspectives, 30*(4), 170–174.

Waxman, B. F. (1994). Up against eugenics: Disabled women's challenge to receive reproductive health services. *Sexuality and Disability, 12*(2), 155–171.

Weber, M. (1958). *The Protestant ethic and the spirit of capitalism* (T. Parsons, Trans.). New York: Scribner's. (Original work published 1904–1905)

Weenolsen, P. (1988). *Transcendence of loss over the life span.* New York: Hemisphere.

Wegman, M. E. (1992). Annual summary of vital statistics. *Pediatrics, 92*, 743–754.

Weick, A. (1994). Overturning oppression: An analysis of emancipatory change. In L. Davis (Ed.), *Building on women's strengths: A social work agenda for the twenty-first century.* New York: Haworth Press.

Weiss, R. S. (1973). *Loneliness: The experience of emotional and social isolation.* Cambridge, MA: MIT Press.

Welsh, R. (1985). Spanking: A grand old American tradition? *Children Today, 14*(1), 25–29.

Werner, C., Altman, I., & Oxley, D. (1985). Temporal aspects of homes: A transactional perspective. In I. Altman & C. Werner (Eds.), *Home environments* (pp. 1–32). New York: Plenum.

Werner, E. (1984). Resilient children. *Young Children, 40*(1), 68–72.

Werner, E., & Smith, R. (1982). *Vulnerable, but invincible: A longitudinal study of resilient children and youth.* New York: McGraw-Hill.

Werner, E. E., & Smith, R. S. (1992). *Overcoming the odds: High risk children from birth to adulthood.* Ithaca, NY: Cornell University Press.

Wesley, C. (1975). The women's movement and psychotherapy. *Social Work, 20*, 120–124.

West, J. (Ed.). (1991). *The Americans with Disabilities Act.* New York: Millbank Fund.

West, M., & Sheldon-Keller, A. (1994). *Patterns of relating: An adult attachment perspective.* New York: Guilford.

Wheeler, H. (Ed.). (1973). *Beyond the punitive society.* San Francisco, CA: Freeman.

Whiting, B. B., & Whiting, J. W. (1975). *Children of six cultures: A psycho-cultural analysis.* Cambridge, MA: Harvard University Press.

Widmayer, S., Peterson, L., & Larner, M. (1990). Predictors of Haitian-American infant development at twelve months. *Child Development, 61*, 410–415.

Widmer, M. A., Ellis, G. D., & Trunnell, E. P. (1996). Measurement of ethical behavior in leisure among high- and low-risk adolescents. *Adolescence, 31*, 397–408.

Wilburn, K. O., & Bates, M. L. (1997). Conflict resolution in America's schools. *Dispute Resolution Journal, 52*(1), 67–71.

Willer, D. (1987). *Theory and the experimental investigation of social structures.* New York: Gordon and Breach.

Wilner, S., Secker-Walker, R. H., & Flynn, B. S. (1987). How to help the pregnant woman stop smoking. In M. J. Rosenberg (Ed.), *Smoking and reproductive health* (pp. 215–222). Littleton, MA: PSG Publishing.

Windle, M. (1990). Longitudinal study of antisocial behaviors in early adolescence as predictors of late adolescent substance use: Gender and ethnic group differences. *Journal of Abnormal Psychology, 99*(1), 86–91.

Winstead, B., Derlega, V., & Montgomery, M. (1995). The quality of friendships at work and job satisfaction. *Journal of Social and Personal Relationships, 12*, 199–215.

Winters, W. G. (1993). *African American mothers and urban schools: The power of participation.* New York: Lexington Books.

Witkin, S., & Gottschalk, S. (1988). Alternative criteria for theory evaluation. *Social Service Review, 62*, 211–224.

Wittenberg, J. (1990). Psychiatric considerations in premature births. *Canadian Journal of Psychiatry, 35*, 734–740.

Wolfe, J. R. (1993). *The coming health crisis: Who will pay for the care of the aged in the twenty-first century?* Chicago: University of Chicago Press.

Wolfner, G., & Gelles, R. (1993). A profile of violence toward children: A national study. *Child Abuse and Neglect, 17*, 197–212.

Woody, D. (1996). *The influence of race and gender on psychological and social well-being: Testing the null hypothesis with a middle-class sample of men and women.* Unpublished doctoral dissertation, Virginia Commonwealth University, Richmond.

*World almanac and book of facts 1997.* (1996). Mahwah, NJ: World Almanac Books.

Wuthnow, R. (1994). *Sharing the journey: Support groups and America's new quest for community.* New York: Free Press.

Young, R. F., & Olson, E. A. (1991). *Health, illness, and disability in later life: Practice issues and interventions.* Newbury Park, CA: Sage.

Yu, V. Y. H., Jamieson, J., & Asbury, J. (1981). Parents' reactions to unrestricted parental contact in the intensive care unit nursery. *Medical Journal of Australia, 1,* 294–296.

Zahr, L. K., Parker, S., & Cole, J. (1992). Comparing the effects of neonatal intensive care unit intervention on premature infants at different weights. *Developmental and Behavioral Pediatrics, 13*(3), 165–172.

Zastrow, C., & Kirst-Ashman, K. K. (1997). *Understanding human behavior and the social environment* (4th ed.). Chicago: Nelson-Hall.

Zelnik, M., & Shah, F. K. (1983). First intercourse among young Americans. *Family Planning Perspectives, 15*(2), 64–70.

Zigler, E. F., & Finn-Stevenson, M. (1995) The child care crisis: Implications for the growth and development of the nation's children. *Journal of Social Issues, 51,* 215–231.

Zill, N., Moore, K. A., Smith, E. W., Stief, T., & Coiro, M. J. (1995). The life circumstances and development of children in welfare families: A profile based on national survey data. In P. L. Chase-Lansdale & J. Brooks-Gunn (Eds.), *Escape from poverty: What makes a difference for children?* (pp. 38–59). New York: Cambridge University Press.

Ziolko, M. E. (1993). Counseling parents of children with disabilities: A review of the literature and implications for practice. In M. Nagler (Ed.), *Perspectives on disability* (2nd ed.) (pp. 185–193). Palo Alto, CA: Health Markets Research.

Zipper, I., & Simeonsson, R. (1997). Promoting the development of young children with disabilities. In M. Fraser (Ed.), *Risk and resilience in childhood* (pp. 10–33). Washington, DC: NASW Press.

Zuravin, S. J. (1986). Residential density and urban child maltreatment: An aggregate analysis. *Journal of Family Violence, 1,* 307–322.

Zuravin, S. J. (1989). The ecology of child abuse and neglect: Review of the literature and presentation of data. *Violence and Victims, 4,* 1010–1020.

# GLOSSARY/INDEX

**Biological rhythms** Biological events that occur on a regular basis and are in synchronization with cycles in the environment. The body goes through many different biological rhythms, such as wake/sleep and cellular renewal. With age, the synchronization with some of these cycles becomes more difficult, thus limiting the body's adaptive capacity, 266

**Biopsychosocial approach** An approach that considers human behavior to be the result of interactions of integrated biological, psychological, and social systems, 18

Birth. *See* Childbirth

**Birthing center** A nonhospital setting established to provide labor and delivery and postpartum services for the low-risk maternity patient, her family, and her significant other(s), 87

Blume, Judy, 190

**Bonding** Development of an emotional attachment between parent(s) and offspring through frequent and close physical contact, 88

**Boundary** An imaginary line of demarcation that defines which human and non-human elements are included in a given system and which elements are outside of the system, 42

Bowlby, J., 131–132

Brain development, 124, 125

**Braxton-Hicks contractions** Intermittent painless contractions of the uterus that may occur every 10 to 20 minutes after the third month of pregnancy, 99

Brazelton, T. Berry, 124

Breastfeeding, 88–89

Bronfenbrenner, Uri, 42

*Brown v. Board of Education,* 159

**Bulimia nervosa** An eating disorder characterized by a cycle of binge eating; feelings of guilt, depression, or self-disgust; and purging, 215

**C**

Cancer, 250

Cardiovascular system, 268

Caregiving, for elderly individuals, 276–277

"Caretaking Decisions for Jessica, Alexia, and Steven Jr." (case study), 119–120

"Carl's Struggle for Identity" (case study), 184–185

**Cellular aging theory** Biological theory of aging proposed by Hayflick (1987). Cells cannot replicate themselves indefinitely, and replication of cells slows with age. Because human cells can only divide approximately 50 times, the biological limit of the human life span is about 110 to 120 years. Also termed the Hayflick theorem, 267

**Central components** In Levinson's seasons of adulthood theory, the relationships that have the greatest significance in the life structure at a particular point, 228

"A Change of Plans for Tahesha Gibbon" (case study), 80–81

Child abuse

effects of, 143–145

factors contributing to, 175–176

Childbearing. *See also* Childbirth; Conception; Pregnancy

at-risk newborns and, 104–110

problem pregnancies and, 103–104

sociocultural organization of, 85–89

special parent populations and, 110–112

Childbirth

breastfeeding following, 88–89

education regarding, 87

hospital stays for, 87–88

place of, 87

traditions of, 86

Child care

attachment and, 133, 134

effects of quality, 166–167

features of quality, 134

promotion of quality, 146–147

**Child maltreatment** Physical, emotional, and sexual abuse and neglect of children, most often by adult caregivers. Definitions vary by culture and professional discipline, but typically entail harm, or threatened harm, to the child, 171

Children. *See* Adolescents; Infants; Neonates; Older children; Young children

**Chlamydia** A sexually transmitted disease caused by *Chlamydia trachomatis* or *T-strain Mycoplasma*. Symptoms appear in one to three weeks after contact and include vaginal itching and discharge in women (most women remain asymptomatic) or a thin, whitish discharge in men (approximately 30 percent remain asymptomatic), 206

**Chorion villi testing (CVT)** Procedure involving cervical insertion of a catheter into the uterus to obtain a piece of the developing placenta for chromosomal analysis, 109

Chromosomal aberration, 107–108

**Chromosomes** Threadlike structures composed of DNA and proteins that carry genes and are found within each body cell nucleus, 94

**Chronological age** An individual's age measured in the chronological time that has elapsed since birth, typically in years, 266

**Classical conditioning theory** A theory in the social behavioral perspective. Sees behavior as the result of the association of a conditioned stimulus with an unconditioned stimulus, 57

Play
  in infants and young children, 134–135
  team, 169
  types of, 135
**Pleiotropy principle**   The ability of a single gene to have many effects, 107
**Pluralistic theory of social conflict**   Suggests that there is more than one social conflict going on at all times, and that individuals often hold cross-cutting and overlapping memberships in status groups. Suggests that these cross-cutting memberships prevent the development of solidarity among members of oppressed groups, 46
**Positivist perspective**   An approach to human behavior in which the findings of one study should be applicable to other groups; complex phenomena can be studied by reducing them to some component part; scientific methods are value-free, 26
**Post-traumatic stress disorder**   A set of symptoms experienced by some trauma survivors, including reliving the traumatic event, avoidance of stimuli related to the event, and hyperarousal, 176
Poverty
  child abuse and, 144
  infants and young children and, 137–138
  marginalization in labor market and, 249–250
  older children and, 170–171
  rate of, 170
  relative, 171
  schools in areas with high rates of, 165
**Power of attorney (POA)**   A person appointed by an individual to manage his/her financial and legal affairs. A POA can be limited (for a limited time period), general (no restrictions), or durable (begins after reaching a specified level of disability), 283–284
Power relationships, 46, 54
Preconceptual stage, 126
Pregnancy. *See also* Childbearing; Childbirth
  abortion and, 90–92
  adolescent, 101–102, 205–206
  contraception and, 89–90
  delayed, 103
  developmental tasks for, 100–101
  early adulthood, 102
  ectopic, 91, 104
  infertility treatment and, 92–94
  miscarriage and stillbirth and, 104
  normal fetal development and, 97–100
  reproductive genetics and, 94–97
  social meaning of, 86
  undesired, 104

**Premature birth**   A fetus born any time prior to 37 weeks of gestation, 105
Premature infants, 105–106. *See also* **Neonate**
**Preoperational stage**   The second stage in Piaget's theory of cognitive development. Young children (ages 2 to 7) use symbols to represent their earlier sensorimotor experiences. Thinking is not yet logical, 126
**Prepubescence**   Developmental period prior to the commencement of physiological processes and changes associated with pubescence, 162
Preschoolers. *See* Young children
**Primary memory**   Part of memory, limited in capacity, that is used to organize and temporarily hold information. Also termed short-term memory, 270
**Primary sex characteristics**   Physical characteristics that are directly related to maturaton of the reproductive organs and external genitalia, 188
**Primipara**   A woman who has delivered only one infant of at least 500 grams (20 weeks gestation), whether the child is alive or dead at the time of birth, 99
**Process theoretical approach**   An approach to the study of adulthood that does not involve discrete stages, focusing instead on the continuous transaction of various biological, psychological, and sociocultural processes, 232–233
**Proposition**   An assertion about a concept or about the relationship between concepts, 25
**Prosocial behavior**   Behavior that elicits and demonstrates positive social regard, is indicative of social competence, and requires interpersonal sensitivity, 157
Prostaglandin, 91
**Psychodynamic perspective**   Concerned with how internal processes motivate human behavior, 53
  central ideas of, 53
  criticisms of, 54
**Psychological age**   Age measured by the skills that people use to adapt to changing biological and environmental demands, skills such as intelligence, memory, emotions, and motivation, 30
Psychological distress, 233
Psychological distress theory, 233
**Psychological time**   Age-related adaptive capacities, such as memory and learning; may be measured by the time needed to complete a psychological event, 266–267
**Psychosocial crisis**   In Erik Erikson's psychosocial life span theory, a predictable turning point in the life cycle that is produced by a combination of physiological changes and societal demands, 227
Psychosocial development theory, 128–130
Psychosocial life span theory, 227–228

# TO THE OWNER OF THIS BOOK

We invite your reactions to the book as well as your questions and sugestions for improving it. Send us a note via e-mail or write your comments below and mail them in the attached self-addressed envelope.

Elizabeth D. Hutchison
Virginia Commonwealth University
ehutch@atlas.vcu.edu

## BUSINESS REPLY MAIL
FIRST CLASS MAIL   PERMIT NO. 150   THOUSAND OAKS, CA

Pine Forge Press
at Sage Publications Inc.
P.O. Box 5084
Thousand Oaks, CA 91359-9924